Praise for the Second Edition

'Writing with clarity, authority and insight Bjola and Kornpro[bst offer an introduc]tion to the study and practice of diplomacy. The welcome se[cond edition updates schol]arship and tackles the emerging issues that are defining our [field, from the ongoing] crises in Syria and Ukraine. No less significantly, the volume also considers new techniques of diplomacy from social media to the emergence of cities as foreign policy actors. This book is an invaluable guide to a vital field.'

Nicholas J. Cull, *Professor of Public Diplomacy,*
University of Southern California

'In many ways superior to the original, the revised edition updates the evolution and transformation of diplomacy, more balanced in theory and practice, wide in scope and succinct in narration, a rich menu for both students and practitioners of diplomacy.'

Zhang Qingmin, *Professor and Chair, Department*
of Diplomacy Peking University

'Adopting a broad understanding of diplomacy and taking us on an exciting tour – from foreign policy implementation to ethics, from bilateral engagements to plurilateral and paradiplomatic ones, from traditional channels to new forms of diplomatic communication – *Understanding International Diplomacy* is a welcome and valuable addition to the expanding field of diplomatic studies. It provides an excellent introduction and essential textbook for both the reflexive practitioner and the intellectually curious student of diplomacy.'

Costas M. Constantinou, *Professor of International*
Relations, University of Cyprus

Praise for the First Edition

'An invaluable volume for all those studying the critical endeavour of diplomacy in today's changing world.'

Javier Solana, *former NATO Secretary General, ex-European Union*
High Representative for Common Foreign and Security Policy

'In this fascinating book, Bjola and Kornprobst offer a fresh perspective on the study of diplomacy as a form of institutionalized communication. Drawing insight from multiple disciplines, it presents a sophisticated overview of both the history and contemporary practice of diplomacy. The cases studies add texture to a theory-driven account of what remains a critically important dimension of international life.'

Ian Johnstone, *Fletcher School of Law*
and Diplomacy, Tufts University, USA

'*Understanding International Diplomacy: Theory, Practice and Ethics* deserves a prominent place on the bookshelf of every serious student of diplomacy. Corneliu Bjola and Markus Kornprobst have produced a study that is simultaneously sophisticated and accessible. Their conception of diplomacy as institutionalised communication captures its similarities to, but also its differences from, other forms of transnational dialogue, and allows them to explore changes in the character of diplomacy in the contemporary world in a richly-textured fashion. Scholars and practitioners alike will draw on the authors' insights for years to come.'

William Maley, *Director, Asia-Pacific College of Diplomacy, The Australian National University*

'Bjola and Kornprobst have done the academic and diplomatic communities the great service of producing a clear text which deals not only with what diplomacy and diplomats do, but with how they contribute to making the international world as it is and as it ought to be.'

Paul Sharp, *University of Minnesota, USA*

'All those concerned with the study or teaching of diplomacy and foreign policy will want to consult this excellent book, which comprehensively discusses the most relevant and topical aspects of the subject; a precious teaching tool as well as a valuable handbook.'

Basil Germond, *Lancaster University, UK*

'*Understanding International Diplomacy: Theory, Practice and Ethics* fills in gap in the study of diplomacy and will be a useful addition for those interested in the conduct of international relations.'

Nabil Ayad, *Director, London Academy of Diplomacy, University of East Anglia, UK*

Understanding International Diplomacy

This textbook provides a comprehensive introduction to the study of international diplomacy, covering both theory and practice. The third edition has been updated and revised, with new chapters on the digital turn, contemporary crises, and power shifts in modern diplomacy.

By integrating historical traditions from Europe, China, and the Middle East with modern diplomatic challenges, this book:

- Traces the evolution of diplomacy from its historical foundations to its modern institutionalised form, examining how shifting power dynamics, technological revolutions, and geopolitical crises have shaped its trajectory
- Examines theoretical perspectives on diplomacy as a communicative practice, exploring how diplomats interpret and project power, negotiate international norms, and sustain diplomatic agency in an increasingly fragmented world order
- Analyses diplomacy in the digital age, investigating how new technologies, social media, and artificial intelligence reshape diplomatic interactions, redefine state and non-state engagement, and challenge traditional diplomatic norms in a rapidly evolving global information environment.

This new edition offers an up-to-date, accessible, and authoritative overview of how diplomacy works and, indeed, ought to work in a globalised world. It will be essential reading for students of international diplomacy and is highly recommended for students of crisis negotiation, international organisations, foreign policy, and international relations.

Corneliu Bjola is Professor of Digital Diplomacy at the University of Oxford, UK, and the Head of the Oxford Digital Diplomacy Research Group. His most recent publications include the *Oxford Handbook of Digital Diplomacy* (2023) and *Digital International Relations: Technology, Agency and Order* (2023).

Markus Kornprobst is Professor of International Relations at the Vienna School of International Studies, Austria. He is the author of *Irredentism in European Politics* (2008) and *Co-managing International Crises* (2019) and co-editor of ten books and publishes in leading journals in diplomacy and international relations.

Understanding International Diplomacy

Theory, Practice and Ethics

Third Edition

Corneliu Bjola and Markus Kornprobst

LONDON AND NEW YORK

Designed cover image: © Getty Images

Third Edition published 2026
by Routledge
4 Park Square, Milton Park, Abingdon, Oxon OX14 4RN

and by Routledge
605 Third Avenue, New York, NY 10158

Routledge is an imprint of the Taylor & Francis Group, an informa business

© 2026 Corneliu Bjola and Markus Kornprobst

The right of Corneliu Bjola and Markus Kornprobst to be identified as authors of this work has been asserted in accordance with sections 77 and 78 of the Copyright, Designs and Patents Act 1988.

All rights reserved. No part of this book may be reprinted or reproduced or utilised in any form or by any electronic, mechanical, or other means, now known or hereafter invented, including photocopying and recording, or in any information storage or retrieval system, without permission in writing from the publishers.

Trademark notice: Product or corporate names may be trademarks or registered trademarks, and are used only for identification and explanation without intent to infringe.

British Library Cataloguing-in-Publication Data
A catalogue record for this book is available from the British Library

ISBN: 978-1-032-77917-1 (hbk)
ISBN: 978-1-032-77916-4 (pbk)
ISBN: 978-1-003-48540-7 (ebk)

DOI: 10.4324/9781003485407

Typeset in Times New Roman
by Apex CoVantage, LLC

Contents

Illustrations ix
Acknowledgements xi
Abbreviations xii
Preface to the Third Edition xiv

PART I
Introduction 1

  1 Why and How to Study Diplomacy? 3

PART II
Tracing Diplomacy 15

  2 Historical Evolution 17
  3 Central Themes of Diplomatic Thought 37
  4 Expansion and Contraction of Diplomacy 54

PART III
Mapping Diplomacy 79

  5 Contexts of Diplomacy 81
  6 Tasks of Global Diplomacy 100

PART IV
Explaining Diplomacy 121

  7 Making Judgements 123
  8 Making Relations 140
  9 Making Order 157

PART V
Remaking Diplomacy   171

10 The Digital Turn   173

11 Crises in the Inter-epoch   190

12 Diplomatic Power   201

PART VI
Conclusion   221

13 The Philosophy of Diplomacy   223

Glossary   *238*
References   *246*
Index   *270*

Illustrations

Figures

3.1	*The Ambassadors* (1533) by Hans Holbein the Younger	42
6.1	Interplay of Diplomatic Contexts and Diplomatic Tasks	101
13.1	Leonardo Da Vinci: Study of the Proportions of the Human Body (Known as the Vitruvian Man)	226

Tables

1.1	Diplomatic Theory versus Foreign Policy Analysis	5
1.2	Methods for Studying Diplomacy	6
3.1	Mediation Approaches	45
6.1	Explaining Success and Failure of Mediation	114
10.1	Digital Crisis Management Stages	176
13.1	Posthumanist Perspectives and Their Implications for Diplomacy	234

Textboxes

2.1	Medieval Diplomats	19
2.2	The Rise of Resident Ambassadors in Italy	20
2.3	Greek Diplomatic Missions	22
2.4	The Policy of Diplomatic Prestige	26
2.5	The Concert of Europe in Action	29
2.6	Diplomatic Ranking	31
3.1	Shils' Dimensions of Tradition	39
3.2	Gadamer's "Fusion of Horizons"	40
4.1	2005 World Summit Outcome: Responsibility to Protect	59
4.2	Agenda 2063	65
4.3	The Early Response to COVID-19	70
4.4	Human Trafficking	74
5.1	Persona Non Grata	85
5.2	2012 Attacks on US Diplomats	87
5.3	Diplomatic Asylum and Julian Assange	89
5.4	Graphic Public Allegations versus Tact and Communicative Genre	92
5.5	Routines of Selectively Sending Peace Concepts from New York to Conflict Zones	94

5.6 The Idea of Europe	96
6.1 The Diplomatic Cable	103
6.2 Limitations of Scholarly Perspectives on Negotiation	110
6.3 The Making of the Nuclear Prohibition Treaty	112
6.4 Former Heads of State as Mediators	115
6.5 Sports and Music Diplomacy	118
6.6 Techniques for Learning from One Another	119
7.1 From Microfoundations to Anthropomorphisation	125
7.2 Appeasement	129
7.3 Security Council Resolution 1973	131
7.4 Diplomacy and Communicative Action	134
7.5 The Underlying Rules of the Diplomatic Game	136
8.1 US-Iranian Relations	144
8.2 Jean Monnet	146
8.3 Metis	147
8.4 The League of Nations, Promises of Horizontality, and Persisting Verticality	150
8.5 Kissinger, China, and the United States	152
8.6 Dag Hammerskjöld on the International Civil Servant	153
9.1 Henry Kissinger, 1923–2023	159
9.2 Towards an International Agency for Artificial Intelligence?	162
9.3 An Ever More Polarising World Order?	165
9.4 Polyplexity and Nuclear Governance	166
11.1 Srebrenica	193
11.2 United Nations Reform	195
11.3 The Multilateralism Index	197
12.1 Kennan's 'Long Telegram' (1946): Four Dimensions of Knowledge	207
12.2 Francesco Guicciardini's Diplomatic Method	213

Acknowledgements

We would like to extend our sincere thanks to Andrew Humphrys at Routledge, whose invaluable support was essential in bringing the third edition of this book to publication. We are deeply grateful to the blind peer reviewers for their insightful and constructive feedback, which has greatly enriched our work. Our special appreciation goes to Moges Zewiddu Teshome for his outstanding research assistance. We are also indebted to the Oxford Department of International Development and the Vienna School of International Studies for providing the stimulating and intellectually vibrant environments that enabled us to complete this project.

In writing this book, we have drawn significant inspiration from our students. Their engagement, curiosity, and contributions to our class discussions have profoundly shaped our thinking, and it is with them in mind that we have undertaken this work. It is to them that we dedicate this book.

Abbreviations

ABM	Anti-Ballistic Missile
ACLED	Armed Conflict and Event Data
ANC	African National Congress
AI	Artificial Intelligence
ASEAN	Association of Southeast Asian Nations
APEC	Asia-Pacific Cooperation
AU	African Union
CSTD	UN Commission on Science and Technology for Development
CTBTO	Preparatory Commission for a Comprehensive Nuclear-Test-Ban Treaty Organization
EPLF	Eritrean People's Liberation Front
EU	European Union
ExComm	Executive Committee
FDI	Foreign Direct Investment
FPA	Foreign Policy Analysis
GCC	Gulf Cooperation Council
HR	High Representative of the Union for Foreign Affairs and Security Policy
IAEA	International Atomic Energy Agency
ICBL	International Campaign to Ban Landmines
ICC	International Criminal Court
ICEM	Intergovernmental Committee for European Migration
IGAD	Intergovernmental Authority on Development
IGN	Intergovernmental Negotiations
ILC	International Law Commission
ILO	International Labour Organization
IMF	International Monetary Fund
INF	Intermediate-Range Nuclear Forces
IOM	International Organization for Migration
IPCC	Intergovernmental Panel on Climate Change
LAWS	lethal Autonomous Weapons Systems
MAGA	Making America Great Again
MDG	Millennium Development Goal
MFA	Swedish Ministry for Foreign Affairs
NATO	North-Atlantic Treaty Organization
NGO	Nongovernmental organisation
NPT	Treaty on the Non-Proliferation of Nuclear Weapons

OAS	Organization of American States
OSCE	Organization for Security and Co-operation in Europe
QUAD	Quadrilateral Security Dialogue
SALT	Strategic Arms Limitation Treaty
SALW	Small arms and light weapons
SCO	Shanghai Cooperation Organisation
SDG	Sustainable Development Goal
START	New Strategic Arms Reduction Treaty
TPLF	Tigray People's Liberation Front
TPNW	Treaty on the Prohibition of Nuclear Weapons
UN	United Nations
UNCTAD	UN Conference on Trade and Development
UNDESA	UN Department of Economic and Social Affairs
UNDP	UN Development Programme
UNESCO	UN Educational, Scientific, and Cultural Organization
UNFPA	UN Population Fund
UNEP	UN Environment Programme
UNHCR	UN High Commissioner for Refugees
UNICEF	UN Children's Fund
UNITAR	UN Institute for Training and Research
UNFCCC	UN Framework Convention on Climate Change
UNGA	UN General Assembly
UNMEER	UN Mission for Ebola Emergency Response
UNODC	UN Office on Drugs and Crime
UNRWA	UN Relief and Works Agency
UNSC	UN Security Council
UNSTO	UN Sciences and Technology Organization
WHO	World Health Organization
WTO	World Trade Organization

Preface to the Third Edition

This is the third edition of this book. The first one was published in 2013, the second in 2018, and now the third in 2025. While we did a rather comprehensive update for the second edition, the revisions for this new edition have been far-reaching. We have thoroughly updated chapters, rewritten entire chapters, and added new chapters. So, why all these revisions?

There are four reasons. First, the world does not stand still. Since we published the second edition, world politics has rushed from one crisis to the next. Russia has invaded Ukraine and annexed huge territories in eastern Ukraine. New civil wars with disastrous humanitarian consequences have started, including in Ethiopia (especially Tigray) and Sudan. Since Hamas's attack on Israel in October 2023 and the latter's heavy-handed response, the Middle East has become a major global crisis hotspot yet again. The COVID-19 pandemic killed millions of people worldwide and had severe economic repercussions for many states. While more and more natural disasters linked to climate change happen, diplomacy has continued to struggle to find ways to implement the 2015 Paris Agreement. Speaking about diplomacy, this institution has not remained unchanged in recent years either. The rise of populist governments in many parts of the world reconfigures diplomacy, pushing it away from subtle language and tact towards the grandstanding of leaders at the expense of career diplomats. Multilateralism and, with it, international organisations are in crisis. Member states made a lot of far-reaching promises when they agreed to the 2024 Pact for the Future, including the Global Digital Compact. In principle, this is to be welcomed. Living in the time of the Fourth Industrial Revolution, diplomacy needs to figure out how to reap the benefits of technological innovation while, at the same time, keeping its destructive potentials at bay. But a compact is not binding and the promises made in such documents are often not kept. The United Nations (UN) remains sidelined when it comes to addressing the crises of our times.

Second, the study of diplomacy continues to broaden and deepen. Gone are the days when the discipline of international relations neglected agency in general and diplomacy in particular. Studies of diplomacy have opened up new pathways for international relations theory and vice versa. The practice turn, for example, comes immediately to mind. In other disciplines, too, research on diplomacy has had a broader impact. Research on public diplomacy, for example, has found its way into more generic theories in the field of communications. Changes in the publication landscape are telling when it comes to this increasing interest in studying diplomacy. Since we published the first edition, numerous new publishing outlets have been created for books, such as the Routledge New Diplomacy Studies Series, the Brill Research Perspectives in Diplomacy and Foreign Policy, and the Palgrave Macmillan Series in Global Public Diplomacy. Many thought-provoking articles on diplomacy have been published in leading journals in the disciplines of International Relations, communications and history, to name but a few. This new edition provides an overview of these new research developments.

Third, the evolving technological landscape presents a profound challenge to global stability. The rapid development of artificial intelligence (AI), quantum computing, and cyber-warfare capabilities has heightened geopolitical tensions, exacerbating competition between major powers such as the United States, China, and Russia. The global digital sphere has become both a battleground and a diplomatic arena, with cyber-attacks, espionage, and the weaponisation of misinformation influencing political outcomes worldwide. While the 2024 Global Digital Compact outlined ambitious aspirations for digital governance, these remain largely aspirational, as states struggle to reconcile national security concerns with the need for global cooperation. Moreover, the digital divide is deepening, further entrenching disparities between developed and developing nations in terms of access to technological innovation. As diplomatic practice adapts to this emerging reality, questions remain as to how international norms and legal frameworks can adequately address the intersection of technology, security, and statecraft. The task of diplomacy is no longer merely to manage state-to-state relations but to navigate an increasingly complex web of digital, economic, and strategic interactions that defy traditional diplomatic frameworks.

Fourth, as academics, we made our own new experiences while dealing with diplomacy. We were engaged in research projects on tech diplomacy, secret diplomacy, digital diplomacy, crisis diplomacy, and diplomatic peace. We thought hard about what digital international relations – both as a subject to be studied and as a way to reinvent the discipline of International Relations – might look like. We taught students, trained diplomats and advised foreign ministries in Africa, the Caucasus, Central Asia, Europe, and the Middle East. This was always a two-way communication process. We learnt a lot from our encounters with colleagues, students and diplomats. This applies in particular to how to make sense of change in international relations and diplomacy, more precisely the technological underpinnings of it, the reconfiguration of diplomatic agency, and the future of world order. Furthermore, our own learning process continues to make this book more 'global' in outlook, and we discuss case studies from various world regions.

Our overriding aim, however, remained the same. Across all its editions, this book serves as a gateway to the study of diplomacy, offering both a foundational understanding and a lens through which to explore its evolving complexities. It lays bare the mechanics of diplomacy – deciphering its legal frameworks, dissecting the competing theories that seek to explain its practice, and interrogating the ethical dilemmas that diplomats inevitably confront. But beyond that, our deepest hope is that this book provokes fresh thinking, challenging readers to see diplomacy not just as a relic of statecraft but as a dynamic force shaping the world's political, economic, technological and security landscapes. In an era where diplomacy is both more necessary and more contested than ever, we invite readers to engage critically with this ancient institution – one whose reinvention may well determine the course of global affairs.

Part I
Introduction

1 Why and How to Study Diplomacy?

Why Study Diplomacy?

Few disciplines are as crucial to understanding the future of our world as diplomacy. In an era of shifting power, technological revolutions, and intensifying global challenges, diplomacy is at the heart of every major political transformation.

Europe, traditionally a pillar of multilateralism and diplomacy, faces its own challenges – ranging from internal fragmentation and geopolitical tensions with Russia to redefining its global role in a world where new power centres are emerging. European diplomacy is being tested not only in its neighbourhood, from Ukraine to the Balkans, but also in its ability to act as a bridge between global powers. Europe's longstanding partnership with the United States is entering a period of uncertainty. The United States, which for decades shaped and upheld the international order established after 1945, is increasingly revisiting its role in global governance. Its shifting foreign policy priorities, growing scepticism towards multilateral institutions, and selective engagement with allies raise pressing questions about the future of transatlantic diplomacy. As Washington reassesses its commitment to the postwar international framework it once championed, European states must navigate new diplomatic realities – balancing cooperation with the United States while strengthening their own strategic independence.

Meanwhile, the rise of China and India as global players raises profound questions about whether the redistribution of power from the West to the East will bring stability or turmoil. The outcome will depend not just on military and economic might but also on the skill and strategy of diplomats shaping the world order. The Middle East remains a flashpoint of conflict, with recent escalations – such as Hamas's attack on Israel and Israel's military response in Gaza – rekindling regional instability. The path to de-escalation, conflict resolution, and, ultimately, peace will not be forged through force alone but through tireless diplomatic efforts behind closed doors and on the world stage. Meanwhile, the world's most pressing existential threat – climate change – demands an unprecedented level of diplomatic cooperation. The Paris Agreement stands as a landmark achievement, yet its success hinges on whether diplomats can negotiate and enforce global commitments to sustainability.

The challenges do not end there. Africa's Agenda 2063 outlines a bold vision for the continent's future, but translating these aspirations into reality requires constant diplomatic negotiation – both within Africa and with global powers. Preventing the next pandemic will not be a matter of science alone; it will require diplomatic coordination to strengthen global health governance. From migration to human rights, from technological governance to nuclear diplomacy, the international landscape is shaped by challenges that no single nation can address alone. The question is not whether diplomacy is relevant but whether we are paying enough attention to how it operates, evolves, and ultimately shapes the world around us.

DOI: 10.4324/9781003485407-2

4 *Understanding International Diplomacy*

We find ourselves in an "in-between era" – a world where old diplomatic structures are struggling to keep pace with new global realities. Fresh ideas and new approaches to diplomacy are desperately needed. Yet, while diplomatic challenges evolve, the fundamental nature of diplomacy remains unchanged: How do political communities, often divided by ideology, interests, and culture, recognise, interpret, and project power through communication? This book does not seek to provide a definitive answer, but rather to open the question from multiple angles – historical, legal, cognitive, social, and ethical – so that readers can appreciate diplomacy as a dynamic, multifaceted, and indispensable tool of global engagement.

To unpack these themes, this chapter begins by comparing different ways of studying diplomacy, particularly in relation to fields like foreign policy analysis (FPA). Next, it examines why communication is the foundation of diplomatic practice, shaping everything from negotiation to public diplomacy. The third section expands the analytical toolbox by integrating insights from disciplines beyond International Relations. Finally, the chapter concludes with an overview of the themes explored in the rest of the book, setting the stage for a deep and thought-provoking journey into the art and science of diplomacy.

How to Study Diplomacy?

The study of diplomacy and foreign policy analysis represents two distinct but deeply interwoven approaches to understanding states' behaviour in international relations. Foreign policy analysis seeks to elucidate the *decision-making processes* that guide state behaviour, focusing on the internal determinants that shape foreign policy, from leadership psychology and bureaucratic politics to strategic calculations (Mintz and Sofrin, 2017). Diplomatic theory, by contrast, does not merely examine how states pursue their objectives but also interrogate the *nature of diplomacy itself*, considering it an institution in its own right – one that operates through negotiation, representation, and norm construction beyond the immediacy of state interests (Sharp, 2009). While foreign policy analysis offers insights into the motivations and decision-making processes that drive state behaviour, diplomatic theory reveals the processes through which these actions are negotiated, legitimised, and embedded within the fabric of global politics. To privilege one at the expense of the other is to risk either reducing diplomacy to a mere adjunct of statecraft or neglecting the structural conditions that shape diplomatic agency. By delineating their conceptual and methodological distinctions, it becomes possible to theorise diplomacy not as a passive vehicle for the execution of foreign policy but as a constitutive force in its own right – one that crafts the contours of international engagement and sustains the international order in which states operate.

Diplomatic theory and foreign policy analysis diverge primarily in their focus. While foreign policy analysis concerns itself with the rationales behind state actions, diplomatic theory scrutinises how diplomacy mediates, sustains, and sometimes even subverts these actions (see Table 1.1). Foreign policy theory, particularly in its realist and neorealist manifestations, frames international relations as a perpetual struggle for power, in which foreign policy is a calculated extension of national interest (Smith, 1986). Diplomatic theory, however, considers diplomacy as an *autonomous practice*, one that is not necessarily dictated by the imperatives of foreign policy, but is instead shaped by its own historical, institutional, and discursive logic (Derian, 1987). As Paul Sharp has argued, diplomacy functions not merely as a conduit for state objectives but as an arena where international norms, values, and collective identities are constructed (Sharp, 2009).

A key point of departure is the treatment of *agency and structure*. Foreign policy analysis is predominantly *agency-driven*, emphasising how decisions emerge from the choices of

Table 1.1 Diplomatic Theory versus Foreign Policy Analysis

Aspect	Diplomatic Theory	Foreign Policy Analysis
Primary Focus	Processes and norms of interaction	Decision-making and strategy
Key Actors	Diplomats, international institutions, non-state actors	Heads of state, government agencies, leaders
Methodology	Interpretive, historical, discourse-based	Empirical, decision-making models
Theoretical Foundations	Constructivism, English School, sociological analysis	Realism, liberalism, rational-choice
Main Concerns	Representation, negotiation, mediation, norms	Power, security, national interest

individuals, bureaucracies, and political institutions (Hudson, 2005). Diplomatic theory, by contrast, is often *structuralist in orientation*, viewing diplomacy as an evolving system of interaction that operates independently of specific national agendas. This distinction is particularly evident in crisis diplomacy, where foreign policy theory interprets crises as breakdowns in decision-making, whereas diplomatic theory sees them as failures in communication, trust, and institutional mechanisms (Bjola, 2016). While foreign policy analysis offers structured models for explaining why states act, diplomatic theory provides a broader, more fluid understanding of international engagement, one that does not assume that power alone dictates state behaviour. The work of James Der Derian is particularly instructive in this regard. His 'Mediating Estrangement' (1987) challenges the notion that diplomacy is merely an adjunct to foreign policy, arguing instead that diplomacy is a force that shapes the very conditions in which foreign policy is conceived and executed. He suggests that diplomacy plays a constitutive role in world politics, structuring interactions between states not through coercion, but through discursive practices and symbolic exchange.

A striking counterpoint to this perspective is offered by Morgenthau, who remains critical of legalistic and idealistic interpretations of diplomacy, contending that any diplomatic engagement must ultimately be judged against the realities of power (Morgenthau, 1948). While Der Derian (1987) considers diplomacy as an independent domain of meaning-making, Morgenthau warns against treating diplomacy as detached from the fundamental struggles of power and survival. This tension – between diplomacy as a constitutive process and diplomacy as an instrument of power – remains one of the most enduring debates in the study of international relations.

Diplomatic theory, however, does not merely provide an alternative to the power-centric focus of foreign policy analysis. It also expands the scope of inquiry beyond the state. Hedley Bull's conceptualisation of diplomacy within *The Anarchical Society* (1977/2002) presents it as a *stabilising force*, one that mitigates anarchy and sustains international order through norms and practices that extend beyond traditional conceptions of national interest. Paul Sharp (2009) develops this notion further, arguing that diplomacy is fundamentally about world disclosure – that is, it shapes the way international actors perceive reality, legitimising certain political orders while marginalising others. This perspective contrasts sharply with rational-choice models in foreign policy analysis, which presuppose fixed interests and calculable strategies. For these reasons, the study of diplomacy requires a distinct methodological approach – one that is necessarily different from the methodologies employed in foreign policy analysis.

As indicated in Table 1.2, diplomatic studies rely on historical analysis, discourse theory, and interpretive methods, prioritising the social and symbolic dimensions of diplomatic interaction.

6 *Understanding International Diplomacy*

Table 1.2 Methods for Studying Diplomacy

Approach	Description	Advantages	Limitations
Historical Analysis	Examining diplomatic traditions over time	Provides depth, context, and patterns	Can be overly descriptive, lacking theoretical rigor
Constructivist Approaches	Exploring diplomacy as a norm-building and identity-shaping practice	Highlights the social and discursive role of diplomacy	Less predictive power than rational-choice models
Case Study Method	Examining individual diplomatic negotiations	Rich empirical data	Case-specific insights may not be generalisable
Comparative Analysis	Comparing different diplomatic traditions	Reveals universal and culturally specific diplomatic behaviours	Risks oversimplification of complex interactions

While this approach offers a comprehensive lens on international engagement, it is not without its limitations. Unlike foreign policy analysis, which formulates structured models to predict state behaviour, diplomatic theory lacks predictive precision and often struggles to account for material constraints such as military and economic imperatives. Its reliance on historical analysis, while rich in context, risks becoming overly descriptive, while constructivist approaches, though illuminating diplomacy's discursive nature, provide little explanatory traction in moments of crisis. The case study method, though empirically robust, yields insights that are often too context-specific to be generalised, and comparative analysis, while useful in identifying patterns across traditions, tends to flatten complexity in pursuit of broad typologies. These methodological constraints reflect the inherent fluidity of diplomacy – an art of negotiation and representation that resists rigid theoretical codification.

Despite these limitations, the study of diplomacy provides a critical corrective to the assumptions of foreign policy analysis, offering a perspective that is not merely focused on power but on the mechanisms of global political order. As Paul Sharp (2009) points out, diplomacy is not merely about negotiation – it is about constructing the very realities within which international politics unfolds. Similarly, Der Derian (1987) challenges us to rethink diplomacy in a world characterised by estrangement and crisis, urging scholars to move beyond state-centric models and explore diplomacy as a force of global transformation. This imperative is particularly evident when considering non-Western diplomatic traditions, which often diverge from the legalistic and institutional frameworks dominant in Western thought. From Kautilyan realpolitik (*Arthashastra*, c. 4th century BCE) and Confucian relationalism (Confucius, *Analects*, c. 5th century BCE) to Middle Eastern mediation practices (Dutta and Dabhade, 2014), these alternative traditions foreground pragmatism, strategic ambiguity, and informal networks of influence, challenging universalist assumptions about how diplomacy is conceptualised and practised across cultures.

The study of diplomacy therefore necessitates a broad yet analytically rigorous approach, one that moves beyond conventional statecraft to interrogate the evolving nature of diplomatic interaction, negotiation, and representation. This volume engages with diplomacy not simply as a function of state interest but as a constitutive force in shaping international order, offering a framework that situates diplomacy within its historical, procedural, and theoretical dimensions. It examines how diplomacy has been both a *structured institution and a fluid practice*, evolving in response to shifting geopolitical realities, economic transformations, and technological innovations. The study of diplomacy requires an appreciation of its contextual underpinnings – its codification in legal frameworks, its role in conflict mediation, and its function as a stabilising force within an anarchic international system. At the same time, diplomacy is inherently contingent, continually reshaped by shifting power asymmetries, the rise of new diplomatic actors, and the evolving landscape of global norms. By integrating the methodological approaches outlined earlier – historical analysis, constructivist inquiry, comparative studies, and case-based research – the volume provides a multi-layered understanding of diplomacy, acknowledging its role as both an instrument of strategic action and a medium of discursive and symbolic exchange.

How to Define Diplomacy?

Diplomacy is best understood as the institutionalised practice of communication among internationally recognised actors, through which they negotiate, manage, and distribute public goods.

Unlike ad hoc political exchanges, diplomatic engagement is shaped by historical precedents, procedural conventions, and cultural expectations that define its legitimacy and efficacy. It is neither static nor uniform but a dynamic field of interaction where power, recognition, and governance intersect. To fully grasp its nature, three interrelated dimensions must be considered: diplomacy as institutionalised communication, diplomacy as a process of recognition, and diplomacy as a mechanism for producing and distributing public goods.

Diplomacy as Institutionalised Communication

Diplomatic communication is not simply an exchange of information; it is a regulated and performative process, structured by formal rules, rituals, and expectations that define how actors interact. Its institutionalisation ensures that diplomatic engagement remains predictable, legitimate, and continuous, even in moments of crisis. This structured nature serves several key functions:

- It reinforces *continuity and order* in international relations, ensuring that even adversarial states maintain channels of dialogue. This allows rivals to de-escalate tensions through diplomatic backchannels, maintain communication during crises, and engage in negotiations without immediately resorting to coercion or military confrontation.
- It establishes a *shared framework of engagement*, reducing the unpredictability of international interactions by embedding diplomacy in a recognised legal and normative structure. By codifying acceptable behaviour and diplomatic precedence, this framework mitigates misinterpretation, fosters reciprocity, and ensures that even asymmetrical power relationships operate within an agreed set of constraints.
- It incorporates *symbolic and performative dimensions*, where gestures such as treaties, summits, and protocol-bound meetings communicate meaning beyond direct negotiation. State visits, diplomatic receptions, or joint declarations often serve to reinforce alliances, project stability to domestic and international audiences, and cultivate trust before substantive negotiations even begin.

While Adam Watson (1984) famously defined diplomacy as an institution of dialogue, its communicative function extends far beyond mere exchange. Diplomacy operates across multiple registers, encompassing not only *negotiation* – the crafting of agreements, peace treaties, and alliances through bargaining – but also *coercive diplomacy*, where pressure, threats, or sanctions are employed to achieve strategic aims. Beyond these, diplomacy also involves *symbolic and declarative acts*, such as declarations of war, diplomatic recognitions, and public statements that shape international legitimacy. This broad communicative spectrum highlights diplomacy's dual nature – it is both a tool for cooperation and a mechanism of strategic influence. It is neither inherently peaceful nor neutral; rather, it serves as an arena where interests are advanced, power asymmetries are managed, and international authority is contested. The same diplomatic frameworks that facilitate conflict resolution can also be leveraged for strategic gain, alliance-building, or geopolitical coercion, underscoring diplomacy's central role not only in maintaining stability but also in shaping the dynamics of global competition.

Recognition as the Basis of Diplomatic Agency

Diplomacy operates within a system of recognition, where legitimacy is granted to specific actors based on their standing within the international order. Traditionally, diplomacy was exclusively state-centric, with sovereign states recognised as the sole legitimate participants in diplomatic relations. This exclusivity was codified in frameworks such as the Vienna Convention on Diplomatic Relations (1961), which formalised the role of embassies, diplomatic immunity, and accreditation. However, contemporary diplomacy has outgrown its state-centric confines. Recognition now extends to a wider set of actors, including:

- *International organisations*, such as the UN Secretariat, the European External Action Service, and the African Union Commission, engage in diplomacy as supranational entities, facilitating multilateral negotiations, setting global norms, and coordinating responses to transnational challenges, often acting as mediators or institutional diplomats beyond the direct interests of any single state.
- *Transnational advocacy groups*, such as Amnesty International and Greenpeace, engage in diplomacy by lobbying governments, influencing international organisations, and shaping global norms through political pressure, public campaigns, and direct participation in multilateral negotiations.
- *Multinational corporations* conduct corporate diplomacy, negotiating trade agreements, influencing regulatory frameworks, and engaging with states and international bodies to protect their economic interests, secure market access, and shape global business governance.

Diplomatic recognition is neither fixed nor universal – it is historically contingent and politically contested. What constitutes a legitimate diplomatic actor shifts over time, reflecting changes in global governance, power hierarchies, and normative structures. The Westphalian model privileged sovereign states; contemporary diplomacy increasingly recognises pluralistic networks of authority, challenging traditional diplomatic hierarchies. Understanding diplomacy today requires an awareness of these evolving structures, where new actors, new arenas, and new modes of engagement continuously reshape the diplomatic landscape.

Diplomacy as the Production and Distribution of Public Goods

Beyond communication and recognition, diplomacy serves a fundamental role in the creation, management, and allocation of public goods – the resources, institutions, and norms that sustain international stability. Historically, diplomacy was narrowly focused on security, ensuring the survival of states against external threats. Over time, however, its scope has expanded to include:

- *Economic Diplomacy* – The negotiation of trade agreements, financial stability, and development assistance. It requires diplomats to mediate between protectionist and free-market policies, resolve disputes over tariffs and subsidies, and facilitate investment flows while ensuring economic cooperation aligns with national and regional priorities.
- *Environmental Diplomacy* – The management of global challenges such as climate change and resource sustainability. It necessitates balancing economic growth with environmental commitments, addressing transboundary pollution and resource management disputes, and securing binding international agreements that hold states accountable for ecological preservation.
- *Health Diplomacy* – The coordination of international responses to pandemics and health crises. It involves negotiating equitable access to vaccines and treatments, strengthening cross-border disease surveillance, and fostering cooperation between states and international health organisations to mitigate global health threats.
- *Humanitarian Diplomacy* – The governance of migration, human rights, and post-conflict reconstruction. It requires diplomats to mediate refugee protection agreements, negotiate humanitarian access in conflict zones, and reconcile sovereignty concerns with international legal obligations to protect vulnerable populations.
- *Tech Diplomacy* – The governance of digital infrastructure, cybersecurity, and AI ethics in global affairs. As digital technologies increasingly shape global interactions, diplomacy now extends into areas such as internet governance, data privacy negotiations, and the regulation of emerging technologies like AI, quantum computing, and autonomous systems.

As global interdependence deepens, many public goods that were once the sole responsibility of nation-states have become transnational concerns, requiring diplomatic frameworks that extend beyond individual state interests. Issues such as climate governance, financial stability, and global health security cannot be managed unilaterally; they demand cooperative, multilateral, and networked diplomatic responses that bring together states, international organisations, corporations, and civil society. However, this transformation presents profound challenges. Diplomats must navigate competing priorities, balancing national sovereignty with collective global obligations, often in areas where institutional mechanisms lag behind global realities, leaving governance gaps that require diplomatic improvisation and innovation. Moreover, as public goods transcend national borders, their legitimacy must be established beyond the state, expanding diplomacy into non-traditional arenas, from corporate boardrooms negotiating digital trade rules to transnational platforms shaping cybersecurity governance.

This shift does not simply broaden the diplomatic agenda; it raises fundamental questions about the very nature of diplomacy itself. As the boundaries between state and non-state actors blur, and as diplomatic functions become increasingly digitised, decentralised, and informal, the traditional foundations of diplomacy – sovereign embassies, international treaties, and state-to-state negotiations – are no longer sufficient on their own. Instead, they are being complemented, and in some cases challenged, by alternative diplomatic spaces, ranging from digital diplomacy to corporate influence networks. Whether these developments signal a fundamental transformation of diplomacy or its fragmentation into a more diffuse and contested practice remains an open question – one that underscores the need for an adaptive and forward-looking understanding of diplomacy in the contemporary world.

Broadening Horizons for Studying Diplomacy

The purpose of this book is neither to advocate for a singular theoretical perspective nor to construct an entirely new one. Rather, *it seeks to equip the reader with a broad analytical toolbox for understanding diplomacy*, offering a range of conceptual and methodological lenses through which to examine both how diplomacy functions and how it ought to function. The intention is not to impose a definitive framework but to enable the reader to navigate and critically engage with the diverse intellectual traditions that inform diplomatic studies. To further this goal, we encourage readers to expand their exploration beyond the material presented here, aided by curated recommendations for further reading.

While many of the concepts in this book are drawn from established literature on diplomacy, we deliberately extend our reach beyond conventional disciplinary boundaries. In this way, the book mirrors existing textbooks in summarising the state of the art, yet it also ventures into intellectual terrain that has often been overlooked in diplomatic studies. Many of the most valuable insights on diplomacy come not from works explicitly dedicated to the subject but from disciplines such as economics, history, law, political theory, psychology, and sociology. Some of the thinkers discussed here have never written about diplomacy directly, yet their arguments shed light on aspects of diplomatic practice that remain underexplored, under-theorised, or taken for granted. Given diplomacy's inherently multifaceted nature, we adopt an equally multifaceted approach to its study, crossing disciplinary and sub-disciplinary boundaries to construct a richer, more nuanced understanding.

This multi-perspectival approach is also evident in how we engage with research on global governance, foreign policy analysis, and international relations theory. While diplomacy is distinct from global governance, the institutionalisation of diplomatic communication generates unique patterns of interaction, particularly in terms of recognition, legitimacy, and authority. The study of global governance, however, offers essential insights for understanding contemporary diplomacy, as diplomats today must operate within and beyond traditional diplomatic structures, engaging with multiple policy fields and diverse actors, some within and some outside the diplomatic realm. Similarly, while diplomacy and foreign policy analysis are not synonymous, the boundary between them is fluid. Foreign policy analysis traditionally examines policy formation within domestic settings, while diplomatic studies focus on how these policies are pursued internationally. Yet as Hedley Bull rightly observed, the study of diplomacy cannot ignore policy formation, particularly in an era where the lines between domestic and international policymaking are increasingly blurred. Diplomacy is not merely the execution of foreign policy; it is a site of political contestation, strategic adaptation, and policy innovation.

Finally, we also examine the intersections between diplomatic studies and broader debates in international relations theory. Of particular relevance are approaches that take agency seriously, exploring how diplomats and diplomatic institutions both shape and are shaped by the structural conditions in which they operate. Diplomacy is inherently agent-driven, foregrounding the work of diplomats as key actors in global politics. Yet diplomats do not operate in a vacuum; they are embedded in institutional, legal, and historical contexts that both enable and constrain their actions. Understanding diplomacy, therefore, requires an appreciation of both its agentive dimensions and the structural forces that define its possibilities and limits. This book, then, is not simply a survey of existing theories of diplomacy but an invitation to think across disciplinary boundaries, engage critically with competing perspectives, and explore the evolving nature of diplomacy in an increasingly complex and fragmented world.

Overview

The book is structured into four interconnected parts, each addressing a fundamental dimension of diplomacy: its historical and conceptual evolution, its core functions and tasks, its role in shaping and maintaining international order, and its adaptation to contemporary challenges such as digital transformation and crisis diplomacy. The structure moves from historical and theoretical grounding to practical applications and future-oriented discussions, balancing conceptual insights with empirical case studies. The book provides a comprehensive and critical exploration of diplomacy, examining how it has evolved, how it operates today, and how it must adapt to an increasingly complex global environment.

The first part of the book establishes the historical and conceptual foundations of diplomacy. Chapter 2 traces the institutionalisation of diplomacy from its origins in the ancient world, particularly in Egypt, Greece, and China, through the Treaty of Westphalia and the Congress of Vienna, up to the emergence of modern multilateral diplomacy. The development of permanent embassies and the professionalisation of diplomatic practices are examined alongside the twentieth-century transformations driven by the establishment of the League of Nations, the UN, and other international institutions that have shaped contemporary diplomatic norms. This historical grounding provides insight into how diplomacy has been shaped by shifting power structures and global events.

Building on this foundation, Chapter 3 explores the themes of tradition, mediation, and power in diplomacy. It examines how tradition functions as a stabilising force through the reproduction and reinterpretation of diplomatic norms, practices, and knowledge across generations. Drawing on the perspectives of Edward Shils and Hans-Georg Gadamer, the discussion highlights how diplomatic traditions evolve through a fusion of historical meanings with contemporary contexts, ensuring both continuity and adaptation. The role of mediation in addressing estrangement and fostering connection is examined through the works of James Der Derian, Georg Simmel, and Paul Sharp, emphasising how diplomacy navigates the inherent fragmentation of international relations. The discussion of power in diplomacy considers Friedrich Meinecke's concept of raison d'état, which focuses on state survival and pragmatism, alongside Adam Watson's raison de système, which emphasises the need for systemic equilibrium and shared norms. The dual approach of Henry Kissinger, which balanced tactical engagement with strategic vision, is explored as an example of how diplomacy operates at the intersection of short-term state interests and long-term global stability.

The expansion and contraction of diplomacy is the focus of Chapter 4, which examines how the scope of diplomatic engagement has changed over time. The post–World War II period saw a dramatic expansion in diplomatic issue areas, incorporating topics such as development, human rights, environmental diplomacy, migration, and health governance. However, since the early 2000s, a counter-trend of contraction has emerged, as traditional great-power diplomacy has reasserted itself, limiting the influence of non-state actors such as nongovernmental organisations (NGOs). The chapter highlights the growing mismatch between the demand for global governance and the limited diplomatic capacity to supply it, analysing how the geopolitical and geo-economic landscape is shaping the scope of diplomatic action.

The second part of the book maps out the contexts in which diplomacy operates and the tasks diplomats perform. These contexts shape diplomatic actions, and, in turn, diplomatic actions reshape the context. Chapter 5 introduces the structural contexts of diplomacy, distinguishing between foreground and background factors, as well as procedural and substantive dimensions. The procedural foreground remains anchored in the 1961 Vienna Convention on Diplomatic Relations, which establishes the dos and don'ts of diplomatic engagement.

The procedural background includes unwritten norms, such as tact, diplomatic authority, and communicative genre, which influence how diplomacy is conducted. The substantive foreground focuses on peace and conflict resolution, emphasising restraint, compromise, and dialogue as key diplomatic objectives. Meanwhile, the substantive background consists of practical how-to-do knowledge, which varies across different historical and cultural traditions. This chapter illustrates how these elements interact, often generating tensions – especially around the principle of sovereign equality, where formal diplomatic principles sometimes clash with geopolitical realities.

Moving to diplomatic practice, Chapter 6 examines the four core tasks of diplomacy: messaging, negotiation, mediation, and dialogue. Diplomats function as messengers, both internally between embassies and ministries and externally to foreign counterparts and the public. External messaging includes public diplomacy, strategic narratives, and forms of soft power engagement. Diplomats are also negotiators, with some approaches emphasising strategic bargaining and others highlighting the interpersonal, skill-based art of negotiation. Where parties fail to reach agreements by themselves, mediation becomes essential, requiring impartiality and trust-building to facilitate agreements. Finally, dialogue represents the most open-ended diplomatic function, where diplomats are expected to engage in reciprocal communication and reconsider their initial positions. However, as the chapter highlights, true deliberative dialogue is rare, with most diplomatic discussions being less demanding forms of interaction, such as polylogue. The chapter concludes by examining how diplomatic tasks both reproduce and reshape the broader contexts in which they occur.

The third part shifts focus to explaining how diplomatic outcomes are shaped by decision-making processes, relational transformations, and international order-building. Chapter 7 explores how diplomats make decisions, contrasting different logics of action. Rational choice models conceptualise diplomats as expected utility maximisers, calculating the best possible outcomes. Psychological approaches challenge this assumption, emphasising heuristic shortcuts and bounded rationality. The logic of appropriateness posits that diplomats follow established norms rather than engaging in purely instrumental decision-making. The logic of argumentation highlights how diplomats construct arguments and adjust preferences by communicating with one another. Finally, the logic of practice shifts attention to habitual doings that shape diplomatic decision-making. This chapter critically examines these perspectives, showing how different modes of decision-making influence crisis diplomacy.

The construction and transformation of diplomatic relationships are the focus of Chapter 8. Diplomatic relations exist along two continua, one from proximity to distance and the other from horizontality to verticality. The chapter examines how diplomatic relations evolve through détente, rapprochement, and entente, and explores the persistence of hidden hierarchies in international relations despite formal claims of sovereign equality. Moving to broader systemic issues, Chapter 9 investigates the role of diplomacy in constructing and maintaining world order. Three main conceptualisations of order are analysed: polarity, in which the world is understood as unipolar, bipolar, or multipolar; order as a system of rules; and order as deeply seated background knowledge. The chapter introduces the concept of polyplexity, which acknowledges the complexity of world order as a constellation of regional, functional, and overlapping governance structures. The limitations of diplomacy in managing this complexity are critically assessed.

The final part of the book focuses on how diplomacy functions today and how it should operate in the future, addressing the role of diplomatic power and crisis diplomacy. Chapter 10 explores how digitalisation reshapes crisis diplomacy, public engagement, and negotiations.

Digital crisis communication, analysed through Arjen Boin's crisis management framework, accelerates response but challenges message control. Public diplomacy, influenced by Erving Goffman's dramaturgical model, balances performance and strategy in managing state narratives. Digital negotiations, shaped by increasing transparency, create risks of leaks and manipulation, requiring states to adopt confidentiality strategies. AI, encryption, and digital media introduce new diplomatic opportunities and vulnerabilities, necessitating recalibrated approaches to influence and authority in a hyper-connected world. How diplomacy copes with permacrisis and polycrisis is the subject of Chapter 11, which argues that contemporary world politics is best understood as an inter-epoch, characterised by power transitions and technological disruptions. Diplomacy struggles to manage two types of crises: policy crises, which disrupt specific diplomatic issue areas, and institutional crises, which undermine the legitimacy of global governance mechanisms. The chapter discusses the co-management of crises, emphasising the difficulty of building consensus among actors with diverging repertoires and interpretations of global challenges.

Chapter 12 examines diplomatic power in three dimensions: epistemic, symbolic, and strategic. Epistemic power shapes diplomacy through knowledge control and intelligence framing. Symbolic power, influenced by Ernst Cassirer, constructs legitimacy via myths, narratives, and representation. Strategic power, as theorised by Francesco Guicciardini and Raymond Aron, operationalises influence through negotiation and statecraft. In the digital age, these dimensions intersect with AI-driven narratives, digital governance, and control over critical infrastructures, making technological supremacy central to diplomacy. The book concludes in Chapter 13 with a philosophical perspective on diplomacy inspired by Da Vinci's *Vitruvian Man*, illustrating how its epistemic, symbolic, and strategic dimensions do not function as isolated forces but as interdependent elements within a proportioned and evolving system of influence. This model underscores the need to understand diplomacy not as a collection of discrete strategies but as a structured discipline, where knowledge, legitimacy, and negotiation exist in dynamic equilibrium, sustaining order while adapting to shifting global conditions.

Part II
Tracing Diplomacy

2 Historical Evolution

Chapter objectives

- To provide readers with a structured understanding of the historical evolution of diplomacy, focusing on its key themes – representation, communication, and conflict management – up to World War I.
- To identify and analyse the pivotal transformations in diplomatic practices across different historical periods and cultural contexts.
- To evaluate the contributions and challenges of diplomacy in fostering international cooperation, resolving conflicts, and adapting to changing geopolitical dynamics.

Introduction

Diplomacy, derived from the Greek word diploma (a double-folded document, often signifying a letter of recommendation or privilege), originates from the earliest human efforts to engage and negotiate with neighbouring communities. These interactions aimed to establish boundaries, foster mutual understanding, and manage co-existence, marking the nascent stages of organised diplomatic practice (Carrió-Invernizzi, 2014). Diplomacy, as with other human institutions, was a deliberate invention, not a universal tradition, reflecting the distinct needs and norms of diverse societies.

Since the 3rd millennium BCE – often considered the starting point of what we recognise today as international relations and diplomacy (Cohen, 2001) – diplomatic practices have developed unevenly across regions. Each society crafted its unique approach to representation, communication, and conflict resolution, shaped by its governance structures, cultural priorities, and geopolitical realities. This lack of uniformity extended to the roles and significance of diplomats, whose influence expanded and contracted over time, often reflecting shifts in the broader international system (Hare, 2015). Diplomatic practice, thus, remains historically and geographically contextual, evolving as a pragmatic response to recurring challenges and volatile geopolitical climates.

This chapter explores the evolution of diplomatic practices through three interconnected themes: representation, communication, and conflict management, weaving these themes across the historical periods of ancient, medieval, and modern diplomacy (up to World War I). The analysis begins by examining representation, focusing on the roles, characteristics, and institutionalisation of diplomats as these evolved over time. It then explores communication, highlighting the tools, methods, and cultural nuances that enabled diplomatic engagement across different eras. Finally, it considers conflict management, tracing the mechanisms employed to resolve disputes and maintain order in increasingly complex international systems.

DOI: 10.4324/9781003485407-4

While European diplomacy, particularly its modern institutionalisation, forms the core of the discussion, examples from non-Western contexts are integrated throughout to provide a comparative perspective. This approach emphasises the adaptability of diplomacy, illustrating how historical traditions and regional contexts have shaped its evolution into a dynamic and multifaceted practice.

Representation Procedures

Diplomatic practices in ancient civilisations were deeply influenced by power asymmetry, shaping interactions between states and leaders. In the Greek city-states, no single polity dominated or faced overwhelming external threats. This relative balance of power allowed for diplomatic engagement based on relative equality. By contrast, the diplomatic systems of Egypt, Rome, Persia, and China were driven by the need to assert, establish, and maintain political, religious, or military superiority over their neighbours, often creating hierarchical relations rather than horizonal ones.

In the Ancient Near East, diplomatic practice reflected the realities of fragmented regional power structures. Envoys, typically of high rank, acted as messengers between "Great Kings" to manage inter-kingdom relations. Their missions were strictly defined, with a focus on the delivery of messages and the negotiation of treaties. However, these envoys were exposed to significant risks, such as imprisonment or assassination, as there were no established protections akin to modern diplomatic immunity. The host sovereign retained extensive control, dictating the envoy's movements and the terms of their stay, which further underlined the precarious nature of early diplomacy (Sofer, 2013: 3). Egyptian diplomacy, as reflected in the Amarna Letters, reveals a similarly structured approach. Pharaohs maintained an active correspondence with rulers of neighbouring powers, referring to one another as 'brothers' to signify nominal equality. However, Egypt's monopoly on prestige goods, particularly gold, allowed its rulers to negotiate from a position of strength, often forcing concessions from their counterparts. This system exemplified the duality of diplomacy as both a stabilising mechanism and a projection of hegemonic power (Munn-Rankin, 2004: 13).

In the Greek system, diplomacy introduced specific classifications of representatives. The *angelos* (messenger) and *keryx* (elder) undertook short-term missions, often chosen for their oratorical skills and maturity to address host councils persuasively. However, their actions were tightly restricted by elaborate instructions from the sending state, limiting their ability to adapt to changing conditions (Murray, 1855: 9). The *proxenos* (→ glossary), in contrast, resided in their own state while acting on behalf of another, facilitating trade, offering hospitality, and occasionally advising on political matters (Hamilton and Langhorne, 1995: 9–10). This role underscored the cooperative and relational aspects of Greek diplomacy. Nonetheless, key features of modern diplomacy, such as immunity and formalised protocols, were absent, leaving envoys reliant on customary codes of religion and hospitality for their safety.

Roman diplomacy was built upon Greek traditions but introduced greater institutionalisation. Roman envoys, termed *nuntii* or *oratores*, were often selected from the senatorial class and operated under strict mandates from the Senate. Their primary task was to negotiate agreements and report back for ratification. Over time, the growing complexity of the empire saw the emperor assume direct oversight of diplomatic activities, symbolising Rome's centralised authority. This blend of pragmatic negotiation and symbolic dominance characterised Roman diplomacy, with the empire using it as a tool to reinforce control and legitimacy across its vast territories.

During the medieval period, diplomacy in Europe evolved significantly, driven by the influence of the Catholic Church and the legal frameworks established by canon and Roman law.

> **Textbox 2.1 Medieval Diplomats**
>
> The nuncius was sometimes instructed to engage in propagandizing, fomenting revolts and breaking unfriendly relations. In the formation of the League of Friuli (1384), Venice sent nuncii to Friuli, towns dependent on that city, and the church of Aquileia, urging them to resist foreign encroachment. Even more, a state that felt itself injured could employ nuncii to deliver a protest, an ultimatum or even a declaration of war. They were also sent in times of war to an ally to coordinate efforts against the common enemy (Queller, 2004: 195).

Early envoys, known as *nuncii* (→ glossary), served as intermediaries carrying messages and exploring opportunities for treaties (see Textbox 2.1). Their immunity was rooted in religious doctrines, granting them protection as representatives of sovereigns (Murray, 1855: 13). However, as political and economic relations grew more intricate, the limitations of the nuncius model became evident. This led to the rise of the *procurator*, an official with "plena potestas" (full powers), capable of independently negotiating and concluding agreements. The professionalisation of these roles marked a critical step in the institutional development of diplomacy (Hamilton and Langhorne, 1995: 27). The growth of trade during the medieval period led to the development of the consular system, with consuls overseeing commerce and resolving disputes. Early examples include Marseille establishing consuls in Tyre and Beirut in 1223. By the 15th and 16th centuries, treaties like the Capitulations between Christians and Muslims expanded consular functions, granting jurisdiction over nationals in the Byzantine Empire. Consuls, appointed as state representatives, gained privileges and immunities, cementing their role in protecting trade and diplomacy (Chatterjee, 2007: 250).

The early modern period witnessed the establishment of the resident ambassador, a transformative innovation in diplomatic practice. Originating in the Italian city-states during the Renaissance, this system institutionalised continuous representation, allowing rulers to gather intelligence on neighbouring states more effectively. It was at this time that European diplomacy professionalised. "It was the Byzantines who taught diplomacy to Venice; it was the Venetians who set the pattern for Italian cities, for France and Spain, and eventually for all Europe" (Nicolson, 1988: 24–5). Byzantine diplomacy exemplified a highly developed system, integrating ceremonial grandeur with strategic negotiation. Envoys were carefully trained in foreign customs and political contexts, while elaborate ceremonies emphasised Byzantine superiority. This strategic use of symbolism not only reinforced the empire's dominance but also influenced diplomatic practices in the broader European sphere.

The Peace of Westphalia in 1648 marked a turning point in diplomatic history, codifying principles of territorial sovereignty and non-interference. This settlement not only ended decades of religious conflict but also provided the foundation for the modern state system. The principle of raison d'état (→ glossary), championed by Cardinal Richelieu, further solidified this shift by prioritising state interests over personal or religious loyalties. The establishment of the new office of resident ambassador was based on the need of rulers to know as much as could be known about the internal affairs of the neighbouring states (see Textbox 2.2). The potential instability of the governments of the early sovereign states led them to frantically attempt to prevent subversion "pursued by diplomatic agents plotting with opposition groups" (Hamilton and

> **Textbox 2.2 The Rise of Resident Ambassadors in Italy**
>
> Italy was the model of what Europe as whole was soon to become. The five large powers, Milan, Venice, Florence, the Papacy and Naples remained in an unstable equilibrium while small states like Lucca, Mantua and Ferrara were protected against aggression only by the mutual jealousies of their powerful neighbors. Resident ambassadors thus proved their usefulness by serving as a check and as a means of raising the diplomatic alarm when any power threatened to upset the balance. Their widespread establishment helped avert crises by making possible rapid realignments in the patterns of alliances.
>
> (Mattingly, 2004: 222)

Langhorne (1995: 33). Resident ambassadors were expected to acclimatise themselves to local conditions to assess to what extent they could intervene in local political intrigues. In addition, resident ambassadors were expected to watch the safety of their fellow countrymen and to aid them in their business abroad.

The social background of early resident ambassadors varied widely, influencing the quality of diplomatic practice. English residents, typically gentry of modest descent, were generally seen as competent. French representatives, often lower-ranking nobles, apparently excelled at seizing strategic opportunities. Spanish envoys, drawn from the high nobility, earned a reputation for skill and effectiveness, while Venetian diplomats, though from leading families, tended to focus excessively on detailed but often irrelevant reporting. Dutch representatives, coming from diverse social backgrounds, were seen as less effective in managing day-to-day diplomatic interactions (Carter, 2004). Over time, it became evident that the success of diplomacy depended heavily on the personal qualities of ambassadors. As one observer noted, "The fate of nations very often hangs on the judicious conduct of a diplomatist. His success depends almost entirely on the confidence and esteem which he inspires" (Murray, 1855: 43).

Resident ambassadors were held to exacting standards. They were expected to master Latin, the diplomatic *lingua franca* of the time (→ glossary), and to navigate suspicion by appearing congenial and tactful. Ambassadors were required to demonstrate erudition, cultivate influential relationships, and exercise patience, particularly when negotiations demanded prolonged discussions. Their private conduct had to be impeccable, avoiding any hint of scandal or impropriety, as such missteps could undermine their mission and the standing of their home state (Nicolson, 1988: 35–6). Failure to meet these expectations often led to tensions, including refusals by sovereigns to receive ambassadors. Such refusals might stem from prior misunderstandings, a desire to avoid ceremonial obligations, or personal grievances against the envoy (Murray, 1855: 57).

The increasing need for control over diplomacy led Cardinal Richelieu to establish France's first foreign ministry, the Ministère des Affaires Étrangères, in 1626. Richelieu justified this centralisation by emphasising the importance of carefully selecting ambassadors and punishing those who exceeded their authority. He argued that effective negotiations required a unified direction, especially given the complexities of 'continuous negotiation', which often led to contradictions and misunderstandings when left uncoordinated (Richelieu, 1961: 355).

While the resident ambassador system became a cornerstone of European diplomacy, its adoption elsewhere was gradual and uneven. For instance, Suleyman the Magnificent sought to engage with Europe but maintained the Ottoman Empire's belief in its natural superiority, delaying the acceptance of European-style diplomatic practices. Similarly, Russia, straddling Asiatic and European influences, only reciprocated France's ambassadorial overtures in 1615, decades after the first French envoy arrived in Moscow (Hamilton and Langhorne, 1995: 37). Pre-colonial Africa also developed sophisticated diplomatic systems, countering the perception of the continent as *terra nullius* before European colonisation. African rulers employed ambassadors with plenipotentiary powers, akin to European procurators, as well as messengers who transmitted orders but lacked negotiating authority. These systems emphasised respect for envoys, reflecting the rational and coherent nature of African diplomatic relations (Irwin, 1975: 93; Smith, 1989: 141).

The Westphalian international order further professionalised diplomacy, necessitating a skilled and educated diplomatic corps. Aristocratic origins dominated the composition of these corps, enabling a corporate identity that transcended national affiliations. Throughout the 19th century, the network of international diplomatic relations continued to expand to the extent that by 1914 there were 41 British missions abroad, 19 of which were outside of Europe (Hamilton and Langhorne, 1995: 110). However, the global adoption of the Westphalian model was often contentious. In Asia and Africa, local rulers resisted external influences, finding European political structures incompatible with their own traditions. In some cases, European powers resorted to military force to secure representation, particularly in the Far East, where permanent diplomatic missions were established under coercive circumstances.

The evolution of diplomatic representation reflects a response to the shifting demands of geopolitical contexts, shaped by power dynamics, growing complexity, and institutionalisation. Ancient diplomacy addressed power asymmetry, with states like Egypt asserting dominance while Greek city-states fostered horizontal engagement. In the medieval period, the introduction of procurators and consuls tackled the increasing complexities of trade and law, while the Renaissance formalised diplomatic engagement through the institution of resident ambassadors. This progression demonstrates the need for both adaptability and structure: power drove the foundations of early diplomacy, complexity required more sophisticated methods, and institutionalisation – exemplified by the establishment of foreign ministries – brought coherence to diplomatic practice. The evolution of diplomatic representation thus reveals the enduring interplay of pragmatism and innovation in managing relations between states.

Communication Methods

The evolution of diplomatic communication has been shaped by the interplay of language, ceremonial gifts, and symbolic gestures, each serving distinct but complementary roles in establishing and maintaining state relationships. These elements reflect the cultural, political, and historical contexts in which they were employed, offering insights into how states navigated power dynamics and articulated intent.

Language as a Diplomatic Tool

Language has consistently been at the heart of diplomatic interactions, providing the medium for articulating political objectives, negotiating treaties, and addressing conflicts. In the Ancient Near East, the use of a common diplomatic language, such as Akkadian, facilitated communication across diverse states. This shared linguistic framework, coupled with the expertise of scribes, ensured the accuracy and continuity of diplomatic correspondence (Malchow, 2016: 103). The reliance on written agreements formalised relationships and provided a tangible record of commitments. The Amarna Letters, a remarkable collection of diplomatic correspondence from the 14th century BCE, exemplify how written agreements were used to formalise relationships and maintain enduring records of commitments. These clay tablets, inscribed in Akkadian cuneiform, capture the exchanges between the Egyptian Pharaoh and the rulers of prominent powers such as Babylon, Assyria, and Mitanni, as well as smaller yet strategically significant city-states like Byblos and Ugarit (Moran, 2002).

In ancient Greece, language became an instrument of public discourse and debate. Treaties were not only drafted but also publicly ratified, reflecting the democratic ethos of Greek city-states (Nicolson, 1988: 9). The precision and clarity demanded in these public assemblies underscored the importance of language in diplomacy. This tradition continued in Rome, where the *jus fetiale* process (→ glossary) codified the language of war declarations, ensuring that all actions were justified through clear and lawful verbal statements. The college of *Fetiales* informed the enemy of the grievances of Rome, and if nothing happened after a fixed period, then a declaration of war would be made at the border of the enemy's territory and a javelin (cornel wood spear) would be cast into his land (Hamilton and Langhorne, 1995: 14).

In the early medieval period, principals used messages to communicate with each other in order to prepare for personal meetings. In this communication process, the nuncius was often described as a 'living letter', because he was supposed to communicate the messages "in a way that was as near a personal exchange as possible" (Hamilton and Langhorne, 1995: 24). The significance of the use of a nuncius instead of a letter laid in the meanings a person can convey beyond the written word. Indeed, his attitude, his actual wording and his responses to questions were of vital importance to the communication between principals. Letters of instructions were particularly important in the case of negotiations as they provided specific guidelines and often the exact words the envoy had to use for extracting and making concessions.

Before the 15th century, Latin was the prevailing mode of diplomatic communication both in terms of written treaties and oral exchanges. With the decline of the Holy Roman Empire and the deepening of religious fragmentation, the use of Latin among diplomats became rare and negotiations through interpreters became more common. While French became frequently used by the Russian nobility, by the end of the 17th century, Russia also had an excellent service of foreign language, which included fifteen translators (*perevodčik*) and fifty interpreters (*tolmach*) of Latin, Italian, Polish, Romanian, English, German, Swedish, Dutch, Greek, Tartar, Persian,

---

Textbox 2.3 Greek Diplomatic Missions

The sophistication of the Greek diplomatic system is illustrated by the fact that diplomatic negotiations were conducted orally and in accordance with some publicly controlled rules:

> The several members of an Embassy (there were often as many as ten Ambassadors in a single mission) would each deliver a set speech to a foreign monarch or Assembly, much as happens in the ordered international conferences of today. If the negotiations resulted in a treaty, the terms of that treaty were engraved in a pure attic on a tablet for all to see. Its ratification was accomplished by the public exchange of solemn oaths.
>
> (Nicolson, 1988: 7)

Arab, Turkish, and Georgian. Most often they were foreigners in Russian service or former prisoners of war (Zonova, 2007: 13). It was only in the 18th century that French had grown to be the dominant diplomatic language, a status it had retained until the end of World War I when it gradually became replaced by English.

The main duty of the resident ambassador was to gather information regarding domestic political conditions in the host state and report back relevant developments to chancelleries at home. To this end, ambassadors were required to build close relationships with the individuals with whom the power rested, form good channels of communication between the two governments, and advise the sending government on the best course of action. Resident ambassadors generally enjoyed a significant degree of discretion in pursuing their missions. They alone could decide at what moment and under what terms their instructions could be best executed and they could interpret the purposes and motives of one government to the other (Nicolson, 1988: 82–3).

The reports they sent back were "very detailed, seemingly filled with political trivia and endless verbatim accounts of conversations that the resident had" (Hamilton and Langhorne, 1995: 33). This style of reporting was maintained so that the secretaries and clerks in the chancellery could identify important connections that were neglected by the resident ambassador on the spot. However, the ever-growing volume of diplomatic exchanges between diplomatic residents and home chancelleries was not accompanied by the development of an effective and competent bureaucratic administration. This had often the effect of slowing down the pace of diplomatic relations and of even misplacing texts of treaties. The creation of the foreign affairs ministry spearheaded by Richelieu therefore represented a logical and necessary step for streamlining diplomatic activity.

Technological advancements began to reshape diplomatic language in the 19th century with the invention of the telegraph. This innovation drastically reduced communication times between capitals, enabling states to coordinate actions and exchange information with unprecedented speed. For instance, during the Crimean War, the telegraph played a pivotal role in facilitating real-time military and diplomatic decisions (Roussev, 2021). However, the need for concise and secure communication introduced new challenges, such as the development of coded language and diplomatic ciphers. The advent of the telephone in the late 19th and early 20th centuries further revolutionised diplomatic communication by enabling direct verbal exchanges between leaders and diplomats. This immediacy allowed for real-time negotiation and clarification of issues but necessitated written records for documentation, as spoken conversations lacked permanence. Together, the telegraph and telephone augmented the efficiency of diplomatic language, complementing traditional written correspondence and enriching the means of negotiation.

Ceremonial Gifts in Diplomatic Exchange

The exchange of gifts has been a hallmark of diplomacy, serving as a means to express respect, consolidate alliances, and communicate intentions. In the Ancient Near East, "opulent gifts" were central to diplomatic missions, symbolising the importance of the relationship and the esteem in which the counterpart was held (Cohen, 1996: 14). These offerings, often comprising rare and luxurious items, conveyed a message of goodwill and underscored the status of both the giver and the recipient. In Chinese diplomacy, the tribute system institutionalised the practice of gift-giving as a symbol of hierarchical relationships. States brought tributes to the Chinese court as an acknowledgement of China's superior status. For example, in 57 BCE, an emissary from Wa (ancient Japan) presented a tribute to the Han emperor, receiving a seal and ribbon in return – symbols of recognition and legitimisation within the Chinese world order (Fogel, 2009: 9).

These exchanges reinforced the centrality of China in regional diplomacy and provided a framework for maintaining stability (Beeson, 2014: 26).

Gift-giving has historically served both material and symbolic functions in diplomacy, acting as a tool to convey authority, reinforce hierarchies, and establish enduring bonds through cycles of obligation and reciprocation. By carefully selecting items of cultural, symbolic, or material significance – such as rare artefacts, exotic animals, or technological marvels – states projected their power, sophistication, and intentions. These exchanges were more than displays of wealth; they were deliberate acts to shape perceptions of political standing and establish relational dynamics. For instance, the Mughal court in India incorporated gifts from European traders into their ceremonial frameworks, using them as both signs of submission and markers of imperial favour. Similarly, in Tokugawa Japan, gifts were embedded in diplomatic rituals, allowing foreign actors like the Dutch East India Company to navigate the political hierarchies of the Shogunate while pursuing commercial interests (Tremml-Werner, Hellman and van Meersbergen, 2020).

Gift-giving has long played a pivotal role in bridging intercultural divides and managing conflicts, functioning as a diplomatic tool to navigate complex relationships and power dynamics. As Neumann (2021) points out, gifts serve not merely as tokens of goodwill but as social and political ordering devices, embedding the giver and recipient in cycles of reciprocity that establish and sustain relationships. A key aspect of diplomatic gift-giving is its inherent ambiguity, which enables parties to interpret gifts in ways that align with their own agendas. This ambiguity often facilitates diplomacy in contentious scenarios, as the same gift can simultaneously signify submission, reciprocity, or partnership depending on the context. One notable case involves the Byzantine practice of requiring 'barbarian' rulers to send royal family members to Constantinople. (Neumann, 2021: 188). While this could be interpreted as an act of submission, the sending polity might view it as a strategic move to ensure the safety of their heirs or to strengthen ties through cultural and political integration. For the Byzantines, the presence of a foreign royal served as a mechanism to assert dominance, while for the sending rulers, it offered an opportunity to influence or benefit from the Byzantine court's resources and prestige.

In medieval Europe, gift-giving became a strategic tool for diplomacy. The selection and presentation of gifts were meticulously planned to reflect the wealth, power, and intentions of the sending state. A notable example is the Spanish King Philip III's mission to the Safavid court in Persia, where gifts included luxurious textiles, silverware, spices, and exotic artefacts. The careful curation of these items, which "had been discussed for over two years and compiled with utmost care", included the king's personal property, underscoring the significance of the mission (Siebenhiiner, 2013: 532). Gifts were not merely tokens of goodwill; they were political statements that could influence the outcome of negotiations.

Ambassadors also enjoyed distinct privileges that greatly facilitated their ability to access information and communicate effectively. Chief among these was diplomatic immunity, which granted them protection from physical harm, exemption from civil or criminal indictment, and the freedom to practice their religion privately. These immunities were rooted in a combination of religious, legal, and practical considerations. Religiously, ambassadors were seen as sacred representatives of their sovereign, acting on behalf of a higher authority. Legally, Roman law codified diplomatic protections, later expanded by canon law to include ambassadors' residences, with violations punishable by excommunication. Over time, legal precedents under the doctrine of extraterritoriality further reinforced these privileges (Hamilton and Langhorne, 1995: 41, 45). Practically, states respected the safety of envoys on a reciprocal basis, recognising that immunity was essential to mitigate the risks posed by long and perilous journeys during the Middle Ages. As Mattingly (1955: 48) observed, diplomatic law aimed to ensure that ambassadors had every privilege necessary for fulfilling their duties, but it was not designed to shield abuses of these privileges, just as it did not protect a tax collector who resorted to blackmail.

The tradition of ceremonial gift-giving, a hallmark of diplomacy for centuries, also evolved with technological advancements. In the industrial era, gifts began to reflect the technological and industrial prowess of the sending state. For instance, during the late 19th and early 20th centuries, gifts often included innovative inventions, machinery, or products that showcased a nation's technological achievements. These items symbolised not only goodwill but also the sender's modernity and progress. An example of this is the exchange of technologically advanced gifts between the United States and Japan in the late 19th century. The United States gifted Japan a steam engine model and two telegraph sets, symbolising industrial progress and the desire to foster modern relations. Japan, in turn, reciprocated with intricate works of art that highlighted its cultural sophistication (Fullilove, 2018). These exchanges underscored the blending of traditional and modern values in diplomatic gift-giving, where symbolic and technological significance converged.

Symbolic Gestures in Diplomatic Practice

Symbolism has played a crucial role in diplomacy, providing a non-verbal means of communication that complements and enhances verbal exchanges. In their diplomatic communications, the Byzantines "adhered to the strategy of the indirect approach, incorporating delays with avoidance of the unnecessary resort to force" (Sofer, 2013: 8). The Empire frequently emphasised its political and military superiority, its longevity, grandeur, and the contrasting fates of its enemies. In order to impress and subdue 'barbarians', great attention was paid to diplomatic ceremony, including showing visitors around majestic palaces and churches or dazzling them with lavish welcoming receptions in the throne room. "The treatment of ambassadors throughout a visit was designed to impress, without allowing them to associate in any way with other than official persons or to see anything which it was not decided that they should see" (Hamilton and Langhorne, 1995: 16). The Byzantium Empire was, perhaps, the first to institutionalise the training of diplomatic envoys, who were recruited and carefully trained to understand and honour manners and customs of their hosts, to observe situations abroad and report back to their sovereign, as well as negotiate terms with their hosts (Sofer, 2013: 8). Bribery, flattery, and marriage were tools used to avoid war and the Byzantines also used information about barbarian potentates and prominent persons of various ranks to build alliances and thwart military invasions (Shepard, 2004).

On the other side of the globe, the Chinese diplomatic dominance of the Sino-Japanese relations started to be challenged in the 7th century. In 607, the Japanese mission to China tried to establish parity in diplomatic status by referring to the Japanese ruler as "the son of heaven in the land of the rising sun" and to the Chinese ruler as "the son of heaven in the land of the setting sun" (Wan, 2010: 155). The Chinese emperor did not accept the letter. However, shared Confucian values enabled a high degree of mutual acceptance and a reduced sense of threat. Consequently, the Japanese did not think that they should challenge the existing Chinese world order, a fact reinforced by Japan's economic conditions in which continued commerce with other Asian states was seen as vital. Diplomatic intercourse between China and neighbouring states had both practical and ceremonial aspects. Face-to-face meetings were held out in the open, often in locations considered sacred in nature. "This outdoor element suggests an origin of the custom at an epoch of less confident interstate relations, when rulers dared not open their capitals or cities to other rulers accompanied by retinues" (Britton, 2004: 619). These meetings

> **Textbox 2.4   The Policy of Diplomatic Prestige**
>
> In the early 16th century, the powers in Europe were France, ruled by Francis I, and the Holy Roman Empire, led by Charles V. Henry VIII of England needed desperately to forge an alliance with one of the parties. In 1520, Henry and Francis I agreed on a meeting near Calais, France. In attempting to outshine the other, the kings spared no expense in their displays of wealth. They erected pavilions made with cloth of gold (real filaments of gold sewn with silk to make the fabric), organized jousts and other competitions of skill and strength, and banqueted each other lavishly, in all ways trying to outdo and outspend one another. This ostentation earned the meeting the title "Field of the Cloth of Gold". The feasting ended abruptly when King Henry challenged King Francis to a wrestling match, which ended in Francis throwing Henry to the ground and besting him. The meeting, which took place over three weeks (June 7–June 24, 1520), nearly bankrupted the treasuries of France and England, and was useless politically. Francis and Henry signed no treaty, and a few weeks later Henry signed a treaty of alliance with the Holy Roman Emperor, Charles V. Within a month, the Emperor had declared war on Francis, and England had to follow suit.
>
> (Russell, 1969)

served to negotiate war, peace, intervention, and defence; affirm friendly relations; and agree marriage unions.

By the Renaissance, symbolic gestures became integral to the institutionalisation of European diplomacy. The arrival of ambassadors, the presentation of credentials, and the conduct of state visits were all carefully choreographed to communicate status, power, and intent. These practices not only reinforced the legitimacy of diplomatic missions but also shaped perceptions of the states involved. Much attention was paid to the affirmation of an ambassador's elite background by ceremonial. First, diplomatic ritual was a clear measure of the aspirations and responses to status recognition among the parties (see Textbox 2.4). The sending state could demonstrate its wealth and power and its rating of the importance of the recipient by the lavishness of the mission and the seniority of its head. The receiver, on the other hand, said something about its standing by the quality of reception offered, the grandeur of accommodation, the nature of celebrations, and the value of the gifts. Indeed, "the envoys of powerful or friendly governments enjoyed far more distinguished honours than were granted to others" (Murray, 1855: 36).

Technological advancements have amplified the impact of symbolic gestures in diplomacy. The introduction of photography and videography allowed ceremonial acts to reach global audiences, enhancing their symbolic power. The televised handshake (Glass, 2019) between Egyptian President Anwar Sadat and Israeli Prime Minister Menachem Begin during the Camp David Accords (1978) exemplifies this, symbolising reconciliation and hope on a global stage. In the modern era, digital technology has introduced new forms of symbolic gestures. The careful design of virtual meeting spaces, with curated backdrops and protocols, continues the tradition of projecting power and intent, albeit in a virtual setting. These visual and spatial choices not merely are aesthetic but also serve as strategic tools for status signalling. During the COVID-19 crisis, leaders employed carefully orchestrated visuals to communicate authority, stability, and influence, leveraging the symbolic power of their surroundings to compensate for the absence of physical presence. Such practices underscore how virtual summitry has become a vital platform for maintaining and projecting diplomatic hierarchies in an increasingly digital world (Danielson and Hedling, 2022).

Language, ceremonial gifts, and symbolic gestures have long served as the foundational pillars of diplomacy, embodying the shifting priorities and complexities of state interactions across historical periods. Language offered the precision and clarity required for negotiation and agreement, facilitating the articulation of political intent and the codification of commitments. Ceremonial gifts and symbolic gestures, by contrast, conveyed layers of meaning that extended beyond words, encapsulating respect, power dynamics, and relational hierarchies. Together, these elements wove a multidimensional tapestry of diplomatic practice, where material exchanges and performative acts complemented verbal agreements to create durable frameworks for diplomatic relations. Over time, these practices have evolved in response to cultural, technological, and political shifts, yet their core functions remain central to understanding the intricacies of statecraft and the enduring art of diplomacy.

Conflict Management

Diplomatic practices of conflict management have developed over centuries, influenced by varying cultural, religious, and political frameworks. From the sacred oaths of ancient Mesopotamia to the balance-of-power strategies of the Concert of Europe (→ glossary), societies have sought to resolve disputes and mitigate tensions through innovative methods.

Religious Foundations

In the Ancient Near East, the arbitration of grievances, negotiation practices, and the sacralisation of treaties through religious oaths were integral to diplomatic conduct. Ancient rulers perceived their counterparts as "brothers" within an international kinship system, creating tangible moral and political attachments. Dynastic diplomacy, involving marriages to solidify alliances, further strengthened these bonds (Cohen, 1996). In Mesopotamia's Sumerian city-states of the 3rd millennium BCE, some of the earliest examples of diplomatic negotiation and oaths of allegiance emerged (Malchow, 2016: 103). Similarly, in ancient Greece, treaties were reinforced by oaths under the guardianship of Zeus, embodying divine authority and moral obligations (Nicolson, 1988: 9). Ethical principles shaped international conduct, as evidenced by rules prohibiting poisoned weapons, respecting truces, and protecting sanctuaries (Phillipson, 2001: 182–91).

The rules of 'civilised conduct' developed by ancient Greeks included fair treatment of prisoners, non-use of poisoned weapons and treacherous stratagems, observance of truces and armistices, prohibition of warfare during religious festivals or athletic contests, as well as inviolability of important temples, sanctuaries, and embassies (Phillipson, 2001: 182–91). In addition, Greeks developed the first forms of international organisations. Festivals such as the Olympic Games represented "a period of deliberately controlled international relations" (Hamilton and Langhorne, 1995: 11), during which agreements on cooperation were frequently discussed. For pacific conflict resolution, arbitration was a quite customary device. Indeed, 46 cases of dispute arbitration had been adjudicated between 300 and 100 B.C. (Nicolson, 1988: 8). The designated arbiter was either another state or an individual – often a philosopher of good reputation or even a victor at the Olympic Games (Murray, 1855: 9).

During the medieval period, the Catholic Church emerged as a key actor in conflict management. Canon and Roman law became instruments for adjudicating disputes and framing the doctrine of just war, influenced by the writings of St Augustine, Thomas Aquinas and Hugo Grotius. The canonists determined the (un)justness of war and breakers of peace and they framed rules of diplomatic conduct. While many diplomatic relations in the Middle Ages were conducted under the form of private law whereby ratification was not obligatory or even customary, agreements made by *nuncii* or procurators without full powers could become binding only on formal approval by principals (Queller, 2004: 211), a practice that still resonates today with the process or ratification of international treaties.

The rise of Islam in the 6th century brought about non-Christian understandings of the legal procedures and justifications for conflict management. Written in the 9th century, the Islamic Law of Nations made a clear distinction between Dar al-Islam (the territory of Islam) and Dar al-Harb (territory of war, inhabited by all those of non-Islamic faith). A state of war was assumed to exist between the two until when the former would conquer the latter. Many rulers in the Middle East had ideologies of kingship that asserted the legality and legitimacy of their rule over various – often overlapping – audiences. The Mamluk sultans – who ruled Egypt and Syria from 1250 to 1517 –, saw themselves, for instance, as the martial guardians of Islam and Islamic society. These conflicting ideologies introduced intolerance into their – rather frequent – diplomatic exchanges, which was "the most prominent arena both for expressing legitimacy, and for denigrating the claims of rivals" (Broadbridge, 2008: 6).

Competing religious conceptions of conflict management also emerged in Latin America. In the second quarter of the 15th century, the Aztec and Inca were able to conquer vast amounts of territory in a relatively short period of time. These conquests were successful because Aztec and Inca had manipulated traditional religious concepts and rituals in such a way that it gave them decisive advantages over their competitors. For example, Aztec elites were increasingly obsessed with legitimising their ancestry and emphasised the militaristic cult of war and human sacrifice of their culture. Also, they portrayed their migration history and current occupations in terms of the will of the Mexica patron deity (Conrad and Demarest, 1984: 25–7). Similarly, the Inca used a 'psychology of submission' and propaganda to remind the subjects of the empire's power (Ogburn, 2008: 225).

Power and Realpolitik

Conflict management has been deeply intertwined with power dynamics and pragmatic strategies. Persian kings, for instance, practised preventive diplomacy to maintain a balance of power among Greek city-states, mediating wars to prevent the emergence of a dominant power (Rung, 2008). Similarly, the Romans used treaties not only to establish peace but also to enhance their military strength. By 264 BC, more than 150 separate treaties had been concluded, which greatly increased Rome's military strength, since, rather than requesting tribute, Rome demanded contingents of soldiers to supplement its armies (Campbell, 2001: 4). By the late Republic, the introduction of new treaty forms forced federated states to recognise the *maiestas populi romani* and surrender control over foreign policy to the Roman Senate (Nicolson, 1988: 16). The Romans also created the *praetor peregrinus* in 242 BCE, who was expected to settle disputes of commercial nature between foreigners or between a foreign party and a Roman citizen based on *jus gentium* (the law of nations).

Considering ancient Chinese diplomacy, some authors suggest the heavy influence of Sun Tzu's *Art of War*, written around 500 BCE, which emphasises the idea that victory should be ensured by subduing the enemy without fighting. It is a matter of constraining the movement of the enemy and achieving victory by attacking moral and mind through "indirection and the manipulation of the enemy's perceptions of the structure of the conflict" rather than through physical domination (Johnston, 1998: 26). "This has given Chinese strategic behaviour a distinctive minimally violent character" and this has arguably been the case throughout Chinese history all the way from Sun Tzu's time (Johnston, 1998: 22).

In Europe, the conclusion of secret treaties was the preferred method of protecting or advancing state interests in line with the doctrine of raison d'etat (→ glossary), but was also a major source of diplomatic tensions. In 1516, Henry VIII of England entered into negotiations with Charles V of Spain directed against Francis I of France, whereupon Charles made a secret treaty with Francis. In 1668, England and the Netherlands made a secret treaty to force Louis XIV of France to make peace with Spain, but that made no impression on him. Louis had already made a secret treaty with the Emperor of Austria by which they were to divide the Spanish dominions on the death of the then king. In 1815, after Napoleon had been banished to Elba, the Allies met in Congress at Vienna to readjust the map. During the Congress, England, France, and Austria entered a secret treaty directed against Russia and Prussia, their putative allies. The secret was so little that the Czar knew of it immediately after the treaty was signed. Napoleon III secretly proposed to Bismarck that France should be given Belgium and Luxemburg as the price of his friendship to the new German Confederation (Low, 1918: 211–12).

In time, great powers increasingly recognised the need for direct meetings to prevent dangerous escalation of diplomatic tensions. Conference diplomacy had its modern origins in the congresses of Osnabrück and Münster that restored peace in Europe through the 1648 Peace of Westphalia after thirty years of religious conflict (see also Chapter 3). This was followed by the congress of Utrecht in 1712–1713 that brought together 83 plenipotentiaries to resolve the issue of European hegemony brought about by the question of the Spanish succession (Meerts and Beeuwkes, 2008). Most importantly, the Concert of Europe (→ glossary) established in the aftermath of the 1814 Vienna settlement of the Napoleonic Wars introduced the practice of regular face-to-face consultation among the leaders of the Great Powers (Great Britain, Austria, Prussia, Russia, and France). The five powers met on 41 occasions to address a number of thorny diplomatic issue concerning matters in Spain, Greece, and Belgium. In so doing, the congress system helped prevent a direct conflict between great powers until the Crimean War in 1856 (see Textbox 2.5).

Textbox 2.5   The Concert of Europe in Action

The London Conference on Grecian Affairs (1827–32), an ongoing conference at the ambassadorial level and the first of its kind, was set up to solve the Greek Question (preventing the Greek rebellion against the Ottoman rulers from descending into a great power war) once and for all. The ambassadors negotiated a French occupation of the Greek mainland, and the constitution, frontiers, population, and even king of the new state. Such a thing – jointly midwifing the birth of a nation-state – had never been done before. On top of that, here it was done deliberatively: proposals were put forward and debated out of the heat and light of high politics. Because the negotiators did not constantly have to keep their eye on Russia, they could freely discuss the problem. Moreover, the minutes and final protocols were made public, and were referred to by the Great Powers in the war diplomacy.

(Mitzen, 2005: 413–14)

The patterns of diplomatic engagement among European powers during the 18th and 19th centuries were described by Harold Nicolson as the 'old diplomacy' (→ glossary) on the basis of five characteristics. In the first place, Europe was regarded as the most important of all continents. Indeed, it was generally understood that no war could become a major war if none of the five major European powers were involved. Secondly, the Great Powers were greater than the Small Powers, since they "possessed a more extended range of interests, wider responsibilities, and, above all, more money and more guns" (Nicolson, 1988: 74). This global hierarchy did, however, imply a third principle, namely that the Great Powers had a common responsibility for the conduct of the smaller powers and the maintenance of peace. A joint intervention by the Great Powers in a small-state conflict was generally accepted to prevent the conflict from developing in a Great-Power crisis.

Fourth, the preservation of peace in the Westphalian international order required a professional diplomatic service of high standards of education and experience. The composition of diplomatic corps during this period was predominantly of aristocratic origin, a fact that allowed diplomats to develop a corporate identity independent of their national identity. Fifth, 'continuous and confidential' negotiation was essential for successfully managing relations between the main powers. This was made possible by the fact that the parties generally remained rational and courteous, since public expectations and time pressure had little influence on negotiations. In turn, this resulted in agreements that were "no hasty improvisations or empty formulas, but documents considered and drafted with care" (Nicolson, 1988: 77).

The methods of the 'old diplomacy' were gradually exported by European powers all over the world. Throughout the 19th century, the network of international diplomatic relations continued to expand to the extent that by 1914, there were 41 British missions abroad, 19 of which were outside of Europe (Hamilton and Langhorne, 1995: 110). As more and more non-Western countries adopted the system, it has gradually been modified, growing progressively less European and more global in nature. The expansion of diplomatic relations was however often complicated by local or regional political situations. In Asia, and to some extent in Africa, local rulers were often reluctant to open their countries to alien influences and political structures were sometimes irreconcilable with the Westphalian principle of territorial sovereignty. On the other hand, in the Far East, European powers needed, at times, to employ their superior military capabilities to secure permanent representation.

Symbolism and Legitimacy

Symbolism and the projection of legitimacy have long been central to diplomatic practices in conflict management. Throughout history, rituals, ceremonies, and symbolic acts have played a vital role in establishing authority and conveying status on the international stage. In ancient China, Sun Tzu's principles of indirection and manipulation were complemented by Confucian-Mencian ideals that linked domestic stability to international peace If rulers are able to ensure a stable and harmonious society – one in which capable officials are employed, just and sound laws are enforced, a high moral code is upheld, economic burdens on the people are kept to a minimum, there is political order, sound socioeconomic conditions, and members of each level of the social hierarchy are content – then it is argued, foreign adversaries will not provoke violent conflict but rather peacefully submit to the ruler of this land (Johnston, 1998: 63).

During the medieval and early modern periods, ceremonial precedence became a key aspect of European diplomacy. Symbolic ceremonial was understood to send precise messages about the relationship between the parties involved and to indicate the significance of the matters discussed. Also, relationships between the several permanent embassies were established through

Textbox 2.6 Diplomatic Ranking

A dramatic diplomatic incident caused by precedence rivalry happened in London on September 30, 1661, on the occasion of the state entry of the Swedish ambassador. The Spanish ambassador de Watteville sent his coach with a train of about forty armed servants. The coach of the French ambassador, Comte d'Estrades was also on the spot, escorted by 150 men, of whom forty carried firearms. After the Swedish ambassador had landed and taken his place in the royal coach, the French coach tried to go next, and on the Spaniards offering resistance, the Frenchmen fell upon them with drawn swords and poured in shot upon them. On learning of this incident, King Louis XIV sent instructions to his own representative at Madrid to demand redress. In case of a refusal a declaration of war was to be notified. The King of Spain, anxious to avoid a rupture, recalled de Watteville from London and announced that he had prohibited all his ambassadors from engaging in rivalry in the matter of precedence with those of the Most Christian King. The question was finally disposed of by the "Pacte de Famille" of August 15, 1761. Article XVII stipulated that at Naples and Parma, where the sovereigns belonged to the Bourbon family, the French ambassador was always to have precedence, but at other courts the relative rank was to be determined by the date of arrival. If both arrived on the same day, then the French ambassador was to have precedence.

(Satow, 1979: 17)

ceremonial, meaning that "each ambassador would struggle for the highest position relative to others on all occasions, but never more so than at formal court functions" (Hamilton and Langhorne, 1995: 64). This element of diplomacy was taken very seriously (see Textbox 2.6). The Pope tried to settle the issue of diplomatic precedence by producing a memorandum in 1504 in which he placed himself first, followed by the kings of France, Spain, Aragon, and Portugal. The Congress of Vienna finally settled the issue in 1815 by establishing precedence among diplomatic envoys according to the date they presented their credentials. The Congress of Aix-la-Chapelle in 1818 further clarified that representatives at conferences must sign treaties in alphabetical order.

Marriages played an important role in managing diplomatic relations by bolstering the legitimacy of new sovereigns, creating durable political alliances and managing crises. Marriage negotiations between Elisabeth I and the Duke of Anjou were framed by both domestic considerations regarding the settlement of the question of the dynastic succession and larger European issues involving England's relationship with Spain (Mears, 2001: 458–9). The Habsburg Empire staked out its claims to European hegemony by actively pursuing a diplomatic strategy of embedding dynastic unions into a web of political alliances, peace treaties, and cordial diplomatic relations (Fichtner, 1976: 247). The British attempt in the 1840s to coax the French and Spanish governments into settling the marriage question of Queen Isabella of Spain and her younger sister, the Infanta Luisa Fernanda, in a way that suited London, Paris, Madrid, and Vienna was part of the strategy to maintain the precarious diplomatic equilibrium among the main European powers (Guymer, 2010).

Status dynamics in diplomacy have historically been expressed through elaborate rituals and hierarchical practices, serving as essential tools to communicate legitimacy, intentions, and power dynamics between states. In colonial contexts, European diplomats blended their own traditions with local customs to assert dominance while maintaining a veneer of respect for indigenous practices. For instance, in British interactions with Indian princely states, ceremonial gift exchanges, public durbars (royal courts), and the display of imperial regalia emphasised the British Empire's supremacy while simultaneously validating the local rulers' status within their own domains (Mcleod, 1994). These practices not only bolstered British authority but also allowed Indian princes to preserve a degree of cultural and political identity, fostering cooperation under the framework of indirect rule.

Similarly, in Sino-European diplomacy, the practice of kowtowing – a ritual act of deep respect traditionally expected at the Chinese imperial court – became a contentious symbol of status negotiation. European diplomats often resisted this practice, as in the case of Lord Macartney's embassy to China in 1793, where Macartney declined to perform the full kowtow, instead offering a compromise of bowing to the emperor in line with European norms of respect (Chen, 2023). This act encapsulated the dual objectives of asserting European equality while acknowledging the symbolic authority of the Chinese emperor. Through such rituals and symbolic gestures, diplomats conveyed messages of power, respect, and intent, navigating the intricate dynamics of status and sovereignty.

Institutional Mechanisms

Modern institutional mechanisms for conflict trace their roots to European congresses such as the Peace of Westphalia (1648), which introduced the principle of territorial sovereignty, and the Congress of Vienna (1815), which institutionalised face-to-face negotiations among great powers. The Concert of Europe further emphasised regular consultations to prevent escalation, holding 41 meetings before the Crimean War in 1856 (Hamilton and Langhorne, 1995: 136). World War I (1914–1918) marked a turning point in diplomatic practices, exposing the inadequacies of "old diplomacy". Critics attributed the war's outbreak to several factors: secret treaties, imperial rivalries, arms races, and the relentless pursuit of balance-of-power policies (Hamilton and Langhorne, 1995: 136). These issues underscored the dangers of opaque decision-making and unrestrained realpolitik. US President Woodrow Wilson seized this moment to advocate for a new approach, often referred to as 'new diplomacy' (→ glossary). In essence, the American diplomatic creed rested on "the belief that it was possible to apply to the conduct of external affairs, the ideas and practices which, in the conduct of internal affairs, had for generations been regarded as the essentials of liberal democracy" (Nicolson, 1988: 84).

Wilson proposed three guiding principles that remain influential: public accountability to ensure foreign policy aligns with popular consent, self-determination as a means of extending liberal rights to sovereign entities, and collective security to deter the arbitrary use of force. These ideas, encapsulated in his Fourteen Points (Wilson, 1918) (→ glossary), challenged traditional European diplomatic norms, where diplomacy was often seen as a royal prerogative or an elite domain requiring confidentiality and expertise. Despite Wilson's optimism, European policymakers expressed scepticism about the practicality of excessive transparency and public involvement in diplomacy. They argued that diplomacy required a degree of secrecy to function effectively, particularly in resolving sensitive international disputes. Furthermore, the historical context of European diplomacy – shaped by centuries of war and conflict – reinforced the notion that foreign policy was a specialised field, distinct from domestic governance.

Wilson's principles materialised in the establishment of the League of Nations (→ glossary), an ambitious attempt to institutionalise collective security. The League sought to prevent conflict by obligating member states to resolve disputes through arbitration and conciliation before resorting to war (League of Nations, 1924). Its Covenant introduced groundbreaking provisions, such as the prohibition of conquest and the limited use of force for self-defence. However, the League's inability to enforce its rules and secure the participation of key powers, such as the United States, ultimately led to its failure. Many of the League's principles were later revived in the UN Charter after World War II. Article 2(4) of the Charter prohibited the threat or use of force, except under specific circumstances like self-defence (Article 51) or collective security (Chapter VII). The introduction of the veto system (→ glossary) ensured the participation of major powers by granting them the ability to block resolutions against their interests. While this system incentivised great-power involvement, it also allowed these powers to circumvent accountability, often undermining the UN's authority.

Wilson's principle of self-determination, though revolutionary, also revealed significant limitations. Its strict application risked endless political fragmentation in regions with entrenched ethnic or religious divisions, as seen in the Kurdish population's quest for statehood (Watch, 2003). Additionally, self-determination sometimes fuelled irredentist claims, leading to regional instability. Examples include Nazi Germany's annexation of the Sudetenland in 1938 and Russia's annexation of Crimea in 2014, both justified under the guise of protecting ethnic or national self-determination. Lastly, if the 'consent of the governed' is a principle of great relevance not only for domestic but also international politics, does the international community have a responsibility to implement it in countries where the principle is lacking or is deficient? The Responsibility to Protect doctrine adopted at the UN World Summit in 2005 suggests that states are no longer protected by their sovereignty if they fail to protect their citizens from genocide, war crimes, ethnic cleansing, and crimes against humanity (UN General Assembly, 2005).

The idea of collective security also faced challenges. Wilson's last of his Fourteen Points called for the establishment of a "general association of nations . . . for the purpose of affording mutual guarantees of political independence and territorial integrity to great and small states alike" (Wilson, 1918). This was supposed to build on and reinforce the other two diplomatic components of the new diplomacy. At the individual level, public scrutiny of diplomacy served to restrain the risky behaviour of diplomatic elites by making foreign policy decision-making more transparent and accountable. At the domestic level, self-determination took aim at removing sources of political oppression, which were seen as a major cause of war. Finally, at the systemic level, collective security pledged to prevent military competition between states by facilitating mutual trust, international cooperation, and peaceful settlements of international disputes.

While the first two components have become entrenched in diplomatic practice, signs of erosion are evident with the rise of authoritarian states and their propensity for wars of conquest, as illustrated by Russia's wars of aggression against Ukraine and Georgia. Similarly, the principle of collective security remains precarious, despite two notable efforts at institutionalisation: initially through the League of Nations and subsequently, in the aftermath of World War II, through the UN. While the principle of collective security aimed to replace the balance-of-power system with cooperative international governance, its success depended on the willingness of major powers to uphold shared principles. The League of Nations and, later, the UN struggled to reconcile the tension between formal equality among states and the practical realities of great-power dominance.

Current debates concerning the extension of the concept of collective security to matters involving pre-emptive action and humanitarian intervention underscore the challenges inherent in constraining power through institutional frameworks. The UN Security Council's capacity to authorise such interventions, as delineated in Articles 41 and 42 of the UN Charter, often hinges less on legal provisions and more on the concurrence of its five permanent members (P5). The paralysis observed in situations like the war in Ukraine highlights the Security Council's limitations, particularly when a P5 member is directly involved in a conflict (Hathaway and Patrick, 2024).

In this context, the ongoing intergovernmental negotiations (IGN) on Security Council Reform represent a crucial opportunity to address these systemic shortcomings. As the 79th session of the General Assembly approaches with a series of plenary meetings in early 2025, the focus has shifted to finding consensus on contentious issues such as equitable representation, the expansion of permanent and non-permanent seats, and the use of veto power (UN General Assembly, 2024). The IGN discussions are occurring against the backdrop of an intensely polarised geopolitical environment, where some states are openly challenging the rules-based international order through force. This has intensified calls for a more representative and effective Security Council capable of responding to contemporary threats.

For the UN to remain relevant in this context, it must balance the competing interests of its member states while safeguarding the principles of international law. The IGN process highlights the need for pragmatic solutions that reflect the geopolitical realities of the 21st century. This includes fostering greater inclusivity by increasing representation for underrepresented regions such as Africa, small island states, and emerging economies, as well as addressing the disproportionate influence of the P5. Ultimately, the true test of the IGN process and the UN's collective security framework lies in its ability to adapt and remain effective amidst the shifting tides of international politics. Strengthening the Council's legitimacy and functionality will require not only structural reforms but also a renewed commitment to multilateralism and the principles enshrined in the UN Charter. In an era of contested global order, this is both an urgent necessity and a profound diplomatic challenge.

The challenges facing the UNSC reform process underscore the broader tensions confronting the Wilsonian principles that have shaped international diplomacy for over a century. While debates around collective security reform reveal the limits of institutional frameworks in constraining power, they also highlight the fragility of the liberal international order rooted in transparency, public accountability, and the rule of law. This order, once heralded as a cornerstone of global governance, is increasingly under strain from authoritarian resurgence, intensified geopolitical rivalries, and the reassertion of unilateralism.

These developments raise critical questions about the future of the Wilsonian framework and whether the liberal international order it underpins is undergoing a fundamental transformation. The rise of alternative visions – driven by multipolar power centres and divergent governance models – suggests the potential emergence of a new set of rules and principles. These nascent frameworks may either complement or supplant existing norms, reflecting the realities of a fragmented and contested global landscape. These questions will be explored in greater depth in the fourth section of this volume, which examines the remaking of diplomacy in response to the transformational dynamics of the 21st century.

Summary

- *Representation – Power balanced by Pragmatism:* Representation in diplomacy has historically balanced assertions of power with practical adaptations to geopolitical contexts. Ancient diplomatic systems, such as those of Egypt and Rome, projected hierarchical dominance, while Greek city-states embraced horizontal engagements rooted in relative equality.

The Renaissance institutionalised representation through resident ambassadors, integrating intelligence-gathering and continuous negotiation into statecraft. Cardinal Richelieu's centralisation of diplomatic activities exemplified the strategic pragmatism that transformed representation into a tool for navigating the complexities of sovereign states and international order.

- *Communication – Clarity through Symbolism:* Diplomatic communication reflects the interplay between the precision of language and the resonance of symbolism. In ancient diplomacy, shared languages like Akkadian facilitated treaty negotiations, while rituals and gifts conveyed intent and status. The evolution of communication, from oral traditions to written agreements and modern technologies like the telegraph, underscores the enduring need for clarity and adaptability. Symbolic acts, such as Byzantine ceremonies or the French dominance of diplomatic language, highlight how states leveraged cultural and linguistic frameworks to manage relations and assert legitimacy.
- *Conflict Management – Strategy meets Structure:* Diplomatic conflict management has evolved through strategic frameworks and institutional innovations. Ancient practices relied on moral and religious codes, such as the sacred oaths of Mesopotamia and Greece, to mediate disputes. The medieval period introduced legal and canonical frameworks, while the Renaissance and Westphalian systems emphasised territorial sovereignty and balance-of-power dynamics. Modern conflict management, as exemplified by the Concert of Europe, institutionalised collective approaches, blending pragmatic strategies with structural mechanisms to maintain stability and prevent escalation.

Study Questions

- How did power asymmetry shape ancient diplomatic practices, and how did these differ between civilisations such as Egypt, Rome, and Greece?
- In what ways did religion influence diplomatic conflict management in the ancient and medieval periods, and how did these methods evolve by the Renaissance?
- What factors contributed to the late development of permanent diplomatic institutions, such as resident ambassadors, by the 15th century?
- How did diplomatic immunity develop in the modern period, and what protections existed for envoys in earlier eras?
- What role did symbolic gestures, such as ceremonial gift exchanges and rituals, play in conveying legitimacy and power in diplomatic practices?
- How did communication methods, from the oral traditions of nuncii to the technological advancements of the telegraph and telephone, transform the efficiency and dynamics of diplomacy?
- What was the significance of the Concert of Europe in 19th-century conflict management, and how did it shape subsequent practices in conference diplomacy?
- How relevant are Wilson's ideas of collective security and public accountability in addressing contemporary global challenges, such as authoritarianism and unilateralism?

Recommended Further Reading

Berridge, Geoff, H. M. A. Keens-Soper, and Thomas G. Otte. 2001. *Diplomatic Theory from Machiavelli to Kissinger*: *Studies in Diplomacy*. Houndmills, Basingstoke and New York: Palgrave.
    This book offers an introductory guide for students to four centuries of diplomatic thought through the writings of a major scholars, statesmen, international lawyers, and historians.

Fletcher, Catherine. 2015. *Diplomacy in Renaissance Rome: The Rise of the Resident Ambassador*. Cambridge: Cambridge University Press.

This volume offers an investigation of the envoy's role during the Renaissance, a pivotal period for the development of diplomacy. Drawing on archival sources and insights from social and cultural history, the author argues for the centrality of the papal court – and the city of Rome – in the formation of the modern European diplomatic system.

Hamilton, Keith, and Richard Langhorne. 1995. *The Practice of Diplomacy: Its Evolution, Theory, and Administration*. London and New York: Routledge.

This volume tracks the historical development of diplomatic relations and methods from the earliest period up to their current transformations in the late 20th century, showing how they have changed to encompass new technological advances and the needs of modern international environments.

Ikenberry, G. John, ed. 2009. *The Crisis of American Foreign Policy: Wilsonianism in the Twenty-First Century*. Princeton: Princeton University Press.

This provocative collection examines and the traditions of liberal internationalism that have dominated American foreign policy since the end of World War II.

Satow, Ernest Mason. 1979. *Satow's Guide to Diplomatic Practice*. 5th ed. London and New York: Longman.

An international classic, this volume provides a comprehensive survey of the rules, laws, and conventions covering the conduct of diplomacy, not only between individual nations but also through international organisations.

3 Central Themes of Diplomatic Thought

Chapter Objectives

- To explore how tradition and historical legacies anchor diplomatic practice while enabling adaptation to change.
- To examine diplomacy's role in bridging estrangement, mediating tensions, and fostering resilience in international relations.
- To analyse the balance between state interests (raison d'état) and systemic stability (raison de système) in shaping global diplomacy.
- To synthesise tradition, mediation, and power as interwoven elements that define diplomacy's evolving role in a complex world.

Introduction

As discussed in the previous chapter, diplomacy draws its enduring institutional strength and relevance from centuries of practice, evolving constantly in response to dynamic political, social, and technological transformations. Identifying and critically examining foundational themes such as tradition, mediation, and power not only illuminates the principles guiding diplomatic conduct but also sharpens our understanding of its evolving role in a world of accelerating complexity. Tradition, mediation, and power are not isolated constructs but deeply interwoven elements that underpin the diplomatic profession. Tradition connects contemporary practice with historical precedence, anchoring the identities of states and diplomats in legacies that confer legitimacy and continuity. Mediation reflects diplomacy's role as an agent of bridging different forms of estrangement among diverse actors and ensuring the resilience of diplomatic relationships. Power, the driving force behind diplomacy, is reflected in strategies of projection and restraint, skilfully balancing state interests with overarching global priorities. Together, these themes furnish a lens through which diplomacy can be studied as a dynamic and adaptive practice.

Engaging with the themes of tradition, mediation, and power provides profound insights into the foundational logic of diplomacy. Tradition, as articulated by Edward Shils and Hans-Georg Gadamer, functions as both a repository of accumulated practices and a dynamic process of reinterpretation. Shils highlights tradition's role in conserving and transmitting knowledge, norms, and practices across generations, ensuring societal cohesion while allowing for gradual adaptation. Gadamer complements this with his concept of the 'fusion of horizons', emphasising how historical meanings are actively engaged with and reinterpreted in light of contemporary circumstances. Together, their perspectives demonstrate how tradition anchors diplomatic conduct in historical continuity while enabling it to adapt to evolving geopolitical realities.

DOI: 10.4324/9781003485407-5

Mediation, drawing on the works of James Der Derian, Georg Simmel, Zygmunt Bauman, and Paul Sharp, addresses the estrangement inherent in international relations. Der Derian frames estrangement as both a precondition for and a product of diplomatic practices, emphasising the role of narratives in constructing and perpetuating otherness. Simmel's concept of social distance underscores the dual role of the diplomat as both insider and outsider, capable of bridging divides while maintaining impartiality. Bauman's notion of liquid modernity illustrates how globalisation intensifies feelings of alienation, requiring adaptive and flexible approaches to mediation. Sharp adds depth by categorising diplomatic encounters into moments of discovery, re-encounter, and ongoing negotiation, highlighting the dynamic and relational nature of estrangement. These perspectives reveal mediation's capacity to reconcile tensions between universal aspirations and particularist realities, navigating differences while fostering resilience in international relationships.

Power, as explored through the lenses of Friedrich Meinecke, Adam Watson, and Henry Kissinger, represents the strategic interplay between state-centric interests and systemic stability. Meinecke's concept of raison d'état focuses on the necessity of power-driven statecraft for survival, often prioritising national interests above ethical considerations. Watson's raison de système shifts the emphasis to systemic stability, advocating for shared norms and prudential responsibility among states to maintain an international order. Kissinger's dual approach of 'zooming in/zooming out' bridges these perspectives, demonstrating how effective diplomacy requires both a strategic vision for global stability and the tactical acumen to address localised challenges. This nuanced understanding of power highlights its role in balancing immediate priorities with long-term responsibilities, ensuring that diplomacy operates effectively at the nexus of state survival and systemic equilibrium.

This chapter is structured around these three interrelated themes. It begins by examining the role of tradition in shaping diplomatic norms and practices, incorporating the insights of Shils and Gadamer. The second section explores mediation as a tool for addressing estrangement, drawing on the works of Der Derian, Simmel, Bauman, and Sharp. Finally, the chapter concludes with a detailed analysis of power, integrating the ideas of Meinecke, Watson, and Kissinger to illuminate its manifestations and implications in contemporary diplomacy. Together, these sections provide a comprehensive framework for understanding diplomacy as a dynamic and adaptive practice.

Tradition in Diplomacy: Continuity, Transformation, and Adaptation

Tradition, as articulated by Edward Shils and Hans-Georg Gadamer, represents a dynamic interplay of continuity and reinterpretation, weaving the past into the fabric of the present. Shils, in *Tradition* (1981), emphasises its role in conserving and transmitting knowledge, norms, and practices across generations, ensuring societal cohesion while allowing for gradual evolution. Gadamer, in *Truth and Method* (1960), complements this view by framing tradition as a hermeneutic process, where historical meanings are not merely inherited but actively engaged with, creating a fusion of past and present horizons. Together, these perspectives provide a robust theoretical foundation for understanding tradition not as a rigid inheritance but as a transformative system, shaping collective identity and guiding action.

For Edward Shils, tradition serves as the medium through which societies conserve the accumulated wisdom of generations, embedding the past into the practices and norms of the present. Tradition, in this sense, is far from static; it is an active process of "possession" where individuals and groups inherit, embody, and re-enact established customs and practices. This generational transmission ensures the durability of cultural, intellectual, and social frameworks while allowing them to evolve over time. Shils highlights that tradition's strength lies in its ability to persist across at least three generations. It takes this length of time for practices and norms to become ingrained and accepted as self-evident by those who inherit them. The process involves not just the passive reception of ideas but their active assimilation, whereby successive generations adapt inherited traditions to their contexts, ensuring their relevance. This intergenerational dynamic is critical in transforming what might otherwise be ephemeral into something enduring. Generations play a dual role in tradition: they are both its preservers and its innovators. The older generation safeguards the core of the tradition, transmitting its values and practices to the younger generation. Meanwhile, the younger generation, while often inured to the foundational elements of the tradition, subtly reinterprets or modifies these elements in response to contemporary challenges. This dynamic ensures that tradition remains vibrant and responsive rather than stagnant.

Languages, as a form of tradition, provide a compelling example of generational transmission. Latin, for instance, has been preserved as a "dead language" yet continues to be taught in schools and universities. Its endurance across centuries is due to its perceived value as a repository of classical thought and as a foundation for understanding modern languages. Generations of educators and scholars have actively maintained its relevance by integrating its study into broader curricula, ensuring its survival even in a world where it is no longer spoken.

Diplomacy itself is an example of a tradition shaped and reshaped by generations. The norms and practices of modern diplomacy – such as the use of ambassadors, formal protocols, and multilateral negotiations – were established over centuries. Cardinal Richelieu's establishment of France's Ministry of Foreign Affairs (MFA) in 1626, the first of its kind, established the role of the foreign minister and formalised key diplomatic practices. Since then, generations of diplomats have built on these foundations, adapting them to the changing needs of global politics. Today, while the symbolic elements of diplomacy, such as ceremonies and protocol, remain, modern challenges like digital diplomacy require innovative approaches that reinterpret these traditions.

Gadamer's perspective on tradition complements and deepens Shils' framework by emphasising its interpretive and dialogical nature. Gadamer nuances the notion of tradition as a mere transmission of fixed content, viewing it instead as an ongoing dialogue between the past and the present. Central to his argument is the concept of the "fusion of horizons", which describes the interaction between historical and contemporary perspectives. This process of engagement allows inherited meanings to be reinterpreted in light of present circumstances, ensuring that

---

Textbox 3.1 Shils' Dimensions of Tradition

Shils (1981) argues that tradition operates across several dimensions.

- It is both descriptive, reflecting the actual behaviours and beliefs of a society, and normative, prescribing what ought to be done to maintain social order and cohesion.
- It is symbolic, providing a sense of identity and belonging, and practical, offering concrete tools and strategies for navigating societal challenges.
- It also balances continuity and change: while its core elements provide stability, it evolves through creative adaptation, ensuring its relevance in a changing world.

> **Textbox 3.2   Gadamer's "Fusion of Horizons"**
>
> Gadamer's concept of the "fusion of horizons" (Horizontverschmelzung) is a central idea in his philosophical hermeneutics. It describes the process of understanding as an active, dialogical interaction between the historical context of a text, tradition, or event (the "horizon" of the past) and the perspective of the interpreter (the "horizon" of the present).
>
>> The horizon of the present is continually in the process of being formed because we are continually having to test all our prejudices. An important part of this testing occurs in encountering the past and in understanding the tradition from which we come. Hence the horizon of the present cannot be formed without the past. There is no more an isolated horizon of the present in itself than there are historical horizons which have to be acquired. Rather, understanding is always the fusion of these horizons supposedly existing by themselves.
>>
>> (Gadamer, 1960: 442–3)

tradition remains a living, dynamic force. For Gadamer, tradition is not only a source of authority but also a mode of understanding, shaping how individuals and societies make sense of their world. Hans-Georg Gadamer's concept of the "fusion of horizons" is exemplified in his analysis of classical texts and their enduring relevance.

Gadamer argues that understanding these works involves more than merely reconstructing their historical context. Instead, the act of interpretation integrates the perspectives of the past and the present, creating new meaning. This interpretive process ensures that classical texts, although originating in specific historical and cultural circumstances, continue to speak to contemporary audiences. A paradigmatic example is the study of Homeric epics. While rooted in the oral traditions and heroic values of ancient Greece, the *Iliad* and *Odyssey* have been reinterpreted across centuries to address modern themes, such as the nature of leadership, war, and human resilience. Each era brings its horizon of understanding to these texts, allowing them to remain vital and relevant.

In the realm of diplomatic tradition, the "fusion of horizons" (→ glossary) is similarly evident in the adaptation of age-old diplomatic practices to technological advancements, such as the rise of digital diplomacy. The historical horizon of diplomacy is deeply rooted in face-to-face interactions, formal protocols, and the symbolic rituals that define statecraft. For centuries, these practices relied on personal presence and ceremonial exchanges to establish trust and build relationships. However, the contemporary horizon, shaped by technological innovation, has redefined the context in which these practices occur. Digital platforms now enable virtual summits, online negotiations, and real-time crisis communication, transforming how diplomacy operates while maintaining its core principles. For instance, during the COVID-19 pandemic, world leaders and diplomats turned to video conferencing for critical discussions, demonstrating that the essence of dialogue and relationship-building persisted even as the medium changed. This adaptation required reinterpreting traditional norms of confidentiality, trust, and formality to fit digital environments, such as ensuring secure communication channels and navigating the nuances of virtual presence.

The interplay between Shils' and Gadamer's theories illuminates the multifaceted nature of tradition and its enduring significance. Shils emphasises the durability of tradition through its capacity to preserve and transmit, while Gadamer highlights its flexibility through the interpretive act of reimagining the past. These perspectives converge in their recognition of tradition's dual role as a stabilising and adaptive force. Tradition, as Shils describes, provides a framework for continuity, embedding individuals in a collective identity shaped by shared norms and practices. Gadamer adds depth to this by showing how that framework is continuously redefined through engagement with historical meaning, allowing tradition to respond to new contexts without losing its essence.

The descriptive and normative dimensions of tradition, central to Shils' analysis, find resonance in Gadamer's hermeneutics. Shils' view that tradition reflects both what is done and what ought to be done aligns with Gadamer's argument that tradition shapes understanding by framing both the factual and the prescriptive. For example, in the context of diplomacy, traditional norms such as respect for sovereignty and non-interference are descriptive, as they reflect historical practices, but they are also normative, as they prescribe standards of conduct for modern states. Gadamer's notion of the fusion of horizons explains how these norms, while rooted in the past, are reinterpreted to address contemporary challenges, such as navigating the complexities of digital diplomacy. Similarly, the symbolic and practical dimensions of tradition in Shils' framework are enriched by Gadamer's emphasis on the interpretive act. Shils describes how traditions provide both symbolic meaning, through rituals and ceremonies, and practical utility, through codified practices like diplomatic protocols. Gadamer adds that these functions are not separate but intertwined, as the symbolic significance of tradition informs its practical application.

In diplomacy, for instance, the ceremonial presentation of credentials is not merely a symbolic act; it establishes the legitimacy and mutual recognition essential for practical negotiations. The dialogical engagement with tradition ensures that such rituals retain their relevance even as the contexts in which they occur evolve. Perhaps most striking is the convergence of Shils' emphasis on continuity and Gadamer's focus on creativity within tradition. Shils argues that tradition persists through the active re-enactment of its core elements, while Gadamer shows how this re-enactment involves reinterpretation, blending stability with innovation. Together, they reveal how tradition accommodates change without abandoning its foundational principles. In diplomacy, this balance is evident in the way long-standing norms are adapted to meet new challenges, such as the emergence of non-state actors or the impact of globalisation. The creative reinterpretation of diplomatic practices ensures that the tradition remains a vital and effective mechanism for international engagement.

Hans Holbein's *The Ambassadors* (1533) (see Figure 3.1) offers a vivid representation of the dimensions of tradition as articulated by Shils and Gadamer. It captures the continuity of diplomatic norms, the descriptive reality of early modern statecraft, and the symbolic and practical tools of the trade. The aristocratic and clerical roles of the figures illustrate the 16th-century reality of diplomacy as a preserve of the elite, with power closely tied to social and religious hierarchies. Their representation conveys not only individual authority but also the broader legitimacy of the states and institutions they served. However, this elitist framework has evolved; modern diplomacy now emphasises inclusivity, meritocracy, and professionalism, reflecting a shift in the normative structures of the tradition. The painting also embodies both the descriptive and normative dimensions of tradition. Descriptively, it depicts the social realities of early modern diplomacy, including the intellectual and cultural sophistication expected of its practitioners. Normatively, objects such as the partially obscured crucifix and scientific instruments highlight the moral and intellectual ideals that framed diplomatic practice. While the religious emphasis has faded, intellectual rigour and adaptability to complex challenges remain central to modern diplomacy.

42 *Understanding International Diplomacy*

Figure 3.1 The Ambassadors (1533) by Hans Holbein the Younger.

Moreover, *The Ambassadors* illustrates the interplay between symbolic and practical aspects of tradition. The scientific instruments and globe underscore the practical knowledge necessary for navigating a rapidly expanding world, including the newly discovered Americas. These tools represent both the practical challenges of diplomacy and its symbolic engagement with the broader currents of exploration and knowledge. The painting's creative incorporation of contemporary advancements, such as geographic discoveries and scientific progress, reflects how tradition adapts to maintain its relevance. While much of the painting's portrayal of diplomacy is specific to its historical context, several elements remain relevant. The emphasis on intellectual preparation, cultural awareness, and the symbolic power of presentation are enduring aspects of the diplomatic tradition. The tools and symbols of Holbein's ambassadors – whether books, instruments, or attire – reflect qualities still valued in modern diplomacy: knowledge, adaptability, and the ability to navigate complex symbolic landscapes. At the same time, the painting serves as a reminder of what has changed. The elitist and exclusionary aspects of diplomacy, rooted in aristocratic and clerical privilege, have largely been replaced by norms of inclusivity and meritocracy. The religious undertones, while significant in the 16th century, are less central in a secularised international order. By examining the painting through the lens of tradition, we thus gain insights into both the enduring and evolving aspects of diplomacy, understanding it as a dynamic practice that bridges history and innovation, past and present. In doing so, Holbein's work remains a testament to the resilience and adaptability of the diplomatic tradition.

Mediation and the Challenge of Separateness

Strangeness serves as a critical concept for understanding the complexities of human and diplomatic relations, where the negotiation of distance – relational, structural, or systemic – is fundamental. Combining the works of Paul Sharp and James Der Derian, whose contributions directly address diplomacy, with those of Georg Simmel and Zygmunt Bauman, who approach strangeness from broader sociological perspectives, allows for a multidimensional analysis. While Sharp and Der Derian frame strangeness within the mechanisms of international interaction, Simmel and Bauman provide insights into the structural and systemic conditions that underlie and shape these diplomatic processes. This synthesis enriches the study of diplomacy by connecting its practical challenges with broader theoretical frameworks, highlighting the interplay between human experience, societal conditions, and international engagement.

Paul Sharp identifies strangeness (→ glossary) as an inherent condition of human relationships, where separateness arises from prioritising one's immediate community over those perceived as outsiders. This relational distance shapes the dynamics of diplomatic encounters, where the unfamiliarity or otherness of others generates tensions and opportunities. For Sharp, strangeness is not merely a matter of geography or identity but a profound emotional and moral reality that influences how individuals and states interact. The recognition of this condition underscores the importance of understanding strangeness as a defining characteristic of international relations. Sharp categorises diplomatic interactions into three types of relationships: encounter, discovery, and re-encounter.

Encounter relations, as Sharp describes, occur when groups meet for the first time, bringing their distinct experiences into contact. The interaction between Hernán Cortés and Montezuma II in 1519 illustrates such a relationship, where the fascination with the 'other' quickly gave way to conflict and conquest. This type of strangeness highlights the volatility of initial encounters, where the absence of shared norms can lead to misunderstanding and domination. *Discovery relations* involve efforts to render disparate cultures intelligible to one another. An example is Nixon and Kissinger's diplomatic breakthrough with China in the 1970s, which required both sides to navigate strangeness and build a strategic framework for cooperation. This form of engagement demonstrates how strangeness, when mediated effectively, can transition from unfamiliarity to mutual understanding. *Re-encounter relations* focus on maintaining distinctions within ongoing relationships. The post-Brexit dynamic between the UK and the European Union (EU) exemplifies this, as the UK seeks to define its sovereignty while managing its historical and geographical ties to the EU. Strangeness in this context reflects the challenges of balancing separation with interdependence.

James Der Derian offers a critical perspective on strangeness, framing it as *estrangement* that is both a precondition for and a product of diplomatic practices. He argues that diplomacy, while appearing to bridge divides, often institutionalises and perpetuates difference by emphasising the "otherness" of groups or states. This process creates a cycle where strangeness becomes essential to maintaining the need for mediation. For Der Derian (1987), estrangement is embedded in narratives and practices that frame certain entities as distinct or inferior, thereby justifying intervention or negotiation. A historical example is the 'civilising mission' of European colonial powers, where colonial diplomacy constructed colonised peoples as 'other', rationalising governance and exploitation under the guise of benevolence. Even post-colonial diplomatic structures, such as the Mandate System of the League of Nations, reinforced this estrangement by institutionalising unequal relationships. Der Derian's analysis underscores how diplomacy can simultaneously manage and perpetuate strangeness, making it a central dynamic of international relations.

Georg Simmel provides a sociological lens on strangeness through his concept of *social distance*. For Simmel (1950), social distance is not merely a physical measure but a relational and symbolic construct that determines how individuals and groups interact. Strangers are unique figures within a social system because they are both inside and outside the group. They participate in its functions but remain distinct, enabling them to mediate and connect different social spheres. This duality of belonging and separateness makes the stranger a pivotal figure for boundary negotiation. Simmel's concept of social distance highlights the tension between proximity and detachment. The stranger is close enough to understand the group's dynamics but distant enough to offer objectivity. For example, itinerant traders in medieval societies facilitated economic and cultural exchanges precisely because their position as outsiders allowed them to navigate multiple social worlds without full assimilation. In diplomacy, this dynamic is mirrored in the role of diplomats, whose effectiveness often depends on maintaining a delicate balance between integration and detachment. Neutral mediators, such as Switzerland's diplomats during Cold War negotiations, leveraged this "stranger" status to act as impartial brokers, bridging ideological divides without aligning with either side. Simmel's insights into social distance reveal how strangeness can be both a source of tension and a tool for connection, making it highly relevant to diplomatic mediation.

Zygmunt Bauman's concept of *liquid modernity* offers a systemic perspective on strangeness, emphasising the transformative effects of modernity on social relations. In liquid modernity (Bauman, 2000), traditional structures such as communities, identities, and institutions lose their stability, giving way to a world characterised by constant change and uncertainty. This fluidity generates profound feelings of alienation, as individuals and states struggle to find permanence or cohesion in an environment where relationships are transient and transactional. Bauman argues that globalisation intensifies this condition by fostering superficial connections that often amplify, rather than mitigate, differences. The erosion of stable structures leads to a form of systemic strangeness, where the interconnectedness of the globalised world coexists with deep alienation and fragmentation. Bauman uses the example of consumer relationships to illustrate the ephemeral nature of modern connections. He argues that individuals, much like consumers selecting products, engage with others based on convenience and utility. This dynamic reduces relationships to transactions, where commitment is replaced by flexibility and disposability. For instance, Bauman discusses how friendships and intimate bonds are increasingly mediated by technology, creating networks that are broad but shallow, reinforcing a sense of alienation even in the midst of apparent connection.

This framework, when applied to diplomacy, highlights how states increasingly adopt flexible, short-term approaches to alliances and agreements, reflecting the fragmentation and alienation Bauman associates with liquid modernity. Bauman's concept is particularly reflected in the Trump administration's transactional approach to diplomacy, which prioritised short-term national interests over enduring alliances and multilateral commitments. Actions such as the renegotiation of NAFTA into the USMCA, withdrawal from the Paris Climate Agreement, and demands for North-Atlantic Treaty Organization (NATO) allies to "pay their fair share" exemplify this pragmatic, impermanent ethos. Bauman's notion of relationships defined by flexibility and disposability resonates here, as traditional frameworks of trust and stability gave way to

Table 3.1 Mediation Approaches

Type of Mediation	Focus	Strengths	Challenges
Relational Mediation	Managing emotional and moral distance to transform strangeness into understanding.	Highly adaptable to diverse contexts; transforms volatile dynamics into cooperative frameworks.	Unpredictable relational dynamics; risks of superficial engagement.
Critical Mediation	Interrogating narratives and institutional processes that perpetuate estrangement.	Fosters inclusive frameworks and addresses systemic roots of division.	Resistance from entrenched power structures; difficulty shifting deep-seated perceptions.
Structural Mediation	Leveraging the mediator's dual role as insider and outsider to connect disparate groups.	Provides objectivity and impartiality; builds trust in polarised contexts.	Balancing detachment and engagement; requires significant skill to maintain neutrality.
Adaptive Mediation	Adapting to fluid and transient relationships shaped by systemic challenges.	Emphasises flexibility and innovation in dynamic diplomatic landscapes.	Ensuring that short-term solutions align with long-term goals.
Transformative Mediation	Linking immediate conflict resolution with systemic transformation.	Offers a holistic approach to both surface-level conflicts and deeper systemic issues.	Balancing immediate conflict resolution with broader systemic change.

fleeting partnerships shaped by immediate returns. This erosion of stable structures in favour of transactionalism disrupted the cohesion of international alliances, embodying the systemic fragmentation and alienation that Bauman associates with liquid modernity. In this way, the Trump administration's diplomacy illustrates how the fluid, fragmented dynamics of liquid modernity increasingly reshape global relations.

The exploration of strangeness through the perspectives of Sharp, Der Derian, Simmel, and Bauman underscores its complexity as a defining feature of diplomatic relations. Sharp highlighted the emotional and moral dimensions of relational distance, Der Derian critiqued the institutional perpetuation of estrangement, Simmel examined strangeness as a structural condition rooted in social distance, and Bauman situated it within the systemic fragmentation of liquid modernity. Building on these insights, distinct forms of mediation emerge at their intersection – relational, critical, structural, adaptive, and transformative – each featuring unique strategies for addressing estrangement (see Table 3.1).

Relational mediation focuses on the management of emotional and moral distance, transforming strangeness into understanding through tailored engagement. It is grounded in Paul Sharp's exploration of encounter, discovery, and re-encounter relations, emphasising the dynamic and evolving nature of diplomatic relationships. The Camp David Accords between Egypt and Israel in 1978 exemplify this form of mediation. U.S. President Jimmy Carter's mediation addressed the deep emotional and moral estrangement between Egyptian President Anwar Sadat and Israeli Prime Minister Menachem Begin. The accords were significant not only for their practical outcomes but also for their ability to transform a volatile relational dynamic into a platform for peace. This example highlights the potential of relational mediation to reframe strangeness as a foundation for cooperation. Relational mediation's strength lies in its adaptability to diverse contexts, whether first encounters, ongoing dialogues, or attempts to redefine historical relationships. However, its challenges include the unpredictability of relational dynamics and the risk of superficial engagement that fails to address deeper estrangement.

Critical mediation interrogates the narratives and institutional processes that sustain estrangement. James Der Derian's emphasis on the role of diplomacy in institutionalising difference provides the theoretical foundation for this approach, which seeks to expose and dismantle the structures that perpetuate division. The Truth and Reconciliation Commission (TRC) in South Africa is a prime example of critical mediation. Following the end of apartheid, the TRC aimed to deconstruct the narratives of racial otherness that had underpinned systemic oppression. By creating a space for victims and perpetrators to recount their experiences, the commission addressed the deep-seated estrangement within South African society. This process highlighted how critical mediation can move beyond immediate conflict resolution to confront the systemic roots of division. The challenge of critical mediation lies in overcoming resistance from entrenched power structures and shifting deeply rooted perceptions. However, its opportunity lies in fostering more inclusive and equitable frameworks for international engagement, making it a transformative tool for post-conflict societies.

Structural mediation leverages the unique position of the mediator as both an insider and outsider, enabling them to navigate boundaries with impartiality. Georg Simmel's concept of social distance informs this approach, emphasising the mediator's ability to connect disparate groups while maintaining a degree of detachment. A striking example of structural mediation is the role of Finnish diplomat Martti Ahtisaari during the Aceh peace process in Indonesia (2005). Finland's neutrality and Ahtisaari's outsider status allowed him to act as a credible intermediary between the Indonesian government and the Free Aceh Movement. His position enabled him to bridge divides while maintaining objectivity, facilitating a peace agreement that ended decades of conflict. Structural mediation's theoretical strength lies in its emphasis on the mediator's positionality, which provides both challenges and opportunities. While neutrality can enhance trust, maintaining the delicate balance between engagement and detachment requires significant skill. When executed effectively, structural mediation offers a powerful means of bridging divides in polarised contexts.

Adaptive mediation responds to the systemic challenges of liquid modernity, where relationships and alliances are transient and shaped by shifting priorities. Zygmunt Bauman's analysis of fragmentation and transience underpins this approach, emphasising the need for flexibility and innovation in diplomatic mediation. The EU's response to the migration crisis of 2015 demonstrates the application of adaptive mediation. The EU coordinated a multifaceted approach, negotiating agreements with Turkey and other transit countries to manage migration flows. While these agreements were temporary, they reflected the EU's ability to adapt to rapidly changing conditions, balancing immediate needs with broader regional considerations. Adaptive mediation's key insight is its emphasis on flexibility as a core diplomatic skill. However, its challenges include ensuring that short-term solutions do not undermine long-term goals. By embracing systemic fluidity, adaptive mediation enables diplomats to navigate complex and rapidly evolving environments.

Transformative mediation synthesises the relational, critical, structural, and adaptive approaches to address the deeper conditions that sustain estrangement. This form of mediation focuses on linking immediate conflict resolution with systemic transformation. The Dayton Accords of 1995, which ended the Bosnian War, offers an example of transformative mediation. While the accords successfully stopped the conflict, they also established a framework for governance that sought to address the systemic causes of division in Bosnia and Herzegovina. This dual focus on immediate resolution and long-term transformation reflects the potential of transformative mediation to address both surface-level conflicts and their deeper systemic roots. The challenge of transformative mediation is balancing immediate conflict resolution with the broader goal of systemic change. However, its theoretical strength lies in its holistic approach, which connects micro-level interactions with macro-level reforms, offering a pathway for sustainable peace.

The Power Nexus: State Interest vs. Systemic Stability

The Concept of the raison d'état

The concept of *raison d'état* (→ glossary), or reason of state, emerges as a cornerstone of the traditional understanding of power in diplomacy. Rooted in the political realities of early modern Europe, raison d'état encapsulates the idea that the survival and well-being of the state are paramount, overriding moral and ethical considerations when necessary. This doctrine found its clearest articulation during the tumultuous periods of the Thirty Years' War, a protracted conflict fought primarily in Central Europe (1618–1648) over religious, political, and territorial disputes involving major European powers. Cardinal Richelieu, serving as Chief Minister to Louis XIII of France, was a pivotal figure in this era. A statesman and cleric, Richelieu is credited with consolidating royal power, suppressing internal dissent, and fortifying France against external threats. His strategies were rooted in the principles of raison d'état, which he used to justify actions aimed at securing the state's survival and enhancing its influence on the European stage.

The origins of raison d'état lie in the organic conception of the state as a living entity that must continually grow and adapt to survive. Richelieu elaborated on this extensively in his *Political Testament*, advocating for centralising authority and prioritising the state's survival above all else. He argued that effective governance demanded foresight, pragmatism, and the subordination of individual or moral considerations to collective state interests. Influenced by Machiavellian pragmatism (articulated in *The Prince*, published in 1532), raison d'état emphasises maintaining and expanding power as the primary objectives of governance. State leaders, in this framework, are obligated to act decisively, even ruthlessly, to secure their nation's interests, invoking necessity as a key justification. Richelieu's assertion that "internal disharmony invites external disaster" reflects the doctrine's focus on internal stability as essential for external strength. This was particularly evident during the Thirty Years' War, as France faced religious conflicts and the threat of encirclement by Habsburg powers. Raison d'état provided Richelieu with a pragmatic framework to centralise authority, suppress dissent, and strategically position France within a volatile European balance of power, safeguarding its sovereignty while expanding its influence.

The enduring features of raison d'état include:

- *Necessity as a guiding principle*: State actions are judged not by their moral value but by their necessity for survival and power maintenance. This principle prioritises decisive action to address existential threats, often invoking the logic of "the ends justify the means".
- *Primacy of power*: The acquisition, preservation, and expansion of power are central goals. This encompasses both hard power, such as military strength and economic resources, and soft power, including diplomacy and cultural influence, to maintain a competitive edge.

- *Strategic vision*: Leaders must balance short-term necessities with long-term objectives to sustain their state's position. This involves foresight in anticipating geopolitical shifts, managing alliances, and crafting policies that ensure enduring stability and influence.
- *Amoral pragmatism*: Ethical concerns are secondary to the imperatives of statecraft. This feature reflects a willingness to employ deception, coercion, or opportunism when required, as long as it aligns with the overarching goal of securing the state's survival and prosperity.

The classical practice of diplomacy under the aegis of raison d'état emphasised the importance of professional skills and intelligence. Thinkers like François de Callières highlighted the role of prudence – not just as a caution but also as a calculated, dexterous ability to navigate complex situations. Diplomats were expected to possess deep contextual understanding and foresight, placing individual events within broader strategic frameworks. Francesco Guicciardini, a contemporary of Machiavelli, provided additional insights by emphasising the importance of historical awareness and pragmatic flexibility in statecraft. His writings highlighted the interplay between human agency and structural constraints, urging statesmen to adapt to the ebb and flow of political fortune. The 18th and 19th centuries further institutionalised these principles, as seminal works like Satow's (1917) *A Guide to Diplomatic Practice* drew heavily on this foundation, emphasising the need for both strategic acumen and moral flexibility.

Cardinal Richelieu coined the term 'raison d'état' during a period of intense religious strife, where internal discord threatened France's stability and external encirclement by the Habsburgs loomed large. As the geopolitical context evolved, so did the doctrine. The rise of colonialism, nationalism, and technological advancements – particularly in military capabilities – introduced a more belligerent tone to raison d'état. This shift is recognised by Friedrich Meinecke, a German historian and political theorist, who portrayed the doctrine as a relentless pursuit of power driven by necessity and survival in a zero-sum world. Meinecke is best known for his work *Machiavellism: The Doctrine of Raison d'État and Its Place in Modern History* (1924/1957), where he analysed the historical development of state-centric power politics and the ethical dilemmas they pose. Living in the aftermath of World War I and during the rise of nationalist movements in Germany, Meinecke's analysis was shaped by the turbulence of his era, reflecting a deep concern about the destructive potential of unchecked state ambitions and the moral compromises inherent in raison d'état. Meinecke's interpretation emphasised the mechanical and often ruthless dynamics of state behaviour, prioritising power expansion and self-preservation over moral considerations. This evolving doctrine reflects the interplay of pragmatic adaptation and historical forces, demonstrating its enduring relevance in guiding statecraft.

The decline of the 'French Method' of diplomacy, characterised by secretive bilateral negotiations and power-centric strategies, marked a significant shift in the practice of international relations. As Harold Nicolson noted, the emergence of new powers and ideologies in the 20th century, particularly the rise of the United States and the ideals of Woodrow Wilson, introduced a fundamentally different approach to diplomacy. Wilsonian principles emphasised transparency, collective security, and international cooperation, standing in stark contrast to the power-driven methods of earlier European diplomacy. This shift represented a transition from the Realpolitik approach to a framework that sought systemic stability and mutual survival, embodying what would later be conceptualised as raison de système. Nicolson's critique underscored the importance of this evolution in adapting diplomacy to a rapidly changing and increasingly interconnected global order.

The Concept of the raison de système

The 20th century saw the emergence of *raison de système* as a counterbalance to raison d'état. This concept acknowledges that while pursuing state interests is essential, it must be balanced with the imperative to sustain a functional international system. The idea is closely linked to the English School, a leading theoretical approach in international relations, which emphasises the pivotal role of shared norms, values, and institutions in shaping an international society that can mitigate the inherent anarchy of the global system. The horrors of two world wars and the advent of nuclear weapons underscored the catastrophic consequences of unchecked state-centric ambitions, prompting a re-evaluation of traditional power dynamics.

Raison de système (→ glossary), advocates for "prudential responsibility" among states, particularly great powers, to uphold the stability of the international order. As Adam Watson, a prominent figure of the English School, argued, all members of international society share a vested interest in preserving the system's viability. Conceptually, international society is distinct from the international system in its emphasis on shared norms, rules, and institutions that shape interactions among states, fostering order and cooperation. By contrast, the international system encompasses a broader array of state interactions, often characterised by power struggles and competition without the framework of common norms. The notion of international society underscores the importance of cooperation, crisis management, and systemic stability, marking a progression from zero-sum competition towards mutual survival and co-existence.

Other key figures of the English School, including Hedley Bull and Martin Wight, expanded on the concept of raison de système by exploring how international society balances the preservation of state sovereignty with the pursuit of systemic stability. Bull's concept of the "anarchical society" highlights the delicate balance between state sovereignty and systemic order. Institutions such as diplomacy, international law, and great power management serve as mechanisms for promoting co-existence without undermining the independence of individual states. Wight's typologies of international systems – from Hobbesian (conflictual) to Grotian (cooperative) – illustrate the potential for raison de système to guide states towards more collaborative arrangements. Building on this, Alexander Wendt's three models of international relations – Hobbesian, Lockean, and Kantian – add further depth to the understanding of systemic dynamics. The Hobbesian model reflects a world of relentless conflict and power struggles, akin to Wight's conflictual systems. The Lockean model introduces a moderated rivalry where states recognise each other's sovereignty, aligning with the Grotian concept of co-existence. Finally, the Kantian model envisions a cooperative international society driven by shared norms and values, highlighting the aspirational potential of raison de système to foster deeper integration and mutual support among states.

Key features of raison de système include:

- *Systemic stability*: Ensuring that the international order remains resilient and functional by addressing emerging threats and maintaining balance among powers.
- *Interdependence*: Recognising that states' interests are deeply interconnected through trade, environmental concerns, and global security, making unilateral actions potentially destabilising.
- *Institutions*: Leveraging international organisations and established norms to mediate conflicts, facilitate cooperation, and maintain accountability among states.
- *Long-term sustainability*: Balancing immediate national interests with the collective goal of creating a stable and sustainable global order for future generations.

The evolution of raison de système reflects the lessons of history, where the excesses of raison d'état often led to destructive outcomes. For instance, the EU's post-Brexit strategy exemplifies the application of systemic thinking, as unity among member states was prioritised to mitigate the challenges posed by the UK's departure. Similarly, the Cold War's logic of mutual survival and strategic arms control highlighted the necessity of balancing national interests with global security. In contrast, recent events like Russia's attack on Ukraine showcase the dangers of a state operating purely on raison d'état without regard for systemic stability. Russia's unilateral aggression undermines the international society, revealing the fragility of raison de système when revisionist powers reject its principles. Similarly, the transactional approach of the Trump administration – favouring bilateral deals over multilateral commitments – tested the resilience of systemic norms. Both cases underscore the importance of reinforcing raison de système to manage the balance between state interests and the collective stability of the international order.

The interplay between raison d'état and raison de système illustrates the evolving nature of power in diplomatic thought and its impact on international societies. Barry Buzan, a distinguished scholar in the field of International Relations and an influential thinker associated with the English School, discusses how the balance between these doctrines produces varying forms of international societies, each reflecting different degrees of competition and cooperation:

- *Competition*: A society characterised by strong raison d'état and weak raison de système, where power struggles dominate, and cooperation is minimal. This reflects a Hobbesian dynamic, with states acting unilaterally to maximise their own security and influence, often at the expense of systemic stability. Historical examples include the Thirty Years' War, where fragmented European states operated under the constant threat of conflict, prioritising self-preservation over collective security.
- *Co-existence*: Here, strong raison d'état is moderated by a growing influence of raison de système, leading to an international society where sovereignty is respected, and rivalries are tempered by the need for limited collaboration. This aligns with a Lockean model of moderated rivalry and mutual recognition among states. The Cold War exemplifies this balance, with the United States and USSR maintaining a tense co-existence through strategic arms control agreements and mutual deterrence.
- *Cooperation*: In this model, raison d'état becomes less dominant, while raison de système strengthens significantly. States prioritise systemic stability and shared interests, creating a Grotian society where collaboration in areas like trade, security, and environmental governance becomes the norm. The post-Cold War period, particularly the 1990s, showcases this model with the expansion of international institutions like the World Trade Organization (WTO) and the establishment of cooperative frameworks for addressing global challenges.
- *Convergence*: The highest level of systemic influence occurs when raison de système is dominant and raison d'état weakens significantly. This Kantian model envisions states sharing deep norms and values, aspiring to integration and collective identity, as seen in examples like the EU. The EU's efforts to harmonise legal, economic, and political systems among its members illustrate the convergence model in practice.

Understanding the roles and missions of diplomats in varying types of international societies shaped by the balance of raison d'état and raison de système requires an exploration of how their functions adapt to competitive, co-existence, cooperative, and convergence models. This adaptation not only highlights the evolving nature of diplomacy in global governance but also underscores the interplay between state-centric imperatives and systemic cooperation.

In competitive societies, characterised by strong raison d'état and weak raison de système, diplomats play a crucial role in safeguarding state interests. They focus on intelligence gathering, alliance building, and crisis management to counter rival powers, embodying the strategic and survival-oriented dynamics of a Hobbesian environment. Their actions reflect the relentless prioritisation of national security over systemic stability. In co-existence societies, where strong raison d'état is moderated by a growing influence of raison de système, diplomats operate in a context of tempered rivalries. Their mission is to maintain peace and uphold sovereignty through establishing communication channels and negotiating agreements that prevent conflict escalation. This role is well-illustrated by Cold War–era arms control negotiations, where diplomats navigated a Lockean framework of moderated competition and necessary cooperation.

In cooperative societies, where raison de système gains prominence over raison d'état, diplomats emphasise trust-building and collaborative efforts. Their primary functions shift towards multilateral engagement, managing global institutions, and addressing shared challenges such as environmental governance and economic interdependence. The post-Cold War expansion of international organisations like the WTO underscores the centrality of diplomacy in fostering systemic stability within a Grotian society. In convergence societies, dominated by raison de système with a diminished influence of raison d'état, diplomats take on the role of architects of integration. They harmonise legal, economic, and political frameworks among states, fostering deeper alignment and shared identity. The EU serves as a prime example, where diplomacy is instrumental in creating cohesion among member states through the development of shared norms and values.

Kissinger's Approach to the Power Nexus

How can the issue of power, particularly as framed by the balance between raison d'état and raison de système, be effectively navigated by diplomats operating within these dual frameworks? This question finds a compelling exploration in the methods of Henry Kissinger, whose approach serves as an intriguing case for examining the dynamics of power in diplomacy. Kissinger's dual strategy of "zooming in/zooming out" (→ glossary) reflects his nuanced ability to navigate between raison de système and raison d'état, tailoring his approach to the specific demands of each context. Zooming out involves assessing the broader geopolitical landscape, allowing negotiators to understand systemic forces, long-term trends, and the strategic environment within which states operate. This perspective is essential for framing negotiations in a way that aligns with overarching goals of stability and balance, ensuring that individual agreements contribute to the broader international order. On the other hand, zooming in requires focusing on immediate issues, interpersonal dynamics, and the granular details of negotiation. This level of engagement is vital for building trust, resolving specific grievances, and crafting actionable agreements that address pressing concerns. Kissinger's method underscores the necessity of integrating these two perspectives; systemic stability cannot be achieved without addressing localised tensions, and localised solutions risk failure if they are not aligned with the broader strategic context. By seamlessly shifting between these levels, Kissinger demonstrated that effective diplomacy requires both a vision for the global order and the tactical skill to manage its immediate challenges.

Kissinger's broader geopolitical strategy often emphasised raison de système, particularly in efforts to stabilise the global order. For example, his advocacy for détente with the Soviet Union during the Cold War highlighted the importance of systemic stability. By negotiating arms control agreements such as the SALT talks, Kissinger sought to embed long-term security into the international system, recognising that unchecked competition risked destabilising the entire structure. This strategic 'zooming out' showcased his commitment to fostering an equilibrium that transcended immediate national interests. Kissinger's tactical engagements often required a focus on raison d'état, where immediate state interests took precedence. His shuttle diplomacy in the Middle East during the 1970s provides a clear example. Engaging directly with leaders like Anwar Sadat and Golda Meir, Kissinger addressed immediate security concerns and territorial disputes. These focused 'zooming in' efforts were instrumental in brokering agreements that, while serving US interests, also contributed to regional stability, thus linking short-term state objectives to longer-term systemic goals.

Kissinger's negotiations with China further illustrate his dual approach. While strategically prioritising raison de système by fostering US-China rapprochement as a counterweight to Soviet influence, Kissinger tactically leveraged the conflicts in Vietnam and Korea to underscore US geopolitical interests. In Vietnam, Kissinger used the ongoing conflict as a demonstration of US resolve, signalling to China that America was willing to confront communist expansion but also open to pragmatic dialogue. Kissinger tactically used the stability of South Korea to assure China of US interest in regional balance while making it clear that America's alliances in the region were non-negotiable. This approach allowed Kissinger to emphasise US strength and reliability as a partner, reinforcing the broader systemic goal of counterbalancing Soviet influence.

Kissinger's methods reveal a nuanced understanding of how raison de système and raison d'état interact in practice. His emphasis shifted according to the context, demonstrating that effective diplomacy requires not only strategic vision but also tactical adaptability. This dual approach offers valuable insights for diplomats navigating the complexities of different forms of international societies, where the interplay between power dynamics and systemic stability remains a central challenge.

Summary

- *Tradition as continuity and adaptation*: Tradition in diplomacy provides a stabilising framework through the reproduction and reinterpretation of norms, practices, and knowledge across generations. Edward Shils emphasised its role in embedding authority in established norms, while Hans-Georg Gadamer's concept of the "fusion of horizons" illustrated how tradition evolves by integrating historical meanings with contemporary contexts. Examples range from the enduring use of rituals to the adaptation of diplomatic protocols for digital diplomacy.
- *Mediation as estrangement and connection*: Mediation addresses the estrangement inherent in international relations, functioning as a bridge between conflicting or estranged entities. James Der Derian critiqued how diplomacy institutionalises estrangement, while Georg Simmel and Paul Sharp highlighted the role of social distance and relational dynamics in facilitating diplomatic connections. Zygmunt Bauman's concept of liquid modernity emphasised the need for adaptability in navigating a fragmented and transient global environment. Mediation extends beyond conflict resolution, fostering resilience and cooperation.
- *Power as strategy and balance:* Power in diplomacy operates at the intersection of state interests and systemic stability, reflecting both immediate priorities and long-term responsibilities. Friedrich Meinecke's raison d'état focused on state survival and pragmatism, while Adam Watson's raison de système emphasised the importance of systemic equilibrium and shared norms. Henry Kissinger exemplified the integration of these perspectives through his dual approach of 'zooming in/zooming out', balancing tactical engagements with strategic global objectives, such as in his negotiations with China and during the Cold War.

Study Questions

- How does tradition shape modern diplomatic practices, and what roles do reproduction and reinterpretation play in its evolution?
- In what ways does diplomatic mediation reconcile estrangement in international relations, and how do theories by Der Derian, Simmel, and Bauman contribute to this understanding?
- How do raison d'état and raison de système differ in their conceptions of power, and how can diplomats navigate their interplay in global governance?
- What lessons can be drawn from Kissinger's dual approach to diplomacy, particularly in balancing tactical priorities with systemic stability?

Recommended Further Reading

Bull, Hedley. 1977. *The Anarchical Society: A Study of Order in World Politics*. New York: Columbia University Press.

Bull's seminal work explores how international society emerges within the anarchic global system, focusing on the balance between sovereignty and systemic stability. His analysis of institutions like diplomacy provides a crucial framework for understanding how order is maintained in international relations.

Der Derian, James. 1987. *On Diplomacy: A Genealogy of Estrangement*. Oxford: Basil Blackwell.

This critical work examines the role of estrangement in diplomacy, highlighting how narratives of "otherness" shape diplomatic practices and relations. Der Derian's insights provide a foundational understanding of mediation as a process that both perpetuates and reconciles estrangement.

Kissinger, Henry. 1994. *Diplomacy*. New York: Simon & Schuster.

Kissinger's landmark text traces the historical evolution of diplomacy from the Westphalian system to the late 20th century. It provides critical insights into the strategic balancing of power among states, with a particular focus on the interaction between state-centric interests and systemic equilibrium.

Meinecke, Friedrich. 1957. *Machiavellism: The Doctrine of Raison d'État and Its Place in Modern History*. New Haven: Yale University Press.

Meinecke's landmark work explores the historical development of raison d'état as a pragmatic doctrine for state survival, tracing its ethical and political implications across centuries. The book sheds light on the evolution of power in diplomacy, highlighting its centrality in statecraft and its enduring relevance in modern international relations.

Watson, Adam. 1984. *Diplomacy: The Dialogue between States*. London: Eyre Methuen.

Watson introduces the concept of raison de système, emphasising the importance of shared norms and systemic stability in international relations. This text highlights the dynamics of international society and its role in managing the interplay between sovereignty and cooperation.

4 Expansion and Contraction of Diplomacy

Chapter Objectives

- To discuss key tension of today's diplomacy: expansion and contraction.
- To explain expansion: diplomacy reaches into more and more issue areas; increasing diversity of state and non-state actors.
- To explain contraction: move back to security, move back to state and great power politics.

Introduction

This chapter continues to trace the evolution of diplomacy to today. In doing so, it highlights how diplomacy expanded from the end of World War II until the turn of the millennium. As the last chapter already started to hint at, it is an important post-1945 development that the number of issue areas diplomacy got involved in as well as the number of actors (→ glossary) populating the diplomatic stage increased significantly. More recently, however, some of this development has been reversed. Diplomacy appears to be contracting again. Issue areas other than security, and to a lesser extent economics, get increasingly sidelined again, and, overall, actors other than states and other than great powers find it more and more difficult again to assert themselves.

This chapter discusses the expansion and contraction of diplomacy since the end of World War II by zooming in on six major issue areas of diplomacy: war and peace, economics, development, environment, health, and migration. Additionally, we discuss two cross-cutting issue areas that deeply affect all other issues areas: human rights, and science and technology. The discussion of each issue area follows the same pattern: We identify key actors, instruments, and challenges in these fields.

War and Peace

Since the end of World War II, there have been at least four major clusters of security challenges that diplomats sought to address. First, there is the problem of *inter-state conflicts*. Overall, the record still looks favourable. Compared to previous eras, inter-state disputes are much less likely to escalate into war since the end of World War II. Even territorial disputes, which, in the past, had been highly prone to war (Vasquez, 2009), are managed or even resolved peacefully. Given the arbitrariness and the ill-delineation of many borders in Africa, territorial disputes do occur. But there are – with very few exceptions in the Horn of Africa (wars between Ethiopia and Somalia from 1977 to 1978 as well as between Eritrea and Ethiopia from 1998 to 2000) – no inter-state wars over territory. Instead, many territorial disputes are settled through arbitration (including, eventually, the one between Eritrea and Ethiopia). Similar patterns prevail throughout Asia and Latin America. Europe, where territorial wars were rampant in the past, especially in the first half of the 20th century, also has a much better overall record of managing and resolving border disputes than in the past (Kornprobst, 2008).

There are, however, indications that this overall record has come under increasing pressure of late. NATO's intervention against what remained of Yugoslavia in 1999 and the eventual recognition of Kosovo as an independent state by most NATO states (and beyond) was violent as opposed to a peaceful territorial change (such as German reunification or the velvet divorce between the Czech Republic and Slovakia). Russian aggression against Ukraine is reminiscent of wars of territorial conquest of a past that many Europeans thought they had left behind. Russia annexed the Crimean Peninsula in 2014 as well as the oblasts Donetsk, Kherson, Luhansk, and Zaporizhzhia in 2022. While it remains to be seen to what extent attempts at violent territorial change will spill over to other areas in Europe and to other regions of the world, a hardening of positions can be observed in many territorial disputes that have proven to be intractable for a long time.

This applies perhaps first and foremost to China and Taiwan where China postulates a right to reunify Taiwan with mainland China with whatever means it chooses. Territorial disputes between China on the one hand and the Philippines and Japan on the other have also become more volatile with more military incidents on sea and in the air happening. Other volatile disputes include the ones between North Korea and South Korea, India and Pakistan, and Armenia and Azerbaijan. Since Hamas's 2023 attack on Israel, the latter's heavy-handed military measures against Gaza,[1] Hezbollah's reprisals, Israel's military offensives against Lebanon, costly signalling between Iran and Israel, and Israeli bombardments and incursions into post-civil war Syria, the Middle East has become deeply embroiled in crisis yet again.

Second, there is the problem of *intra-state conflicts*. There have been many more intra-state disputes since the end of World War II and these have been much more destructive than inter-state disputes. To list only the deadliest ones between 1945 and 2000, the civil war in Bangladesh in 1971 cost 1.5 million people their lives (of which a million were civilians). Just the first three years (1998–2000) of the war in the Democratic Republic of the Congo alone left 1.5 million people dead. The war that Cambodia's Pol Pot regime waged against its own people killed 1.8 million civilians. Intra-state fighting in the Sudan killed 2 million people between 1983 and 2000 alone. The staggering number of casualties during the Chinese civil war – only for the years of 1946 to 1950 – stands at 6.2 million (5 million civilians). Several internal conflicts killed a million people, again mostly civilians: Ethiopia (1962–1989), Nigeria (1967–1970), Angola (1980–1995), and Afghanistan (1990 and 2000) (Leitenberg, 2006).

In the new millennium, staggering numbers of casualties in intra-state wars have continued. By 2003, armed conflict in the Congo had claimed no less than 3 million lives. From 2012 to 2017 as many as half a million Syrians were killed (Ray, 2024). In Sudan, violence in Darfur peaked from 2003 to 2005, killing about 200,000 people (United States Holocaust Memorial Museum, 2015). The war in Ethiopia's Tigray province, fought by the Ethiopian government with the help of Eritrea from 2020 to 2022, left 500,000 people dead (Ghent University, 2021). Other highly destructive internal wars raged in Afghanistan and Iraq. From 2009 to 2016, monthly civilian casualty numbers in Iraq oscillated between 89 (November 2009) and 1775 (June 2014). These figures are somewhat lower for Afghanistan but also very high (United Nations Human Rights, 2017; ReliefWeb, 2017). It is common in all these civil wars that most casualties are civilians. To emphasise the destructiveness of intra-state wars again, the Tigray War claimed significantly more lives in 2022 than the Russo-Ukrainian one.

Third, challenges posed by *transnational terrorism* have made themselves felt more and more in the post-Cold War era. Much diplomatic attention to counter-terrorism focuses on

Jihadist terrorism. In 1992, a bomb exploded in the Gold Mohur Hotel in Yemen, targeting US soldiers. Al Qaeda claimed responsibility for this attack. More bombings followed. In East Africa, the US embassies in Nairobi and Dar es Salaam were bombed in 1998. By September 2001, international terrorism had reached the United States, when Al Qaeda terrorists hijacked four commercial aircraft and crashed them into the World Trade Center and the Pentagon.

This provoked a massive military reaction by the United States. Even two decades later, the War on Terror, initiated by George W. Bush in the immediate aftermath of the Al Qaeda attacks, is still ongoing. It is estimated that Washington's military campaigns, including the invasions of Iraq and Afghanistan, killed 4.5 million people (Berger, 2023) and displaced about 40 million (Vine, 2021: xix). In the short run, these campaigns gave rise to new terrorist movements, including the Islamic State of Iraq and the Levant (ISIL) or Daesh, which added to the destabilisation of already war-torn countries such as Afghanistan, Iraq and Syria. Transnational terrorist networks stroke against targets in various states allied with the United States in the War on Terror, including Belgium, France, Germany, and the United Kingdom in Europe as well as Ethiopia, Kenya, and Uganda in Africa. In the longer run, counter-terrorist measures by various states and state alliances succeeded, for the most part, in taking away territorial control from terrorists, especially ISIL in Syria. But they continue to carry out terrorist attacks. Boko Haram remains a terrorist organisation able to control considerable swaths of territory in West Africa, including in Benin, Cameroon, Chad, Niger, and Nigeria. There are several other terrorist splinter groups such as ISIS-Sahel and Jama'at Nusrat al-Islam wal-Muslimin in Mali. Since the early 2020s, Al Shabaab has been gaining territory again in Southern Somalia.

Fourth, there is the issue of *transnational organised crime*. This comes in many shapes and forms, which are often causally linked to intra-state wars and transnational terrorism. Revenues from criminal activities fuel armed conflict and vice versa, armed conflict and the breakdown of state authority open the doors for criminal networks. These dynamics can be observed in a number of states and regions in Latin America and Africa. They are probably most prevalent in the Horn of Africa. Cattle rustling, for instance, has become a multi-million business. Lifestock warlords arm groups of youth, who use para-military tactics and equipment to steal as much cattle from victim communities as possible. Operations can be as large as involving 10,000 attackers with automatic rifles, stealing 135,000 head of cattle (ENACT, 2024). Lifestock warlords deliver the meat to the urban markets in the region or fly or ship it to overseas markets (Daghar and Okumu, 2021). The Horn of Africa's considerable mineral wealth attracts a number of actors, international criminal networks very much included, and these exercise very little restraint in chasing people from their land or targeting competitors. Mohamed Hamdan Dagalo ('Hemedti'), after wreaking genocidal havoc in Darfur in the 2000s and before initiating yet another Sudanese civil war in 2022 by fighting Abdel Fattah al-Burhan, had secured control over the gold mines in Jebel Amer. For several years, Wagner's mercenaries helped him to exercise this control. In return, some of the gold revenue went to Moscow, which, in turn, used it to help finance its war against Ukraine. The stream of migrants from states in the Horn of Africa to other states in the region as well as Europe, Gulf states and the Middle East, and Southern Africa has increased steadily since the mid-2000s. In most cases, migrants have to rely on smugglers because otherwise the journey would be unmanageable, and human smuggling, at times, becomes human trafficking, that is, coerced 'for the purpose of exploitation' (UN Convention against Transnational Organized Crime, Art. 3(a)). Very serious cases of coercion and abuse happen on all major routes (Eastern, Northern, and Southern), including abduction, sexual violence and even organ removal.

None of these criminal activities are much in the public limelight. An exception to this rule was the piracy off the Somali Coast. When more and more of these attacks happened in the latter half of the 2000s, and, as a result, a vital global trade route got disrupted, the international community reacted with determined military operations. NATO launched Operation Allied Protector and Operation Ocean Shield, Operation Atalanta was the first naval operation of the EU (EU NAVFOR Somalia), and states otherwise as varied as China, India, Russia, and South Korea also sent ships (Weldemichael, 2019: 171–95).

What does diplomacy do to address these security challenges? The UN Charter lays down the institutional architecture for the maintenance of international peace and security. It endorses what amounts to the paramount norm in international affairs and provides mechanisms to safeguard it. The norm is state sovereignty. The principal instruments to safeguard it are measures for the pacific settlement of disputes (Chapter 6) and enforcement measures (Chapter 7). The latter is supposed to contain the 'teeth' of the UN system, that is, a system of collective security. The Security Council (→ glossary) is the primary organ on matters of security. Apart from cases of self-defence, it is only the Security Council that has the authority to decide upon enforcement measures. There are five permanent members, who have a veto power: China, France, Russia, the UK, and the United States (P5). There are also ten non-permanent members, each of whom is elected for two years.

Within this overall architecture, many more institutional arrangements have been put into place in order to deal with security issues. As far as territorial disputes are concerned, the 1975 Helsinki Final Act is particularly noteworthy. It codified a territorial status quo norm in Europe, which greatly facilitated the resolution of long-standing territorial disputes, such as between Germany and Poland as well as Germany and the Soviet Union. In other regions, too, a notable agreement on the territorial status quo emerged, at least among governments. Upon independence, African states agreed upon the principle of *uti possidetis iuris*. Thus, former colonial borders were accepted as the borders of the newly independent states. The wide acceptance of this principle is what underpins Africa's record of settling border disputes peacefully, oftentimes by arbitration.

The diplomatic infrastructure to uphold peace and avoid peace, however, has always been rather imperfect and has come under additional pressure of late. There are at least five sets of problems: First, these institutions were designed with certain purposes in mind. The UN Charter was meant as vehicle to manage inter-state disputes and not intra-state conflicts. Indeed, the sovereignty principle sits quite uneasily with interventions into the domestic affairs of a state, even if a civil war ravages this state. When the Syrian government waged a merciless war on its own population, including the use of chemical weapons, and invited an external power such as Russia to help target Syrians, the sovereignty principle constituted a mighty wall protecting it from international intervention. The fact that Russia is a permanent member of the Security Council and, therefore, entitled to veto UN Security Council (UNSC) resolutions that could do something about the situation fortifies this wall of impunity even further.

Second, international institutions – above all the UNSC but also regional security organisations – demand from states that they co-manage international crises. They ought to manage crises together, above all the permanent members of the Security Council. This constituted a major problem during the Cold War where on many occasions the Soviet Union vetoed what it saw as resolutions favouring US interests and vice versa. In the last decade, we entered a situation that may amount to a New Cold War (Paul and Kornprobst, 2025). It does not matter whether it is the civil wars in Syria, Libya, Yemen, Ethiopia, or Sudan, the inter-state war between Russia and Ukraine or the wars between Hamas and Israel as well as Hizbollah and Israel, the Security Council either fails to produce any resolutions at all or merely manages to agree on watered down formulations that are ill-suited to defuse a crisis. Permanent members of the Security Council regularly shed their allies from criticism, such as the United States and

Israel. At times, permanent members even lash out against pillars of the UN system themselves. Albeit Russia flagrantly violates the territorial integrity of Ukraine by not only waging a war of aggression but even annexing Ukrainian territories it conquered, the UN, due to Russia's permanent seat at the Security Council, cannot do much.

Third, with arms control and disarmament being in crisis, weapons are readily available to combatants – no matter whether they are state or non-state actors. Perhaps the most well-known piece of art in front of the UN Headquarters in New York is the sculpture entitled 'Non-Violence' by Fredrik Reuterswärd. It depicts a giant gun with an equally giant knot in the barrel. The sculpture serves as a reminder that diplomacy ought to be about preventing violence and armed conflict. It ought to, among other things, take away the means to kill. When it comes to some weapons categories, diplomacy has been quite successful in doing so. Since 1975, the Biological Weapons Convention prohibits the possession and use of biological weapons. In 1997, the Chemical Weapons Convention, in many ways modelled after the Biological Weapons Convention, followed suit. Some violations occur. Syria's chemical weapons attack on its own population serves as a grim reminder. Yet, overall, compliance with these instruments is rather strong. Small arms and light weapons (SALW), empirically speaking, have killed many more people since the end of World War II than heavier weapons categories. Here, the record is much weaker. It is only since 2014 that the Arms Trade Treaty attempts to curb the illicit flow of these arms with more determination, but compliance, especially when it comes to SALW, is weak.

Historically speaking, diplomacy was very active in bringing about nuclear arms control and even in designing avenues of nuclear disarmament. The 1968 Treaty on the Non-proliferation of Nuclear Weapons (NPT), despite its name, was not just a treaty to prevent the proliferation of nuclear weapons but also meant as an instrument to disarm nuclear weapons states and share the benefits of the peaceful use of nuclear energy. A number of bilateral treaties between the superpowers were concluded, including the Anti-Ballistic Missile (ABM) Treaty and the Strategic Arms Limitation Treaty (SALT) I in 1972, the Intermediate-Range Nuclear Forces (INF) Treaty in 1987, Strategic Arms Reduction Treaty (START) I in 1991, the Strategic Offensive Reductions Treaty in 2006, and New START in 2010. From the 2000s, however, this bilateral treaty regime has suffered a number of serious setbacks, including the US's withdrawals from the ABM Treaty in 2006 and the INF Treaty in 2019 as well as Russia's suspension of the New Strategic Arms Reduction Treaty (START) in 2023. Multilateral nuclear arms control and disarmament has been in a state of crisis since the mid-2000s. Non-nuclear weapons states have become increasingly vocal about the failure of nuclear weapons states to negotiate about nuclear disarmament in good faith (Article 6, NPT). They designed their own multilateral instrument, the Treaty on the Prohibition of Nuclear Weapons (TPNW), which came into force in 2021.

Fourth, implementing instruments designed to overcome ever-occurring problems in the field of peace and war does not always come easy. It was especially in the cooperative era of the 1990s that diplomacy proved to be highly productive to re-think some basic parameters of international security. In 1989, Trinidad and Tobago reignited a debate in the General Assembly to establish a permanent international criminal court. In 1998, this new institution had become a reality. The Rome Statute set up the International Criminal Court (ICC) to put an end to impunity for individuals who commit genocide, war crimes, crimes against humanity and/or the crime of aggression. This constituted a major step forward to further justice in international affairs. In the mid-2020s, however, the legitimacy of the ICC has become increasingly contested. When most of the indicted cases were Africans in the 2010s, some African states became increasingly critical of the ICC, alleging an anti-African bias in its procedures. When the ICC issued an arrest warrant against Putin for war crimes committed in Ukraine, Russia hiked up its

> **Textbox 4.1   2005 World Summit Outcome: Responsibility to Protect**
>
> The World Summit postulates the responsibility to protect in two paragraphs. '138. Each individual State has the responsibility to protect its populations from genocide, war crimes, ethnic cleansing and crimes against humanity. This responsibility entails the prevention of such crimes, including their incitement, through appropriate and necessary means. We accept that responsibility and will act in accordance with it. The international community should, as appropriate, encourage and help States to exercise this responsibility and support the United Nations in establishing an early warning capability. 139 The international community, through the United Nations, also has the responsibility to use appropriate diplomatic, humanitarian and other peaceful means, in accordance with Chapters VI and VIII of the Charter, to help protect populations from genocide, war crimes, ethnic cleansing and crimes against humanity. In this context, we are prepared to take collective action, in a timely and decisive manner, through the Security Council, in accordance with the Charter, including Chapter VII, on a case-by-case basis and in cooperation with relevant regional organizations as appropriate, should peaceful means be inadequate and national authorities manifestly fail to protect their populations from genocide, war crimes, ethnic cleansing and crimes against humanity. We stress the need for the General Assembly to continue consideration of the responsibility to protect populations from genocide, war crimes, ethnic cleansing and crimes against humanity and its implications, bearing in mind the principles of the Charter and international law. We also intend to commit ourselves, as necessary and appropriate, to helping States build capacity to protect their populations from genocide, war crimes, ethnic cleansing and crimes against humanity and to assisting those which are under stress before crises and conflicts break out.
>
> (United Nations General Assembly, 24 October 2005)

accusations against the ICC even more. When it announced that Netanyahu is wanted for war crimes and crimes against humanity committed in Gaza, Israel, the United States and many Western allies criticised the ICC severely.

Compared to the ICC, the situation is even more dire with regard to another important diplomatic innovation of the 1990s, that is, the responsibility to protect. In 2005, the World Summit Outcome (see Textbox 4.1), which was adopted by the General Assembly, attempted to formalise humanitarian reasons for intervention when it defines the principle of responsibility to protect. In the context of this principle, sovereignty is not an absolute privilege, but its exercise is linked to a state's responsibility to protect its own population. If a state is not able to do so, it is the responsibility of the international community to help this state. If the state is itself the perpetrator of crimes such as genocide, war crimes, ethnic cleansing, and crimes against humanity, the international community has the responsibility to intervene, if necessary with Chapter 7 measures. This sounds like a far-reaching qualification of the sovereignty norm. However, the usage of the responsibility to protect principle in diplomatic speeches and international documents has decreased markedly in the 2010s. When the Security Council adopted UNSC/1973 (2011), it authorised UN member states to "take all necessary measures to protect civilians" in Libya. Yet Western powers – above all France, the United Kingdom and the United States – interpreted this mandate much too broadly and toppled Muammar al-Gaddafi from power. This was a short-lived victory, to be followed by war and instability in Libya, and the global delegitimation of the principle of the responsibility to protect. The 2024 UN Pact for the Future, although full of big promises to deliver peace, does not use this term. Instead, it vaguely circumscribes it by postulating to "support credible, timely and decisive action by the Security Council . . . to prevent or end the commission of genocide, crimes against humanity or war crimes" (A/RES/79/1, Action 41(b)).

Fifth, the world never stands still. This puts the onus on diplomacy to develop new instruments to address new threats to international security. Diplomacy's track record in doing so is chequered. At a time when digital technology leapfrogs from one major progress to the next, diplomatic debates about how to regulate technologies that affect peace and war remain in their infancy. An instrument regulating lethal autonomous weapons systems (LAWS), although postulated by the UN Secretary-General António Guterres in his 2023 New Agenda for Peace, seems still far away. Great powers who already have LAWS capabilities and are confident that they can develop them further resort to the usual diplomatic trickery to delay the making of rules or make it entirely impossible. Among other things, they quarrel about a definition of what LAWS actually are. The UN Office for Disarmament Affairs, when providing an overview of LAWS, starts with the following sentence, which speaks volumes about these problems: "At present, no commonly agreed definition of Lethal Autonomous Weapon Systems (LAWS) exists" (UNODA, 2023). Another problem that remains insufficiently addressed is transnational crime. Although it is closely linked to war and gross human rights violations, and albeit there is a worrying trend that mercenaries linked to states take part in these criminal activities, transnational crime is still routinely downplayed in diplomatic discourses. In an era that experiences a geopolitical turn and where this geopolitical turn has strong economic components (licit and illicit), this neglect is highly problematic.

Of all the diplomatic issue areas discussed in this chapter, war and peace is the one in which non-state actors struggle the most to leave a mark. Still, there were openings that advocacy groups used successfully. In the cooperative environment of the 1990s, advocacy groups successfully lobbied for prohibiting land mines and cluster munition. The ICC would never have been created without transnational civil society organisations. The responsibility to protect, too, is rooted in ideas pushed forward by advocacy networks. This kind of communicative space for civil society organisations has contracted in recent decades. There was another moment during the making of the TPNW but, overall, civil society organisations find it increasingly difficult to make their voices heard.

There are some indications that very different breeds of non-state actors may become more influential instead. Mercenaries, mentioned earlier several times, may be among these. So may be major tech companies. Starlink Services, LLC, is a case in point. Funded in part by Western governments, it provides the "essential backbone of communication" (Farrow, 2023) for the Ukrainian military in its war against Russia; but only within the confines that the company – and probably Elon Musk himself – sets. A Ukrainian attack on the Russian fleet in Sevastopol, for example, was judged as being beyond these confines. Starlink was shut down just when Ukrainian forces were about to attack the Admiral Makarov frigate. As a result, the attack failed (Kim, 2023). It may very well be that major tech companies will gain privileged access onto the diplomatic stage in years to come. It was not just Trump and Zelensky, who discussed future US support for Ukraine in its war against Russia shortly after Trump had been re-elected president. Musk was on the line, too.

Economics

The foundations of our current economic system go back to US-led efforts to re-organise the international economic system in the mid-1940s. The 1944 Bretton Woods Conference created the International Bank for Reconstruction and Development (usually simply referred to as the World Bank) and the International Monetary Fund (IMF). It was also agreed to set up an International Trade Organization. With the US Congress not ratifying the agreement, the General Agreement on Tariffs and Trade came into being as a substitute. Yet the global economic architecture evolved considerably over time. International organisations (→ glossary) such as the World Bank became important actors on the diplomatic scene as opposed to mere arenas in which state diplomacy takes place (St Clair, 2006). Diplomacy negotiated new international organisations into being, such as the WTO. It also institutionalised less formalised fora designed to discuss and decide about how to develop international economic institutions further.

What started as an informal G5 meeting at the library of the White House with delegations from the United States, Germany, the UK, France, and Japan, has moved via the G6 (+Italy) to the G7 (+Canada), and temporarily further to the G8 (+Russia). In the aftermath of Moscow's annexation of the Crimean Peninsula, the G7 reconstituted itself again without Russia. Parallel to these developments, the G20 have become an important diplomatic forum. Developing out of US President's Clinton's efforts to manage the 1997 Asian Financial Crisis, the G20 are composed of the members of the G7 plus Russia, South Africa, Mexico, Argentina, Brazil, China, South Korea, India, Indonesia, Saudi Arabia, Turkey, the EU, Australia, and, since 2023, the African Union (AU). While G7 and the G20 focus on economic issues, they also deal with adjacent policy fields such as environment, migration, and even security. There is a far-reaching diplomatic consensus that economic issues have profound repercussions for many other diplomatic issue areas.

The states represented in the G20 grouping directly or indirectly (through the EU and the AU) cover about two-thirds of the global population. Still, states are, of course, not the only actors in the economic field. There are a range of other important actors including multinational corporations. As early as in the early 1970s, when the fixed exchange rates of the Bretton Woods system collapsed, the German economist Klaus Schwab founded the World Economic Forum meant to facilitate the exchange between state and non-state actors. Since then, annual meetings take place in Winter in Switzerland. Since 2007, there have also been the annual 'Meeting of New Champions' in Summer in China. More recently, an India Economic Summit has been added to make sure to firmly include another major rising economy in the structure of the World Economic Forum.

It is disputed to what extent multinational corporations eclipse what kinds of states in the international political economy. On the one hand, there have been several studies arguing that about half of the 100 biggest economies in the world are firms and not states (Kaplan, 2000; Dicken, 2007: 38; Mander, 2014: 8). The rise of major tech companies seems to add to this trend. On the other hand, more conservative estimates suggest that multinational corporations make for about a third of the world's economic activity (Roach, 2023: 10). Yet even this more conservative finding still underlines the economic might of private for-profit actors.

In 1999, the idea of a Global Compact between state and non-state actors was introduced by UN Secretary-General Kofi Annan at the World Economic Forum. About 10,000 companies ended up agreeing to uphold the standards formulated in the Global Compact, ranging from human rights to environmental issues. The Global Compact, however, is not a legally binding convention but merely a compact that relies, for the most part, on voluntary compliance. Furthermore, it can be read as simply reminding firms of a body of international law that has long been in place anyway. More critical attempts to keep the might of multinational corporations in check include the World Social Forum that constituted itself in response to the World Economic Forum in 2001. The first meeting took place in Brazil. The World Social Forum, too, meets annually in January, that is, at the same time as the World Economic Forum. Mainly composed of activists and advocacy groups and dedicated to critically interrogating the repercussions of globalisation (→ glossary), it is an important opportunity for NGOs to debate with one another and to diffuse their ideas to a global audience. These ideas, if NGOs are successful in mobilising public opinion, do not stop at the gates of the 'official' international political economy. If NGOs, for example, would not have been as adamant about the eradication of poverty as they have been, a firmly established international organisation such as the World Bank may not have moved its practices into this direction the way it has done in the last decade. This will be further explored in the next section.

Let us have a look at global trade and finance in a bit more depth. International trade has always been an important sub-field of economics, and, historically, it *generated a number of innovations in diplomacy*. Perhaps most notably, diplomatic attempts to facilitate trade led to the creation of what is now often seen as the first international organisation, that is, the Central Commission for Navigation of the Rhine. The organisation was created by the Congress of Vienna in 1815 (and is still in operation). Another important development growing out of trade has been the establishment of free trade zones and regional organisations. The European unification effort has been at the forefront of this development for some time, but regional cooperation and integration schemes are found virtually everywhere in the world by now. In some world regions, there is considerable competition among regional groupings. Take Asia, for example. There is the Association of Southeast Asian Nations (ASEAN), but there is also the South Asian Association for Regional Cooperation (SAARC), and the Asia-Pacific Cooperation (APEC). To some extent, these organisations can simply be seen as sub-regional groupings. But the boundaries between these groupings are very much a political issue. Especially India and China carry out diplomatic skirmishes about who participates in what organisation. Extra-regional powers are of importance, too.

Since the 2010s, there has been an important reconfiguration of international trade and diplomacy struggles to channel it into warranted directions. There are at least two dimensions to it, one ideational and the other one material in nature. The rise of populist leaders and, with it, a populist diplomacy that is geared towards satisfying a leader's constituents rather than the national economic interests of a nation, has shaken the erstwhile strongly shared beliefs about the benefits of free trade. As a result, concluding free trade agreements has become more and more difficult. Trump's first presidency in the United States showed these dynamics rather clearly. A political rhetoric that is all about 'Making America Great Again' (MAGA) and that depicts this national renaissance in zero-sum terms (the greatness of America equals the weakness of competitors), does not easily allow for diplomatic outcomes from which relations between nations benefit more generally. Even already-made diplomatic agreements, for example, the WTO's Appellate Body, became victims of this turn towards zero-sum economics (Bown and Keynes, 2020).

On top of ideas about turning away from free trade, the COVID-19 pandemic was not only a major global health crisis but also 'the largest shock' that the global economy suffered in the 'past 75 years' (International Monetary Fund, 2024: 19). There was a GDP loss in most countries in the world, with the weakest economies affected the most. The Global Supply Chain Pressure index entered a downwards spiral from early 2022 to early 2023 (International Monetary Fund, 2024: 20). Trade, having long been a major regionalising force in regions otherwise as varied as Africa and Europe or the Middle East and East Asia (World Trade Organization, 2015), experienced major disruptions even on the regional level (Altman and Bastian, 2022). The EU shows rather clearly how ideational and material dimensions of trade disruption interact. Once the posterchild of regional integration, the supranational organisation underwent a rather ugly divorce from the UK whose populist leader Boris Johnson used the demarcation from the EU as a vehicle for becoming Prime Minister. Economically, at least in the short run, Brexit leaves both sides worse off.

At the heyday of economic globalisation, the increase in global trade was already remarkable but it paled to global financial flows. There is an obvious reason for this. In the digital age, financial transactions travel fast and effortless. Daily global trading in foreign exchange and interest rate derivatives increased steadily from the 1990s to the late 2000s and have since plateaued at a staggering average of about US$5 trillion. Major players in this game tend to be concentrated in a handful of global cities, such as London, New York, Tokyo, Singapore, and Hong Kong. Given these tremendous flows, scholars ask the question of whether diplomacy is still able to control them in a meaningful way. Those who answer this question in the positive allude to the instruments available for diplomacy to influence financial markets. Many of these instruments are located at the Bank of International Settlements, including the Basel Committee on Banking Supervision, the Committee on the Global Financial System, and the Financial Stability Forum. The IMF and the World Bank, of course, are important organisations as well (Porter, 2009). The G20 also plays an important role (Garrett, 2010).

Yet a quick glance at the last decade shows how volatile global financial markets are and how difficult diplomacy finds it to assume a steering function. The so-called credit crunch started in the United States when the major lenders Fannie Mae and Freddie Mac could no longer continue business without state intervention on 7 September 2008. This was then rapidly felt all over the world. State-funded rescue packages followed, for instance, for the Hypo Real Estate in Germany by 6 October, and a week later for the British banks Royal Bank of Scotland and Lloyds TSB. The EU tightened its financial governance mechanisms, most notably by creating the European Financial Stability Facility and the European Financial Stabilisation Mechanism. But the repercussions of the crisis were still felt even a decade later, especially in countries greatly suffering from the crisis such as Greece.

More clouds started to gather on the global financial horizon. During the heyday of economic globalisation, worldwide foreign direct investment (FDI) went from one record to the next. Since 2018, however, global FDI flows have plateaued (UNCTAD, 2024). COVID-19 as well as Russia's attack on Ukraine and the many economic sanction packages that the West imposed on Russia fuelled inflation. The median country in the world experienced a slight deflation in the early months of 2020 and then an inflation of over 10 percent two years later. There are some indications that the situation has improved since 2023 but, nonetheless, the outlook remains much more volatile than, say, three decades ago (International Monetary Fund, 2024: 53).

Recent changes in the international political economy move economics and security closer together. In line with beliefs into zero-sum economics as well as the material reality that our new tech economy needs to be fuelled by many natural resources not readily available in some of the rich countries in which these new technologies are developed, there has been a recent geopolitical turn in economics. The World Economic Forum defines geo-economics as "the application of power politics by economic means" and "a contest waged via global trade and investment rather than on a traditional battlefield" (World Economic Forum, 2024). It remains to be seen whether geo-economics will add a new aspect of the national interest to what the diplomat is expected to do, whether diplomats will succeed to channel geoeconomics into directions that are reconcilable with existing international law, or whether diplomacy will be eclipsed by unilateral state behaviour and/or perhaps even the rise of tech giants (Feldstein, 2021).

Development

Early on, diplomacy privileged an understanding of development as a *national economic issue*. When decolonisation occurred in the late 1950s and early 1960s, there was plenty of optimism about the economic trajectories of the newly independent states of the global South. In a highly influential article, Walt Rostow likened this trajectory to a plane taking off from the ground (Rostow, 1960). Rapid industrialisation was considered to be the fuel powering this take-off. World Bank and IMF, although originally created for the reconstruction of war-torn Europe, were supposed to be major facilitators of this endeavour. They funded, for instance, major infrastructural projects that were considered to provide the necessary prerequisites for industrialisation, such as major dams and highways. The take-off, however, did not happen, especially not in the poorest areas of the global South that required development the most.

In the face of these failures, global diplomacy struggled to adopt a new lens through which to look at development. By the 1980s, a network of economic experts, Western donors and international institutions (World Bank and IMF) had replaced the focus on the national economy with an emphasis on *integrating developing economies into the world economy*. Structural adjustment programmes were supposed to be the principal means for achieving this goal. On the conditionality of reducing government expenditure, opening up domestic markets for imports, and taking measures to build more export-oriented economies, developing states received loans from the World Bank as well as other bilateral and multilateral creditors. Sometimes referred to as Washington Consensus, this seeming paradigm (→ glossary) shift, however, did not change the record of international developmental policies around. Those states and people who were in need the most profited the least from the opening of markets in the aftermath of the Cold War (→ glossary). They were simply not ready to compete on an equal footing in the global economy from one moment to the next. On the contrary, structural readjustment programmes often made things worse. Cutting government expenditure, for example, caused major problems for healthcare systems in many developing states.

In the late 1980s, a new prism arrived. It revolved around the concept of *good governance*. This prism is considerably different from the aforementioned approaches. It is a broader lens through which to look at development. There is not just a rather technocratic and narrow understanding of a global free market economy, but there is an emphasis on the political dimensions of development. Albeit defined somewhat differently in different documents and contexts, there are certain key features that are common to most, if not all, interpretations of good governance. These include the rule of law and democracy (at times only implicit), a transparent and efficient state bureaucracy, human rights and sustainability, and justice and the absence of corruption.

Good governance became a frequently used concept. By 2000, when the EU and developing states from the African, Caribbean, and Pacific regions signed the Cotonou Agreement, good governance already made a self-evident early entry into the document. The AU even established a peer-review mechanism, which is meant as an intra-African check on African governments and their performance with regard to good governance. The AU also includes good governance among its seven aspirations identified in the Agenda 2063 (see Textbox 4.2).

Three concepts closely associated in diplomatic discourse with good governance are *human development, sustainable development*, and *human security*. These concepts illustrate how different the current understanding of development is from the Washington consensus and the early dream of rapid modernisation. Human development puts the human being at the centre. Conceptually speaking, development is no longer simply considered a macro-economic exercise whose successes and failures can be observed in macro-economic data such as GDP and exports. But measures of successes and failures are, ultimately, about how close human beings come to

> **Textbox 4.2   Agenda 2063**
>
> Agenda 2063 of the African Union (AU) is, to date, the most ambitious African development document. The Agenda is a vision for how to develop that is organised into seven aspirations:
>
> 1. A prosperous Africa, based on inclusive growth and sustainable development
> 2. An integrated continent, politically united, based on the ideals of Pan Africanism and the vision of Africa's Renaissance
> 3. An Africa of good governance, democracy, respect for human rights, justice and the rule of law
> 4. A peaceful and secure Africa
> 5. Africa with a strong cultural identity, common heritage, values and ethics
> 6. An Africa whose development is people driven, relying on the potential offered by people, especially its women and youth and caring for children
> 7. An Africa as a strong, united, resilient and influential global player and partner.
>
> The Heads of State and Governments of the AU adopted the Agenda in January 2015. Ten-year implementation plans, drawn up by the African Union Commission and defining goals and targets are meant to help implement the Agenda.

developing their potentials. The emphasis on sustainable development also marks an important conceptual departure. Successes and failures of development are not only to be measured in the here and now, but also in the future. This has important repercussions for how to deal with environmental resources. The concept of human security provides a bridge between the diplomatic fields of peace and war on the one hand and development on the other. As defined in the influential UNDP's 1994 Human Development Report, human security is about freedom from want and freedom from fear. The Report underlines that development is inescapably intertwined with these two basic freedoms. By the mid-1990s, the concept of good governance had become more and more influential in diplomatic discourse. The UN General Assembly (UNGA) endorsed the concept in 1996 (United Nations General Assembly, 1995–1996).

By the early 2000s, these new development concepts had given rise to a new paradigm of development, which is referred to as the capability approach. Coined mainly by the economist Amartya Sen and the philosopher Martha Nussbaum, the capability approach distinguishes beings, doings, and functionings. Being is about what an individual can be as a person and doing what he or she is actually able to do given a set of circumstances. Development is about enlarging the capabilities of what an individual can do. These doings cannot be measured but functionings can, for example in terms of decreasing poverty or improving public health (Stewart, 2013).

In 2000, the General Assembly adopted the UN Millennium Declaration. The Declaration featured a substantial section on development and – in contrast to many other comparable documents – set clearly defined targets of development and a timeline when these targets ought to be met. The Millennium Development Goals (MDGs) listed eight functionings by which developmental progress was to be measured. This included the postulate to halve the proportion of people in the world whose income is less than 1$ a day, of people suffering from hunger, and of people with no access to safe drinking water by 2015 (United Nations General Assembly,

2000–2001: Para.19). The results were encouraging and discouraging at the same time. They were encouraging because some regions of the world – most notably South-Eastern Asia and Eastern Asia – were rather successful in making progress in reducing extreme poverty and its repercussions. At the same time, however, they were also discouraging because progress in other regions, especially Sub-Saharan Africa, Southern Asia, and the Caribbean but also the Caucasus and Central Asia remained far removed from meeting the Millennium targets.

Building on the MDGs, the UNGA adopted A/RES/70/1 in October 2015. This resolution outlines the Sustainable Development Goals (SDGs). There are seventeen goals: (1) no poverty, (2) zero hunger, (3) good health and well-being, (4) quality education, (5) gender equality, (6) clean water and sanitation, (7) affordable and clean energy, (8) decent work and economic growth, (9) industry, innovation and infrastructure, (10) reduced inequalities, (11) sustainable cities and communities, (12) responsible consumption and production, (13) climate action, (14) life below water, (15) life on land, (16) peace, justice, and strong institutions, and (17) partnerships for the goals. There are, overall, 169 targets, to be met by 2030. Implementation of the SDGs is regularly assessed and every four years the SDG Summit brings together heads of state and government to discuss the progress made. The 2023 Sustainable Development Goal Report, however, paints an alarming picture. Written eight years after states had agreed to the goals and seven years before they were supposed to be implemented, the report finds that "of the approximately 140 targets that can be evaluated, half of them show moderate or severe deviations from the desired trajectory. Furthermore, more than 30 per cent of these targets have experienced no progress or, even worse, regression below the 2015 baseline" (United Nations, 2023a: 10).

The shift from narrow economic to broader politico-economic understandings of development was facilitated by the increasing recognition of NGOs by nation-states as actors on the diplomatic scene. Recognition comes in various shapes and forms. There is the issue-based stamp of approval, for instance, when the UN accredits an NGO for a particular endeavour such as the High-Level Dialogue on Financing for Development. But there is also the more general stamp of approval that applies to major NGOs. Development NGOs such as Oxfam, CARE International, and Save the Children International have a global distribution of offices. While most offices are geared towards helping at the locales where help is needed there are also offices in major decision-making centres such as New York that are reminiscent of an embassy or a permanent mission of a state. Similarly to the latter, the head of such an office is usually titled 'Representative'. Representatives of states and influential NGOs tend to follow similar rules and routines in their interactions.

NGOs contributed to broadening understandings of development. Development NGOs tend to take a more holistic approach, often very much informed by what happens at the local (or micro) level. In the 1980s, this approach very much clashed with the structural adjustment directives of traditional donors, and NGOs were very vocal about it. The move to human development and the capabilities approach takes some of the long-time criticisms raised by NGOs into account. Other criticisms remain unaddressed, which makes for a continuation of the notable tensions between development NGOs on the one hand and governmental and inter-governmental donors on the other.

Despite all this conceptual and agential broadening in the development field, however, the empirical record remains disappointing. Developing poor regions of the world continued to be a major challenge. Some causes of this have been around for a long time. It is one thing for diplomacy to prepare ambitious documents and for summit diplomacy to celebrate their adoption. But it is another thing altogether to follow up on the promises made in these documents. Funding, for instance, is always a major issue. Poverty reduction and investments in public health do not come cheaply and the poorest nations simply do not heave the means to make it happen without the wealthier ones. Another problem is the frequent relegation of developmental issues under other diplomatic concerns, most importantly security and economics. With the turn towards geopolitics and geoeconomics, the openings for international development become more limited.

This turn is anything but confined to Western donors. Take Africa, for example. Wealthy Gulf states such as Saudi Arabia and the United Arab Emirates have the economic means to reach deeply into domestic politics at the Horn of Africa. Many African governments pursue a hedging strategy; they opportunistically cooperate with the United States and China, oftentimes doing so not primarily to serve the national interest of their countries but to make sure that they stay in power. Russia plays an important role in West Africa and the Horn of Africa. In future, more rising global powers are likely to leave their mark on Africa – not only for reasons of prestige and perhaps even some limited sense of South-South solidarity but also, very much in a geo-economic vein, for the sake of exploring Africa's mineral wealth. Yet such a 'New Scramble for Africa' (Ewalefoh, 2022), sparking yet another round of exploiting the continent, would be entirely out of sync with diplomatic promises to work towards sustainable development.

Environment

Although a fairly new arrival on the diplomatic scene, environmental diplomacy has burgeoned since the 1970s. Arguably, the 1949 Scientific Conference on Conservation and Utilization of Resources was the first international forum for discussing environmental issues. On a general level, the 1972 UN Conference on the Human Environment (Stockholm Conference), and, on a more specific level, the Third UN Convention on the Law of the Sea (UNCLOS) in 1974 were important steps towards institutionalising global environmental governance. By the late 1990s, there had already been more than 200 international environmental treaties in place. Many more have been added since, and many more are to be expected in the future.

There are a *host of different actors* in this field. NGOs, ranging from general environmental NGOs such as Greenpeace to more specialised ones such as the Rainforest Action Network, play an important role by providing information and putting pressure on state actors by raising awareness as well as mobilising publics. In order to exchange information and engage in dialogue with one another, but also in order to make their voices being heard, environmental NGOs exhibit a strong tendency towards coalition-building. The Climate Action Network (CAN), for instance, is a network consisting of over 700 international and national NGOs. This tendency of coalition-building and networking is found in issue areas other than the environment as well.

States are represented not only by foreign service diplomats but increasingly by 'new' diplomats from environmental ministries and agencies as well. The reason for this is obvious. Environmental issues often require highly specialised expertise, and this requirement is not always easily met by foreign services, whose personnel is primarily trained in general terms. For the same reason, scientists are very important actors on the environmental stage as well. In this field, politics ultimately has to rely on cutting-edge research that identifies environmental problems as well as their causes, and proposes steps to mitigate or overcome these problems.

Within the UN, environmental issues are to be dealt with by the UN Environmental Programme (UNEP), which is based in Nairobi. The creation of UNEP in 1972 was one of the outcomes of the Stockholm Declaration. UNEP is active in three large environmental issue areas: *climate*, *nature*, and *pollution*. Very briefly put, activities on climate revolve around studying, monitoring and mitigating climate change as well as reducing carbon emissions. Nature ranges from protecting biodiversity to sustainable lake management. Pollution is about reducing chemicals and waste. UNEP's activities started with countering pollution. As early as in 1973, state parties agreed upon the Convention for the Prevention of Pollution from Ships. Countering pollution still is an important activity of UNEP and of environmental diplomacy more generally. In 2013, states adopted the Minamata Convention, which controls usage and emissions of mercury. In 2022, states agreed to an ambitious timetable to negotiate a plastic convention by the end of 2024.

When it comes to nature, the 1992 Convention on Biological Diversity is an important cornerstone. It links the conservation of biological diversity to sustainable development. More recently, despite increasing diplomatic deadlock in other diplomatic fields, states moved on to protect marine biodiversity. In 2022, they adopted the Agreement under the UN Convention on the Law of the Sea on the Conservation and Sustainable Use of Marine Biological Diversity of Areas Beyond National Jurisdiction (BBNJ). The agreement protects almost two-thirds of the oceans, that is, those marine areas that are beyond national jurisdiction.

No environmental issue receives as much public and diplomatic attention as climate change. While the Stockholm Conference in 1972 may be seen as an important early encounter with this issue, the creation of the Intergovernmental Panel on Climate Change (IPCC) in 1988 marks the starting point for a more sustained diplomatic engagement with this field. The IPCC is an expert body, composed of world-renowned climatologists who are appointed by their respective governments. On December 21, 1990, the General Assembly adopted Resolution 45/212, which set up a negotiation committee on climate change. Two years later, all of these efforts yielded an important outcome. The 1992 UN Framework Convention on Climate Change (UNFCCC or Rio Declaration) was signed, in which the state parties agreed to monitor their carbon dioxide emissions. In 1997, the parties negotiated the Kyoto Protocol, which set legally binding targets for the reduction of greenhouse gases.

From the late 1990s to the mid-2010s, diplomacy encountered plenty of difficulties to move forward. The Kyoto Protocol only entered into force in 2005. Several climate change summits, such as in Copenhagen in 2009 and Durban in 2011, did little more than to avert a collapse of the global environmental regime. The 2015 Paris Agreement was a new landmark document agreed upon by 195 states. Having been swiftly ratified by the overwhelming number of state parties, it entered into force a year later and more detailed negotiations on how to implement it proceed annually in the format of the Conference of the Parties (COP). Even when the United States announced in mid-2017 that it would withdraw from the Agreement, these detailed negotiations continued to go ahead as scheduled. The Paris Agreement, similarly to other recent global agreements, criss-crosses issue areas. There are notable overlaps, for example, between the SDGs and the Paris Agreement.

But the Paris Agreement has its major weaknesses, too. For one, pledges made by the parties are insufficient. Given these pledges, the goal of keeping climate change at bay with 1.5 degrees of warming in this century cannot be achieved. Current pledges point towards a range of 2.5 and 2.9 degrees (United Nations Environment Programme, 2023). Furthermore, it remains, mildly put, far from clear whether parties keep their promises. More than 140 countries have set themselves net-zero targets by now, that is, to come as close to zero greenhouse gas emissions as possible. This includes the biggest polluters such as China, the United States, India and the EU states (United Nations, 2023b). Yet it is unclear how close to zero they really will move in years to come.

No other diplomatic field has experienced as much expansion as the environmental one in the last fifty years. This applies to the number of issues considered, instruments adopted, and the number of actors involved in it. At UNEP's 50th birthday, there were almost 5,000 people involved in adopting the political declaration. Out of which 3,400 were present in person while 1,500 followed the event online. Most of them represented non-state actors. This ranges from major oil companies, eager to protect their business model, to environmental advocacy networks. Greta Thunberg made it from an unknown schoolgirl to a highly influential global spokesperson on the environment thanks to social media. Science diplomacy is of key importance because our knowledge about what is happening in our environment in general and climate in particular is produced by science. Experts and non-experts (career diplomats very much included) need to find a way to meaningfully talk to one another.

At the same time, diplomacy finds it very difficult to provide the kind of governance needed to meet the demand. The Union of Concerned Scientists summarises the situation on climate change very well: hotter, wetter, and more extreme. In most areas of the world, temperatures are on the increase. This leads, among other things, to deforestation and desertification. It also makes ice sheets and glaciers melt. This makes sea levels rise. More extreme weather events are happening such as hurricanes, tornadoes and cyclones (Union of Concerned Scientists, 2023). All of this threatens natural and socio-political systems on which the people of this world depend. The people of Tuvalu are witnessing how the sea swallows their land. Droughts become more frequently in Ethiopia and Somalia, threatening the livelihood of pastoralists. Sea level rise projections show that many major urban centres worldwide are under risk of flooding due to rising sea levels. This includes Bangkok (Thailand), Amsterdam (Netherlands), Ho Chi Minh City (Vietnam), New Orleans (United States), Manila (Philippines), London (United Kingdom), Shenzhen (China), Hamburg (Germany), and Dubai (United Arab Emirates) (Igini, 2022). Given these problems, there really would be plenty of need for stronger and more effective governance mechanisms.

Aside from political will and at times even doubting the science, there appears to be a coordination problem. Take desertification, for example. There are at least eight international organisations and UN agencies addressing the issue: the Food and Agriculture Organization of the UN (FAO), the International Fund for Agricultural Development, the Sahel and West Africa Club, the Sahara and Sahel Observatory, the UN Environment Programme (UNEP, especially the Drylands and Development Center), the UN Institute for Training and Research (UNITAR), the permanent secretariat of the UN Convention to Combat Desertification, and the World Bank. This institutional thickening in the field is, in principle, to be welcome. Yet it also causes some problems of coordination and even competition.

Health

The institutionalisation of health as a field of diplomatic activity goes back to the 19th century. From the mid-19th to the mid-20th centuries, 20 international sanitary conferences took place. They were meant to curb the cross-border spread of cholera and the plague. In 1907, the *Office international d'hygiène publique* was created. After World War I, the League of Nations Health Organization was founded, to be succeeded by the World Health Organization (WHO) in the aftermath of World War II. The latter's Constitution remains the most foundational document on global health today. Article 1 sets the bar high: "Health is a state of complete physical, mental and social well-being and not merely the absence of disease of infirmity". The same article also defines health, thus defined, as human right "of every human being without distinction of race, religion, political belief, economic or social condition".

A number of documents build on the WHO Constitution. The 1951 International Sanitary Regulations are about how to prevent and contain the spread of six communicable (infectious) diseases: cholera, plague, relapsing fever, smallpox, typhoid, and yellow fever. The 1969 International Health Regulations kept the focus on a narrow list of known communicable diseases but smallpox dropped out of the list. This highly contagious and deadly disease, estimated to have killed about 80 to 90 percent of the local population in Latin America in the aftermath of European conquest (Watts, 1999: xiv), was declared eradicated by the World Health Assembly in 1980.

In the early 2000s, the SARS outbreak – SARS-CoV-1 – shocked the world. Even though the numbers of infected people, fatalities, and states remained limited, the spread of SARS to every continent in the world underlined a risk that epidemiologists had highlighted for a long time. Growing interdependence and globalisation (including more and more air travel), as well as the encroachment of human beings into areas previously uninhabited by humans, increases the risk of the global spread of communicable diseases. SARS was a zoonotic virus, that is, a virus that was transmitted from an animal to humans. Then it spread quickly in and around China, and from there to other states worldwide.

Diplomats and medical experts came together and worked on strengthening the International Health Regulations. Thoroughly revised in 2005, these regulations feature at least two important innovations: First, there is no given list of communicable diseases any more. Any disease, including an unknown one that causes a serious outbreak, is covered by the 2005 International Health Regulations. This is an important lesson from SARS. The disease, being unknown previously, was not on the list of diseases of the previous version of the International Health Regulations. Second, the 2005 version includes the Public Health Emergency of International Concern (PHEIC). Meant to be the loudest alarm bell that the WHO can ring, PHEICs are to be determined by the WHO Director-General, after having been advised by a panel of experts (Emergency Committee), in cases in which there is 'an extraordinary event' that constitutes a "public health risk to other States through the international spread of disease" and that "potentially require[s] a coordinated international response" (IHR, 2005: Art 1).

It took, however, much too long to sound this alarm bell when SARS-CoV-2, causing the disease COVID-19, started to spread globally (see Textbox 4.3). Between December 2019 and

---

Textbox 4.3 The Early Response to COVID-19

Medical doctors in China exchanged concerned messages from early December 2019 onwards about the spread of a dangerous virus. Initially, some of them thought that they were in the midst of another SARS outbreak, which China had experienced two decades before. They were actually not far off. What would soon be dubbed SARS-CoV-2 shares a number of features with SARS-CoV-1. Yet Chinese authorities reacted swiftly, making discussions disappear on social media platforms such as Weibo and likened medical expertise to spreading rumours. Even when it became increasingly clear to the authorities that a serious unknown disease was spreading quickly, there was still no reporting to WHO although, according to the 2005 International Health Regulations, this ought to happen within 24 hours. China only started to report – and even then only piecemeal – on December 31, 2019. Precious time was lost. The WHO Director-General Tedros Adhanom Ghebreyesus did not act swiftly either. He only convened the Emergency Committee, in charge of advising him whether to determine a PHEIC or not, for the first time on 22 and 23 January. The discussions were shaped less by the criteria to determine a PHEIC listed in the International Health Regulations than by highly demanding benchmarks for scientific certainty, including how many generations of human-to-human transmission it takes to determine a PHEIC. Given these highly

> demanding benchmarks, the Emergency Committee delivered a split opinion. Only on 29 January, the Committee almost unanimously recommended that a PHEIC ought to be declared. Even the highly demanding benchmarks were fulfilled. Overall, therefore, it took about eight weeks from the first indications of a fast-spreading serious disease to the point when the WHO finally rang its loudest alarm bell. And even then, there was not much reaction among states. Only when Tedros declared COVID-19 a pandemic another five weeks later did more serious counter-measures gain momentum. Time is of the essence for pandemic prevention, preparedness and response. The early response to COVID-19 was simply much too slow.

March 2022, the disease is estimated to have killed about 20 million people worldwide (Wang et al., 2022). Negotiations for a new Pandemic Treaty are on their way. But it remains far from clear whether diplomats and medical experts will be able to agree on an instrument that, according to the latter, really could make a difference. At a minimum, three recurring problems need to be addressed: First, WHO requires its own reporting capacities. Under current global health law, WHO does not have the authority to monitor the outbreaks of diseases by itself. It needs to rely on member states to do so (or be invited by a member state). Reporting that a dangerous disease emanates from one's own country, however, does not come easy to state representatives. Trained to uphold the national interest, avoiding economic disruptions caused by quarantine measures very much included, diplomats tend to downplay the seriousness of a disease outbreak. Second, diplomatic practices in Geneva put the bar for determining PHEICs too high. In recent years, these were less and less about 'risk' of international spread and more and more about scientific certainty that such spread has occurred. By the time such certainty is established, precious time to curb a disease outbreak early on may be lost. Instead, the precautionary principle – here determining a PHEIC in cases of serious outbreaks of diseases even with partial as opposed to conclusive medical evidence about the severity and transmission patterns – would make for a much better compass. Third, the WHO requires adequate funding. The organisation is already barely able to fulfil its basic functions. Assessed contributions have not been increased in years and the WHO relies extensively on voluntary funding provided by state and non-state actors with their specific interests and concerns in mind. It will not be possible for the WHO to take on additional tasks such as monitoring if the funding situation does not improve significantly (Kornprobst and Strobl, 2024).

According to foundational documents of global health, the field is to be much more than merely keeping dangerous communicable diseases at bay. It is what WHO, following the 1978 Alma Ata Declaration, refers to as a strategy of 'Health for All'. Such a comprehensive view of health, fully in sync with understanding health as human right, is clearly visible in the Millennium Development Goals and the Sustainable Development Goals.

As global health statistics show, however, a lot remains to be done if we want to be able to at least somehow approximate the Health-For-All postulate. Wealth and poverty (as well as peace and war) remain strongly correlated with health and sickness along a number of indicators. Maternal mortality remains very high (between 500 and 999 per 100,000 live births) in 13 countries in what is to the WHO the African Region and the Eastern Mediterranean Region (World Health Organization, 2023: 15). Of the 2.3 million neonatal deaths worldwide (newborn does not survive first month), almost half happen in Africa and more than a third in Central and Southern Asia (World Health Organization, 2023: 18). Overall, the implementation of health-related SDGs proceeds much slower compared to the MDGs.

Global health statistics are also telling about another worrying trend. Even though diplomatic discourse strongly focuses on communicable diseases, non-communicable ones are on the rise and they claim more lives than communicable ones. This is a pattern that can be observed throughout WHO regions. While non-communicable diseases caused 61 percent of global deaths (this is equivalent to about 31 million people) in 2000, this figure rose to 74 percent (or 41 million) in 2019. Four major non-communicable diseases (in this order) mainly account for these figures: cardiovascular disease, cancer, chronic respiratory disease, and diabetes (World Health Organization, 2023: 10).

Global health issues oftentimes remain sidelined in national foreign services. Thus, national ministries of health and development, development agencies, international organisations and agencies, and locally, nationally, and transnationally operating non-governmental organisations are important players in this field. Given the many different actors in this issue area, coordination is an important challenge. Take, for instance, just the number of international organisations and agencies dealing with the problem of HIV/AIDS: UN Children's Fund (UNICEF), World Food Programme, UN Development Programme (UNDP), UN Population Fund (UNFPA), UN Educational, Scientific, and Cultural Organization (UNESCO), WHO, World Bank, UN Office on Drugs and Crime (UNODC), and the International Labour Organization (ILO). In order to coordinate at least the work of the UN agencies and their affiliates in this field, the UN created the Joint UN Programme on HIV/AIDS (Seckinelgin, 2005).

Occasionally, diplomacy stops marginalising global health and, securitising the spread of a communicable disease, may at times even come up with determined responses. The 2014 Ebola outbreak in West Africa illustrates this well. S/RES/2177 (2014) states that this situation "constitutes a threat to international peace and security". In order to curb this threat, the resolution authorised the UN Mission for Ebola Emergency Response (UNMEER). At least three aspects of this resolution are worth emphasising: First, the Security Council, originally envisaged to decide upon matters of war and peace, dealt with a health issue. Second, the Security Council used legal language that is usually reserved for attempts to de-escalate or end armed conflicts. Third, the Security Council set up the first UN field mission focusing on health issues.

All too often, however, traditional diplomacy *dismisses global health as low politics*. Thus, many non-state actors play key roles in this field. This ranges from individual medical experts, say those on the roster of the Emergency Committee, to those working for Doctors without Borders, from the Bill & Melinda Gates Foundation – one of the biggest donors in global health, well ahead of most states – to the vaccine alliance Gavi, and from the International Red Cross and Red Crescent Movement to pharmaceutical companies. Relations between some of these actors have been fraught with friction ever since. At the First Sanitary Conference, the eleven state delegations (it was still a very colonial world) were each composed of two members with voting rights: a diplomat and a doctor. The two, however, often could not agree and cast their votes differently. By the time of the Second Sanitary Conference, the voting rights of the medical doctors were gone. The problem, however, remains. Doctors have the medical expertise and diplomats have the toolbox to make international cooperation happen where this is necessary. The two have to work together (Kornprobst and Strobl, 2021).

Migration

The globalisation of world politics has gone hand in hand with major increases of migration flows. Between 1970 to 2000, the number of international migrants worldwide rose from 82 million to 175 million. Within this time period, the 1990s account for most of this marked increase (International Organization for Migration, 2018: 394). This trend continued unabated. By 2024, the figure stood at 281 million. As a percentage of the world population, this remains still rather small: 3.6 percent are migrants. The United States, Germany, Saudi Arabia, Russia, and the UK have been the top-five destination countries in the early 2020s (International Organisation for Migration, 2024).

Migrants are mixed in terms of their skill levels. This includes low, intermediate and high skill. Migration of the latter category leads to the so-called brain drain, which amounts to a serious impediment for developing economies. There are numerous countries, in which at least a third of people with a tertiary education live outside the country in which they were born. This includes Belize, Barbados, Congo (Brazzaville), Ghana, Guyana, Jamaica, Cambodia, Mozambique, Mauritius, Seychelles, Tonga, Trinidad and Tobago, Saint Vincent and Grenadines, the US Virgin Islands, Samoa, and Zimbabwe (Dumont, Spielvogel and Widmaier, 2010). For many sending countries, remittances sent to families back home by migrants have become a major economic factor. In 2024, migrants transferred no less than US$831 billion (International Organisation for Migration, 2024).

In international law, there is no agreed-upon definition of migrant. The term is either used as referring to persons who left their country of origin voluntarily or as a generic term for persons who are living outside the country of their origin irrespective of the motives for doing so. Yet there is an agreed-upon definition of refugee. In the 1951 Convention Relating to the Status of Refugees (Refugee Convention), a refugee is defined as someone who is persecuted, for instance, based on race, religion, nationality, or political opinion, forcing the person out of its country of origin. The number of refugees has increased significantly from 1970 to 1990. In 1970, there were 5.3 million refugees worldwide. By 1980, the figure had risen to 9.6 million and, by 1990, to 12.3 million. After this peak, the number decreased to 9.5 million in 2000 (International Organization for Migration, 2018: 309). Yet from then onwards, the figures increased enormously. By 2023, there were 36,4 million refugees. Even these high numbers pale compared to the ones of internally displaced persons, that is, those fleeing their homes to other parts of their country of origin. There are 62.5 million. Overall, there are 110 million people in the world who were forced to flee their homes (United Nations High Commissioner for Refugees, 2023). This makes for a post–World War II record number. This record is closely linked to the increase of inter-state and intra-state wars, both in terms of absolute numbers and their destructiveness.

The diplomatic institutionalisation of this issue area *has kept up neither with migration flows nor the increasing number of displaced people*. During World War II, the UN Relief and Rehabilitation Administration was set up, replaced by the International Refugee Organization in the aftermath of World War II, which in turn was soon replaced by two institutions: The UN High Commissioner for Refugees (UNHCR) and the Intergovernmental Committee for European Migration (ICEM). The latter's name gives away the original primary purpose of these institutions, that is, the management of the large numbers of refugees and displaced people in war-torn Europe. The ICEM was reformed in 1989 and renamed International Organization for Migration (IOM). The 1951 Convention to the Status of Refugees (Refugee Convention) remains the key international accord on the rights of refugees, and, thus, marks the perimeter within which the UNHCR's activities ought to take place.

The diplomatic community has been slow to add to these instruments. In 1990, the UN International Convention on the Protection of the Rights of All Migrant Workers and Members of Their Families was adopted but it remains poorly ratified. Apart from the IOM and the UNHCR, there are no major international organisations that focus on migration issues. Many organisations address particular aspects, which causes difficulties of coordination. These organisations and agencies include the ILO, UN Conference on Trade and Development (UNCTAD),

74 *Understanding International Diplomacy*

Textbox 4.4   Human Trafficking

Human trafficking is the trade of humans for the purpose of forcing them into exploitative relationships. The UN Protocol to Prevent, Suppress and Punish Trafficking in Persons, especially Women and Children, lists the following forms of exploitation: "prostitution and other forms of sexual exploitation, forced labour or services, slavery or practices similar to slavery, servitude or the removal, manipulation or implantation of organs" (Article 3a). Since human trafficking is a highly clandestine activity, it is difficult to get precise data on how many people get trafficked each year. Some time ago, the ILO estimated that there are close to 2.5 million trafficked persons at any given point in time. Since human trafficking is the third largest transnational criminal industry (third only to drug dealing and arms trafficking), it is likely that these numbers have increased further. Two-thirds of trafficked persons are women, to be followed by girls (13 percent), men (12 percent) and boys (9 percent).[2] According to current data by the UNODC, most victims are trafficked for purposes of sexual exploitation (79 percent). Forced labour amounts to 18 percent. Other forms of exploitation, including organ removal make up the rest.[3] Countering human trafficking is a very difficult task. There are international organisations that address the problem, most notably the ILO, UNODC and UNICEF. The 1998 Rome Statute constituting the International Criminal Court lists the forms of abuses associated with human trafficking as crimes against humanity. But with many states not enacting law required for curbing trafficking and not dedicating sufficient resources to the cause, it is unlikely that these international efforts will eradicate human trafficking – and catastrophic violations of human rights that come with it such as slavery – any time soon.

UNDP, UN Department of Economic and Social Affairs, UNESCO, UNFPA, UNICEF, UNITAR, UNODC – Textbox 4.4 explains why it is part of this list – and the World Bank. The UN Relief and Works Agency for Palestine Refugees in the Near East (UNRWA), founded in 1949, is a special case because its mandate is confined to a particular group of refugees, that is, the nearly 6 million Palestinians who are registered as refugees in Gaza, Palestine and surrounding states. Coordinating the many activities of these organisations does not come easy. The first instrument meant to do so was the Global Migration Group. In 2018, it was replaced by the UN Network on Migration.

In the latter part of the 2010s, there seemed to be some movement towards diplomatic solutions to migration problems. In 2016, the General Assembly adopted A/RES/71/1, which is also referred to as the New York Declaration for Refugees and Migrants. The resolution vows to address the root causes of migration and ensure that "the human rights and fundamental freedoms of all persons, in transit and after arrival" are protected (New York Declaration for Refugees and Migrants, 2016: Art. 26). The New York Declaration also pledges to negotiate further details on the implementation of the goals formulated in the resolution. The outcome of this pledge are two compacts, one on migration and one on refugees. The Global Compact for Safe, Orderly and Regular Migration lists 23 objectives on how to curb push factors of migration, safeguard human rights at different stages of migration, and create conditions of successful integration. The compact, being a compact, however, is not legally binding. The same applies to the Global Compact on Refugees, meant to ease pressures on host countries, enhance self-reliance of refugees, expand access to third-country solutions, and support conditions for a safe return to countries of origin.

The refugee compact, being rather defensive and geared towards the interests of receiving states, was less controversial than the migration compact, which is more forward-looking. Only Hungary and the United States, both at the time governed by populist right-wing governments, voted against the refugee compact. The Czech Republic, Hungary, Israel, the United States, and Poland cast their vote against the migration compact. These votes against the compact highlight that domestic politics, in many states in the Global North, has turned against immigration. This gives rise to national policies of fortifying nation-state borders rather than to meaningful diplomatic deliberation and negotiation about how to address the many different forms of migration and their causes.

Crosscutting Areas

The aforementioned are merely a selection of issue areas that form something akin to functional international sub-orders in which there is a considerable amount of diplomatic activity. There is always some spill-over among these sub-orders. When a health issue becomes securitised, for example, actors, on an ad-hoc basis, come to draw linkages from war and peace to health. Yet there are also areas that are frequently entangled with many others. Two of these cross-cutting areas are especially noteworthy: human rights as well as science and technology.

On the one hand, human right makes for its own diplomatic field. There is a so-called International Bill of Rights, comprised of the Universal Declaration of Human Rights, the International Covenant for Civil and Political Rights, and the International Covenant for Economic, Social and Cultural Rights. Many other conventions, treaties, and legal instruments are grouped around this Bill of Rights. There are Charter-based mechanisms to ensure human rights compliance, most importantly the Human Rights Council. Additionally, there are treaty-based mechanisms, which encompass the Committee on the Elimination of Racial Discrimination, Committee on Economic, Social and Cultural Rights, Human Rights Committee, Committee on the Elimination of Discrimination against Women, Committee against Torture, Committee on the Rights of the Child, Committee on Migrant Workers, Sub-committee on the Prevention of Torture and Other Cruel and Inhumane or Degrading Treatment or Punishment, Committee on the Rights of Persons with Disabilities, and the Committee on Enforced Disappearances. Much of the further development of the human rights field takes place in Geneva. This is also where the UN High Commission for Human Rights is located.

On the other hand, the human rights field is closely intertwined with a host of other issue areas. A day before the Universal Declaration of Human Rights was adopted in December 1948, the General Assembly agreed to the Convention on the Prevention and Punishment of the Crime of Genocide. This convention has very clear repercussions for the field of war and peace. More generally speaking, international humanitarian law is very much underpinned by human rights. When this body of law was further developed in the 1990s, the lens of human security was put to use. What mattered, according to human rights advocates and like-minded states was not the usefulness of landmines or cluster munition for national security but their threat to human security. These kinds of weapons cannot distinguish between combatants and non-combatants, which is a cornerstone in international humanitarian law. The aforementioned overview of diplomatic issue areas abounds with other examples. There was mention of the right to development and the right to health. Migrants have, like anyone, a 'right to life, liberty and security of person', as the Universal Declaration put it in 1948. These examples could be extended almost indefinitely. It is no exaggeration to write that the human rights field, especially in the 1990s, was something akin to the engine of progress in many diplomatic issue areas. More recently, however, the human rights field has become increasingly contested. At the same time, it has struggled more and more to keep up its role of helping advance other areas of diplomatic cooperation.

When it comes to science and technology, things are rather different. Not a single issue area discussed earlier remains untouched by ever-accelerating scientific and technological innovations. To give but a few examples, arms control needs to discuss how to regulate autonomous and semi-autonomous weapons, the so-called Fourth Industrial Revolution fundamentally transforms the global economy, implementing SDGs depends, in no small measure, on using already available and soon-to-be available technologies, finding ways to cut greenhouse gas emissions is, first and foremost, a technological challenge, monitoring and treating diseases is revolutionised by digital technologies, and questions about how to reconcile new technologies with human rights abound. Diplomacy, in other words, ought to talk a lot about science and technology.

But it hardly does. Merely the contours of a diplomatic issue area on science and technology are visible. It is not a fully fledged field yet. For sure, there is the UN Sciences and Technology Organization (UNSTO) and the UN Commission on Science and Technology for Development (CSTD), which is a subsidiary body of the Economic and Social Council. Since 2020, the UN Secretary-General appoints a Tech Envoy. There are discussions on science and technology in various diplomatic issue areas. Lethal autonomous weapons (LAWS), for instance, are discussed within the framework of the Convention on Certain Conventional Weapons, which dates back to 1980, that is, at a time when the technological breakthroughs of today, especially in digital technology, was entirely unimaginable. The 2024 Pact for the Future includes a Global Digital Compact. But the document is not binding and leaves out the more difficult issues arising from the digital age, including the implications of digital technology for matters of war and peace.

It is highly questionable to what extent these slow and partial attempts to govern technological innovation are sufficient to shape the tech world of today – not even to speak of anticipating changes for the future. Diplomatic hesitation to define rules ultimately empowers great powers to use their tech edge to keep others at a distance and major tech companies to look out for their benefits more or less unrestrained by international norms.

Summary

- In the post–World War II era, there was a steady expansion of diplomatic issue areas for many decades. Many issue areas were added to traditional activities in the fields of war and peace as well as economics. This includes development, environment, health, migration, human rights, and, up to a point at least, science and technology.
- Since about the turn of the millennium, there are indications of contraction. While there is more and more demand for global governance, *the diplomatic supply for this governance decreases* in areas ranging from the environment to science and technology and from health to development.
- The expansion of diplomatic issue areas came with a *multiplication of actors* on the diplomatic stage. There were no longer just traditional diplomats working for an MFA but also representatives from other ministries, experts, international bureaucrats, advocacy groups, and corporations.
- More recently, there is the counter-trend of *traditional diplomacy, especially great power diplomacy, asserting itself again more strongly*. Non-traditional actors find it more difficult again to have a voice. This applies especially to NGOs. Furthermore, geopolitical and geoeconomic premises circumscribe *more narrow boundaries even on what traditional diplomacy can accomplish*.

Study Questions

- What diplomatic issue areas are there? How are they related to one another?
- What is the role of the general diplomat in a diplomatic system that deals more and more with specialised policy fields and issues?
- What indications are there for diplomacy to assume a larger and what for it to assume a smaller role in shaping various issues areas?
- What are, from an ethical point of view, the most urgent world problems to be dealt with by the diplomatic community? And what kind of diplomacy would be appropriate to do so?

Recommended Further Reading

Chasek, Pemela, and David Downie. 2020. "Actors in the Environmental Arena." In *Global Environmental Politics*, edited by Pamela Chasek and David Downie, 51–104. London: Routledge.

This chapter discusses traditional and non-traditional diplomatic actors in the environmental field.

Chatterjee, Charles. 2020. *Economic Diplomacy and Foreign Policy-Making*. Basingstoke: Palgrave Macmillan.

This book addresses the evolution of diplomacy in the international political economy, including the international development field.

Kickbusch, Ilona, and Austin Liu. 2022. "Global Health Diplomacy: Reconstructing Power and Governance." *Lancet* 399 (10341): 2156–66.

This state-of-the-art overview of global health diplomacy discusses persistent problems and ways of how to overcome them.

Kittichaisaree, K. 2020. *International Human Rights Law and Diplomacy*. London: Edward Elgar.

This comprehensive study addresses the human rights field and how it has expanded to shape other diplomatic fields.

Kornprobst, Markus. 2023. "Diplomatic Peace." *The Hague Journal of Diplomacy* 18 (4): 475–508.

The article analyses how diplomats define peace and war, and discusses how these diplomatic promises to work towards peace and stay away from war shape various diplomatic issue areas.

Notes

1 The war between Gaza and Israel is, legally speaking, not an inter-state war because Gaza is not a recognised state, but the confrontation has certain resemblances with asymmetric inter-state wars, including the determination to fight out contradictory claims of over control over territory. A similar caveat applies to the disputes between China and Taiwan. Most states in the world do not recognise Taiwan as a state (or Taiwan as representing China).
2 P. 11. www.unodc.org/documents/Global_Report_on_TIP.pdf
3 P. 6. www.unodc.org/documents/Global_Report_on_TIP.pdf

Part III
Mapping Diplomacy

5 Contexts of Diplomacy

Chapter Objectives

- To identify the contexts that constrain as well as enable diplomats to perform their tasks, and make diplomacy in the first place.
- To differentiate between foreground and background layers as well as substantive and procedural dimensions of contexts.
- To discuss procedural foreground provisions, especially the 1961 Vienna Convention on Diplomatic Relations, and procedural background provisions on tact, communication, and authority in diplomacy.
- To examine substantive foreground provisions and background elements, especially those on the nexus of diplomacy and peace.

Introduction

Diplomats draw from contexts (→ glossary) in order to orient themselves and perform their tasks. These contexts make diplomacy possible in the first place. This chapter discusses these contexts by making two kinds of distinctions: foreground and background layers (Adler, 2019; Kornprobst and Strobl, 2024) as well as procedural and substantive dimensions (Bull, 1995: 13–19; Müller, 2004: 425) of context.

Our differentiation of foreground and background is similar to the one between demiurgic and autopoietic (Anter, 2007: 26; Tsekeris, 2009). The foreground consists of designed institutions. In classic Greek democratic theory, it would be the *dēmiourgós* (those who work for the people) who negotiate laws into being. In international relations, it is diplomats who are entrusted with designing and negotiating agreements. The background is about all those elements constituting diplomatic encounters that usually stay implicit, even to the extent that many diplomats cannot reflect upon them. Adler (2019) introduces the concept of background to the study of international relations by borrowing from John Searle (1980), who uses the concept as a generic term for all those elements structuring communication that are not explicitly voiced in this communication. These evolve over time, and this evolution is always conditioned by what is already there. Backgrounds, therefore, are autopoietic (self-producing and self-reproducing) to a considerable extent.

Foreground and background each are comprised of procedural and substantive elements. The 1961 Vienna Convention on Diplomatic Relations remains the key instrument for the procedural design of diplomacy. It regulates the rights and obligations of diplomats posted abroad as well as sending and host states. Yet there are many other procedural instruments as well. Rules of procedure, for example, are very important. They are actually of such high salience that the Security

DOI: 10.4324/9781003485407-8

Council, for example, has been operating for almost eight decades merely with Provisional Rules of Procedure (S/96/Rev. 7). Agreeing on rules of procedure is always a somewhat delicate issue because some rules may lend themselves a bit more to stalling any kind of progress (such as the comprehensive consent rule at the Conference on Disarmament that even extends to the agenda of what is to be discussed) than others. Substantive foreground provisions range from definitions of terms, say what a chemical weapon is (and what categories there are) or what counts as greenhouse gas emissions, to obligations such as the elimination of such weapons or emissions thus defined.

Procedural and substantive background elements are much more difficult to detect for the researcher, and it is difficult for diplomats to reflect upon them because, for the most part, they take them very much for granted. But these elements do matter, too. Diplomacy's procedural background elements are about tact, communicative genre and authority. Tact is at the core of standards of behaviour that diplomats get socialised into early on in their careers. Diplomatic communication forms its own genre. Words are carefully chosen to signify messages. Authority is about who is widely regarded to be entitled to speak out and who is not. Substantive background elements are those prejudgements that diplomats use to anchor diplomatic communication on a particular topic. These range from entire lenses or paradigms to stand-alone epistemic understandings and normative beliefs. Take chemical weapons, for example. Are they to be discussed through the lens of national or human security? What actually are the effects of what kinds of chemical devices for the human body? Does this make them a category of inhumane weapons to be banned or simply another kind of weapon, *en par* with new generations of highly destructive conventional weapons?

These questions already strongly hint at the heterogeneity of the background. There can be all kinds of quarrels about how to interpret a foreground institution. But when it comes to the background, there is usually much more contestation. The lenses with which actors look at international politics oftentimes to not easily converge.

This chapter first deals with procedural dimensions of the background. We discuss the procedural foreround, elaborating on the 1961 Vienna Convention, and follow up with the procedural background, focusing on tact, communicative genre and authority. Then, we move on to the substantive dimensions of the background. Again, we begin with the substantive foreground, illustrating our main points by discussing how diplomats define peace in key General Assembly documents. We stick to the question of peace when we examine the substantive background, highlighting heterogeneity and contestation.

Procedural Foreground: Looking at the Vienna Convention

Diplomacy boasts lots of procedural foreground provisions, ranging from grand principles to highly detailed decision-making procedures. For introducing the reader to the procedural foreground, we focus on the former and, with it, on the Vienna Convention on Diplomatic Relations, which was adopted in 1961 and came into force in 1964. The convention remains the most foundational document in diplomatic law.

In the 17th century, the Dutch legal scholar and philosopher Hugo Grotius already postulated two important principles: "Now there are two rights of ambassadors which we see are everywhere referred to the law of nations. The first is that they be admitted, the second, that they be free from violence" (Grotius, on the Right of Legation, in Berridge, 2004: 101). But it was only in the early 19th century, when the Concert of Europe put pressure on states to put their communication channels on more solid legal ground, that attempts to codify the evolving customary diplomatic law found its first more influential codified expressions. In 1815, the

Vienna Regulation was an important move towards codification of existing practices. Resolutions adopted by the Institute of International Law in 1895 and 1929, the Havana Convention regarding Diplomatic Officers in 1928, and the Harvard Draft Convention on Diplomatic Privileges and Immunities of 1932 followed (Denza, 2008: 1–12).

In its very first session in 1949, the International Law Commission (ILC) included the codification of diplomatic law on its list of codifying tasks. The ILC is an important institution. Many international conventions have been drafted by it. Composed of legal experts with various backgrounds – academic, diplomatic corps, international organisations, and so forth – its members are elected by the General Assembly for the duration of five years. In the early 1950s, Yugoslavia took the initiative in the UN General Assembly, and advocated for prioritising the codification of diplomatic law. With this initiative finding a friendly response from other member states, the General Assembly requested the ILC to work on a draft convention. The Commission drafted articles for such a convention, and, by 1958, redrafted them, taking into account comments by the General Assembly and 21 member states. This prepared the ground for a conference in Vienna, where negotiations among the 81 participating states were concluded successfully between March 2 and April 14, 1961. The Vienna Convention was signed on 18 April. It is to date by far the most comprehensive attempt to codify diplomatic law. It has been ratified by almost 190 states. To the few states who have not ratified it, the Convention applies as customary law.

The Vienna Convention is very much a product of its time. In the 1950s and 1960s, world politics was still understood – almost exclusively – as *inter-state politics*. Thus, the Vienna Convention is all state embassies and diplomats authorised to speak on behalf of sovereign states (→ glossary: sovereignty). Denza puts it very well, when she writes that the Convention is all about codifying "the rules for the exchange of embassies among sovereign States" (Denza, 2008: 1). To what extent the Convention contains novel elements and to what extent it merely codifies customary law is not entirely undisputed among legal scholars. While Denza writes about a 'progressive codification' (Denza, 2008: 5) of customary law, Brown downplays the 'progressive' and puts more emphasis on the codification (Brown, 1988). But these differences in scholarly opinion are anything but large. It is clear that exercises in codification of already-existing customary law played a major role in writing the Convention.

Four Major Provisions

There are four major provisions: First, mission premises (and the private residences of heads of missions) are *inviolable*. According to Art 22 of the Convention, this inviolability does not only mean that the mission (such as an embassy) ought not to be entered without the consent of the head of the mission (such as an ambassador). It also means that the host country has the obligation to protect the "premises of the mission against any intrusion or damage and to prevent any disturbance of the peace of the mission or impairment of its dignity". Second, there is the often-quoted *diplomatic immunity*. The overarching goal of the Convention is to ensure the functionality of the embassy. This cannot be achieved just be protecting the premises of the embassy. But protection has to be extended to the diplomats working in the embassy as well. The Convention does this in a fairly strong fashion. Again, not only is the host state obligated not to violate the diplomat's rights. According to Article 31, the diplomat ought to enjoy immunity from criminal jurisdiction and, with some exceptions, also civil and administrative jurisdiction. According to Article 29, the host state is also obligated to protect the diplomat against attacks from non-state actors within its territory; it has to "prevent any attack on his person, freedom or dignity". Third, the host state has the duty to *protect the communication lines* between the embassy and its sending state. Some of the stipulations of Article 27 sound rather antiquated. There is talk about the 'diplomatic bag', how it is to be transported on an aeroplane, how it is to be off-loaded and so on. But the gist of Article 27 is as important as ever. With diplomacy being all about communication, the functionality of an embassy cannot be guaranteed without the protection of this communication. Yet note that Article 27 is about the communication between embassy and sending state. There is no right of embassies to communicate at free will in the host country. Fourth, embassies *ought not to interfere* in the domestic affairs of their host country. The Convention does not bestow rights only to embassies and obligations only to host states. There are also stipulations where this balance reads the other way round. Non-interference belongs to this category. Diplomatic missions, as envisaged by the Convention, are vehicles for facilitating state-to-state communication with 'state' standing for the upper echelons of the executive (especially foreign ministries and chief executive). They are not vehicles that entitle a mission to try to politically influence the broader public in the host country.

When Brown (1988) writes about the Vienna Convention as "one of the surest . . . multilateral regimes in the field of international relations", he has the Convention's compliance record in mind. All in all, this compliance record has been – despite some ambiguous formulations and the continuing relevance of customary law to interpret the Convention – very solid. This does not mean, however, that the regime is free of contestation. This contestation is often partly due to the evolving nature of law and partly due to states as well as individual actors trying to get the justice that suits them best.

An important contested case pertaining to diplomatic immunity was General Augusto Pinochet's arrest in London in October 1998. That month, the Spanish judge Baltasar Garzón set a chain of events in motion that indicates a major change in international law. He issued an international arrest warrant against Pinochet for crimes committed during the General's 17-year reign of terror in his native Chile. Garzón justified this warrant with crimes (94 counts of torture featured prominently) committed against Spanish citizens. Although this cast aside – for legal reasons – compelling evidence for thousands of cases of murder and torture during Pinochet's reign in Chile for the time being, the consequences were felt soon. UK magistrates, applying the European Convention on Extradition, arrested Pinochet. The General tried to make a case before the High Court that the arrest warrants against him were null and void, most importantly because of Article 39 (2) of the Vienna Convention, which guarantees former heads of state to remain immune from the criminal jurisdiction of foreign states (Bianchi, 1999: 255). It was only in March 1999 that the Lords came to a decision. They ruled that Pinochet could be extradited but only be prosecuted for crimes that he committed after 1988. This is when the UK had incorporated legislature for the UN Convention against Torture in the Criminal Justice Act. On the one hand, this qualification amounted to a major drawback. It threw out much of what Pinochet was supposed to stand trial for. This drawback became even bigger when the Lords ruled a year later that Pinochet had to be set free for medical reasons.

On the other hand, however, the decision signalled a move towards *universal jurisdiction*. Some crimes are just so horrendous that they warrant jurisdiction by domestic courts over individuals even if their alleged crimes were committed outside of the boundaries of the state within which this court is located and the individuals are not otherwise associated with this state (e.g., by citizenship or permanent residency). For some time thereafter, it was especially Spanish courts that exercised universal jurisdiction in a number of cases. Most of these were about atrocities committed by military governments against their own population in Latin America in the 1970s and 1980s: Guatemalan officials involved in the genocide against the Ixil Maya population of the country, El Salvadoran officials for the murder of six Jesuit priests, and an Argentine naval officer for crimes against humanity during the so-called Dirty War that the military junta waged against its own population. In 2009, the Spanish Parliament enacted a bill that restricted universal jurisdiction. While this did not signal the end of universal jurisdiction, it qualified it in significant ways (Langer, 2015).

Yet similar, and at times stronger provisions, are found in other countries. In September 2005, for example, a Belgian court indicted Hissène Habré, the former Chadian dictator, for crimes against humanity, torture, and war crimes. Again, diplomatic immunity did not protect him. Habré ended up being tried in Senegal. In May 2016, he was found guilty of rape, sexual slavery and unlawful killings and sentenced to life in prison. It is also noteworthy in this regard that the International Criminal Court has, thus far, indicted four sitting heads of state or government: Libya's Muammar Gaddafi, Sudan's Omar al-Bashir, Russia's Vladimir Putin and Israel's Benjamin Netanyahu. Diplomatic immunity no longer guarantees protection from international criminal investigations if these include atrocity crimes.

Contestation about alleged cases of diplomatic interference into domestic affairs abound but tends to be less spectacular than the aforementioned case on diplomatic immunity. Democratisation efforts by Western countries in the Global South are sometimes met with staunch rejection. In extreme cases, these accusations are accompanied by declaring a diplomat who allegedly interfered with domestic affairs *persona non grata*. Textbox 5.1 elaborates on this diplomatic institution. In 2008, for example, Hugo Chavez – in his very own determined rhetorical fashion – declared US ambassador Patrick Duddy *persona non grata* and expelled him from Venezuela. Thereafter, the US Chargé d'Affairs John Caulfield became the target of Chavez's ire for allegedly

---

Textbox 5.1 Persona Non Grata

Given the immunity granted to diplomats in the Vienna Convention, there is only so much host countries can do to diplomats they accuse of misdoings. Yet Article 9 of the Convention codifies one of the sharpest weapons available in such cases: to declare a diplomat *persona non grata*. The sending state then ought to recall such a diplomat to his or her capital. If this does not happen, the Convention reserves the right to "refuse to recognize the person concerned as a member of the mission". Yet this last sanction is rarely applied. In diplomatic practice, declaring a diplomat *persona non grata* amounts to expelling this diplomat from the host country. To some extent, such declarations are a barometer of the general atmosphere of international relations. In cooperative eras, these declarations occur rarely. In 1996, for example, Canada threw out a Ukrainian vice-consul for alleged drunk driving and similar offenses. In 2004, Mexico declared a Cuban diplomat *persona non grata* after Castro had declared that Mexico's prestige had 'turned into ashes'. In 2005, a Czech diplomat had to leave Belarus due to alleged sexual misconduct. In less cooperative eras, there are many more cases in which diplomats were declared *persona non grata*. During the Cold War, this happened frequently. In 1971, for instance, Britain sent 105 Soviet citizens home, many of them diplomats. They were accused of spying. Moscow reacted in kind. Judging by what has been happening since the 2010s, we may be experiencing a New Cold War. In 2016, the US government accused 35 Russian diplomats of hacking computer networks of a number of organisations and declared each of them *persona non grata*. Russia retaliated and sent 35 US diplomats home. Since Russia's war on Ukraine, hundreds of Russian diplomats, often accused of spying, have been made to pack their bags. Again, Russia responded in kind.

meeting with exile Venezuelan oppositional groups in Puerto Rico. While Chavez's reaction may be extreme and, of course, fuelled by a principled stance against the United States, there really is a tension between democratisation efforts and the diplomatic non-interference norm. Western states often try to bypass this tension by delegating democratisation tasks to agencies not officially or only indirectly linked to the government. The German political foundations, especially the Konrad-Adenauer-Stiftung, Hanns-Seidel-Stiftung, Friedrich-Ebert-Stiftung, and Friedrich-Naumann-Stiftung, are such entities. The National Endowment of Democracy in the United States and the British Westminster Foundation for Democracy serve similar purposes (Kleiner, 2010: 82).

Aside from these cases of contestation, there are also a few clear-cut and widely recognised problems of compliance with the Vienna Convention. Again, it is important to emphasise that the compliance record, all in all, is strong. But there are at least three exceptions that are worth mentioning. First, while states, all in all, comply with the stipulation that mission premises are inviolable, there are cases where this inviolability is violated. The most headline-producing event in this regard was, without much doubt, the Iran Hostage Crisis. In the wake of the Iranian Revolution, a crowd of about 5,000, most of them reportedly Islamist students, marched onto the US embassy on 1 November 1979. That day, the crowd eventually dispersed peacefully. Three days later, it was an altogether different matter. About 3,000 protestors gathered, including a large group of armed individuals, self-identifying as 'Muslim Student Followers of the Imam's Party'. They stormed the embassy and took 52 American citizens hostage. Negotiation, mediation, and even the condemnation of the act by the International Court of Justice (→ glossary) did little to resolve the crisis quickly. It took 444 days for the hostages to be finally released (Barker, 2006: 9). In 2011, there was suddenly again a lot of mentioning of the Iran Hostage Crisis, when Iranian protestors, shouting 'Death to England!', forced their way into the British Embassy in Teheran. Again, many of them were students. Yet this time, there was merely damage to the building and the British diplomats were detained only very briefly. Note that what was at issue in both cases was not so much that the Iranian state directly attacked the mission premises. But the Iranian state – in the 1979 case much more so than in the 2011 case – failed to protect the mission premises. This, too, constitutes a violation of the Vienna Convention.

Recently, the number of attacks on mission premises has increased. In 2024, Israel bombed the Iranian embassy in Damascus, Syria, killing several officers of Iran's Revolutionary Guard Crops. The same year, Ecuadorian special forces stormed the Mexican embassy in Quito to take an opposition politician into custody who had sought refuge there. Both cases are clear-cut violations of diplomatic law in general and the Vienna Convention in particular.

Second, despite diplomatic immunity, there are cases in which diplomats become targets. In 1979, the Iranian government failed not only to protect the US mission premises, but, of course, also US diplomatic personnel. But there is a long list of worse treatment of diplomats (and innocent bystanders). US diplomats have been especially frequently targeted. On 18 April 1983, a suicide bombing against the US embassy in Beirut left more than 60 people dead, including 17 American citizens. Fifteen years later, an even more destructive attack hit the US embassy in Nairobi. On August 7, 1998, a terrorist truck bomb killed almost 300 people and wounded as many as 5,000. Al-Qaeda claimed responsibility for the attack (US State Department, 2022). Twelve of them were American citizens. These cases are no violations of the Vienna Convention unless one would want to make the unrealistic claim that the Lebanese and Kenyan governments could have prevented such an attack. In 2012, there was a series of attacks on US embassies. Textbox 5.2 discusses these at greater length.

Textbox 5.2 2012 Attacks on US Diplomats

In June 2012, a small cinema screened the movie *The Innocence of Bin Laden* in Los Angeles. The anti-Islamic film depicts Prophet Muhammad, among other things, as coward and child molester. In July, a user with the pseudonym 'sam bacile' uploaded some clips taken from the film on the online portal YouTube under the titles *The Real Life of Muhammad* and *Muhammad Movie Trail*. Yet the radical group hiding behind the pseudonym left a mark with its amateurish film only in early September when the Egypt-based Salafist television channel *Al-Nas* broadcasted Arab translations of the YouTube clips, vilified them, and turned its rage against the West in general and the United States in particular. From then, protests spread across the Islamic world. In the early evening of 11 September, protesters stormed the yard of the US embassy in Cairo, tearing down the US flag. Egyptian riot police prevented a further escalation. Later this evening, gunmen – heavily armed with rocket-propelled grenades and anti-aircraft guns – started firing on the US consulate in Benghazi (Libya) out of a group of protestors. For about an hour, they succeeded in taking over the main consulate building, killing four Americans, including the US Ambassador to Libya, Christopher Stevens. Elsewhere in the region (Tunisia, Sudan, Lebanon, Iraq and Yemen) and beyond it (Afghanistan, Pakistan, and Indonesia) angry protests took place but did not escalate to the extent they did in Benghazi.

Yet, to be sure, it is not only US diplomats that are subjected to ill-treatment. In 2002, for instance, African ambassadors requested better protection from the Russian authorities for their personnel in Moscow. They were concerned about racist attacks. This concern was substantiated when Ghana's ambassador, Francis Y. Mahama, was beaten up when he went for a walk in a park in Moscow (Kleiner, 2010: 130). During the 2012 attacks on US diplomats, embassies and diplomats of allied nations (e.g., France, Germany, and the UK) were under siege, too. Situations of internal strife and civil war can be dangerous for diplomats. The Sudanese Civil War, especially the urban warfare ravaging Khartoum, puts diplomats at risk. In 2022, the EU Ambassador was assaulted in his residence (Jamal, 2023). In Myanmar, Singaporean diplomats were shot at when they accompanied a humanitarian aid mission to Shan State in 2023 (Al Jazeera, 2023).

Third, while the aforementioned two exceptions to the strong compliance record of the Vienna Convention occur rarely, host states are often rather eager to find out what messages embassies send back and receive from their capitals. During the Cold War, the FBI went as far as to build a tunnel underneath the Soviet embassy in order to tap communication lines (Denza, 2008: 11). The US diplomatic offensive prior to the 2003 Second Gulf War showed that this kind of spying was still alive and well in the post-Cold War era. On 2 March 2003, the Observer published an article based on a leaked memo written by a top official of the US National Security Agency, which orders to step up surveillance operations "particularly directed at . . . UN Security Council Members (minus US and GBR, of course)" (Beaumont, Bright and Vullyami, 2003). It seems that the operations were primarily directed against Angola, Cameroon, Chile, Mexico, Guinea, and Pakistan (then non-permanent members of the Security Council). But the aforementioned quote leaves China, and Russia, and even the long-standing US allies France and Germany (then also a non-permanent member) also in the equation.

The opposite problem occurs, too. Some embassies and consulates take advantage of the inviolability of mission premises by spying on the host state. Due to online publications of large quantities of data by WikiLeaks as well as leaked documents provided by the whistleblower Edward Snowden to several media outlets, the US National Security Agency (NSA) was severely criticised by much of the diplomatic community and beyond in the mid-2010s. The data demonstrate that the United States systematically spied on a number of high-ranking government officials in host states. This put a strain on the diplomatic relations between the United States on the one hand and many US allies and non-allies on the other. Washington had been as busy spying on its friends as on its foes, in some cases for decades.

Updating the Vienna Convention?

We have seen from the aforementioned text that the Vienna Convention is at the core of codified diplomatic law. Following a *functional approach* – postulating a set of norms that guarantees the functioning of residence embassies – it is a pillar on which modern diplomacy is built. Although there are some notable problems with implementation, all in all the compliance record is strong. This has probably quite a bit to do with the fact that the drafters of the Vienna Convention did not pluck its stipulations out of thin air. For the most part, they codified what had been customary law for a very long time already. They codified what has been taken for granted by the diplomatic community for a long time.

The Vienna Convention, however, is very dated. Today's diplomacy cannot be reduced to the functionality of the resident embassy. Customary diplomatic law and a host of other norms that do not qualify as law but, nevertheless, have important effects (see later in the text) have developed since the drafting of the Vienna Convention. New actors and new processes, often underpinned by globalisation and global governance (→ glossary: governance), have taken shape over time. Most of all, the stipulations about protecting communication lines in the Vienna Convention are archaic. While the Vienna Convention goes on and on about how diplomatic mail is to be packaged and loaded on to a plane, there is, of course, nothing about electronic messaging. While, in our days, digital diplomacy – including digital public diplomacy – is actively practised, the Vienna Convention is all about analogous communication. The Convention was drafted at a time when today's telecommunications technology was still unimaginable.

It is, therefore, no coincidence that there are calls for a thorough overhaul of the Vienna Convention or a new convention altogether. Siracusa, for example, cautions that, international organisations and even transnational corporations – as well as their role in diplomacy – should be included in such a convention (Siracusa, 2010: 1). The role of NGOs would warrant some written specification as well, as, for example, the 2012 diplomatic asylum case of WikiLeaks founder Julian Assange suggests. Textbox 5.3 discusses this case. New rules for digital public diplomacy are badly needed. There is a very thin line between promoting one's country and one's country's views on social media channels on the one hand and interfering into the domestic affairs of a host country on the other. It would be very useful for this line to be specified in an updated Vienna Convention.

For the time being, however, the codification of diplomatic law seems to proceed as slowly as ever. It took hundreds of years for the Vienna Convention to be written, signed and ratified. It may take quite a few more years, probably decades, until the Vienna Convention is updated or a new one enters into force.

Textbox 5.3 Diplomatic Asylum and Julian Assange

In 2012, the case of Julian Assange produced a series of newspaper headlines. Assange is the founder of WikiLeaks, which is a well-known, non-for-profit online platform dedicated to global transparency that published material regularly until 2019. Its radical pursuit of transparency brought it into conflict with nation-states, in particular the United States. WikiLeaks leaked classified information on US interventions and their aftermath in Iraq and Afghanistan, publishing shocking violations of international humanitarian law. WikiLeaks also leaked classified material about Guantanamo Bay. In 2010, the organisation released a host of US State Department diplomatic cables. This suddenly made diplomacy much more transparent than Wilson had postulated (see Chapter 2). The cables were at times not very generous about the host countries and their decision-makers from where US diplomats sent these cables. The United States found itself compelled to apologise in a number of cases. In 2010, the Swedish Chief Prosecutor Marianne Ny issued an arrest warrant on allegations about rape against Assange. Assange, expecting to be extradited from Sweden to the United States and charged for espionage there, looked for ways out. In 2012, he applied for asylum at the Ecuadorian embassy in London. A diplomatic stand-off between the UK and Ecuador followed. Ecuador granted Assange diplomatic asylum. It is very much disputed in international law, however, whether the institution of diplomatic asylum exists, with European diplomats tending to deny and Latin American ones tending to postulate it. In terms of the 1961 Vienna Convention, this was, nevertheless, a fairly clear-cut case. The Ecuadorian embassy was inviolable. Thus, British authorities could not simply go into the embassy and arrest Assange. If the immediate arrest had been a major priority for the UK, it would have had a strong means at its disposal. It could have ceased diplomatic relations with Ecuador. Thus, the embassy building would no longer have been inviolable. Yet the British chose a more elegant route. They waited. When a new Ecuadorian government wanted to improve relations with the West again in 2019, they handed him over to the British authorities.

Procedural Background: Tact, Communication, and Authority

The most frequently quoted diplomacy book of the 17th century, Abraham de Wiquefort's *L'Ambassadeur et ses fonctions* (The Ambassador and his functions), focuses heavily on manners and tact of the diplomat. The book does not try to teach legal rules but standards of behaviour that are supposed to sink into the background of the diplomat. This is, in principle, not all that different from trying to teach a young child to brush her teeth every day in the morning. The expected result of such an exercise is to make this norm a self-evident and unquestioned standard of behaviour. Arguably, François de Callière's *De la manière de négocier avec les Souverains*, published in 1716, focuses even more heavily on manners and tact. The discipline and rules that the author advocates are all about behavioural markers that make a good diplomat. This pattern of writing about diplomacy continued well into the 20th century (Satow, 1917).

Books on diplomacy may not be that heavily centred on manners and tact any more. But the latter are still recognised as highly important by diplomatic practitioners. Diplomatic academies all over the world teach their students and trainees a lot about standards of behaviour. Take, for instance, India's National Institute of Diplomacy. It defines diplomacy in terms of strategy, cooperation, and tact: "In an informal or social sense, diplomacy is the employment of tact to gain strategic advantage or to find mutually acceptable solutions to a common challenge, one set of tools being the phrasing of statements in a non-confrontational, or polite manner" (National Institute of Diplomacy, 2025). Tact, up to a point can be taught. But it is also a function of personality and experience. What can be taught though is protocol. And diplomatic academies and foreign service training institutes around the world put a lot of emphasis on this kind of training. The US Foreign Service Institute, for example, provides a 'hands-on course' on "practical knowledge of international protocol and U.S. representational responsibilities pertinent to Foreign Service life. Upon completion participants will have gained confidence to attend receptions, make introductions, plan seating arrangements for a formal dinner, and adhere to formal dining etiquette" (U.S. Department of State, 2017).

Tact and protocol already include communicative elements, including formulas for how to address an audience (e.g., the generic 'Excellencies, Ladies and Gentlemen'), when to speak, how to voice disagreement in subtle ways, and so on. Indeed, much of diplomatic communication is so formulaic that diplomacy may be seen as a communicative genre in its own right. Niceties are important in the diplomatic communicative genre. There is a time for being antagonistic. Yet usually diplomatic talk filters out a lot of anger, frustration, and antagonism or hides it behind subtle formulations, which are more or less standardised in the diplomatic world. Subtle hints are usually understood by a diplomatic audience.

Employing an English School perspective, Hedley Bull, although not using the term communicative genre, identifies some of its key aspects very well:

> He [sic; the diplomat] seeks always to reason or persuade rather than to bully or threaten. He tries to show that the objective for which he is seeking is consistent with the other party's interests, as well as with his own. He prefers to speak of 'rights' rather than of 'demands', and to show that these rights flow from rules or principles which both states hold in common, and which the other state has already conceded.
>
> (Bull, 1995: 165)

At times, diplomatic nice talk can be shocking for a more general public, not familiar with the diplomatic genre, especially when it takes place in the midst of disaster. To refer to a highly misplaced case of soft talk – which many diplomats, especially in hindsight, find shocking, too – the first Security Council Resolution on the Rwandan Genocide did not use the word genocide at all, and employed merely the word 'condemn' to describe the Security Council's stance towards the unfolding events. It used the expression 'strongly condemn' only once; this was to condemn attacks on UN personnel. The Security Council passed this Resolution, S/RES/912 (1994), on 21 April 1994 (UN Security Council, 1994). This is more than two weeks after the fastest genocide in human history, which cost at least half a million people their lives, had begun.

In our days, the most thoroughly researched aspect of the procedural background is authority. This research is primarily done by constructivist (→ glossary) and critical scholars, who question to what extent the diplomatic stage constitutes a level playing field. Sovereign equality is the most foundational procedural foreground norm. But do actual diplomatic practices live up to this postulate of horizontal inter-state relations? What about relations between states and non-state actors?

Kuus, for example, studies decision-making procedures in the EU. On paper, all member states are equal, and when it comes to external policies outside supranational policy domains, such as security and defence policies, member states decide unanimously. Yet the author argues that the diplomats of some states are widely recognised to have more of a say than the diplomats of other states. Central and Eastern European states, for example, find it more difficult to assert themselves than Western European ones (Kuus, 2013). Pouliot makes a very similar observation when he studies the UNSC. The provisional rules of procedure, mentioned earlier, do not differentiate between permanent and non-permanent members when it comes to drafting resolutions. In practice, however, permanent members, for the most part, serve as penholders of resolutions, thus deeply shaping these resolutions from the very beginning on. There is a 'pecking order' that puts some states atop of others. States form, despite all kinds of reassurances in procedural foreground provisions, a hierarchy and enact it, seemingly self-evidently, over and over (Pouliot, 2016).

Some kinds of authority empower non-state actors. Epistemic authority is among them. Individuals and/or organisations may widely be recognised as experts to be listened to, even when procedural foreground rules do not identify them as actors (Zagzebski, 2012; Sending, 2015). The parties to multilateral and bilateral agreements on nuclear arms control, for example, are states. Foreground provisions merely delegate certain clearly defined tasks to experts such as monitoring tasks to the International Atomic Energy Agency (IAEA). But if one digs a bit deeper, one finds that the entire nuclear order has been profoundly shaped by a handful of thinktanks, most notably the Rand Corporation. Many strategic understandings of nuclear weapons, taken for granted by all nuclear weapons states, originate with this US think tank (Griessl, 2023). The opposite, of course, happens, too. At times, experts are empowered by foreground provisions. Nevertheless, they find it very difficult to make themselves heard. In global health, for instance, medical experts are empowered in numerous key documents including the International Health Regulations. Still, medical expertise is often brushed aside by states who narrowly pursue what they see as their short-term vital economics interests (Kornprobst and Strobl, 2021).

In the last decade or so, many studies have dealt with the configuration of hierarchies in international relations. They are useful for studying relations among state and non-state actors more generally (Baumann and Dingwerth, 2015; Musgrave and Nexon, 2018; Nexon and Neumann, 2018; Mattern and Zarakol, 2016). Yet it is important to keep in mind an important *caveat* that applies to all research on authority and hierarchy. The background is always contested and this applies not only to substantive but also very much to procedural matters. It is, for example, not uniformly the case that medical experts are marginalised by states. While some states take their expertise very seriously, others marginalise it when they perceive a clash between the expert opinion and an economic interest. Nuclear arms control really has been shaped profoundly by think tanks such as the Rand Corporation. But there are also different kinds of experts, civil society movements, and eyewitnesses that put forward very different understandings of arms control and the fact that the Treaty on the Prohibition of Nuclear Weapons that recently came into force testifies that they have a considerable amount of epistemic authority with many states, too.

Populist diplomacy makes for a particularly far-reaching contestation of the dominant procedural background of diplomacy. Portraying themselves as the champions of the people, populist leaders use the diplomatic stage primarily to jockey for the approval of their constituents back home. Demarcating themselves from the 'establishment', they tend to marginalise the own foreign service (and replace key positions in the foreign ministry with people obeying their orders) and place themselves on the diplomatic stage instead. Catering to their constituents, they do not employ all that many niceties. Instead, their kind of communication is often very coarse. Trump, for example, antagonised even long-standing US allies such as Germany. Summit diplomacy was no longer a vehicle for improving relations and confirming friendship. Instead, it was a means to demonstrate disagreement and putting a zero-sum understanding of US interests first. Showcasing his dislike of Angela Merkel was part and parcel of Trump's performances of demarcation from Germany and the EU (Schmidt, 2018).

> **Textbox 5.4 Graphic Public Allegations versus Tact and Communicative Genre**
>
> During its rise to great power status, Chinese diplomacy, for a long time, took tact and diplomatic genre very seriously. Yet from the 2020s onwards, Chinese diplomacy has become much more assertive. The spokesperson of the foreign ministry, Zhao Lijian, postulated a new kind of diplomacy, referred to as 'wolf warrior diplomacy' (borrowing the phrase from a Chinese action movie). China's diplomacy started to occasionally violate the diplomatic procedural background in order to make a big bang statement. In 2020, for instance, Zhao Lijian Tweeted a computer-generated image that depicted an Australian soldier slitting the throat of an Afghan child. The posting happened amidst deteriorating relations between Australia and China in which both sides accused each other of disrupting trade and Canberra criticised Beijing of its lack of co-operation to curb the Covid-19 pandemic. It is not that the post was without any correspondence in real life. There were allegations that Australian soldiers had killed two fourteen-year-old Afghan boys about a decade earlier (BBC News, 2020). But the way the spokesperson and key proponent of 'wolf warrior diplomacy' handled the situation was far removed from the diplomatic communicative genre, and it appears that this was very intentional.

Yet populist diplomacy is not the only challenge to the procedural background. There are many others. Textbox 5.4 discusses a diplomatic incident between China and Australia that, underpinned by technological changes, was not at all 'diplomatic' in the sense of how the procedural foreground circumscribes 'diplomatic'.

Substantive Foreground: Peace, First, and Foremost

The substantive foreground is made up of all designed principles, rules, and decision-making procedures that diplomacy prescribes itself as parameters for the content of what it discusses and negotiates about. The substantive foreground is vast, and the previous chapter has provided a glimpse into it. Substantive foreground provisions range from the prohibition of biological weapons to measures to counter inflation, from the sustainable development goals to agreed benchmarks to cut greenhouse gas emissions, and from health as a human right to non-refoulement of refugees. Yet there is a long-standing and far-reaching agreement in the literature that diplomacy has a general tendency towards peace (Nicolson, 1963; Vincent, 1986; Watson, 1992; Sharp, 2009; Berridge, 2010; Hamilton and Langhorne, 2011; Bjola, 2013). Thus, for the sake of illustrating the substantive foreground, we focus on what provisions there are about peace.

A good place to start is the UN Charter, which is full of foundational substantive foreground principles. It mentions peace no less than 51 times. But it is not quite clear what peace is supposed to mean. The Charter includes narrow and broad notions of peace (Simma et al., 2002: 50) and never defines them in any detail. Article 1 features both of them. On the one hand, there is the maintenance of international peace and security. This formulation, for the most part, points towards military matters and curbing physical violence (Article 1(1)). On the other hand, there is peace understood as 'universal peace'. Here, the connotation of peace is much more all-encompassing. It is associated, for example, with 'friendly relations among nations'.

According to the Charter, the General Assembly is to elaborate on the 'general principles of cooperation in the maintenance of peace' (Article 11(1) UN Charter). This has done extensively from the very beginning in many treaties and declarations. Over time, the General Assembly has broadened and deepened the peace to be pursued by diplomats. Peace is not just about exercising military restraint but also about compromise and even dialogue. Furthermore, the principles attached to military restraint, compromise, and dialogue became more and more demanding.[1]

Apart from self-defence, the Charter only allows the use of military force as a collective security measure, that is, if it is authorised by the Security Council. The General Assembly has repeatedly built upon and enlarged these principles of exercising restraint. The 1970 Friendly Relations Declaration (A/RES/2625 (XXV)) clarifies that not only force but also the threat to use force is out (Article 1). The 1987 Declaration on the Enhancement of the Effectiveness of the Principle of Refraining from the Threat or Use of Force in International Relations (A/RES/42/22, Art. 7) uses a very broad definition of threat. States are to refrain from "attempted threats against the personality of the State or against its political, economic and cultural elements". The 1974 Definition of Aggression (A/RES/3314 (XXX)) defines aggression comprehensively. Invasion (Art. 1a), bombardment (Art. 1b), blockade (Art. 1c), an attack by armed forces more generally (Art. 1d), non-withdrawal of armed forces in violation of the terms of the agreement with the state in which they are stationed (Art. 1e), usage of armed forces deployed in another state against a third state (Art. 1f) and/or wars by proxy (Art. 1e) all constitute aggression.

The General Assembly increasingly applied restraint to intra-state disputes as well. In 1948 already, the Anti-Genocide Convention (A/RES/260(III)[A]) delegitimises a particularly heinous kind of atrocity crime. In 2005, the World Summit Outcome described a procedure to implement the responsibility to protect (A/RES/60/1, Art. 138). Several resolutions broaden the peacekeeping concept, adding more and more civilian, society- and state-rebuilding functions to the existing military ones (A/RES/49/59, Arts. 5–9; A/RES/55/2, Art. II(9); A/RES/67/259, Art. 12). According to the Rome Statute, crimes within the jurisdiction of the International Criminal Court encompass the crime of aggression, war crimes, crimes against humanity, and genocide. These crimes are all highly relevant in intra-state settings.

Yet peace, according to the General Assembly, is not merely about exercising restraint. It is also about meeting in the middle, including in situations in which this kind of compromising is difficult for the parties involved. Chapter 6 of the UN Charter lists a number of instruments for negotiating peaceful settlements of disputes. The list of principles by which compromises have to adhere has much expanded from the times of the formulation of the Charter and its focus on sovereign equality. The 1982 Manila Declaration (A/RES/37/10) clarifies that disputants are to serve the higher purpose of stabilising international order. Furthermore, justice is not to be 'endangered' (Art. 2). From the late 1970s onwards, some UNGA resolutions specify further what justice is supposed to be. The 1970 Declaration on the Occasion of the Fiftieth Anniversary of the UN (A/RES/50/6, Art. 13) likens justice to the rule of international law. The 1977 Declaration on the Deepening and Consolidation of International Détente (A/RES/32/155, Art. 5) identifies 'respect for human rights' and peaceful co-existence as pillars of justice. In the 2000s, three UNGA resolutions used the same formula of "in conformity with the principles of justice and international law" (A/RES/55/2, I(4); A/RES/60/1, I(5), III(77); A/RES/67/1, Art. 3). No declaration is more detailed than the World Summit Outcome (I(5)), when it highlights the following justice principles:

> The right to self-determination of peoples which remain under colonial domination and foreign occupation, non-interference in the internal affairs of States, respect for human rights and fundamental freedoms, respect for the equal rights of all without distinction as

to race, sex, language or religion, international cooperation in solving international problems of an economic, social, cultural or humanitarian character and the fulfilment in good faith of the obligations assumed in accordance with the Charter.

Peace – judging by diplomatic designs – is even more than restraint and compromise. It is also about keeping dialogue going. Among other things, the 1948 Universal Declaration of Human Rights (A/RES/217(III)[A], Art. 26(2)) postulates a more free-flowing communication across national boundaries that enables peoples to learn from one another (A/RES/1962 (XVIII). Fostering 'mutual understanding' is an important goal and the formulation was included in various resolutions (A/RES/32/155, Art. 9; A/RES/33/73, Art. 4). Since the end of the Cold War, the concept of culture of peace has postulated a highly demanding kind of peace. The 1999 Declaration and Programme of Action on a Culture of Peace puts strong emphasis on it: "Recognizing that peace not only is the absence of conflict, but also requires a positive, dynamic participatory process where dialogue is encouraged and conflicts are solved in a spirit of mutual understanding and cooperation" (Preamble). The resolution identifies a range of actors, including "governments, international organizations and civil society" (Preamble) and calls for peace to constitute relations among "individuals, groups and nations" (Art. 4). Those supposed to promote a culture of peace are "parents, teachers, politicians, journalists, religious bodies and groups, intellectuals, those engaged in scientific, philosophical and creative and artistic activities, health and humanitarian workers, social workers, managers at various levels as well as to non-governmental organizations" (Art. 8). In the 2000s, a number of resolutions add civilisational dialogues including the 2000 Millennium Declaration (Art I(6)), the 2001 Global Agenda for Dialogue among Civilizations (A/RES/56/6, Preamble), and the 2015 Agenda for Sustainable Development (Art. 49). Deliberation is not only called for in global politics but also in domestic politics. Reconciliation is a necessary part of peacebuilding (A/RES/51/240, Arts. 161, 170; A/RES/60/1, Art. III 97; A/RES/67/259, Art. 14).

These increasingly demanding conceptualisations of peace are not without consequence. Some aspects of them are applied. They make their way from New York into conflict zones around the world. Other aspects, however, remain marginalised. Textbox 5.5 discusses routines of application and neglect.

Textbox 5.5   Routines of Selectively Sending Peace Concepts from New York to Conflict Zones

Principles of peace arrived at by the General Assembly do make it out of New York. They affect peace processes all over the world. This very much includes situations of intra-state conflict. Yet the application of the principles is always rather selective. Sudan and South Sudan show these patterns all too clearly. Taken together, they have witnessed no less than six major peace agreements in the last two decades. Four of them were about the Sudan: the 2005 Comprehensive Peace Agreement (CPA or Naivasha Agreement), the 2006 Darfur Peace Agreement (DPA or Abuja Agreement), the 2011 Doha Darfur Peace Agreement (DDPA) and the 2020 Juba Agreement. Two of them were meant to put an end to civil wars in South Sudan: the 2015 Agreement on the Resolution of the Conflict in the Republic of South Sudan (ARCSS) and the 2018 Revitalised Agreement on the Resolution of the Conflict in the Republic of South Sudan (R-ARCSS). The agreements, all over 100 pages long, resemble one another in many ways. On the one hand, they echo UNGA formulations very closely, especially provisions on inclusiveness, good governance, democracy and self-determination as well as wealth-sharing, and equitable development and sustainability. On the other hand, these agreements are very peculiar elite compromises. The greater the military might, the better the seat at the negotiating table. Other stakeholders in a peace process remain unrepresented. Thus, many provisions on compromise and dialogue found in General Assembly documents do not make it into these agreements.

Substantive Background: Continuing the Discussion About Peace

In terms of the substantive foreground, therefore, diplomacy likens itself to something that may be referred to as the art of making and sustaining peace. But diplomacy, at times more and at times less, very much struggles to approximate the kind of diplomatic peace that it postulates for itself (Kornprobst, 2023). There are, of course, many reasons for this. Yet some of them are rooted in the substantive background, which is not all that much in sync with the substantive foreground.

Many actors look at international affairs through a particular lens. Scholars conceptualise these lenses in different ways. There are, for example, writings on ideology (Steger, 2008; Búzás, 2022), doxa (Adler-Nissen, 2011; Svendsen, 2020), nomos (Kornprobst and Senn, 2016b; Opitz, 2016), and epistemes (Ruggie, 1993). Most of these conceptualisations deal with procedural and substantive background understandings. Yet research on the episteme (→ glossary) focuses strongly on the substantive side. When Ruggie, borrowing the concept from Foucault, introduced the concept to the study of international relations, he used it to explain epochal change. He researched how the episteme of a territorially demarcated world came into being and what kinds of repercussions this had. These were rather profound. It made it possible for actors to imagine a world of states.

Existing research uncovers lenses of *standing together* and *standing apart*. Pan-Africanism belongs to the former category. The standing apart of African states is likened to outside interference, exploitation and a politics of divide and rule of the continent. Standing together, in strong variants even doing away with African states, by contrast, is seen as possibility for Africa to develop and stand its ground in international relations (Aniche, 2020). Pan-Africanism has always been contested and, thus far, it has not proven to be strong enough to decidedly push forward the supranationalisation of the AU. Yet Pan-Africanism makes itself felt on the global diplomatic stage. African states, for example by organising themselves as a Group of African States at the UN, tend to stick together in international negotiations. This makes a difference. After all, these are 54 states, that is, well over a quarter of UN member states.

Lenses of sticking together and overcoming ideational distances between states have positive effects on their peaceful relations. The Idea of Europe, discussed in Textbox 5.6, shows this very clearly. The strong shared belief that standing apart caused World War II and, more broadly, a history of warfare in Europe, and moving closer together can prevent a relapse into this past, underpins the making of the European unification process and, with it, an era of unprecedented peace. This echoes the UN Charter's foreground provision that friendly relations make for peaceful relations.

Some lenses, however, point into very different directions. In today's world politics, geopolitics is a lens that appeals to more and more actors. Interpretations vary greatly among actors but even a brief sketch of the genealogy of the concept highlights how uneasily it sits with the peaceful pursuit of diplomacy. The partition of Africa in the late 19th century sparked ideas that

> **Textbox 5.6 The Idea of Europe**
>
> The Idea of Europe accepts that Europe consists of distinct nation-states but postulates that these are not autonomous from one another. Their fate is understood as being inescapably intertwined. In the past, Europe had failed to understand this shared fate in the past, causing a series of disasters. Only overcoming the divisiveness of Europe's nation-state borders through co-operation and integration makes it possible for Europe to prevent these tragedies from re-occurring. Historically, the Idea of Europe tended to gain influence among intellectual elites all over Europe after major catastrophes. They used the Idea of Europe to make sense of what happened and to find ways to prevent disasters from re-occurring. Early accounts of the Idea were about state interactions, for instance by Maximilian de Béthune, duc de Sully who wrote during the Thirty Years' War, and the Abbé de Saint-Pierre (2013 [1713]) and Jeremy Bentham (1974 [1789]), who were influenced by the Enlightenment's belief in progress. A seminal statement of the Idea (applied not only to Europe but the world) is David Mitrany's essay *A Working Peace System* (1946), written in the middle of World War II. It is only after World War II that the Idea starts to leave its mark with European diplomacy. Arguably, the Idea is weakening because the generation that experienced the cruelties of World War II has left the diplomatic stage and has been replaced by actors who no longer take this important lesson of European history seriously.

linked the might of a nation to its territorial expansionism. In Germany, Friedrich Ratzel likened the state to an organism whose growth was dependent on territorial expansion. This resonated with Emperor Wilhelm II, who sought to, belatedly, secure more colonial territories for Germany. In Britain, Halford Mackinder wrote more generally about territorial control (including the control over other states). Meant as anti-Wilsonian policy advice for the Conference of Versailles that discussed the post–World War I order, he (in)famously made the following argument: "Who rules East Europe commands the Heartland; Who rules the Heartland commands the World Island [Eurasia, authors]; Who rules the World Island commands the World" (Turner, 2022). This heartland theory left a major impression on Karl Haushofer, Rudolf Hess's professor and mentor, and via Hess on Adolf Hitler.

Needless to say, most interpretations of the geopolitical lens are not as extreme as Ratzel's and Haushofer's and most do have this kind of political impact. Nonetheless, it is important to keep in mind that geopolitics is, at least on the part of great powers, about attempts to territorially reorder the world according to their military and economic interests. This, in our days, usually does not entail postulates to conquer other states, albeit Russia's war of territorial expansion against Ukraine follows the geopolitical prescriptions formulated by Alexandre Dugin, a far-right lecturer and intellectual. But it does encompass attempts to divide up parts of the world into spheres of influence with little regard for what this means for the people involved. Africa may be experiencing another scramble for Africa, mainly due to its mineral wealth. It is interesting to note in this regard that Mackinder identified two heartlands. The one is Eastern Europe. The other one, he argued, is Africa.

Not all elements making up the substantive background are building blocks that, taken together, amount to lenses. There are also a host of fundamental causal and normative understandings that are not contextually linked to one another to form an intersubjective prism.

For example, not only environmental activists but also many actors less inclined to look at the world through a 'green' lens, share notions of climate change and the role human beings play in bringing it about. Pacifists firmly believe that the use of physical force causes more use of physical force down the line but there are also many non-pacifists who subscribe to this cause-effect relationship (Sarrica and Contarello, 2004). Policy proposals for how to counter inflation rely on economic propositions, those on pandemic preparedness and response on medical understandings of how diseases spread, those on implementing the SDGs on the micro-foundations of the capabilities approach, and so on.

Again, however, not all cause-effect relationships found in the substantive repertoire foster peace. 'Qui desiderat pacem, prepararet bellum' is an old Roman maxim. 'Those who want peace, prepare for war'. National security, in this reading, is all about military strength. Great powers have a strong tendency to adhere to this causal belief. The Biden-Harris National Security Strategy features a long part entitled 'Investing in Our Strength'. The first section in this part is entitled 'Investing in Our National Power to Maintain a Competitive Edge' (The White House, 2022). For Xi Jinping, "strengthening and revitalizing the armed forces" is a major priority (Xinhua News Agency, 2017) and he is increasingly prepared to use these forces to showcase military superiority in the South China Sea. Russia's military strategy vows to "ensure the permanent readiness of the Armed Forces, other troops and bodies for deterring and preventing military conflicts" (Pietkiewicz, 2018). Fighting Ukraine is portrayed as fighting for Russia's – and Ukraine's – security against threats emanating from the West. Ultimately, according to Putin, there is no Ukraine; there is a 'historical unity' between Russia and Ukraine (*okraina* meaning periphery) (Putin, 2021). All of this, needless to say, is very far removed from the substantive foreground and its promises of a diplomatic peace.

There are also many normative understandings deeply woven into the substantive context. Some of them support the kind of peace postulated in General Assembly documents. The world, unfortunately, never embraced the civilising kind of habitus of restraint (Elias, 2000; Bjola and Kornprobst, 2007) that the sociologist Norbert Elias postulated in the interwar years. The use of physical violence never came to be generally tabooed as other forms of violence such as the duel. Nonetheless, many actors strongly adhere to background knowledge that thoroughly delegitimises certain forms of physical violence. Henry Dunant, when witnessing the immediate aftermath of the Battle of Solferino, was deeply disturbed about what to him were inhumane practices of leaving thousands of seriously wounded soldiers to die on the battlefield. It inspired him to advocate for codifying the laws of war. The Hague Conventions and Geneva Conventions then put into law several key distinctions and prohibitions, most importantly the fundamental distinction between combatants and non-combatants. The codification of the laws of war continued. Atrocity crimes such as crimes against humanity were added. None of these legal formulations fell from the sky. They are rooted in widely shared background understandings of what is humane and what is inhumane.

Such foundational standards of what is and what is not appropriate in armed conflict are not undisputed either, however. Violating these kinds of standards amounts to a strategy of terrorist organisations. Yet even states tend to push some of these standards aside when they are embroiled in armed conflict. Take Somalia in the early 2000s, for example. Washington engineered an alliance of warlords who eagerly portrayed themselves as anti-Islamist. The warlords were generously paid for their 'services', including for chopped-off heads of supposed Islamists who oftentimes had nothing to do with Islamism. When the warlords could not keep the Islamic Courts Union at bay, Ethiopia, a key US ally in the region, invaded southern Somalia. Civilians suffered greatly. The Union was defeated but radical elements in it founded Al Shabaab in response to the military invasion from outside. From then on, Al Shabaab has been waging its brutal war against civilians in Somalia and neighbouring countries (Kagwanja, 2006: 81–3).

Despite these violations, it is astounding that diplomats always claim to abide by foreground provisions on peace. In January 2024, Sergey Lavrov, after two years of war of aggression waged against Ukraine and its population, made the following astonishing proposition at the Security Council: "Let me remind you that we have never renounced peaceful methods" (Ministry of Foreign Affairs of the Russian Federation, 2024). Analysts of diplomacy should always beware that diplomats' appeals to foreground provisions on peace, such as the peaceful settlement of disputes, are often overshadowed by background understandings such as geopolitics that go in the exact opposite direction. The background at times looms large over the foreground. This is why it is important to study it.

Summary

- Diplomats are embedded in *contexts*. These contexts constitute the diplomat and diplomacy in the first place. Without these contexts, there would be no diplomacy.
- We discussed a two-fold distinction of the components of this concept: *foreground* versus *background*, and *procedural* versus *substantive*.
- Albeit outdated in many ways, the cornerstone of the procedural foreground remains the *1961 Vienna Convention on Diplomatic Relations*. It lists key procedural principles by specifying the dos and don'ts of diplomats and host state institutions.
- The procedural background revolves around *tact*, the diplomatic communicative *genre* and *authority*. There are considerable tensions between the procedural foreground and background, especially when it comes to the principle of sovereign equality.
- The substantive foreground is vast. The set of elements that is emphasised the most is about *peace*. Over time, diplomacy has arrived at more and more comprehensive promises about the peace they are to pursue. It encompasses restraint, compromise, and dialogue.
- The substantive background, too, is much too multifaceted as to allow for a brief summary. Yet our illustration of background understandings of peace highlights that some of the *lenses*, *causal*, and *normative* understandings making up this background are more easily reconciled with foreground provisions than others.

Study Questions

- What are the strengths and weaknesses of diplomatic law in ensuring the functionality of diplomacy in our times?
- Are procedural and substantive foreground provisions in sync with one another?
- Is diplomacy about peace?
- Do epistemes drive regional integration efforts?

Note

1 In what follows, we draw from Kornprobst (2023).

Recommended Further Reading

Constantinou, Costas M., and Fiona McConnell. 2023. "On the Right to Diplomacy: Historicizing and Theorizing Delegation and Exclusion at the United Nations." *International Theory* 15 (1): 53–78.
 This article uncovers a range of inequalities in what we refer to as procedural background.

Denza, Eileen. 2016. *Diplomatic Law: Commentary on the Vienna Convention on Diplomatic Relations*. Oxford: Oxford University Press.

Frequently cited by scholars and routinely used by practitioners, this remains the authoritative commentary on the 1961 Vienna Convention.

Scarneccia, Timothy. 2021. *Race and Diplomacy in Zimbabwe*. Cambridge: Cambridge University Press.

The book, focusing on Zimbabwe's decades-long struggle of liberation from colonialism, shows that racial prejudgements and prejudices are deeply ingrained in diplomatic backgrounds.

Sending, Ole Jacob, Vincent Pouliot, and Iver B. Neumann. 2015. *Diplomacy and the Making of World Politics*. Cambridge: Cambridge University Press.

Many chapters in this edited volume address the evolution of what we refer to as contextual background and link them to the making and unmaking of the foreground. The chapters cover a wide range of issue areas.

Towns, Ann E. 2020. "Diplomacy Is a Feminine Art': Feminised Figurations of the Diplomat." *Review of International Studies* 46 (5): 573–93.

This article discusses what this chapter refers to as procedural and substantive background through a gender perspective.

6   Tasks of Global Diplomacy

Chapter Objectives

- To identify the main tasks of diplomacy.
- To discuss different kinds of performing these tasks.
- To provide an overview of how the literature on diplomacy conceptualises these tasks.
- To relate the tasks to diplomatic contexts.

Introduction

No matter what kind of diplomatic actor and no matter what kind of issue area this actor addresses, it is possible to identify key tasks of diplomacy. This chapter refers to these as *internal messaging*, *external messaging*, *negotiation*, *mediation* and *dialogue*. What all these functions share in common is communication. Doing diplomacy is communicating. At times, this communication is more closed and at other times it is more open. Internal messaging ranges from carrying out instructions for how to communicate with a representative of another state to providing input in strategy and policy formation, external messaging from formulaic praise via public diplomacy to cheap talk, negotiation from the exchange of rigid positions to the art of transforming a negotiation situation, mediation from directive to procedural ways of standing in the middle, and dialogue from a more strategically oriented polylogue to fully fledged deliberation.

All these tasks and their variations along the spectrum of open and closed communication are rooted in the diplomatic context. Procedurally and substantively, they are delineated by the background and regulated by the foreground. Vice versa, carrying out these tasks, and performing them in particular ways, plays its part in reproducing or changing the context. Being a diplomat, to put this differently, has a lot to do with *putting contexts to use in order to communicate*. This, in turn, leaves a mark on the contexts. Figure 6.1 summarises the interplay of context and tasks.

This chapter is organised into five parts. We start with the task of internal messaging, then we deal with external messaging. We continue with discussing negotiation and mediation in some depth. Finally, we focus on dialogue.

Internal Messaging

Diplomats are *messengers*. When it comes to traditional state diplomacy, the usual connotation of the diplomat is someone who sends messages to the representative of another state. We refer to this as external messaging and discuss it in depth in the next section. There is, however, also a

DOI: 10.4324/9781003485407-9

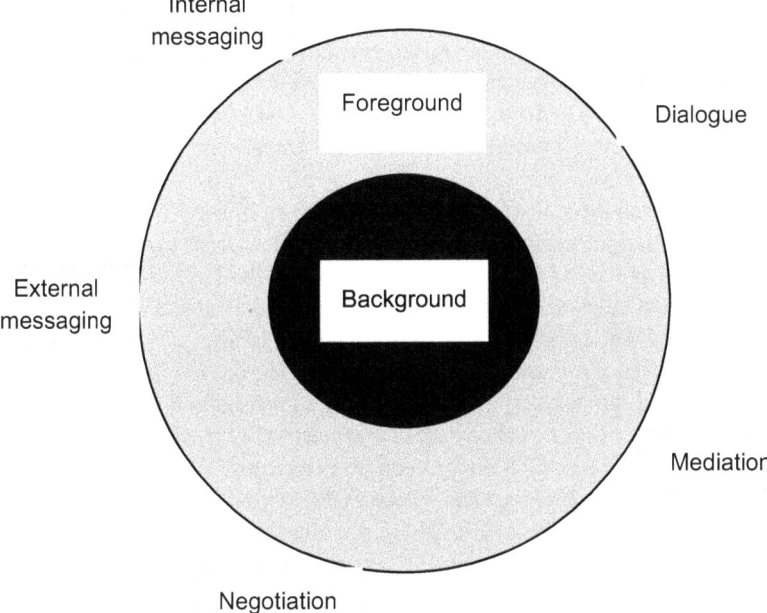

Figure 6.1 Interplay of Diplomatic Contexts and Diplomatic Tasks.

very important category of messaging that is all about exchanging messages within state institutions, oftentimes just inside a foreign ministry. We refer to this as internal messaging.

Any kind of diplomatic communication can be depicted on a spectrum of closed and open communication. In the metaphorical language of rhetorical theory, performing diplomatic tasks ranges from the closed fist to the open hand (Kornprobst et al., 2008). Internal messaging spans the entire spectrum. Consider the following example, which illustrates the closed pole of the spectrum.

On June 21, 1941, Friedrich-Werner von der Schulenburg, the German ambassador to Moscow, was radioed a telegram from Berlin, which was classified as 'state secret' and 'very urgent'. The telegram contained a fateful message to the Soviet government, culminating in the following summary:

> To sum up, the Government of the Reich declares, therefore, that the Soviet Government, contrary to the obligations it assumed,
>
> 1) has not only continued, but even intensified its attempts to undermine Germany and Europe;
> 2) has adopted a more and more anti-German foreign policy;
> 3) has concentrated all its forces in readiness at the German border. Thereby the Soviet Government has broken its treaties with Germany and is about to attack Germany from the rear, in its struggle for life. The Führer has therefore ordered the German Armed Forces to oppose this threat with all the means at their disposal.
>
> (Public Broadcasting Service (PBS), 2009)

Predictably, the declaration of war blamed the victim to be the perpetrator. The last sentence formulates the declaration of war. This, of course, was a very fateful case of external messaging.

But the internal messaging is interesting and consequential, too. The telegram was a detailed instruction to Schulenburg. He was instructed to read the statement and not to 'enter any discussion of this communication'. In the morning of June 22, 1941, Schulenburg went to the Kremlin and, as instructed, conveyed his fateful message to Vyacheslav Molotov, the Soviet foreign minister.

Schulenburg followed these instructions even though he himself was against the declaration of war. Schulenburg had joined the Nazi Party shortly after Hitler came to power. In 1934, he had become Hitler's ambassador to Moscow. In 1939, he had pressured for the Hitler-Stalin Pact, in which the two sides agreed not to attack one another and delineated their spheres of influence at the expense of a number of Eastern European states.

When Molotov asked the German ambassador why Berlin was breaking the Hitler-Stalin Pact, the latter violated the instructions. He did enter a conversation with his Russian counterpart, reputedly replying: "For the last six years I've personally tried to do everything I could to encourage friendship between the Soviet Union and Germany. But you can't stand in the way of destiny" (Public Broadcasting Service (PBS), 2009). Three years later, the *Volksgerichtshof* (People's Court) found him guilty of conspiring to assassinate Hitler near Rastenburg, close to the Eastern front. He was hanged in Berlin-Plötzensee. Diplomats do not always agree with their instructions.

Yet there are, of course, circumstances where diplomats are much freer to communicate internally. When diplomats posted abroad tell their capital what is happening in their host state, for example, they do not simply carry out instructions. They are expected to provide the capital with detailed accounts about what the capital does not know yet. Machiavelli, in his *Advice to Raffaeloo Girolami*, formulates this in a ruthless fashion that is quite characteristic for Machiavelli and geared towards penetrating the secrecy of courts but the gist of it remains applicable in our times:

> To find out all the intrigues, and to conjecture the issue correctly, that is indeed difficult, for you have nothing to depend upon except surmises aided by your own judgment. But as the courts are generally filled with busybodies, who are always on the watch to find out what is going on around them, it is very desirable to be on friendly terms with them all, so as to be able to learn something from each one of them.
> (Machiavelli, Advice to Raffaeloo Girolami, on his departure, 23 October 1522, as ambassador to the emperor Charltes V, in Spain: Machiavelli in Berridge, 2004: 42)

This information-retrieving function is usually confined to details about planned policies. Some of it takes place in the grey area of what the Vienna Convention allows and does not allow, or even beyond. The previous chapter on contexts and diplomatic law alluded to this.

In rare occasions, open internal messaging from the host state back to the capital succeeds in making new meaning. It invents or re-invents what counts as reality. Kennan's 'Long Telegram' has been one of the most influential messages ever sent by a diplomat. It is well worth looking at this document in some depth, too.

In early 1946, the US Treasury was puzzled by Moscow's lack of support of the World Bank and the IMF, which had just been created. The Treasury, as much of the US bureaucracy, still thought of the Soviet Union as an ally. The Soviet scepticism against these new international institutions, therefore, came as a surprise. The Treasury sent a request to the US embassy in

> **Textbox 6.1 The Diplomatic Cable**
>
> Diplomatic cables transmit classified information from an MFA to embassies abroad and vice versa. The term 'cable' goes back to the days in which telegraphs relied on submarine communications cables to transmit messages. In our days, diplomatic cables are sent electronically. From the user's point of view, this is not all that different from sending an email. But the message is encrypted. Diplomatic cables follow their own communicative rules. Messages transmitted from an embassy to the ministry back home, for example, are often characterised by a subject line that attracts attention, the punchline of the message appears early in the cable, overall the message is concise and, of course, the information transmitted is expected to be accurate. Diplomats posted abroad want to make sure that their messages are read and understood. Thus, they take writing these cables and abiding by these style guidelines seriously. Kennan's Long Telegram is an exception in this regard. He intentionally violated the rules and justified this with the need to provide the State Department with an in-depth account of what he perceived to be a momentous turn of events in the Soviet Union.

Moscow to explain this behaviour. This request found its way onto the desk of George F. Kennan, then Deputy Chief of Mission of the United States to the Soviet Union. Kennan started his telegram with apologising for the unusual format and length of the telegram (see Textbox 6.1 for the usual format of a diplomatic cable).

Kennan provided a detailed five-step analysis about the general trajectory of foreign policy. First, he claimed that the beliefs in a 'capitalist encirclement' as well as the impossibility of peaceful co-existence between capitalism and socialism, inevitable in-fighting within the capitalist camp, and the necessity to prevent such infighting in the socialist camp formed the key premises of Moscow's understanding of world politics. Second, he contended that Moscow inferred from this that "everything must be done to advance relative strength of USSR as factor in international society", to deepen and exploit differences among capitalist states, and to stamp out deviant tendencies in the socialist world (such as social democracy). Third, he predicted that Moscow's overt policies would revolve around advancing Soviet power and prestige, for instance in the Third World and in international organisations. Fourth, he forecast that the Soviet Union's covert policies would pay special attention to 'rank and file of Communist Parties', instalment of puppet regimes (e.g., Turkey), and "everything possible will be done to set major Western Powers against each other". These four points taken together, according to Kennan, amounted to a huge challenge:

> In summary, we have here a political force committed fanatically to the belief that with US there can be no permanent modus vivendi that it is desirable and necessary that the internal harmony of our society be disrupted, our traditional way of life be destroyed, the international authority of our state be broken, if Soviet power is to be secure.

Fifth, Kennan elaborated on how the United States should respond to this challenge. At the core of these elaborations is a juxtaposition. The Soviet leadership, Kennan held, was 'impervious to the logic of reason'. But 'it is highly sensitive to the logic of force'. In Kennan's view, therefore, the challenge could be met if the West – and especially the United States – stood firm.

This standing firm would have a military component but it would also encompass putting forward 'a constructive picture of sort of world we would like to see'. The strength to stand firm could only come out of US society: "Much depends on health and vigor or our own society. World communism is like malignant parasite which feeds only on diseased tissue".

Kennan's message was not without consequences. It is a landmark document whose key arguments found their way into the minds of American elites and the public. Some of the channels through which this occurred are quite clear by now. In the summer of 1946, President Truman asked one of his closest advisors, Clark Clifford, to write a report on US foreign policy. Clifford used the Long Telegram as the foundation for his report, which Truman considered very important and helpful. Half a year later, Kennan published an article entitled 'The Sources of Soviet Conduct' under the pseudonym 'X' in *Foreign Affairs*, thus diffusing it to a wider audience. The article bears a strong resemblance to the 'Long Telegram'.

In order to make sure that his idea would have a broad impact in the United States, therefore, Kennan chose the official route through the Department of State as well as an unofficial one via the public and public opinion. This may appear to be a very unusual one but public opinion back home is something that has become increasingly important for foreign ministries and political leaders around the world. If there is trouble at the 'home front', it becomes very difficult to move ahead with important foreign policy issues. In 2013, for example, the EU and the United States started to negotiate a major free trade agreement to be labelled 'Transatlantic Trade and Investment Partnership'. Even though a number of major macro-economic studies showed that the agreement would boost the economies on both sides of the Atlantic, negotiations lacked the necessary momentum and were formally abandoned in the late 2010s amid major criticisms emanating from civil society.

Eying public opinion can become so extreme that leaders use the diplomatic stage not for the sake of meaningfully communicating with other actors on this stage but merely to ensure their own constituents back home of fighting for their interests. When Donald Trump started his speech at the UN General Assembly's General Debate in September 2018, it was all about what he portrayed as his domestic successes ('America's economy is booming like never before') (The White House, 2018). It was not even about international politics. The Assembly's reaction to this was laughter. In other words, he was far from convincing to the audience in the room. But that was not the audience he attempted to please and really speak to. The audience he targeted were his voters and prospective voters, sitting at home in front of their television sets or following coverage of the speech on social media channels with their smartphones in their hands.

External Messaging

External messaging comes in many shapes and forms. We discuss five of them here: epideictic communication, shaming, social fact dissemination, public diplomacy, and cheap talk. Some of them may overlap to varying degrees.

Aristotle identifies *epideictic communication* as a distinct kind of communicative encounter. Its hallmark is that the speaker does not want to arouse any kind of controversy with the audience (Perelman and Olbrechts-Tyteca, 1969). The means for doing so are to praise and blame significant others. In diplomacy, speeches that ritually invoke and reinvoke friendship and enmity in front of an audience that is already convinced of this friendship and/or enmity to another actor are within this communicative category. When an American president meets a British prime minister, for example, the bilateral summit diplomacy is usually geared towards confirming the 'special relationship' between the two nations. Everything is carefully planned in advance. Nice speeches are exchanged, which are all about co-identification and promises to work even more closely together than before. Topics are chosen for discussion that are not controversial between the leaders. At the same time, there is a strong demarcation from other nations. At the 2023 summit in London, for example, Biden and Sunak strongly condemned Russia for waging war against Ukraine (Widakuswara, 2023). Praising and blaming are two sides of the same coin for epideictic communication. Albeit being ritualistic its effects should not be easily dismissed. The 'special relationship' is an important part of the substantive background linking the United States and the United Kingdom together and so is their disidentification from significant others (Vucetic, 2011). Epideixis plays its part in reproducing this relationship.

Shaming is a form of rhetorical force (Mattern, 2005). Another actor is singled out for violating particular foreground standards that are portrayed as being widely shared. Terman (2023), for example, researches whether shaming can make recalcitrant actors comply with human rights. Schimmelfennig (2001) enquires into the EU's enlargement processes, scrutinising to what extent long-time members succeed in diffusing their standards to newer and would-be members. Shaming may go so far as to seek to delegitimise certain actors (Chowdhury and Krebs, 2010), contesting their status of an actor or at least an actor to be listened to. Diplomats may respond to rhetorical forces directed against them in various ways. They employ various strategies to counter stigmatisation (Adler-Nissen, 2014). Shaming in its various shapes and forms also feeds back to the context. If it succeeds in what it was intended to do, it helps bring about compliance with foreground elements. Existing research strongly suggests that this is easier if the relations between shamer and shamed are not too far away from one another to begin with. If they are, shaming strategies are likely to simply increase antagonism. Furthermore, shaming plays its part in reproducing foreground and background elements of those who engage in shaming another actor with these elements.

Social fact dissemination is about attempting to make receivers see the world in a similar light as the sender. NGOs and even IOs have very little genuine decision-making power. The latter usually resides with states. Yet NGOs and IOs can shape how other actors look at international relations. NGOs such as Amnesty International and Human Rights Watch issue regular reports on human rights abuses worldwide. These reports make a difference. In the worst-case scenario, they merely raise awareness but the problem persists. Yet there are even cases in which states, put under pressure by public opinion, revisit their doings. President George W. Bush, for example, was heavily criticised for transferring Al Qaida and Taliban suspects to Guantanamo Bay in Cuba in 2002. The in-depth research and diffusion of the research results by NGOs led to a public outcry against the detention facility. Bush did not yield to the pressure. Obama and Biden sought to close the facility but, lacking backing for their plans in Congress, failed to do so.

International organisations, too, are important disseminators of social facts. Through annual reports, say on economic growth and financial transactions, development and good governance, international migration and transmittances and so on, as well as through more ad-hoc fact-finding endeavours, they contribute to making a global reality. International organisations, as Barnett and Finnemore point out, have a particular kind of authority that predisposes many other actors to listen to them. They are seen as non-political entities serving not themselves but the global community. This makes their word count (Barnett and Finnemore, 1999). A particularly interesting institutional arrangement in this regard is the Preparatory Commission for the Comprehensive Nuclear-Test-Ban Treaty Organization (CTBTO). Lacking the ratification by a number of key states, the Comprehensive Test Ban Treaty (CTBT) has not yet entered into force. But the CTBTO is a de facto international organisation. Using state of the art equipment it detects nuclear weapons tests anywhere in the world. Thus far, it detected six of them.

North Korea tested nuclear devices in 2006, 2009, 2013, twice in 2016, and again one in 2017. The last one was also the one with the largest magnitude (*CTBTO*, n.d.).

Narration and framing are also ways to disseminate social facts. They are frequently employed by traditional and non-traditional diplomatic actors. They put together messages, meant to win over others, including preference changes and, at times even changes of something akin to world views. Scholars employ a variety of concepts in order to understand the dynamics of advocacy. Framing and narration feature prominently among them. Framing is the attempt to make an audience see an issue in light of a few already firmly established ideas (Benford and Snow, 2000; Zeng, Dai and Javed, 2019; Kornprobst, 2019a). This linkage of new (what is to be framed) and old (the components of the frame; at times even the entire frame) can often be summarised in very easy terms. Frames, therefore, sometimes amount to powerful catchphrases. Narration is somewhat more elaborate; it embeds what is argued for in a familiar story that features a plot including heroes and villains, as well as connects past and present (Fisher, 1984; Roberts, 2006; Linklater, 2009).

When social fact dissemination cuts deep, it changes the substantive foreground and at times even the background. The making of the Millennium Development Goals – the Sustainable Development Goals then built upon them – as well as the World Summit Declaration (including the responsibility to protect) illustrates this rather well. Celebrity diplomacy was a major facilitator. Usually, individual members of our nascent global civil society find it extraordinarily difficult to make themselves heard. Owing to their celebrity status, famous actors and musicians are exceptions in this regard. *Qua* their status, very much gained outside of diplomacy and politics, they have the authority to speak. Their talk is often accompanied by powerful images, for example, Angelina Jolie holding a little child suffering from malnutrition. Celebrities use various avenues to exert influence. Some put to use conventional diplomatic ways of doing things. Bono, for instance, did not shy away from intermingling with state leaders. On the very contrary, he looked for contacts with them, knowing very well that his 'power of attraction' can make things happen. He did 'bilateral' diplomacy with George W. Bush, and 'multilateral' diplomacy at international forums debating development and poverty issues. Bob Geldof, by contrast, is aptly described as 'antidiplomat' (Cooper, 2008: 55). There was very little softening diplomatic talk when he cursed and scolded officials from the World Bank, IMF, and Western state development agencies over the provision of humanitarian aid to Africa.

Public diplomacy (→ glossary) has become firmly entrenched in post–World War II diplomatic practice. The term was coined by Edmund Gullion, former dean of the Fletcher School of Law and Diplomacy at Tufts University. The main goal of this kind of diplomacy is to make the own state appear in a good light while communicating with the public of the host state directly. This kind of reputation management is expected to add to the authority of the state to speak out on a range of diplomatic issues but also to make the state appeal to prospective tourists and companies willing to trade and invest in that state. The term nation branding is related to public diplomacy. The war over Nagorno-Karabakh damaged the image of Azerbaijan. Azeri diplomacy then embarked on a national branding campaign, managed by public relations companies, that was meant to reinvent the image of Azerbaijan. Embassies abroad portrayed it as a peaceful country with a great history, going back over 5 millennia. At the same time, it was branded as a rising economy full of opportunities for investors (Imran, 2018). This re-branding paid off economically. Tourist numbers increased considerably and trade went up significantly, especially when the EU sealed a major gas deal with Baku.

There is at times a very thin line between public diplomacy and the kind of interference into the domestic affairs of the host state that the Vienna Convention, discussed earlier, prohibits. From a Russian point of view, for instance, Geoffrey Pyatt, US ambassador to Kyiv at the time the Maidan Revolution happened, stepped over this line when his portrayals of the United States as a model of democracy were more and more linked to supporting the revolution, even to the extent that the ambassador discussed names of who should lead post-revolution Ukraine. A number of Western commentators were critical of Pyatt as well (Mearsheimer, 2014).

Public diplomacy, too, feeds back into the context. If the portrayed positive image resonates in the public of the host state, then relations between states can move closer together. States successful in public diplomacy may also increase their authority in international affairs. A particularly interesting aspect of public diplomacy's contextual effects is the reconfiguration of the diplomatic genre. For centuries, diplomats were groomed to talk to diplomats representing other states. With public diplomacy, it is different. The audience is the public on the host stage. This requires different kinds of communicative skills, the management of social media very much included. The trick here is not to simply engage in a monologue but, up to a point, invite the public to join the conversation. The more important public diplomacy becomes – and due to the increasing salience of social media this is bound to happen – the more the diplomatic communicative genre has to be broadened.

Finally, *cheap talk* is also a distinct form of messaging that happens prior and during negotiations. In informal communicative encounters, diplomats get a sense of what the other side wants and expects from the negotiations, and vice versa. Perhaps most importantly, negotiators get a hunch of what the bottom lines of one another are. This kind of information is important for diplomats to get a sense of whether and how negotiations can be successfully concluded (Ramsay, 2011; Trager, 2011). The Vienna Café at the UN in New York, for example, has been a venue facilitating such informal encounters for over four decades. Many of these encounters remain shielded from much of the diplomatic community and the public. Trust is crucial for these kinds of encounters, too. At times, diplomats from different delegations have a history of having negotiated with one another for many years. This may generate the kind of trust that makes it possible for diplomats to tell the other side quite a bit about their expectations and hopes during the negotiations.

Cheap talk prepares negotiations (which are dealt with separately further in the chapter). If it successfully facilitates these negotiations and these lead to a new agreement, then this adds a new element to the diplomatic foreground. Cheap talk also affects the background. Depending on how close or distant diplomatic relations between states are, they find it more easy or more difficult to engage in cheap talk, and this, in turn, plays its part in reproducing relations. Since cheap talk is not just about sending a prefabricated message but exchanging priors more freely before and during negotiations, it is, among these messaging functions, the most open one.

Negotiation

Thompson's definition is helpful: "Negotiation is an interpersonal decision making process necessary whenever we cannot achieve our objectives single-handedly" (Thompson, 2009: 2). It is rather rare in international politics that objectives can be achieved single-handedly. This applies not only to smaller players but also most powerful states. Even in the 1990s when authors wrote about a *Pax Americana* in the world, US diplomats still had to do a lot of negotiating. Even then, Washington was far removed from being able to simply lay down the law in international affairs.

At times, negotiators find it very easy to agree. Consider the simple convergence on the boundaries of spheres of influence in a meeting between Churchill and Stalin. On October 9, 1944, the two leaders discussed future spheres of influence in Moscow. Late in the evening, Churchill put an important item on the agenda: "Let us settle about our affairs in the Balkans". He continued: "We have interests, missions, and agents there. Don't let us get at cross-purpose in small ways. So far as Britain and Russia are concerned, how would it do for you to have ninety per cent dominance in Rumania, for us to have ninety per cent of the say in Greece, and go fifty-fifty about Yugoslavia?" Churchill wrote these figures on a piece of paper. Stalin looked at the list, listened to the translation, paused quickly, "took his blue pencil and made large tick upon it, and passed it back to us". Churchill was rather satisfied with the meeting: "It was all settled in no more time than it takes to sit down". Ultimately, this account, taken from Siracusa (Siracusa, 2010: 55–6), originates with Churchill. Stalin may not have been that passive an actor and other things may have happened a bit differently as well. But the gist of it matches more elaborate studies by historians. It is rather remarkable how easily the two leaders reached an agreement that would impact Europe for decades to come.

Yet oftentimes negotiations are much more drawn out. Since 1995, the parties to the UNFCCC meet as Conference of the Parties (COP) to agree on new landmark agreements and decisions meant to facilitate the implementation of these agreements. These meetings usually take place once a year. Factoring in that these meetings have to be prepared and drafts be circulated before, it is no exaggeration to write that climate change negotiations never really end and hardly ever pause. Once a seeming breakthrough agreement has been adopted, such as the Kyoto Protocol in 1997 and the Paris Agreement in 2015, parties negotiate about further details and implementation. By 2019, COP had agreed to no less than 763 formal decisions (The United Nations Climate Change, n.d.).

None of these decisions, let alone the landmark agreements, come easy. The sheer number of government delegations and delegates suggests already how difficult it is to agree, and even to organise the negotiations from a logistical point of view. The very first COP, COP 1 in Berlin, took place in 1995 and was attended by 757 delegates from state parties. At Kyoto, two years later, the number had increased already to 2,273 (COP 3). By the time COP 11 happened in Montreal in 2005, this figure grew further to 2,809. Again, two years later, at the COP 13 in Bali, it stood at 3,516. In 2009, Copenhagen had to make sure that there was enough room for 10,591 delegates to negotiate COP 15. In 2015, the COP 21 in Paris was attended by 19,260 delegates (The United Nations Climate Change, n.d.). Note what this means for negotiations: Delegations have to be able to agree among themselves, like-minded states and regional groupings of states have to forge joint understandings and positions, and agreement is also required across these like-minded states and regional groupings.

What makes negotiations succeed or fail? Among analysts of negotiations, there are two distinct schools of thought for answering this question. On the one hand, game theory is a scientific approach to explaining and even predicting the outcomes of negotiations. On the other hand, a number of scholarly approaches understand negotiations as an art that does not lend itself easily to prediction.

Game theory has established itself as an influential angle for explaining and predicting negotiations. Game theory asks the question of *how individual players can reach the best possible outcome for themselves while they are locked into a single game with one another*. Using chess as a metaphor provides an entry into the basic conceptual toolkit of game theory. There are two players (actors) sitting on a board (context). They pursue strategies (e.g., a particular opening), in order to win the game (→ glossary). Here, the metaphor reaches its limits. A game such as the often employed prisoners' dilemma is not about winning all the way down. It is about finding a set of strategies and counter-strategies that is configured in a way that no unilateral deviation from it by either one of the players improves a player's pay-off. This set is called a Nash equilibrium. In studies on diplomacy, game theory finds wide application in particular policy fields such as peace and war (Touval and Zartman, 1985) as well as in more general attempts to capture the dynamics of diplomatic negotiations (Putnam, 1988).

Let's stick with these authors briefly. Zartman's explanations of how negotiations can put an end to wars factors in the situation on the battlefield. He maintains that the perception of a mutually hurting stalemate makes a conflict ripe for resolution. It is the opportune moment to start negotiations. In this kind of situation, it has become clear to conflict parties that they cannot militarily defeat the other side, and this stalemate is costly for them. Negotiations are seen as way out of this hurting stalemate (Zartman, 1989, 1995, 2000). The situation on the battlefield may also have been an important aspect in the encounter between Churchill and Stalin. Up to a point, their agreement reflected the military realities of October 1944.

Putnam's two-level games is among the most frequently cited pieces ever published on diplomacy. Game theory usually black-boxes the state. Thus, the game to be played is a game between states. Whatever happens inside the state is not addressed. The anthropomorphised state (heuristically treating the state as if it was an individual) is assumed to have preferences. Putnam rejects the black-boxing of the state. He contends that diplomatic negotiations happen simultaneously on two levels: international and domestic. The diplomat negotiates on the international level. At the same time, governments negotiate with stakeholders and constituents on the domestic level. Only when the win sets overlap across states and across the two levels can diplomatic negotiations be concluded successfully (Putnam, 1988). This framework has been applied by several authors to explain the outcomes of bilateral trade negotiations (da Conceição-Heldt, 2013; Shinoda, 2020).

Things become more complicated, however, when we move from bilateral to multilateral negotiations. The basic insight that international and domestic dynamics matter remains as important as ever. But modelling two-level games for the kind of scale of negotiations that happens on climate change is a difficult thing to do. We are very far removed from a chess game in which two players try to outwit one another.

Conceptualisations of negotiations as an art list a number of factors shaping negotiations. Political Psychology cautions that negotiators are not always the computational machines that game theory makes them out to be. *Emotions* (→ glossary), in particular, matter. They constitute the affective dynamics between players, which, in turn, has repercussions for the selection of their strategies and even their interest formation. *Perceptions* (→ glossary) are important, too. They affect how player A sees player B, including the power that B has in the eyes of A (Goldman and Rojot, 2002: 77).

Another distinct angle looks at the means at the disposal of chairpersons of committees, conferences and so on to shake up stalled negotiations. These means include putting together new package deals, put time pressure on negotiators, and temporarily re-convene negotiations with fewer parties (Steiner, 2004; Odell, 2009; Coleman, 2011). Linda Putnam (2010) formulates an important insight in this regard. Skilful negotiators do not take a communicative situation for granted. They seek to transform it in order to reach agreements. Chairpersonship is very important in this regard. For the chair, it is usually much easier to propose new package deals, re-do the agenda and the time schedule, facilitate smaller informal gatherings, and probe where common ground could be reached.

It is very unlikely that the two landmark climate change agreements at Kyoto and Paris would have been agreed upon without excellent chairpersonship that transformed the negotiations. At Kyoto, the 160 delegates negotiated, towards the end of the two weeks, day and night. An additional day of negotiations was added, resulting in delegates having to rearrange their hotel accommodations and return flights. David Sandalow, having headed the US delegation (and talked into quite a few concessions), reflected about the role of the chair of the Committee of the Whole – the Argentinian Raúl Estrada-Oyuela – afterwards: "Estrada is a grandmaster of diplomacy and the godfather of Kyoto". And he added how important it is to have the right feel

> **Textbox 6.2 Limitations of Scholarly Perspectives on Negotiation**
>
> For all the scholarly angles there are, they cannot capture every nuance of negotiations. François de Callières, for instance, recommended to the negotiator to "drink in such a manner as not to lose control of his own faculties while endeavouring to loosen the self-control of others" (de Callières, 2021[1716]). This may not be the most scholarly of all perspectives but one should not forget that diplomacy is not just about giving prepared grand speeches in great halls but that the moments that move negotiations along are often informal in nature. Depending on setting and cultural differences, this may sometimes include a drink or two. When Konrad Adenauer, West Germany's chancellor travelled to Moscow in 1955 to negotiate about the return of German prisoners of war, he did have this aspect in mind. He ordered his delegation to take plenty of rollmops (pickled herring fillets) with them, and eat them before informal negotiation rounds. He expected these rounds to involve more than a glass of vodka, and hoped for the alcohol-absorbing quality of the fatty fish. What role the fatty fish exactly played is rather unclear, but the negotiations were successfully concluded. The Soviet Union agreed to release the last almost 10,000 German prisoners of war. In return, West Germany agreed to open diplomatic relations with the Soviet Union. The highly sensitive issue of West German recognition of East Germany did not feature in the agreement.

for the negotiations: "It wouldn't have happened without his leadership, excellent judgment and good humor" (Center for International Environmental Law, 2015).

More sociologically inclined approaches elaborate on the intangible aspects of power, for example, by studying the repercussions of *status and prestige* on negotiations (Cohen, 2001). *Occupational culture* is another helpful concept. Diplomats, no matter where they come from, converge around some taken-for-granted ideas about what diplomacy is and how to practice it, including how to negotiate. This facilitates their negotiations (Salacuse, 1998). In the language of the previous chapter, there are convergences around background ideas that constitute diplomacy in general and diplomatic negotiations in particular in the first place.

There are also rather unscholarly angles from which to make sense of negotiations. Textbox 6.2 discusses some of them.

At this point, the reader may object that this overview of negotiation has been rather state-centric thus far. Indeed, there are many actors outside of the foreign services of nation-states who leave their mark on negotiations in world politics. Yet in order to see what they do, we have to go beyond the scholarly accounts of negotiation listed earlier. *Informal networks*, for example, are of key importance for negotiations. They crucially shape negotiations and their outcomes before the negotiations even take place. Usually, it is not just traditional diplomats who make up these networks but there are actors representing NGOs, transnational corporations, international organisations, and so forth as well. It is through the interaction in these informal networks that actors make up their minds about interests and how to act accordingly (Strömvik and Jönsson, 2005). Even more so, actors arrive at interpretations about the world and the seemingly self-evident oughts and ought nots for how to act through interaction in these networks. Some actors occupy nodes in this network that enable them to diffuse their understandings of the world and these actors are not necessarily traditional diplomats.

Actors representing international organisations, for example, have *social construction power*. Barnett and Finnemore correctly point out that they "define shared international tasks (like 'development'), create and define new categories of actors (like 'refugee'), create new interests for actors (like 'promoting human rights'), and transfer models of political organisation around the world (like markets and democracy)". These categories, in turn, form the building blocks of many negotiations (although these negotiations may not always leave their definitions untouched). Note how foundational, and thus consequential, this knowledge is. Whether someone enjoys protection as refugee or is classified as 'illegal alien', to use a US phrase, makes for this person a huge difference. When it comes to defining these categories, international bureaucracies play an important role (Barnett and Finnemore, 1999: 699).

NGOs, too, are often excluded from the actual negotiation processes leading to international agreements, or they are relegated to mere observer status. But *raising awareness* about a problem, at times even putting an issue on the bargaining table in the first place, and *framing* such a problem in a way that it gives the message a punch into the desired direction has a lot to do with the communicative work of NGOs prior to inter-state negotiations. In 1997, total 133 states signed the Anti-Personnel Mine Ban Convention in Ottawa. What looks, at first glance, like a typical inter-state agreement has the authorship of NGOs written all over it. In the 1990s, 'some one thousand NGOs from over sixty countries' started their vigorous campaign to ban landmines. Jody Williams emerged as their coordinator and the resulting International Campaign to Ban Landmines (ICBL) gained more and more momentum (Price, 1998). At the beginning of the momentum was an information campaign. ICBL presented shocking statistics to world opinion. About 500 people, mostly civilians, were killed or maimed by land mines each week. This information campaign was linked to international law and deeper backgrounds. Randomly striking against civilians is incompatible with established *ius in bello*. The campaign gained more and more legitimacy. ICBL became an authority to be listened to, especially after being awarded the Nobel Peace Prize in 1997. By the mid-1990s, the Campaign had found strong resonance among traditional diplomatic circles. States such as Belgium, Canada, and Germany became outspoken proponents of a ban on landmines. Lloyd Axworthy, Canadian foreign minister, seized the right moment and hosted a meeting in Ottawa in December 1997, where the negotiations were concluded successfully.

The Anti-Personnel Mine Ban Convention, arguably adds up to a qualified success. Some major powers, including China, Russia, and the United States have neither signed nor ratified the Convention. Yet 159 states have done so, and this makes for a significant step forward. Note that the convention succeeded not only in adding an arms control agreement to the contextual foreground. It was also successful in reaching down into the background. Traditionally, the reference point of arms control is state security. The Mine Ban Convention, by contrast, is underpinned by human security. Equally important, NGOs are traditionally sidelined during debates on arms control. During debates on banning landmines, however, they were very much actors in their own right. Since the Mine Ban Convention, debates on a number of other arms control instruments have experienced similar moves towards human security and inclusive governance. This gave rise to tangible outcomes such as the 2008 Convention on Cluster Munition and the 2017 Treaty on the Prohibition of Nuclear Weapons (Kornprobst and Senn, 2016b; Kornprobst and Senn, 2017). Textbox 6.3 provides an overview of the making of the latter. In both cases, however, a number of states, including great powers, have decided to remain outside these instruments. Today's debates about how to regulate autonomous and semi-autonomous weapons are structured by clashes between the lenses of national and human security that are very similar to persisting debates on landmines, cluster munition and nuclear weapons.

> **Textbox 6.3 The Making of the Nuclear Prohibition Treaty**
>
> In 2010, the President of the International Committee of the Red Cross (ICRC), Jakob Kellenberger, gave a speech to the diplomatic corps in Geneva, which may be seen as the beginning of the Humanitarian Initiative. This Initiative made a double move: Procedurally, it included many actors routinely pushed aside when it comes to discussing nuclear weapons. This ranged from eyewitnesses of the nuclear attacks on Hiroshima and Nagasaki to scientists explaining and modelling the disastrous humanitarian consequences of different kinds of nuclear attacks and accidents. Substantially, the Initiative echoed earlier arguments on landmines and cluster munition. Nuclear weapons cannot distinguish between combatants and non-combatants, which is the cornerstone of international humanitarian law. The lens that this Initiative put to use was about human security and not national security. From 2010 onwards, support for the Initiative grew and grew. By 2016, the overwhelming majority of parties to the Nuclear Non-proliferation Treaty (NPT) had decided to negotiate a binding instrument to ban nuclear weapons. Not since the signing of the NPT in 1968 have so many states joined forces to change the legal foundations upon which the nuclear field is based. Nuclear weapons states and those non-nuclear weapons states under the nuclear umbrella of the United States distanced themselves from the Initiative in oftentimes harsh terms. They held on to understandings of national security and with it a deterrence logic. Nevertheless, the Initiative went ahead. In July 2017, the negotiating parties agreed upon a treaty to ban nuclear weapons. Four years later, the Treaty on the Prohibition of Nuclear Weapons (TPNW) passed the ratification hurdles and entered into force.

Mediation

Leading negotiations to the conclusion of an agreement is often a rather complicated task for the parties on the bargaining table. This is why they sometimes accept the involvement of third parties, who are not directly involved in the conflict and try to facilitate the negotiations. Such involvement is called mediation. Christopher Mitchell provides a useful and broad definition of this diplomatic task: It is an "intermediary activity . . . undertaken by a third party with the primary intention of achieving some compromise settlement of issues at stake between parties, or at least ending disruptive conflict behaviour" (Mitchell, 1981: 287). In principle, any conflict may be mediated in the diplomatic realm. The conflict may be about an economic, environmental, health issue and so on as long as this issue is deemed to have an international dimension. In practice, mediation efforts about security issues are the most visible. Thus, most of our empirical illustrations in this section are taken from this issue area.

Focusing on states, the literature on mediation lists several reasons why mediators offer their facilitating role to conflicting parties. One of them is *standing* in the international community. De Callières contends that mediation raises a state's prestige. "Nothing is more proper to raise the reputation of his power, and to make it respected by all nations" (de Callières, 2004). The current, more empirically inclined literature on mediation also looks at prestige and mediation but draws the causal arrow in the opposite direction. Great powers – that is, states with a lot of prestige in the sense de Callières was writing about it – get more frequently involved in mediation than small and middle powers. Taken together, these arguments may suggest a more complex hypothesis in which the link between prestige and mediation runs both ways. Great powers, *qua* their great power status, feel the need to get involved as mediators much more often than smaller powers do, and this, in turn, may contribute to them reproducing this great power status.

Aside from prestige, states may also mediate because they are *concerned about the destabilising repercussions* of continuing conflict for the international system. Washington's longstanding mediation efforts in the Middle East, especially between Israel and Palestine, fall under this rubric. Former US President Bill Clinton, for instance, was adamant about his opinion that resolving this conflict would have important positive consequences not only for the whole of the Middle East but also for world politics. Among other things, he expected such a resolution to siphon off fuel for the agitation and terrorist campaigns by Islamic fundamentalists.

Not only states engage in mediation. But also international organisations – on the global and regional levels – often have mediation tasks *enshrined in their charters and other key constitutive documents*. Chapter VI of the UN Charter, dealing with the pacific settlement of disputes, puts emphasis on mediation in Article 36, that is, the first article of this chapter. In his Agenda for Peace, Boutros Boutros-Ghali also stresses the importance of mediation and underlines approvingly that, in UN practice, "frequently it is the Secretary-General himself who undertakes the task" (Boutros-Ghali, 1992). Regional organisations such as the AU, Arab League, and the EU prescribe to their members to seek mediation if disputes in the region arise. At times, the interpretation of this mandate to mediate is so strong that it violates what may be seen as a key characteristic of mediation, that is, that the parties to a conflict agree to the mediation effort. The Arab League's move to dispatch an observer mission to Syria in late 2011 and especially its January 2012 recommendation to replace Bashar al-Assad's regime with an inclusive power-sharing agreement occurred despite al-Assad's constant attempts to deny the Arab League a meaningful role in the conflict.

NGOs and NGO-like entities engage in mediation, too. They can do so with major success. Having a considerable amount of religious authority, for example, the Catholic church is sometimes an active mediator. The Community of Sant-Egidio helped to bring the decades-old Mozambican civil war to an end. In the early 1990s, the Community mediated between the *Frente de Libertaçao de Moçambique* (Frelimo) and the *Resisténcia Nacional Mocambicana*. In 2002, the parties signed a peace agreement at the seat of the Community in Rome. Sant-Egidio also mediated in conflicts in Albania, Algeria, and Kosovo. Some bishops engage in mediation efforts, perhaps most notably Samuel Ruiz in Mexico, Monsengwo in Zaire, and Carlos Felipe Ximenes Belo in East Timor (Sampson, 2007: 299).

There are different types of mediation. Some of these types qualify even if we were to use a narrower textbook definition of mediation that puts heavy emphasis on voluntary agreement by the conflicting parties. But not all of them would do. Bercovitch and Kadayifci (2002), looking at the strategies employed by the mediators, distinguish three types. First, there are *communication-facilitating strategies*. Mediators confine themselves to passing on messages from one conflicting party to the other. They may also add credible information of which the conflict parties had previously been unaware. Second, there are *procedural strategies*. Assuming less of a passive role, mediators attempt to create an environment in which negotiations can be led to a successful conclusion. This ranges from suggesting places and times for negotiations to an agenda-setting function. Even something as seemingly mundane as the right place for negotiations may play a major facilitating role. Third, there are *directive strategies*. Assuming a distinctly active role, mediators strongly intervene in the negotiation process, for instance by providing incentives and issuing ultimatums.

114 *Understanding International Diplomacy*

Any of these types, but in particular the first one, may be closely associated with a peculiar kind of negotiation. While back-channel (→ glossary) negotiations are not necessarily associated with mediation, they often are. Facilitating communication frequently has something to do with opening up communication channels between conflict parties that are shielded from the public limelight and interference from possible spoilers within the conflict parties. This shield has a number of advantages. It makes it possible for leaders – usually via their closest advisors – to explore a range of options that would otherwise be unthinkable.

Take the 1993 Oslo Accords, for example. The main goal of the Norwegian mediators, especially Terje Rød-Larsen and Mona Juul, was to establish an informal back-channel through which the Israeli and Palestinian leaders – Yitzak Rabin and Yassir Arafat – could freely talk about possible avenues for peace. Rabin and Arafat chose Simon Peres and Mahmoud Abbas, respectively, as chief negotiators. During twelve rounds of negotiations Peres and Abbas not only realised that the other side was prepared to make concessions that had previously been deemed unthinkable but also that they developed an interpersonal relationship that would prove crucial for moving the negotiations along. All of this happened at a time when even talking to who was widely taken to be the enemy still risked a major backlash at home. The shield also has disadvantages though. Not trying to include possible spoilers early on can upset the negotiation process at a later stage or make the implementation impossible. Related to this, leaders and especially their close aides involved in the back-channel negotiations may overestimate what is possible; they may engage in group-think (Carcasson and Putnam, 1997). The Oslo Accords bear some of these scars. The negotiations were completed in August 1993 and then signed in Washington on 13 September 1993. But implementation collapsed amidst strong and determined domestic opposition in Israel and Palestine. This opposition cost Rabin his life, when he was killed by the right-wing extremist Yigal Amir.

Most of the literature on mediation attempts to identify the causes of success and failure of mediation. Notwithstanding the problems to define what success in negotiations actually is (see previous section), many different explanations are provided. Table 6.1 outlines the most frequently discussed ones among these. Some of them are in notable tension to one another, while others are complementary.

The literature puts strong emphasis on *impartiality*. Berridge, in his overview of classical writings on diplomacy comments on an important agreement among the authors: "They are unanimous that a mediator is, *by definition*, impartial" (Berridge, 2004: 4). Vattel is also adamant about impartiality. A "mediator should observe an exact impartiality" (Vattel, 2004: 189).

Table 6.1 Explaining Success and Failure of Mediation

Explanatory Focus	Key Explanations
Mediator	Impartiality
	Experience
	Power
Mediation	Robustness
	Information
Conflict	Ripeness
	Regime type
Mediator and Parties	Positive identification
	Legitimacy

Wicquefort, writing about an instruction manual for a diplomat engaging in mediation, formulates the same postulate in even more absolute terms. This manual has to

> recommend to him first, and above all things, indifference, without which all his offices would be useless; in which the legate ought to be so exact that not only no partiality should be discovered in his conduct, but also that none should be observable in the actions or words of his domestics.
>
> (Wicquefort, 2004: 133)

Impartiality, in short, tends to be seen as a *sine qua non* for successful mediation. Other explanations focusing on the mediator are also influential, although by far not as influential as impartiality. There is the argument that the mediator's experience makes a major difference; it bestows authority on him or her (Kleiboer, 2002). On these points – impartiality and authority, see also Textbox 6.4. There is the contention that the mediator has to *represent a powerful entity* with plenty of resources at its hands. Strong states are expected to be more successful mediators than weak ones (Greig, 2001). Other hypotheses focus on the types of mediation as outlined earlier. On the one hand, there is the opinion that mediation strategies have to be *more robust* than merely facilitating information. When it comes to robustness, the authors have directive mediation in mind (Beardsley, 2008). On the other hand, there is also the view that the provision of *credible information* facilitates mediation (Kydd, 2006). Trying to reduce the tension between these two hypotheses, there is also a middle-ground argument proposing that only high-quality information facilitates mediation; otherwise information-facilitating mediation is less likely to be successful than more robust strategies (Savun, 2008).

Some hypotheses suggest that it is actually not the mediation but *the conflict itself* that is the main determinant of the outcome of mediation efforts. There is again the argument that conflicts

---

Textbox 6.4 Former Heads of State as Mediators

Former heads of state can fulfil important mediation functions. Once heads of state leave office, their efforts are no longer as closely tied to the national interest as before. This makes them appear impartial to conflict parties. Furthermore, they may have acquired a considerable amount of authority while being in office. Taken together, impartiality and authority can make a difference. Scandinavian former heads of state have a great tradition in doing so. Among these, Martti Oiva Kalevi Ahtisaari, former President of Finland, probably stands out the most. He mediated in conflicts as different as Indonesia, Iraq, Kosovo, and Namibia. In 2008, he received the Nobel Peace Prize for his efforts. In Africa, Nelson Mandela used his authority very skilfully after having stepped down as South African President. In the early 2000s, for example, he mediated in Burundi. Mandela, too, is a Peace Nobel Prize laureate. He also received many other awards and honours. Among these is the UNGA's 2009 move to declare 18 July Mandela Day (his birthday). Former US President Jimmy Carter's mediation efforts are very noteworthy, too. For the most part, they concentrated on the Middle East. But he also mediated in other regions, for instance between Colombia and Ecuador and in Sudan in the mid-2000s. The AU, setting up the Panel of the Wise, created an innovative institution that, among other things, performs important mediation tasks. It is made up of former high-ranking government officials, including some former heads of state and government.

have to be ripe for resolution. Greig and Diehl, for example, make an intriguing point about enduring rivalries. They suggest that mediation has little chance early and late in the rivalry. The most promising window is in the middle, circa 25 years into the rivalry (Greig and Diehl, 2005). Furthermore, some authors submit that regime type matters. Democracies are considered more amenable to conflict resolution by mediation than authoritarian regimes (Bercovitch and Kadayifci, 2002).

Finally, there are also arguments focusing on the *relationship between the mediator and the conflict parties*. Positive identification between conflict parties, on the one hand, and the mediator, on the other, it is argued, generates trust and thus facilitates mediation. This positive identification can be rooted in religion (Bercovitch and Kadayifci-Orellana, 2002) or other, more malleable cultural bonds (Carnevale and Choi, 2000). Another approach stresses the legitimacy of the mediator. Legitimacy, as other intangible resources to make mediation work, is generated through the interaction between mediators and conflict parties (Jabri, 1996).

In the new millennium, mediation has undergone significant changes. Most importantly, it has become rather common that there is no longer just one mediator but a group of mediators. When Russia annexed the Crimean Peninsula in 2014, half a dozen states participated in attempts to mediate between Russia and Ukraine. By 2016, the number of co-mediators struggling to put the Syrian War to an end had increased to almost 20. Since the outbreak of civil war between the Rapid Response Forces and the Sudanese Army in 2022, the number of mediators has steadily increased. Early on, Saudi Arabia and the United States joined efforts to try to mediate. In contrast to previous efforts to mediate in Sudan, they sidelined the Intergovernmental Authority on Development (IGAD). Yet Kenya was adamant that the regional organisation should have its part to play. Chad and Egypt, not part of IGAD but as neighbouring states very much affected by the war, muscled in by creating their own mediation group, labelled the Neighbouring Countries Initiative, which includes Chad, Egypt, the Central African Republic, and Libya. All of this left the AU, the Arab League, the UN and interested states such as Qatar – always eager to counter Saudi Arabian initiatives and vice versa – out of the picture. Thus followed the Extended Mechanism that includes well over 20 states, the AU, the Arab League, the EU, and the UN (Chughtai and Murphy, 2023).

The proliferation of mediators adds political complexity to mediation. Many of these states and even state groupings join in order to serve what they see as their interests. These may not at all amount to impartially putting an end to a civil war. Many regional players – and beyond – fuel the civil war by providing weapons and otherwise siding with one of the warring parties. The first public statement by the Extended Mechanism speaks volumes about this problem: Participants "stress the need for countries of the region, and beyond, to maintain neutrality and to refrain from providing military, political or financial support to the belligerents in Sudan" (ReliefWeb, 2023). Thus far, however, some self-appointed mediators have made matters worse rather than help settle the dispute. Especially Saudi Arabia and the United Arab Emirates conduct themselves more as proxy warriors than as mediators.

Dialogue

It is widely agreed upon that dialogue is one of the main functions of diplomacy. Watson (2020) even goes so far as to equate diplomacy with 'dialogue between states'. As discussed in the previous chapter, foreground provisions frequently postulate dialogue. General Assembly documents routinely liken peace to dialogue, and this is a kind of dialogue that is not supposed to be confined to states. It ought to be much broader, establishing open communication among multiple stakeholders.

In diplomatic practice, however, the term 'dialogue' is frequently relegated to euphemistic usage. All too often it amounts to little more than a nice way of effectively ending a conversation amid disagreement, especially in multilateral settings. Alternatively, it is also used as a synonym of 'okay, we disagree but let's keep on talking' with the 'keep on talking' being a euphemism for 'I'll try to teach you!' The so-called critical dialogue of the EU with Iran in the 1990s illustrates this well. The EU embarked on this policy hoping to be able to teach Iran something about human rights. The policy may be understood as an exercise in norm diffusion.

In scholarly usage, by contrast, dialogue is the most demanding form of communication. Theorists such as Gadamer, Bakhtin, Bernstein, and Ricoeur contend that dialogue is about approaching communicative encounters with an open mind. The point about dialogue is not to win one's argument and it is certainly not to dismiss other perspectives prematurely. On the very contrary, dialogues require their participants to be prepared to revisit their cherished beliefs and the way they employ these to make sense of a given situation. They need to be eager to learn from different points of view. Put differently, engaging with the views of the other is a chance to get rid of, or at least revisit, one's own prejudgements and prejudices. Literally speaking, *diá* is a preposition that indicates movement from somewhere to somewhere else[1] and *lógos* means word but also reason and logic. Metaphorically speaking, therefore, it could be translated as moving from one line of reasoning to another one. This metaphorical reading of the term is very close to what theorists have in mind when they write about dialogue.

Although dialogue understood in scholarly terms does not come at all easy to diplomats trained much more to disseminate messages and asking concessions in return for own concessions, we do find instances of more or less dialogue in some diplomatic encounters. Less dialogue can be conceptualised as *polylogue*. It is an open form of communication in which it is unclear who the interlocutor and the audience are. There are multiple communicators. They are strategic to varying degrees but, at the same time, again to varying degrees, they are prepared to revisit some of the priors with which they entered the communicative encounter (Kristeva, 1977; Kerbrat-Orecchioni, 2004). Even if some revisiting of priors occurs, actors do not forgo their previous lines of reasoning altogether. Multiple actors enter the communicative encounter with multiple (*poly*) understandings (*lógos*) and, even if they revisit some of them, they keep a considerable amount of this heterogeneity.

Although the concept of polylogue has not made it into literature on diplomacy yet, there are several diplomatic practices in which polylogues are at work. *Track-two diplomacy* (→ glossary) is among these. The concept was coined by Joseph Montville, a career diplomat in the American Foreign Service. Reflecting upon the troubled communication between the United States and the Soviet Union during the Cold War, he postulated that there should not be only one track of diplomacy, that is, from government to government, but also a second unofficial one that involves parliamentarians, private citizens, activists, scholars, religious communities and so on. Since there is a plethora of different types of untraditional diplomats involved in track-two diplomacy, Diamond and McDonald write about multi-track diplomacy. In their terminology, the first track is the official government-to-government route whereas the other tracks are distinguished by the type of the non-traditional diplomats dominating the track. Track-three, for example, is about the business community, track-nine about the media (Diamond and McDonald, 1996).

For Montville, the key advantage of track-two diplomacy is that it does not require the posturing that is needed in track-one diplomacy. The latter, in his opinion, is about standing firm and not showing weakness. The former, by contrast, can experiment and explore, and is much more open-minded. To put this differently, there is much more room for dialogue in track-two than in track-one diplomacy. Take the South African case, for example. From 1980 to 1985, moderate white South Africans and members of the African National Congress (ANC) explored ways for how to put an end to apartheid. This brought together people from various walks of life, ranging from business executives to freedom fighters, from parliamentarians to activists, and from scholars to ANC officials. These rather unstructured explorations were crucial. They reduced the threat perceptions on both sides. Even the normative contours of a new and inclusive South African identity were taking shape during these talks, many of which took place outside of South Africa (e.g., in Zambia). This case illustrates well how successful track-two diplomacy can be, especially if the actors involved seize the opportunity to step into the shoes of the other, question dominant orthodoxies, and dare of talking novelty into being. Changing a racially defined definition of being a South African into the rainbow nation is no small feat. These talks, which at times came to approximate the ideal of a dialogue to a considerable extent, were an important contribution to re-thinking South African identity.

Science diplomacy may also be seen as a polylogical communication. Multiple actors take part in these encounters, ranging from traditional diplomats representing states to independent scientists. The issues that these actors address are often rather profound, which makes science diplomacy a kind of polylogue that has a distinct potential for leaving a mark on the contextual background. When the United States (NASA), Russia (Roscosmos), Japan (JAXA), Canada (CSA), and 19 EU member states plus Norway, Switzerland, and the United Kingdom (ESA) co-operate to run the International Space Station, then polylogical encounters on research results and their meaning for international affairs can have very far-reaching consequences. It is interesting to note in this regard that this kind of cooperation has continued thus far despite deteriorating relations between Russia and the West in the last decade.

There are many other polylogical diplomatic encounters. Textbox 6.5 deals with two of them: sports and music diplomacy.

Textbox 6.5 Sports and Music Diplomacy

There are many different routes for track-two diplomacy. Some of these even encompass what may be labelled sports diplomacy. In the early 1970s, President Nixon and his advisor Henry Kissinger sought a rapprochement with China in order to contribute to China's moving away from the Soviet Union. Given the ideological differences and the recent history of these two states – the Korean War, in which Americans and Chinese soldiers fought one another about two decades before – this rapprochement was anything but an easy diplomatic task. Track-two initiatives proved important to break the old mould. The so-called Ping-Pong Diplomacy was part of these initiatives. From 11 to 17 April 1971, the American ping-pong team played fun matches against the Chinese team, and visited various tourist sites in China. Reflecting on this ice-breaking event, the Chinese leader Choi En-Lai said: "Never before in history has a sport been used so effectively as a tool of international diplomacy" (Graham and Kelley, 2009). In the 1990s, a case of music diplomacy attracted major attention. Washington's attempts to dissuade North Korea from acquiring nuclear weapons in the Six-Party Talks (China, Japan, North Korea, Russia, South Korea, United States) were accompanied by an internationally broadcast visit of the New York Philharmonic Orchestra in Pyongyang in February 2008. In this case, however, track-two initiatives could not prevent the collapse of track-one negotiations. On April 14, 2009, North Korea announced they would never participate in such Six-Party Talks. Despite major diplomatic upheavals between North Korea and South Korea, the two countries have engaged in sports diplomacy since the mid-1950s, for example by organising joint Taekwondo demonstrations.

> **Textbox 6.6 Techniques for Learning from One Another**
>
> Gadamer was adamant that dialogue is about engaging with each other's arguments. Careful listening (or reading) is only the starting point of engaging with an argument. The next step involves asking clarifying questions in order to improve on one's understanding of the other's argument. The counterpart then answers these questions in a comprehensible manner. If the questioner discovers what seems to him or her weaknesses in the statement of the answerer, the questioner does not use these as pretext to dismiss the argument of the answerer. On the very contrary, the questioner tries to get deeper into the thought constructs of the answerer and proposes, based on his or her reading of the other's background, ways to overcome the weaknesses. This last step is crucial. What may appear as a weakness in someone else's argument is not the end of dialogue. In a way, it is only the beginning because it prompts the questioner to familiarise him- or her-self with the background of the other (Gadamer, 1960).

More dialogue can be conceptualised as deliberation. A thought-provoking study on the end of the Cold War suggests that even high-level inter-state diplomacy sometimes makes actors change their minds fundamentally. Risse argues that Soviet leaders were persuaded in top-level talks, especially by the US and West German sides, that German reunification and incorporation in NATO would not pose a threat to the Soviet Union (and certainly a lesser one than a neutral one, Washington contended). Not having fixed preferences itself, the Soviet leadership was open to listen to good arguments (Risse, 2000).

At times, deliberation involves a larger number of actors. It can play an important role for the formation and re-formation of advocacy networks, for example. Before the campaign that eventually led to the establishment of the International Criminal Court gained more and more momentum, some of the actors that would later become key advocates engaged in a plurilogue. This shaped the general direction of the campaign in various ways. In other words, there are 'islands' (Deitelhoff, 2009) of dialogue in international politics. Linking up with other forms of talk, these islands can be rather consequential.

Summary

- Diplomats are *messengers*. Messaging happens internally, for example, from an embassy to the MFA in the sending state, and externally, for example, from sending and hosting state. External messaging comes in many shapes and forms, including epideixis, shaming, social fact dissemination, public diplomacy, and cheap talk.
- Diplomats are *negotiators*. While some scholars conceptualise negotiations scientifically as games, others understand them as an art. In former explanations, preferences and strategy feature prominently, whereas the latter also pays careful attention to interpersonal relations, experience, and skills.
- *Mediation* comes in where negotiating parties cannot reach an agreement by themselves. There are also several contending explanations but they converge on the importance of impartiality, which is considered something akin to a *sine qua non* for successful mediation.
- *Dialogue* is the most open form of communication. Diplomats are, in principle, prepared to revisit the priors with which they entered a communicative encounter with others.

Even though diplomats talk a lot about dialogue, they often do not practice it, and if they do they are more likely in engaging in less demanding forms of dialogue (polylogue) than more demanding ones (deliberation).
- *Context makes the performance of diplomatic tasks possible, and, vice versa, these diplomatic doings shape the context.* Oftentimes, this comes down to the reproduction of context. Yet more open forms of communication have the potential to change the foreground and even the background.

Study Questions

- Is messaging describing the world or making it?
- How does game theory help us understand the dynamics of negotiations?
- What are the advantages and disadvantages of back-channel diplomacy?
- What are the dos and don'ts of mediation?
- How do NGOs make a difference on the diplomatic scene?

Note

1 We would like to thank Iver Neumann for pointing this out.

Recommended Further Reading

Adler-Nissen, Rebecca, and Kristin Anabel Eggeling. 2022. "Blended Diplomacy: The Entanglement and Contestation of Digital Technologies in Everyday Diplomatic Practice." *European Journal of International Relations* 28 (3): 640–66.

This article discusses how technological developments change diplomatic practices and even something that we refer to in this book as procedural background.

Berridge, Geoff R. 2022. *Diplomacy: Theory and Practice*. Cham: Springer Nature.

This often-cited and recently updated textbook on diplomacy deals with negotiation and mediation in great detail.

Jönsson, Christer. 2022. "Theorising Diplomacy." In *The Routledge Handbook of Diplomacy and Statecraft*, edited by B. J. C. McKercher, 13–26. London: Routledge.

The author discusses how diplomatic tasks have evolved in recent decades and what this means for making sense of diplomacy.

Neumann, Iver B. *At Home with the Diplomats: Inside a European Foreign Ministry*. Itaca: Cornell University Press, 2017.

This anthropological study of diplomacy is full of insights into how diplomats perform their tasks, especially how they conduct what we refer to as internal messaging, that is, communicative encounters within a foreign ministry.

Rana, Kishan S. 2023. "Why Reforms Are Needed in Bilateral Diplomacy: A Global South Perspective." In *The Palgrave Handbook of Diplomatic Reform and Innovation*, edited by Paul Webster Hare, Juan Luis Manfredi-Sánchez, and Kenneth Weisbrode, 81–108. Cham: Springer International Publishing.

This chapter written by a practitioner turned scholar postulates revisiting and reforming a range of diplomatic tasks in order to make for more productive bilateral and regional relations.

Part IV
Explaining Diplomacy

7 Making Judgements

Chapter Objectives

- To introduce the reader to different scholarly logics of action (→ glossary).
- To differentiate different approaches to conceptualise these logics.
- To discuss strengths and weaknesses of these approaches in explaining diplomatic decisions and decision-making.

Introduction

With the exception of the extreme form of messaging in which the diplomat is reduced to delivering a message from one capital to the next, every task listed in the previous chapter requires from the diplomat to make up his or her mind about what to do. This ranges from writing instructions for colleagues posted abroad to framing messages for the purposes of public diplomacy, from negotiation to mediation, and from cheap talk to dialogue.

In other words, diplomats have to make judgements. Subsuming particulars under universals, they come to orient themselves in a situation (Kornprobst, 2019b). Consider the speech by Martin Kimani, Kenyan Ambassador to the UN on 22 February 2022, that is, the day Russia invaded Ukraine. His reasoning was based on three clusters of universals: the UN Charter, African history, and world history. When it came to the Charter, he repeatedly invoked the universals of sovereignty and territorial integrity. Learning the lessons from African history to him was about accepting borders inherited from 'dead empires', forgo irredentism and work together to overcome the divisiveness of borders instead. World history, finally, cautions against the 'relentless assault of the powerful'. Given that Kimani subsumed the particulars of the situation in Ukraine under these universals, Kimani condemned Russia's war against Ukraine (Kimani, cited in Kenya Digital News, 2022).

Scholars conceptualise the making of diplomatic judgements very differently. Some seek to predict how diplomats choose while others seek to trace decision-making processes in depth. Some factor in how diplomats interact with others to make up their minds while others do not. Some study what is explicit in processes of judgement while others seek to uncover what remains implicit.

This chapter introduces the reader to a broad analytical toolbox to study diplomatic judgements, highlighting strengths and weaknesses of different approaches. We take the tools of this toolbox from various disciplines, including political science, economics, psychology, and sociology. Since the tools we discuss are at times rather abstract, we frequently refer to important 20th and 21st-century events, and the diplomatic decisions made in order to deal with them as illustrative cases. These events share in common that they pushed decision-makers into addressing the balance between diplomatic and military responses, which helps us to highlight the strengths and weaknesses of the approaches we discuss.

This chapter is organised into six sections. First, we deal with rational choice and discuss its strengths and weaknesses by taking a look at how the Cuban Missile Crisis came to be eventually de-escalated by diplomatic means. Second, we provide an overview of contending approaches in political psychology. Here, our illustrative case is the diplomatic run-up to the Second Gulf War in 2003. Third, we address the logic of appropriateness and employ it to analyse continuities and discontinuities of Germany's usages of coercive diplomacy since re-unification. Fourth, we direct our attention to the logic of argumentation and evaluate its explanatory power by putting the diplomatic driving forces of the end of the Cold War under scrutiny. Fifth, we outline the logic of practice and probe its explanatory strengths and weaknesses by applying it to Norwegian diplomatic crisis management.

Rational Choice

Rational choice remains the dominant perspective for how to study the making of decisions in the Social Sciences. On the purely individual level – how actors arrive at a decision without taking the actions of others into consideration – the key term of this perspective is *expected utility*. Let us look at this concept, and how it is linked to other concepts, in a bit more depth by scrutinising the key assumptions on which theorising on expected utility is based. First, the starting assumption is that actors have *desires* that they want to attain. Second, some of these desires are more important for the individual than others. In technical language, the individual *rank-orders preferences* by attributing different degrees of utility to them. It is assumed that the individual does this consistently during a decision-making situation, that is, it does not change the rank-ordering. Third, the individual calculates which action *maximises* its utility.

This is a straight-forward mechanism of choice. It becomes more complicated though when we factor in a common feature of decision-making situations, that is, uncertainty. Uncertainty means that an actor's calculations cannot generate certainty about which maximum utility can be attained. Here we have to add a fourth assumption. An individual can only calculate which maximum utility is to be *expected*. Thus, the individual does not calculate its utility but merely its expected utility. Calculations of expected utility include the factor of likelihood and how to deal with it, that is, whether to be more risk-prone or more risk-averse.

On the interactive level, the key concept that the rational choice perspective adds to the aforementioned is *strategy* ($\rightarrow$ glossary). It is rare that individuals can get what they want without taking into consideration what others may do. Individuals have to think of the moves that others may make and choose their moves accordingly because the interplay of moves and counter-moves crucially affects the pay-offs in a given decision-making situation. Similarly to a chess player choosing a particular opening to a game, individuals are assumed to plan their moves. Such a plan is called a strategy (Green and Shapiro, 1994). Game theory, already alluded to in the previous chapter, is an especially rigorous and formal device to understand how the interplay of such strategies can lead to an agreement between actors (Morrow, 1994). Textbox 7.1 discusses how scholars apply rational choice to study diplomacy in general and international relations more generally.

Rational choice is the dominant perspective in diplomatic studies. Authors use it more or less rigorously. On the one end of the spectrum, game theory makes for a very rigorous analytical tool. On the other end of it, scholars make rational choice not explicit but rely on it in order to explain empirical decision-making. The next section discusses strengths and weaknesses of rational choice by discussing the 1962 Cuban Missile Crisis. During the crisis, John F. Kennedy,

> **Textbox 7.1   From Microfoundations to Anthropomorphisation**
>
> Decision-making as conceptualised by rational choice can be applied to diplomacy on different levels. Staying true to its individualist premises, rational choice can be applied to how individual diplomats choose in decision-making situations. Depending on the preference ranking and strategy, the individual diplomat may serve the national interest while interacting with diplomats representing different states. But he or she may also be selfish in terms of how to further his or her career, putting their own needs ahead of those of the nation. Rational choice can also be applied to collective actors. In this case, the rational actor is anthropomorphised. The collective actor is analysed as if it were an individual one. This way, a department in the foreign ministry may become an anthropomorphised actor, eager to further its agenda at the expense of other departments. Much more common, a state is anthropomorphised and ends up being portrayed as a single actor on the diplomatic stage. Note that rational choice scholars do not claim that their assumptions – including stable preference-ranking during a decision-making situation and treating collective actors as if they were individuals – are true. They merely consider them heuristically useful simplifications of reality.

then US president, estimated the odds of a nuclear exchange as "between 1 out of 3 and even" (Allison, 1969). What explains why he, ultimately, let diplomacy rather than a military solution of the crisis prevail?

Cuba, 1962

On October 14, 1962, US air reconnaissance showed very clearly that a build-up of Soviet missiles was happening in Cuba. Khrushchev had decided to secure Cuba not only with defensive missiles (surface-to-air) but also with offensive ones (ground-to-ground). This triggered an intense crisis in which diplomacy ultimately won out against military options. Starting 24 October and facilitated by UN Secretary-General U Thant, the leaders of the superpowers, Nikita Khrushchev and John F. Kennedy exchanged signals for how to de-escalate the crisis. Most importantly, Robert Kennedy, the president's brother and close advisor, and Anatoly Dobrynin, the Soviet Ambassador in Washington, reached an informal agreement that the Soviet Union would ship all its missiles back from Cuba in exchange for the United States withdrawing its missiles from Turkey. By the end of the year, this agreement had been implemented.

How come that diplomacy prevailed in the end? Graham Allison, in his seminal article 'Conceptual Models and the Cuban Missile Crisis', starts off with applying a rational choice framework to the Cuban Missile Crisis. The first step in this application is to conceive of the state as a unitary decision-maker. The state is anthropomorphised and treated as if it was behaving as a rational individual actor with 'rational' standing for the conformity with the key assumptions of rational choice outlined earlier. The second step concerns the identification of preferences. Allison, as many authors writing on diplomacy and international relations, does so 'in an intuitive fashion' (Allison, 1969: 694). He observes that national security was the overriding interest for the United States. He specifies that, in the context of deterrence, MAD, and the Cold War, this meant that the military balance must not shift in favour of the Soviet Union.

President John F. Kennedy, helped by his advisors in the Executive Committee (ExComm), discussed six strategies for how to respond to the Soviet challenge. The first strategy that was scrutinised was to do nothing. Starting from the premise that the Soviet build-up of missiles in Cuba does not change the military balance between the United States and the Soviet Union, this strategy aims to downplay the issue and not to provide Khrushchev with a 'public relations' victory. Second, Washington could exert diplomatic pressure on Khrushchev in order to persuade him to remove the missiles from Cuba. Various diplomatic routes would be possible for such an endeavour, including a direct (bilateral) approach or an indirect one via the UN or the Organization of American States (OAS). Third, the United States could secretly approach Fidel Castro. The goal of such an approach would have to be to lure him away from the Soviet orbit. The fourth strategy that was debated was the most militarily determined one. The United States would invade Cuba, remove the missiles itself, and bring the island back into its sphere of influence. Fifth, the US Air Force would take out the missiles through a surgical airstrike. Sixth, the US Navy would conduct a naval blockade of Cuba, making it impossible for Soviet ships to deliver more missiles and other hardware necessary for the build-up to Cuba.

Next, the analyst dissects these strategies, determining which one provides for the maximum pay-off, given what the other side is likely to do. As Allison puts it, this is not all that complicated in this case. On the one hand, some strategies are too limited and cautious as that one could expect them to make a difference. 'Do nothing' only helps if one really does not infer the necessity of the withdrawal of the missiles from the primacy of national security. Given the geographical proximity of missiles in Cuba, however, their withdrawal should be strongly preferred. Exclusively relying on 'diplomatic pressures' is a set of moves that is not very promising either. Absent any military posturing, it is unclear how the United States would be able to project the necessary pressure on the Soviet Union to withdraw its missiles from Cuba. The 'secret approach to Castro' is also a set of moves that is likely to fail. Independently of whether Castro could be convinced to leave the Soviet sphere of influence (which is highly unlikely), the missiles were guarded by Soviet soldiers. Thus, the key for removing them lay in Moscow and not in Havana. On the other hand, some strategies were too risky; they could have pushed the world over the brink into nuclear disaster. This applies most clearly to the 'invasion' option. Invading Cuba could have prompted the Soviet Union to retaliate in like-minded fashion, for instance a move against West Berlin or Turkey. From there, things could have spilled easily out of control. The 'surgical airstrike' was somewhat less risky. But it would still have involved killing Soviet soldiers, guarding the missiles with all the potential of further escalation of the crisis. It was also not entirely clear whether such a surgical airstrike would really be able to destroy all Cuban missiles. The sixth strategy, that is, the naval blockade, was situated in the middle of the spectrum of too little and too much resolve. It shows United States' determination for the Soviet Union to remove the missiles but, at the same time, gives the Soviet Union time to react and keep face. In other words, the blockade option provides an opportunity for diplomacy to diffuse the dangerous situation.

Allison aptly summarises the explanation for the choice of the blockade from the perspective of the rational actor model with the sentence: "The blockade was the United States' only real option" (Allison, 1969: 698). Indeed, he has a point. From a rational choice point of view, we should not be too surprised that John F. Kennedy opted for the naval blockade (or quarantine, as it was labelled for legal reasons), and, ultimately, for a diplomatic resolution of the crisis. In fact, from a rational choice point of view, the Cuban Missile Crisis was not that dangerous after all. It would have been irrational for either party – the United States or the Soviet Union – to escalate the crisis further. Given the pervasive effects of MAD on the preferences and strategies of the two parties, an escalation was very unlikely to occur.

Yet we detect reasons to doubt this firm conclusion as soon as we open up the black-box called state and look into the decision-making mechanisms that happen within the state. Allison, for instance, shows that organisational routines (as opposed to reflective decision-making) deeply influenced decision-making. Perhaps most importantly, the air force, relying on its manuals and unquestioned routines, presumed that an airstrike would be much more extensive than what the ExComm had in mind. With 'surgical' not being in the manuals for how to conduct an airstrike, the airforce sketched a scenario in which airstrikes came to appear too risky to most members of the ExComm. The ExComm was bewildered about the number of sorties required, likely casualties, and likely collateral damage. In the ExComm, this cast serious doubt on this option from the very beginning.

The dynamics among the ExComm members, not explicitly addressed by Allison, also allude to weaknesses of rational choice. Collective deliberations and the social relations that shape these deliberations are outside of the analytical scope of rational choice. Ultimately, it was John F. Kennedy's decision what to do. But the president, far from making the decision by himself, heavily relied on the advice of the ExComm members he trusted the most. It is no coincidence that he went with the naval blockade, to be followed by the diplomatic solution of the crisis. This was the course of events advocated by his brother Robert Kennedy and his security advisor Robert McNamara. These two ExComm members he trusted the most. Seen in this light, it is also no coincidence that Robert Kennedy took care of leading the crisis to its diplomatic conclusion by reaching agreement on what to do with the Soviets.

Otto von Bismarck predicted the outbreak of World War I with anything but a rationalist argument. He feared that 'some damned foolish' thing in the Balkans would at some stage lead to a major European war (Siracusa, 2010: 32–3). To put this differently, diplomatic history is full of examples in which diplomatic moves did not follow the rigorous rationality assumptions put forward by rational choice. Let us, however, not lose sight of the strengths of rational choice amidst all these *caveats* against all too stringent assumptions of rationality. The rational choice perspective provides for a parsimonious explanatory framework. Rational choice scholars are very much aware of the fact that they simplify the world in order to be able to explain it (Keohane, 1988: 379). In other words, these scholars do not believe that their assumptions are true. They merely defend them as being useful for conducting research.

It is up to the reader to judge under what circumstances rational choice provides for a fruitful perspective to explain diplomatic decisions. The following sections introduce the reader to major alternative perspectives. We start with psychological approaches. Scholars embracing these approaches and students of rational choice share, for the most part, a consequentialist logic of action. They seek to understand how selfish individuals, reflecting upon the consequences of their actions, figure out what to do. But psychological approaches conceptualise this 'figuring out what to do' very differently. We then move on to logics of action other than consequentialism: appropriateness, argumentation, and practice.

Psychological Approaches

Since there is a plethora of angles for studying the psychology of leading diplomats and decision-makers, it is much more difficult to summarise the key unifying assumptions of political psychology than it is with rational choice. Yet whatever political psychologists may disagree about, they share the *rejection of computational goal-seeking*. They criticise rational choice assumptions for what is to them pretending that "the mind has essentially unlimited demonic or supernatural reasoning power" (Gigerenzer and Todd, 1999: 6).

The starting assumption of psychological approaches is that actors arrive at a decision-making situation with a lot of *baggage* (conceptualised, for instance, as schema or operational code). Over time, individuals acquire background knowledge that helps them orientate themselves amidst uncertainty and complexity. The baggage decision-makers acquire is hypothesised to be highly consequential. Actors are not assumed to compute endlessly until they have found the optimal outcome for themselves. Instead, they rely on heuristic devices that tell them when to *stop searching* for alternative options. Herbert Simon's seminal contributions revolve around these stopping rules. His notion of bounded rationality holds that actors do not compute endlessly to maximise but stop to satisfice their expected utility (Simon, 1957). Several approaches build on Simon's work. Prospect theory, for instance, argues that actors are risk-prone in their decision-making when they perceive loss and risk-averse when they perceive gain (Kahnemann and Tversky, 1979; Levy, 2000). Fast and frugal heuristics contends that actors rely on simple heuristics drawn from an adaptive toolbox to make sense of the world; ultimately, a single clue can suffice for an actor to make up his or her mind (Gigerenzer and Todd, 1999). There are also authors who highlight the emotional dimension of all of this. For some authors, emotions are so inescapably intertwined with reason that they simply cannot be kept apart at all. Emotions and reason always go together; or, to put this differently, no reason without emotions (Mercer, 2010).

Psychological approaches zoom in on individual decision-makers such as state leaders. Thus, the scope of these approaches is limited. There is very little on diplomatic actors other than these leaders, not even to speak of actors not representing states. This is a limitation. But it is also a virtue. Given the limited scope, the research conducted by political psychologists is very detailed and full of insights. Linking diplomacy and political psychology, the work of Alexander George (1969) has been especially influential. He conceptualised the 'baggage' as operational codes. This sparked a lively research programme (Holsti, 1970; Walker, 1990; He and Feng, 2013; Haas, 2023).

Iraq, 2003

Let us look at another case where key diplomatic actors situated themselves at the thinning line between diplomacy and war. Yet this time, unlike with the Cuban Missile Crisis, the line was actually crossed. In 2003, the United States and the UK, along with a group of other states dubbed the 'coalition of the willing', terminated diplomatic efforts to convince Saddam Hussein to disclose and dismantle his alleged weapons of mass destruction, invaded Iraq, occupied it, and installed a different regime. How did they come to do so? What are the strengths and weaknesses of psychological approaches for helping us answer this question?

Judging by the sources available to us, Bush and Blair approached the Iraq question with the baggage of historical analogies and metaphors in mind. Taken together, this baggage helped them make sense of Saddam Hussein, Iraq, and what to do. Historical analogies featured very prominently (see Textbox 7.2). None of them featured as prominently as appeasement. Bush and Blair invoked again and again the Munich analogy. The lesson of Munich 1938 ought to be that dictators have to be confronted before it is too late. In 2003, Saddam Hussein, for Blair and Bush, belonged into exactly this category.

Other historical analogies seem to have been important anchors for reasoning as well. Blair, for example, repeatedly referred to the NATO intervention against Serbia during the 1999 Kosovo conflict. In his opinion, the lesson to be learnt from Kosovo was that intervention works. Not only can it effectively counter threats against peace and security but it can also be the first step towards the democratisation of a country. Metaphors with religious connotations were of significance for Bush and Blair as well. The binary opposition of 'good' and 'evil' is a *Leitmotiv* in their speeches and statements. Some authors analysing their decision-making refer to this as their Manichean worldview (Dyson, 2007).

Textbox 7.2   Appeasement

Early morning hours on 30 September 1938, the Führerbau (Leader's Building) in Munich. Adolf Hitler, Neville Chamberlain, Benito Mussolini and Edouard Daladier sign the Munich Agreement on behalf of Germany, the United Kingdom, Italy and France, respectively. Mussolini had officially proposed territorial revisions in favour of Nazi Germany and at the expense of Czechoslovakia, which had been put together by Hitler's foreign service. Chamberlain and Daladier agree to the territorial revisions and convey to the Czechoslovak government, which was not invited to attend the conference, that it would have to fight Nazi Germany on its own if it did not agree to hand over the Sudetenland peacefully. A year later, Hitler showed that the kind of territorial aggrandisement he had in mind much surpassed the Sudetenland. World War II began with Germany attacking Poland. Since then, appeasement has become an important diplomatic lesson, and, at times, also a powerful rhetorical weapon. Appeasing a tyrant does not work. Not confronting a dangerous dictator early enough makes things even worse; it becomes more and more difficult to defeat the tyrant. This really is an important lesson. But it is also a lesson that is prone to be instrumentalised for those trying to mobilise nations to go to war. Portraying someone as Hitler or Hitler-like (e.g., Saddam Hussein) does mobilise people. But whether the portrayal is appropriate or not is an altogether different matter.

The baggage affected Bush's and Blair's interpretation of Saddam Hussein's moves, and their decisions about how to counter his expected moves. Both leaders made up their minds very early that Hussein possessed and further developed weapons of mass destruction, especially biological and chemical ones. In 1997 already, Blair is on record for saying that "I have now seen some of the stuff on this. It really is pretty scary. He [Saddam] is very close to some appalling weapons of mass destruction. I don't understand why the French and others don't understand this" (Dyson, 2006). This assessment sounds remarkably similar to Blair's understanding of the situation six years later. By 'stuff', Blair referred to intelligence. The overestimation of threat based on a highly selective reading of available intelligence persisted. In 2002, the Bush Administration sent Colin Powell to the UNSC in order to present evidence to the world that Iraq was a major threat to international peace and security. Amongst other things, Powell alleged that Iraq was developing unmanned aerial vehicles that were capable of delivering chemical and biological weapons to the United States. As the UN Monitoring, Verification and Inspection Commission later confirmed, these allegations were unfounded (Kerr, 2004).

There is evidence that Bush's and Blair's emotions played their role in all of this. Indeed, no American president could possibly have reacted to 9/11 in an entirely detached manner. For Bush, given his patriotism and deep attachment to the American nation, such an emotionless response was especially unlikely to happen. When Bush declared the end of the war in May 2003, he stressed that the Iraq war had been an important success in the war against terror; with the end of Saddam's regime, an ally of Al Qaeda – ready to provide international terrorists with weapons of mass destruction – had been removed. These allegations of a link between Al Qaeda and Saddam Hussein never withstood the test of any serious scrutiny. But in the wake of Sept 11, 2001, they seemed fully reasonable for Bush and his advisors. The emotional dimension may very well explain at least part of this subjective reasonableness. The language used to describe Saddam Hussein also alludes to this emotional dimension. The term 'evil' has been alluded to above already; it was very frequently used to portray Saddam. The term, of course, has a very clear emotional dimension to it. The same applies to other terms used as well. Blair, for instance, referred to Saddam as 'monster' – again this signals anything but detachment (Kennedy-Pipe and Vickers, 2007).

Psychological approaches provide for important insights into decision-making in general, and Bush's and Blair's misinterpretations and miscalculations in the Iraq case in particular. In hindsight, we know now that Saddam Hussein, after his defeat against the US-led coalition in 1991, did not re-start Iraq's nuclear, chemical, and biological weapons programmes. But psychological approaches, too, have their limits. Two of them are especially worth mentioning. First, doing empirical research and generating the kind of evidence that applying these approaches requires is sometimes a major challenge. David Owen, for instance, contends in an article in the reputable *Journal of the Royal Society of Medicine* that Blair suffers from a psychological state that the author refers to as 'hubris' (Owen, 2006). But how is this to be shown empirically? After all, Blair might not agree to sit down on Owen's couch and provide him with the kind of in-depth information about his decision-making that would provide compelling empirical support for such a claim.

Second, many psychological approaches focus on top decision-makers at the expense of looking at the broader picture of how these decision-makers interact with advisors, organisations, bureaucracies, and the broader public. Leaders, however, consult with others, for instance, trusted career diplomats, and this does not always leave their views unchanged. Furthermore, some leaders are more sensitive to public opinion than others. Among psychological approaches, Janis's concept of 'groupthink' (1972) is an important exception to the tendency to neglect processes of consultation. Some decision-makers keep critical voices out of the inner circles of advisors. Thus, the group finds it quite easy to agree on interpretations of the world and how to act in it. But their perspective is a narrow one, leading to serious misinterpretations. Recent research applies this concept, for example, to a tightly knit group around Putin. This group includes Sergey Lavrov, his long-time foreign minister (Götz and Staun, 2022; Forsberg and Pursiainen, 2017).

The remainder of this chapter deals with more sociologically inclined perspectives. They take the social embeddedness of diplomats making judgements more seriously. Far from being assumed as standing apart, decision-makers are presumed to be rather deeply embedded in social context. A disclaimer is necessary though. In contrast to rational choice and most psychological approaches, these perspectives do not seek to explain the exact decisions that individuals make. Instead, they attempt to understand how what kinds of judgements become conceivable or inconceivable for actors. To put this differently, on a spectrum of approaches to judgements, rational choice would be at the scientific pole of the spectrum, political psychology would be situated a bit further towards the arts, and the sociological schools of thought to follow move us even much closer to the arts.

Logic of Appropriateness

The logic of appropriateness proceeds from a different ontology (theory of being). Consequentialism, and here especially rational choice, de-emphasises the social context in which individuals are embedded. The starting point of analysis is the individual and not communities and their practices that may be meaningful for the individual. The logic of appropriateness proceeds very differently. Assuming human beings to be *deeply embedded in social context*, it stresses the intersubjective ideas in which individuals are embedded. Established ideas are presumed to constitute these individuals as political actors in the first place. March and Olsen hold that this social context is made up of rules. The repertoire of *rules*, in turn, has cognitive and normative dimensions (March and Olsen, 2004: 3).

We have come across the *cognitive* dimension already, although with somewhat different connotations. When psychologists write about heuristic devices such as analogies that make it possible for actors to reason, then they, too, write about this dimension. Yet the logic of appropriateness puts a different twist on them. These cognitive rules are identity-constituting. The Munich analogy, for example, is not just a heuristic clue that an individual has come across at some stage and holds onto because it is considered useful knowledge, but it has sunk in and became part of the identity narrative of the socially embedded individual and the community (or communities) to which this individual belongs. From this scholarly point of view, it is not a coincidence that Munich 1938 featured prominently on the minds of George W. Bush and Tony Blair. This historical lesson is a key ingredient of the dominant American and British identity narratives; they are deeply ingrained in the nation, including its representatives on the diplomatic stage.

For March and Olsen, the *normative* dimension of rules is at least as important as the cognitive one. Ultimately, it is the normative dimension that drives action. Norms tell the socially embedded individual the oughts and ought nots of political conduct. The logic of appropriateness proposes that actors abide by these oughts and ought nots because they constitute their identity. Violating them would amount to violating their very Self (March and Olsen, 1989). Looking through this scholarly lens, Bush and Blair were adamant about putting an end to diplomacy and resort to war among other things because the supposed appeasement of Saddam Hussein would have meant to violate a lesson of history that ought to be at the forefront of every American and British leader, respectively; Chamberlain's monumental error ought never to be repeated again.

Textbox 7.3 alludes to something that is strongly emphasised in latest research on norms (Wiener, 2009; Holzscheiter, 2016). How far norms are shared across actors or not is very much a matter for empirical analysis. Usually, there is plenty of contestation about norms and how to interpret them.

Textbox 7.3 Security Council Resolution 1973

In mid-February 2011, protests in Libya's coastal city of Benghazi escalated when security forces loyal to Muammar Gaddafi fired into the crowd. The escalation led to a civil war, which spread more and more across the country. Gaddafi's targeting of civilians prompted strong responses from the international community. On 26 February, the Security Council adopted S/RES/1970 (2011) in which it strongly condemned the "widespread and systematic attacks . . . against the civilian population", warned that they "may amount to crimes against humanity", and clarified that it was acting under Chapter 7 (enforcement measures) of the UN Charter. The operative clauses refer the situation in Libya to the International Criminal Court, and impose an arms embargo and travel bans against leading figures of Gaddafi's government. With the situation further deteriorating, the Security Council adopted S/RES/1973 in which it reiterated its grave concerns and decided to resort to more robust measures, above all the establishment of a no-fly zone and the authorisation for UN member states to "take all necessary measures . . . to protect civilians and civilian populated areas under threat of attack in the Libyan Arab Jamahiriya".

Among the Security Council members, France, the United Kingdom and the United States (permanent members) as well as Bosnia and Herzegovina, Colombia, Gabon, Lebanon Nigeria, Portugal, South Africa (non-permanent) voted for the resolution. China and Russia (permanent) as well as Brazil, Germany and India (non-permanent) abstained from the vote. While the ensuing NATO intervention in Libya did protect civilians and reiterated this again and again as the purpose of the mission, the intervention also played a crucial role in shifting the military balance in favour of the National Transition Council and against Gaddafi's regime. China, India, South Africa, and especially Russia, therefore, vocally criticised Resolution 1973 and its implementation. Vladimir Putin put this into the following accusatory language: "It [Resolution 1973] is reminiscent of medieval calls for a crusade. It allows for the invasion of a sovereign state" (RIA Novosti, 2011).

Germany, Diplomacy, and Intervention

It is easy to summarise the story of the weighing of diplomacy and military intervention in (West-)German politics before 1993. It tilted very heavily towards the former. Germany, for instance, confined itself to the so-called *Scheckbuch-Diplomatie* (chequebook diplomacy) during the First Gulf War in 1990. It endorsed the US-led intervention against Iraq aimed at liberating Kuwait but did not participate in it, except for providing funds for the war effort. This decision-making for *Scheckbuch-Diplomatie* and against participation in the intervention is anything but self-explanatory. The First Gulf War was a textbook collective security effort; a member of the UN had been attacked and annexed. The UN decided to come to the rescue of this member. Yet, at the same time, deploying German soldiers abroad in order to participate at an enforcement measure was still virtually unthinkable. This applied as much to key political figures including Chancellor Helmut Kohl and his Foreign Minister Hans-Dietrich Genscher as it did to large segments of society.

Two protracted international crises shook this foreign policy consensus. During the onset of the Yugoslav War, German diplomacy assumed that an early recognition of the break-up republics would put an end to the bloodshed. Pressuring other EU members to recognise and doing so unilaterally rather than within the framework of the EU did not stop the worst killing Europe had experienced since the end of World War II. On the contrary, fighting became fiercer, especially in Bosnia. The international community increasingly resorted to coercive diplomacy to put an end to the war. A no-fly zone over Bosnia was one of the means used. This no-fly zone had to be monitored. NATO conducted surveillance flights for doing so; a third of the personnel in charge of the mission was German. Since the First Gulf War, there had been considerable diplomatic pressure by Germany's allies to make Berlin contribute to military operations. The Kohl government eventually succumbed to the diplomatic pressure, especially by the United States. The successor government, even though composed of different parties with much more pacifistic leanings, continued this stance. In 1999, Joschka Fischer decided in his function as foreign minister and together with the social democratic Chancellor Gerhard Schröder to join the NATO intervention against Yugoslavia. The air strikes happened despite the lack of a mandate by the Security Council.

From 2003 onwards, it appeared as if Germany would revert back to its more traditional hesitation to forgo diplomatic efforts and join military campaigns. Not only did Schröder and Fischer refuse to join George W. Bush's 'coalition of the willing' in 2003 but they were also openly critical of Bush's campaign in a manner German diplomacy had not dared to do since the end of World War II. In 2011, the centrist coalition government under Chancellor Angela Merkel and Foreign Minister Guido Westerwelle decided against the humanitarian intervention in Libya. Germany, then with a non-permanent seat at the UNSC, was the only western country not to agree to Resolution 1973 (it abstained), which, in the American, French, and British interpretations, provided the legal basis for the intervention against Muammar Gaddafi. It did not participate in the military intervention, which was spear-headed by France, the United Kingdom and the United States. The cautious and mediation-centred conflict management approach has prevailed in a number of more recent crises as well. This includes Syria and Ukraine.

But then came the Russian invasion of Ukraine. Chancellor Scholz, began a speech at the Bundestag, given a few days after the invasion, with the following words: "24 February 2022 marks a *Zeitenwende* [epochal turning point] in the history of our continent" (Bundesregierung, 2022). He went on to condemn Russia's aggression by juxtaposing it to international law and by likening it to Europe's history of warfare. From this, he inferred the postulate for a new balance between diplomacy and military preparedness, that is, "as much diplomacy as possible without being naïve". The latter he described as negotiating and mediating with someone who is not willing to seek a settlement on the negotiation table (Bundesregierung, 2022). To a considerable extent, the *Zeitenwende* is echoed by other political parties, the media and in public opinion. Yet it is not a unanimous new foreign policy consensus. Similarly to other Western democracies, there is plenty of polarisation in domestic politics. Neither the right nor the left end of the political spectrum share the conviction of a *Zeitenwende*. As long as these political forces remain marginalised, they will not have much of an impact on German diplomacy. But it is not clear to what extent they will remain marginalised in the future.

How well-suited is the logic of appropriateness to explain these decisions about diplomatic and military options? On the one hand, the logic provides explanatory power. Not to repeat the catastrophic wrongs of the past, in particular causing World War II and the Holocaust, is deeply ingrained in the dominant identity narrative of Germany. On the other hand, however, the logic has difficulties accounting for the participation of Germany in joint military efforts in the former Yugoslavia and the *Zeitenwende* that has become a key term in foreign policy discourse. Standards of appropriateness are not carved into stone. They evolve over time. When crises happen, they may even shift. This is to be explained and the logic of appropriateness is not very well attuned to explaining these kinds of changes.

Logic of Argumentation

Thomas Risse contends that there is a third logic of action, which he labelled the logic of argumentation (Risse, 2000). Risse borrows heavily from the social thought of Jürgen Habermas, and more precisely, his theory of communicative action. At first glance, Habermas's framework does not look all that different from the logic of appropriateness. Writing about the significance of a *shared lifeworld* (→ glossary: lifeworld), he places a lot of emphasis on social context. This emphasis is reminiscent of March and Olsen. At a second glance, however, there is a notable difference between the two logics. In Habermas's view, analysing the shared lifeworld alone does not tell us all that much. It merely sketches the repertoire of ideas available to actors to make sense of the world. What is really important for Habermas is how actors, communicating with one another, select certain ideas rather than others from this large repertoire, how they link these ideas together to create arguments, and how they come to the consent that a particular argument is the most convincing one.

> **Textbox 7.4 Diplomacy and Communicative Action**
>
> According to a Habermasian framework, the goal of the diplomats engaged in communicative action is to seek a communicative consensus about their understanding of the situation and the preferred course of action. The way in which diplomats engage in communicative action is by constructively challenging the validity claims inherent in the interests, preferences, and norms driving each other's actions. According to Habermas, any interaction orientated to reaching understanding is defined by three validity claims (Habermas, 1984: 99). The first refers to the truth of assertions made, or the conformity with interpreted facts in the world: the statements made are intersubjectively true. For instance, is Iran close to becoming a nuclear power? If so, how close? The second focuses on the moral rightness of the norms underlying arguments: the speech is right with respect to the existing normative context. Is it right for a diplomat to condemn other countries' violation of human rights while their own government suppresses human rights at home? The third validity claim concerns the truthfulness and authenticity of the speaker: the manifest intention of the speaker is meant as it is expressed. Is the diplomat willing to change their mind and adopt a new position if the arguments presented by the other side are more convincing? The communicative action framework has been applied to various processes of international cooperation, dealing with questions such as why the internalisation of human rights norms occurs (Risse, Ropp and Sikkink, 1999), how inter-civilisational dialogue can take place (Lynch, 2000), how effective is decision-making in the UNSC (Johnstone, 2003), why international negotiations are successful despite the opposition of important powers (Deitelhoff, 2009), or how the use of force can be justified in international politics (Bjola, 2005).

Habermas is a normative scholar. He uses a counterfactual as a benchmark to critique political communication in Western democracies. The counterfactual is the ideal speech situation. Ideally, there should be open access to discourse and those participating in discourse ought not to aim at making their arguments win but to figure out together which argument is *the most convincing* one, no matter who the authors of this argument are. As Habermas puts it, the aim is to let the "force of the better argument" (Habermas, 1984: 161) come to the fore.

Scholars such as Müller (1994) and Risse (2000) make an analytical-empirical logic of action out of this normative framework. They contend that world politics, far from always being about the might of the strong dictating to the weak what they must – or must not – do, sometimes allows for the force of the better argument to prevail. In some cases, actors on the diplomatic scene can convince one another of the better argument. Note how this hypothesis contrasts with rational choice. As discussed earlier, rational choice assumes stable preferences. During a decision-making situation, preferences do not change; they are fixed. Risse suggests that these preferences are not immutable. Communicative interaction among actors can *change their preferences*; during a communicative encounter, actors can be convinced to want something that is different from what they wanted prior to this encounter. Textbox 7.4 elaborates on how to apply this approach to the study of diplomacy in more detail.

The End of the Cold War

The end of the Cold War posed a major puzzle for scholars of world politics. Established theories, emphasising continuity (i.e., stable preferences) rather than change, experienced major shortcomings to explain what happened. Risse's development of the logic of argumentation has to be seen in this context. He provides a number of empirical illustrations for his contention that there are incidences of arguing and preference change in world politics. Mikhail Gorbachev's decision to agree to a unified Germany within NATO is one of them.

Risse submits that Gorbachev and Eduard Shevardnadze, his foreign minister, had been engaged in a dialogue about a new global and European security architecture with Western powers since the mid-1980s. In the course of this dialogue, the parties created a shared lifeworld; the diplomatic encounters made them increasingly share understandings about the shortcomings of the current order and the parameters of a new one.

Gorbachev, Risse continues, approached the German question without a fixed set of preferences. Thus, he was susceptible to US Foreign Minister James Baker's argument that it would be better to have a reunified Germany embedded in Western structures than a neutral Germany that may eventually revert back to pre-1945 policies. He was also susceptible to normative arguments, most importantly the application of the 1975 Helsinki Final Act on the issue of Germany and alliances. According to the Final Act, states ought to choose their alliances freely. In May 1990, when Gorbachev declared his principal agreement with the NATO membership of a reunified Germany for the first time, he did so in response to President George Herbert Bush's framing of the issue in Helsinki terms. In short, the story Risse tells about Gorbachev is one about an uncommitted thinker who was persuaded to fundamentally break with Soviet orthodoxies of foreign policy by what were to him convincing arguments emanating from his Western counterparts.

How convincing is this account? It tells us some important things about one piece of the diplomatic puzzle that ended the Cold War. Open communication can really leave a mark. Yet it is questionable to what extent this more open communication is to be conceptualised by borrowing too much from a framework that is meant to be a counter-factual for criticising modern mass democracies. It is a highly demanding form of dialogue that is not easily found in diplomacy. Polylogues, by contrast, are less demanding but also amount to a fairly open kind of communication that has the potential to change how actors see the world and understand their preferences. Furthermore, the end of the Cold War is a case in which the world order changes fundamentally. This became possible because of a constellation of material and intersubjective forces that goes much beyond a dialogical encounter between heads of state and government. Material structure, for example, the Soviet Union's grave domestic economic problems, provided openings for diplomacy to transform the world.

Logic of Practice

What Habermas is to many students of argumentation, Pierre Bourdieu is to many scholars of practice. Authors on world politics interested in the logic of practice draw heavily from the French social theorist. Bourdieu gained the principal insights into his thought on practice from anthropological research on the Kabyle people in Algeria (Bourdieu, 1977). He amended his framework while researching the French education system (Bourdieu, 1988) and then making a more general social theory out of it (Bourdieu, 1990). But his key concepts, that is, habitus and field, have remained the key ingredients of his theorising.

The *habitus* is about the "generative principles of . . . practices" (Bourdieu, 1998: 8), or, more concretely, the "matrix of perceptions, appreciations and actions" (Bourdieu, 1977: 83) into which the individual has been socialised. This matrix *predisposes* actors to pursue certain practices rather than others. The *field* is about the organising principles of social encounters among individuals: actors participating in these encounters are not equal (power), they agree on what is at stake in these encounters (stakes), and there is a tacit consensus on the basic rules of the encounters (doxa). These organising principles put actors into (unequal) *relationships* with one another. The interplay of habitus and field generates *tacit commonsense*. This tacit commonsense amounts to reasons upon which to act. But, as the 'tacit' already indicates, these reasons are of a peculiar nature. Agents take their reasons for action too much for granted as that they could reflect upon these reasons, not even to speak of debating them among themselves.

To put this differently, no other logic of action puts as much emphasis on what happens *underneath* the radar screen of explicit communicative exchanges as the logic of practice (Pouliot, 2008). Consequentialism, especially rational choice, is all about the individual's processes of reflection. Utility maximisation, or even satisficing, is something about which actors ponder. They reflect and weigh different alternatives. The logic of appropriateness is rule-following but, at least, as it is conceptualised by students of international politics, the actors following these rules tend to be aware of them. Scholarship looks for utterances of these rules by the actors who abide by them in order to generate empirical evidence that these rules matter. The logic of argumentation, too, is very much about reflection. Actors put the social background (lifeworld) to use and debate with others what to do. The Bourdieusian view of practice, by contrast, is rather different in this regard. Actors improvise what to do and this improvisation is, ultimately, what comes naturally to them. They do not reflect upon it. Doing what comes naturally very much includes hierarchies among the actors. Textbox 7.5 elaborates on such hierarchies.

Not all research on practices and related concepts is underpinned by Bourdieu. At least three alternative conceptualisations are noteworthy. First, practices need not be entirely non-reflected doings. This reflection injects agency into theoretical frameworks, including diplomatic agency (Adler, 2005: 2–26). Second, studies inspired by Elias' work on restraint put emphasis on the social psychological foundations of restraints to use force (Bjola and Kornprobst, 2007; Adler, 2008). They are, over a period of time, made, and they are, again over a period of time, also unmade again. Third, there is what Hopf (2010) refers to as the logic of habit. This is, among the approaches to practice discussed here, the one that places the most emphasis on structure.

Textbox 7.5 The Underlying Rules of the Diplomatic Game

Focusing on hidden forms of power, many Bourdieu-inspired studies on diplomacy focus on the hierarchies among actors populating the diplomatic field. In-depth studies deal with hidden power relations at the UN (Pouliot, 2016) and the EU (Kuus, 2013), for example. This research shows that powerful nations tend to be rather successful in translating material power into privileged and very much taken-for-granted hierarchical relationships. Yet even deeply taken for granted rules of the game can change over the *longue durée*. Chapter 3 showed that the diplomatic field has expanded in terms of issue areas and actors involved. This points towards changes in the nomic – that is, deepest – layer of the diplomatic field. It is remarkable, for example, that NGOs have recently even made inroads into the nuclear non-proliferation regime. This does not mean that all non-state actors suddenly enjoy the same status as state actors, or that powerful states lose their privileges from one moment to the other. It does mean, however, that diplomatic hierarchies become more and more complex (Kornprobst and Senn, 2016a, 2017).

Performing Crises

In the past two decades, practice literature has burgeoned in international relations in general and diplomatic studies in particular. Neumann (2002), who was among the first scholars to allude to the nexus of practice and diplomacy mainly by drawing from Bourdieu, has increasingly come to link practice to performances. In a piece with Sending (Neumann and Sending, 2021), he argues that a Foreign Ministry's international crisis management can be understood as habitualised performance geared towards making the state to show presence in domestic and international politics. Studying the case of Norway, they find that diplomats put to use what Bourdieu may call doxa to make sense of a crisis. They pigeonhole a crisis into one of three categories: security crisis, humanitarian crisis or civilian crisis. These categories are hierarchical in nature. Threat is understood as high, medium, and low, respectively. Each category comes with its own repertoire of 'distinct bundles of practices' (Neumann and Sending, 2021: 3). In the case of security crises, these are about producing certainty that the state will be unharmed. Matters are handled in-house and in cooperation with the Ministry of Defence. Military and diplomatic resources are allocated. Humanitarian crises are about assuring domestic and international audiences that Norway is a 'do-gooder'. A considerable amount of the humanitarian work is outsourced to NGOs. For the Ministry, however, diplomatic results (for example reputation, standing, economic interests) are, ultimately, more important than humanitarian ones. Civilian crises are primarily about assuring Norwegians that the state is taking care of them. The Ministry handles this internally. Consular practices are used.

These findings are intriguing. Foreign ministries are bureaucracies. Diplomats get socialised into doing things in certain ways rather than others and this oftentimes becomes like second nature to them. There is not necessarily a lot of reflection. At the same time, the findings cannot be easily generalised. Neumann and Sending's study is based on detailed results from one MFA. Moreover, it would be warranted for further research to embed these findings in a broader context. What about other kinds of crises, such as health, migration, or environment? Do they exist as background categories for foreign ministries? If so, how do they look like? If not, what are the background categories and repertoires being put to use in these kinds of crises? When it comes to the environment, there is a further complicating factor. Traditionally, crises were understood as a sudden escalation of events that puts the burden on decision-makers to deescalate before things might spiral out of control. Climate change, however, is a slow escalation of climate-related events. How does this fit into pre-made crisis categories?

Another set of interesting questions is about the hierarchy of categories. Are security crises always on top? What about crises that come to be securitised such as migration? Is it possible for diplomacy to learn that the outbreak of certain diseases can have even more disastrous consequences than some security crises? What about change more generally? How do these categories change; how the repertoires that are linked to these repertoires? In practice approaches, the context always features dominantly. Categorisations and practices are assumed to be rather sticky, channelling diplomatic encounters in certain directions rather than others. Still, categories and practices do change. Our overview of the evolution of diplomacy in the previous part of the book speaks volumes about such changes. And, finally, during crises, decision-making tends to move up the executive ladder, oftentimes to a head of state or government. Summit diplomacy becomes an important means to defuse crises. What makes these decision-makers tick? To what extent do they follow their own hunches, beliefs, and experiences rather than those having settled among career diplomats?

Summary

- When it comes to studying diplomacy, most authors draw from rational choice assumptions. They conceptualise diplomats as *expected utility maximisers*. Diplomats, therefore, are assumed to calculate how to get what is the best outcome that they, locked into a decision-making situation with other players on the diplomatic stage, can achieve.
- Psychological approaches provide an alternative. Being less optimistic about the computational powers of human beings, they allude to *heuristic shortcuts* that actors use in order to make up their minds. The short-cuts provide actors with clues when to stop searching for alternatives and settle for a particular course of action.
- The logic of appropriateness focuses on the *rules* that make up the social context in which agents are embedded. These rules are assumed to be cognitive and normative in nature. Taken together, they make the world intelligible to them. Actors are assumed to act appropriately, given a set of norms. They do what appears to them as *the right thing to do*.
- The logic of argumentation deals with how agents come to *assemble arguments* from a social background, and how exchanges of arguments come to shape and re-shape how these agents figure out what to do. The latter encompasses changing preferences and even the social background.
- The key contribution of the logic of practice is that is looks at what happens underneath the radar screen of discourse. As far as the logics of consequences, appropriateness, and argumentation are concerned, scholars take for granted that making up one's mind has something to do with reflection. Scholars of practice, by contrast, hold that many things we do, we simply do *habitually*.

Study Questions

- How confident are rational choice and psychological approaches in diplomacy's abilities to make deterrence effective?
- How convincing is the logic of appropriateness in explaining how states come to shift towards more coercive diplomacy?
- Is there room for a logic of argumentation in explaining epochal change in world politics?
- How much of diplomacy is acting upon commonsense?
- Studying crisis management, are there ways to link contending logics of action together?

Recommended Further Reading

Gürkan, Seda. 2021. "Emotions in Parliamentary Diplomacy: Debating the Armenian Genocide in the European Parliament." *Global Affairs* 7 (2): 103–22.

This article discusses how standards of appropriateness shaped the EU's diplomacy via debates in the European Parliament. The author links the logic closely to emotional dimensions of communication.

Kornprobst, Markus. 2019. *Co-Managing International Crises: Judgments and Justifications*. Cambridge: Cambridge University Press.

This eclectic study on political judgements in crisis situations contends that judgements are pushed and shoved over and over by justificatory encounters in domestic and diplomatic settings.

Moshirzadeh, Homeira. 2020. "The Idea of Dialogue of Civilizations and Core-Periphery Dialogue in International Relations." *All Azimuth: A Journal of Foreign Policy and Peace* 9 (2): 211–28.

Moshirzadeh points to the heterogeneity of social backgrounds in international diplomacy and proposes ways to meaningful diplomatic communication amidst this heterogeneity. Opportunities to bridge different sets of taken-for-granted understandings, in her opinion, extend to inter-civilisational dialogue.

Qin, Y. (2020). Diplomacy as Relational Practice. *The Hague Journal of Diplomacy*, 15 (1–2), 165–173. https://doi.org/10.1163/1871191X-15101092

This article argues that diplomacy is primarily a relational practice, with the MFA serving as a key manager of international relations guided by Confucian and Mencian principles of mutual benefit and harmony.

Rathbun, Brian C., Joshua D. Kertzer, and Mark Paradis. 2017. "Homo Diplomaticus: Mixed-Method Evidence of Variation in Strategic Rationality." *International Organization* 71 (S1): S33–60.

This article makes sense of agency by bridging rational choice and political psychology. *Homo diplomaticus* (the diplomatic human being), the authors contend, links together what these scholarly perspectives keep apart.

8 Making Relations

Chapter Objectives

- To discuss diplomatic relations along a spectrum from proximity to distance.
- To uncover diplomatic relations along a continuum from horizontality to verticality.
- To address how these relations are made and unmade.

Introduction

Diplomacy makes relations. Whenever we hear that relations among states are deteriorating, stabilising or improving and so on, diplomacy has something to do with it. This chapter provides an overview of what kinds of relations diplomacy makes and unmakes, and, equally important, discusses how it does so.

We address two dimensions of diplomatic relations. First, we depict relations on a spectrum *from proximity to distance*. By this, we mean what is colloquially referred to as 'good' or 'bad' diplomatic relations. The spectrum is, in other words, not about geographic proximity or distance but about how close or troubled relations are. Second, we investigate relations on a continuum from *horizontal to vertical* relations. To what extent are diplomatic actors equal and to what degree are they hierarchical?

Once we have established these two dimensions, we inquire into how diplomacy makes and unmakes relations. Here, we draw from a number of empirical illustrations of bilateral and multilateral relations. Discussing explanations offered in the literature, we look into processes that lead to minor changes and those that even make major changes possible. When it comes to the latter, we find that there is more to it than diplomacy. Major changes in diplomatic relations are accompanied by major societal changes and identifications in and across nations.

This chapter is organised into six sections: First, we discuss relations of proximity. Second, we move to distance. Third, we direct our analytical gaze at how relations change from proximity to distance and vice versa. Fourth, we uncover horizontal relations. Fourth, we follow up with vertical ones. Fifth, we investigate how relations move from horizontality to verticality and vice versa. Sixth, we summarise our main points.

Proximity

If states would take the UN Charter more seriously and follow up on the promises they make at the General Assembly, inter-state relations would be characterised by proximity. Art 1(2) of the Charter postulates friendly relations. These are understood as necessary conditions for peace: "To develop friendly relations among nations based on respect for the principle of equal

DOI: 10.4324/9781003485407-12

rights and self-determination of peoples, and to take other appropriate measures to strengthen universal peace". At the General Assembly, states have repeatedly elaborated on the postulate of friendly relations. In 1970, the Declaration on Principles of International Law concerning Friendly Relations and Cooperation among states in accordance with the Charter of the UN (A/RES/2625(XXV)) clarifies that friendly relations encompass the 'duty of states to co-operate with one another'. In the 1970s, a number of resolutions follow up on elaborating further on friendly relations. Fostering 'mutual understanding' is an important goal and the formulation is included in various resolutions (A/RES/32/155, Art. 9; A/RES/33/73, Art. 4).

By the 1990s, elaborations on friendly relations become even more demanding. Take, for example, the 1999 Declaration and Programme of Action on a Culture of Peace: "Recognizing that peace not only is the absence of conflict, but also requires a positive, dynamic participatory process where dialogue is encouraged and conflicts are solved in a spirit of mutual understanding and cooperation" (A/RES/53/243, Preamble). The resolution identifies a range of actors, including "governments, international organizations and civil society" (A/RES/53/243, Preamble) and calls for peace to constitute relations among "individuals, groups and nations" (A/RES/53/243, Art.4). Those supposed to promote a culture of peace are "parents, teachers, politicians, journalists, religious bodies and groups, intellectuals, those engaged in scientific, philosophical and creative and artistic activities, health and humanitarian workers, social workers, managers at various levels as well as to non-governmental organizations" (A/RES/53/243, Art.8). In short, friendly relations are about mutual understanding and this mutual understanding ought to go way beyond diplomats and reach deeply into societies.

There are inter-state and even inter-societal relations that come close to these postulates. The Anglosphere is among them. Originating in colonial relations between Britain and settler communities in the Americas and Oceania, today's relations among Australia, Canada, New Zealand, and, even more so, between the UK and the United States are characterised as 'special' (Vucetic, 2011). There may be all kinds of geopolitical incentives to widen this sphere, say to include India, which is a major rising power, but deeply ingrained (and racialised) identity representations stand in the way (Davis, 2018). Within the Anglosphere, diplomatic relations are close and setbacks when they happen are short-lived. This is underpinned by plenty of transnational transactions and linkages, ranging from culture to economics. Among other things, these reproduce a shared identity.

Studies on security communities and alliances also contend that there is more proximity among some states than others. But they disagree about the degree of proximity even though they often study the same case, that is, NATO. From a security community perspective, states making up a security community co-identify to a considerable degree. This co-identification makes it appear as unthinkable for these states to lash out against one another militarily. Co-identification is again something that is not just made and maintained by diplomacy but by societal processes more generally. Deutsch's original formulation of security communities was about the frequency of transactions (broadly speaking, including communicative encounters) across the states that make up this community. Based on his empirical findings, he argued already in 1957 that NATO was not just an alliance. It was a security community. His work on security communities was almost forgotten during the Cold War but sparked plenty of interest again from the 1990s onwards (Adler and Barnett, 1998; Williams and Neumann, 2000).

This was in no small measure because of the peaceful ending of the Cold War. During the superpower rivalry, research on alliances marginalised studies on security communities. Realist scholarship assumed that the existence of NATO and the Warsaw Pact were mutually dependent on one another. NATO, in this logic, was a grouping of states trying to deter the Warsaw Pact from attacking a NATO member, and Warsaw Pact states did the same against NATO. Given this logic, the expectation was that NATO would wither away after the collapse of the Warsaw Pact (Gallagher, 2002; Harries, 1993). When this did not happen, many analysts directed their analytical gaze at security communities.

More recently, there is a resurgence of scholarly interest in NATO as an alliance. This has a lot to do with resurgent great power competition and the Russo-Ukrainian War (Sushentsov and Wohlforth, 2020; Mearsheimer, 2022; Lepskiy and Lepska, 2023). Once more, NATO is seen as an instrument to deter Russian aggression. This view is not confined to academia, of course. Some states have re-thought their strategic role in the world fundamentally since 24 February 2022. Among them are Finland and Sweden, two long-standing neutral states. The Cold War did not even make them question their neutral stance. After the Russian attack on Ukraine, however, they decided to forgo their long-standing neutrality and join NATO (Alberque and Schreer, 2022).

The largest grouping of states – apart from UN member states – to profess relations of proximity to one another is the Non-Aligned Movement (NAM). NAM's key principles were agreed upon at the 1955 Bandung Conference. A joint diplomatic initiative of Egypt, Ghana, India, Indonesia, and Yugoslavia conducted at the highest level – by Gamal Abdel Nasser, Kwame Nkrumah, Jawaharlal Nehru, Sukarno and Josip Broz Tito, respectively – led to the formal establishment of NAM in 1961. NAM states agree on a broad policy agenda, ranging from nuclear disarmament to sustainable development and from a reform of the Security Council to the need for more South-South cooperation. In order to facilitate the latter, the Non-Aligned Movement Centre for South-South Technical Cooperation, headquartered in Jakarta with offices in Cuba, India, and Iran, has been set up. NAM's greatest strength is its size. NAM represents almost two-thirds of UN member states and well over half the world's population. But this enormous size is also its greatest weakness. It amounts to a major challenge to mould meaningful common positions out of this great heterogeneity. Thus, it is not a coincidence that the 2024 Kampala Declaration speaks about the need for reinvigorating NAM (Non-Aligned Movement, 2024).

Distance

Close proximity and great distance are oftentimes two sides of the same coin.[1] Consider the more tightly knit examples of state groupings earlier in the text. The Anglosphere differentiates between those historically part of this sphere and those who are not. Broadening the Anglosphere beyond in-group is nothing that comes natural or easy to the in-group (and probably not to many outgroups either). Literature on security communities and alliances may disagree upon all kinds of things. But they do agree that security communities and alliances develop in response to a threat. To put this more succinctly, in security communities the co-identification comes at the expense of demarcation from significant others. Similarly, the alliance literature holds that alliances form in response to potentially hostile actions on behalf of other states and/or state groupings.

Distant state relations come in different variations. Distances can be constituted by hostile relations. These range from open warfare (such as Russia and Ukraine) to enduring rivalries (say between India and Pakistan). Located further away from the antagonistic extreme of hostility, we find relations that may be dubbed agnostic. There are formal diplomatic relations but very little substance to it. Very few states can afford a network of diplomatic missions in every state they recognise as a state. Much more frequently, embassies are to serve a group of states. The ambassador resides in one of these states, makes occasional visits to the other ones and relies on other aides, for example, honorary consuls, to keep up some kind of presence.

Very few EU member states, for example, have embassies all over Africa. Most of them focus on major players such as the North African states, Ghana, Ethiopia, Kenya, Nigeria, and South Africa. Increasingly, they also 'farm out' diplomatic relations with states considered to be less important to the European Union External Action Service, which has a presence in every singly African state.

Distant relations, above all hostile ones, tend to be sticky. Take the example of the relations between the United States and North Korea.[2] Ever since the Korean War, relations have been hostile. Mending relations is complicated by a range of factors including the politics of memory of the war in both countries and the absence of official relations between them. Thus, diplomatic encounters have to rely on informal channels and intermediaries. Nevertheless, several US administrations attempted to improve relations with North Korea. Their main motive was to diffuse tensions between South Korea, an important ally of the United States in the region, and to dissuade Pyongyang from building nuclear weapons. In the cooperative atmosphere of the 1990s, it seemed that even US-North Korean relations could finally be changed towards the better.

Facilitated by former US President Jimmy Carter, and mainly negotiated by high-ranking officials from the foreign ministries of both countries, Robert Gallucci and Kang Sok Ju, the 1994 Agreed Framework appeared to be a landmark agreement. North Korea agreed to freeze its plutonium enrichment programme and allow for IAEA inspections to verify it. The United States provided a number of incentives, most importantly the promise to build light water reactor power plants (these make diversion of civilian to military uses of nuclear power much more difficult comparing to the existing reactors in North Korea). Both parties also agreed to normalise their relations, seek more cooperation, and work towards the goals of the NPT.

The agreement, however, unravelled in the following years amidst mutual allegations. Progress with building the light water nuclear reactors proved to be very slow. Since it took a long time for an international consortium to be founded and then to secure the funding for it, not much progress happened before 2001. In the meantime, Republicans gained control over the US Senate and voiced their dissatisfaction with the Framework Agreement. Deeply mistrusting the North Korean regime of Kim Jong-il, they considered any kind of attempt of a rapprochement utopian. The US General Accounting Office (1 October 1996) maintained that the Agreed Framework is a 'nonbinding political agreement' or 'nonbinding international agreement' rather than an international treaty or legal document. George W. Bush accused North Korea of being part of an 'axis of evil' in his 2002 State of the Union Address. North Korea responded in no uncertain terms. It ended the freeze on plutonium processing, striving with ever more vigour to acquire nuclear weapons.

A new round of talks started in 2003. The Six-Party Talks brought together the six key players in Northeast Asia: Japan, North Korea, South Korea, as well as the great powers of China, Russia, and the United States. During the talks, North Korea oscillated between cooperative and defiant stances. On the one hand, Pyongyang conducted nuclear tests in 2006 and 2009, and also several missile tests. On the other hand, North Korea seemed again to be susceptible to positive sanctions such as fuel aid and food aid. At various points in time, the state temporarily agreed to nuclear inspections and shut down its Yongbyon nuclear facility. Kim Yong-il died in December 2011, giving hope that the pattern may change under his successor Kim Jong-un. These hopes were short-lived, however. Kim Yong-il's successor, Kim Jong-un, has continued to move the nuclear programme forward.

In the late 2010s, relations went from bad to worse when President Trump announced that he would take a tougher stance on Kim Jong-un, denouncing his regime as 'reckless and brutal' (France Presse, 2017). What followed was an almost unprecedented duel between Trump and Kim in public speeches at home and on Twitter (now X). Trump promised to his constituents to do away with "mad men, shooting rockets all over the place" and asserted that "rocket man should have been handled a long time ago; little rocket man" (Guardian News, 2017). In exchange, Kim called Trump 'dotard' and threatened that he has a nuclear button on his desk (CNN, 2019). Next day, the US president (Trump, 2018) tweeted that he, too, "has a Nuclear Button [sic], but it is a much bigger & more powerful one than his, and my Button [sic] works!"

Only half a year later, the two leaders met in Singapore and, to the surprise of many, agreed upon a declaration to change relations fundamentally. The two sides promised to open up a new chapter in their bilateral relations and work towards peace on the Korean Peninsula, including its 'complete denuclearisation'. Furthermore, North Korea agreed to return the remains of US soldiers fallen during the Korean War (Wootliff, 2018). These were big promises but they were very lofty. While the diplomatic habitus is usually about moving negotiations along carefully and incrementally, and concluding documents that are usable in diplomatic practice afterwards, the process leading to the Singapore Declaration was heavily dependent on the two leaders and they steered clear of making any meaningful commitments. As Andrei Lankov, a North Korea expert, put it: "We expected it to be a flop, but it's floppier than anything we expected. The declaration is pretty much meaningless" (cited in Snyder, 2021).

What is interesting about this case is that different leaders – on both sides – tried to accomplish the same with different means over and over. They wanted to better relations. But no matter what leaders were involved and what means were chosen, they failed. Textbox 8.1 deals with a similar case of failure, that is, US-Iranian relations. While it is possible to change hostile relations into friendly ones, diplomacy alone – such as well-meaning external messaging or negotiations – are not enough. A more profound societal change is needed as well.

Textbox 8.1 US-Iranian Relations

Prior the Iranian Revolution in 1979, relations between the United States and Iran had been close. Since the revolution, however, relations have been fraught with difficulties. The United States has been demonised by successive theocratic Supreme Leaders, who, in no small measure, legitimise their rule by demarcating themselves from the United States. Vice versa, Iran has featured as a major villain in US foreign policy discourse for decades. The states have no official diplomatic relations, which makes opening communication channels very difficult. Yet at times both sides recognise that such open channels are needed. In 2013, the EU's attempts to make the United States and Iran meaningfully speak to one another on Iran's nuclear programme led to the first tangible success. Iran, the P5 and the EU agreed to the Joint Plan of Action. In April 2015, a framework agreement followed. In July 2015, the parties agreed to the Joint Comprehensive Plan of Action (JCPA). The JCPA is a complex document that lays down a multi-phase implementation process. The most important steps are the following: In the first six months, Iran has to remove more than 13,000 centrifuges, reduce its stockpile of low-enriched uranium to no more than 300 kg, disable the core of the Arak heavy-water reactor, and make all necessary arrangements for verification with the IAEA. In the first five years of implementation, Iran had to limit the number of IR-1 centrifuges to 5,060 and limit its research and development of advanced centrifuges. There are a number of steps specified for the first ten, fifteen, and twenty and twenty-five years of implementation. Key provisions such as the commitment not to reprocess spent fuel, continuous surveillance of centrifuge production areas as well as uranium mines and mills, IAEA safeguards and additional protocols and, of course, the ban to pursue nuclear weapons, do not have a time limit. In return, the P5 and the EU agreed to a phased lifting of sanctions. This applies to multilateral sanctions such as those imposed by the Security Council as well as bilateral ones such as those imposed by the United States.

It is interesting to note that the preface of the JCPA addresses the re-making of relations. All parties emphasise that confidence-building is a crucial goal:

> Iran envisions that this JCPOA will allow it to move forward with an exclusively peaceful, indigenous nuclear programme, in line with scientific and economic considerations, in accordance with the JCPOA, and with a view to building confidence and encouraging international cooperation.
>
> The E3/EU+3 envision that the implementation of this JCPOA will progressively allow them to gain confidence in the exclusively peaceful nature of Iran's programme.

The JCPOA, however, became a victim of domestic politics. Donald Trump tried his utmost to derail the implementation of the agreement, sticking to an extreme vilification narrative of Iran. The Iranian leadership responded in kind.

From Distance to Proximity

From the creation of the German state in 1871 to the end of World War II, Franco-German relations were hostile. There were only two variations of this hostility: open warfare and a *guerre froide*, that is, a cold war. This metaphor, later on widely used to describe US-Soviet relations (more about this in the next chapter on international orders), was first used in France to make sense of relations to Germany in the early 1930s (Freedman, 2010).

After the end of World War II, however, relations between the two states changed fundamentally. They did so bilaterally and within the framework of European unification efforts. When it comes the former, the 1963 Élysée Treaty provides the foundation for the Franco-German friendship. The treaty, albeit more declaratory than legally binding in nature, played an important symbolic step for breaking from past cycles of hostility. Since then, many more cooperation agreements have been concluded. They aim not only at improving diplomatic relations but at weaving an ever-tighter network linking the two societies together. The latter is about fundamentally transforming relations in Europe and not just between France and Germany. From the beginnings of the European Coal and Steel Community, integration efforts moved via the European Economic Communities to the European Community and on to the EU. Due to European integration efforts, relations between France and Germany reached a kind of supranational proximity that is almost diametrically opposed to the past relations of utmost distance.

How did European states – France and Germany, but also about two dozen other states – embark on supranationality? Two scholarly perspectives provide two different answers. On the one hand, there are approaches that put emphasis on IGN. Liberal Intergovernmentalism (Moravcsik, 1999), for example, focuses on how state governments – influenced by powerful constituents – act *selfishly*. Integration is understood as something that does not happen in one sweep but is an evolving *process*. National governments are seen as the drivers of integration.

Whether steps of integration are taken or not – say the Single European Act, the Maastricht Treaty, or the Treaty of Lisbon – is up to national governments. This reserves some room for diplomacy. Ultimately, it is up to diplomacy to negotiate these steps. But the outcomes of these negotiations is understood in rational choice terms. There is little wiggle room for diplomacy. Negotiations are, to use a term we employed in a chapter earlier in this volume, not an art. They can be, based on the preferences of the governments, predicted.

On the other hand, there are approaches that borrow from a functionalist logic. For Mitrany, the actors are experts. In his *A Working Peace System*, Mitrany (1946) maintains that experts are the agents of integration, pushing for integration in narrowly confined areas when the functional need arises. Through this integration in a narrowly confined issue area, new functional needs for integration may arise (*spill-over*), and so on. Over time, there would be more and more functional integration in – and across – more and more issue areas. Mitrany even predicted that, over time, *people's loyalty would shift* from the nation-state to the functionally integrating polity. In other words, even the attachment to the nation-state would wither away. Mitrany's work not only influenced generations of scholars but also practitioners, perhaps most importantly Jean Monnet (see Textbox 8.2).

Ernst Haas's *The Uniting of Europe* is the foundational text of neofunctionalism (Haas, 1958). This work can be read as an attempt to introduce politics into functionalist thought. Based on his observations about European integration efforts in the 1950s, he argues that experts and functional integration play an important role. But politics remains in charge of letting functional integration happen. Neo-neofunctionalism (Schmitter, 2004), too, is not just about functional

---

Textbox 8.2 Jean Monnet

Jean Monnet was never a traditional diplomat who moved through the ranks at the French foreign office. Nevertheless, he was a highly influential player on the diplomatic field for many decades. At the Versailles Conference, he was a close advisor to Etienne Clémentel, who was the French minister of commerce and industry. Monnet advocated a much more conciliatory and co-operative peace in Europe but failed with his advocacy. The same year, he became Deputy Secretary-General of the newly founded League of Nations. During World War II, Monnet was a member of France's National Liberation Council in Algiers. Even here, he advocated for a new Europe. The fact that World War II was raging was not a reason for him to forgo his conviction that Europe could only be at peace if its nations would integrate; on the very contrary, it made him hold on to this belief even more. In the aftermath of World War II, Monnet worked for the like-minded Foreign Minister Robert Schuman, and authored the Schuman Declaration in 1950. The Declaration emphasises that "Europe will not be made all at once, or according to a single plan. It will be built through concrete achievements which first create a de facto solidarity". The 'concrete achievements' refer to successful functional integration. The force ascribed to it is formidable; formidable enough for the "elimination of the age-old opposition of France and Germany", which the Declaration considers the *sine qua non* for peace in Europe (European Union, 2020). The functional decision-making organ of the Coal and Steel Community was the High Authority. Monnet became its first president. He also played an important role in the creation of the European Economic Community, mainly through the Action Committee for the United States of Europe, which he founded.

> **Textbox 8.3   Metis**
>
> Although Iver Neumann (2002) tried to familiarise scholars of diplomacy with the concept of 'metis' some time ago, it still remains widely neglected. Metis is the agential power to change relations. It has three defining features: First, someone who has metis knows how to make use of a favourable situation. Metis is the acquired experience to help create and seize opportunities for change. Crises of everyday routines are possible when actors are confronted with social constellations in which the usual indeterminacies of interpreting the world are especially pronounced. In these moments of openness – the technical term used for this in rhetorical theory is *kairos* – actors can change structures. For the most part, these opportunities themselves are none of their doing. The indeterminacies appear mainly because of external circumstances, for example an exogenous shock. Yet actors have some room to enlarge these windows of opportunity. They can spell out the crisis of pre-established meaning that actors are confronted with in a particular situation. Most importantly, metis enables actors to seize these windows of opportunity. Actors who have metis do not lose their orientation when a community experiences situational difficulties in interpreting the world. On the contrary, they understand these indeterminacies as chances for changing the world (Detienne and Vernant, 1991: 295–6; De Certeau, 1988). Thinking about illustrative examples, the authors of the European unification process, especially Schuman and Monnet as well as Adenauer and Hallstein, come immediately to mind. They were determined to break with centuries of enmity between France and Germany. In the late 1940s and early 1950s, the shocks of World War II and the Holocaust constituted an opportunity for these actors to start authoring a new chapter of European history. In doing so, Europe's past disasters became an important Other from which Europeans ought to demarcate themselves as strongly as possible (Wæver, 1996).[3]

pressures but also about political processes involving governments, associations and individuals. This is an important departure from Mitrany. It leaves more room for diplomacy, for example to deal with a crisis such as the sovereign debt crisis. Yet the thrust of functionalist thought stays in place. Functionalist pressures are the key force making nations move closer and closer together; political agents are deeply constrained by these pressures; they 'overshadow' them (Schmitter, 2004: 61).

Many more explanations can be offered for what Haas refers to as the uniting of Europe. The beliefs and agency of leaders as well as how they played their diplomatic cards in an environment that provided an opening for new ideas mattered quite a bit. Textbox 8.3 discusses the concept of 'metis' and what it can do in diplomacy.

Of late, scholarship on the EU has been challenged by explaining setbacks. Literature that emerged in response to an ever deeper (integration) and ever broader (enlargement) European unification process suddenly had to explain the rise of parties and public opinion that endorse nation-states and are highly sceptical of supranationalism in general and the EU in particular. They had to explain why the citizens of an important state – the United Kingdom – (narrowly) voted for Brexit. Overall, this added new facets to the literature on the EU. Recent research, for example, is full of new insights into how public opinion and the resilience of the EU hang together (Howarth and Schild, 2021; Foster and Frieden, 2021). Diplomacy, however, remains confined to the backseat of the analysis in most studies even though it is an important part of the puzzle. Long-ruling right wing populist regimes such as in Hungary and Poland, for example, at times play their diplomatic cards unexpectedly, rather skilfully and effectively, testing out the limits of what they can achieve for themselves without crossing red lines that would mobilise other EU member states to strongly move against them (Hettyey, 2021; Dyduch and Müller, 2021).

From Proximity to Distance and Back

While France and Germany, and with them many other European states, moved from hostility to friendship and, current problems facing the EU notwithstanding, even to supranationality, other empirical examples have moved back and forth between friendship and hostility in a much shorter time frame. Relations between Eritrea and Ethiopia are particularly intriguing. If the creation of Franco-German enmity in the 19th century came with the creation of the German state, the independence of Eritrea from Ethiopia marked the beginning of an Eritrean-Ethiopian friendship.

Eritreans fought for their independence from Ethiopia for three decades. From 1961 to 1974, several independence movements opposed Ethiopia's Emperor Haile Selassie I. After the Ethiopian revolution in 1974, Eritrean liberation movements fought the Derg, the military junta that followed the Emperor. In the 1980s, one movement – the Eritrean People's Liberation Front (EPLF) – came to dominate the resistance. The EPLF defined itself (and the Eritrean people) very much in juxtaposition to Ethiopia. The relations to Ethiopia woven into the identity narrative were one of enmity.

During the fight against the Derg regime, the EPLF came to join forces with the Tigray People's Liberation Front (TPLF). The purposes of their struggles were different. The EPLF fought for Eritrean independence whereas the TPLF sought to replace the Derg regime. Yet facilitated by a common enemy – the Derg – cordial relations developed the two movements. In 1988, they agreed that the TPLF, when it succeeded in ousting the regime, would support a referendum about Eritrean independence. EPLF and TPLF defeated the Derg in 1991. The TPLF stood by its word. A UN supervised referendum about independence was held in 1993, and Eritrea became independent. Ostensibly trying to transform itself into a political party, the EPLF changed its name to People's Front for Democracy and Justice, and moved towards forging a stronger Eritrean national identity. The need for this was all too clear to President Isaias Afwerki. During the independence struggle, he had experienced the splintering of independence movements along ethnic, religious and linguistic lines. Forging a stronger identity – not atypical for a newly independent state at all – was, therefore, important to him. The liberation struggle served as a major source of inventing an identity narrative that was meant to rally Eritreans around the flag. Ethiopia featured prominently in this narrative. Ethiopia is portrayed as an imperialist and expansionist state (Gilkes and Plaut, 1999).

Forging a stronger identity went hand in hand with becoming more assertive on the international stage. Initially, this was done in tandem with the new Ethiopian government. For example, both governments responded to Sudanese attempts to destabilise Ethiopia and Eritrea by supporting rebel movements in these two countries in the same fashion. Addis Ababa and Asmara started to sponsor rebel movements in the Sudan. Yet triggered by the ambiguities of a not yet demarcated border, Eritrea responded with determined force to what Isaias perceived as Ethiopian infringements on Eritrean territory in the border area around Badme.

Friendship had turned into enmity. This enmity was fuelled by a dominant identity narrative that interpreted the present almost exclusively in terms of a selective reading of the past. Eritrean observers of the border dispute believed that "things have not changed since the time of

Menelik II. Ethiopians have always been obsessed with the sea" (Dahli, 2000: 1). Eritrean diplomats echoed this in unequivocal terms, alleging that the "old Ethiopian foreign policy tactic is repeating itself" (Tekle, 2000: 1), and even that "their insane dream is to enslave the Eritrean people as well as plunder the country" (Asghedom, 1999: 1). In short, history came to haunt Eritrean-Ethiopian relations once more. Eritrea interpreted the actions of Ethiopia through the prism of a formerly colonised and subjugated people that had the resolve to fight for its sovereign statehood within its historic boundaries (Kornprobst, 2002).

The Eritrean-Ethiopian War, fought from 1998 to 2000, may have cost as many as 100,000 people their lives. About a third of the Eritrean population was displaced. Without determined outside diplomatic interventions, mainly by the United States but also by the OAU and the EU, it is unlikely that the fighting would have come to an end in 2000 (Prendergast, 2001). Despite all kinds of mediation and arbitration efforts, a political settlement of the border dispute remained elusive, however. This changed dramatically when Abiy Ahmed became Prime Minister in 2018. Domestically, the new prime minister broke the Tigrayans hold on power in Ethiopia. In November 2020, a conflict between the Tigrayan province and the federation spiralled out of control. Abiy Ahmed then resorted to a rather unusual strategy. He settled the border disputes with Eritrea and even signed a friendship agreement with the neighbour. In return, Eritrean soldiers moved into Tigray, helping the federal government and its military to wage a merciless war against Tigray, its civilian population very much included. To Afwerki, the Tigrayans were to blame for the border war twenty years earlier. After the joint attack on the Tigrayans, relations between Ethiopia and Eritrea soured yet again.

The Eritrean-Ethiopian case is very different from the Franco-German one and the making of the EU. But one thing these cases share in common. Explaining major changes on the proximity-distance continuum needs to look at societal factors, including the politics of memory, as much as it needs to study diplomacy. Or, to put this differently, there are all kinds of words in the diplomatic dictionary that describe important points on how states move closer towards proximity. In the language of the past diplomatic lingua franca – French – these include the following: détente (relaxation of tensions), rapprochement (moving closer to one another), and entente (informal alliance). But the diplomatic toolkit only goes thus far to explain how these relations are produced.

Horizontality

When Article 2 of the UN Charter lists the principles upon which the organisation is founded, sovereign equality is the first one that is listed (Art 2(1)): "The Organization is based on the principle of the sovereign equality of all its Members". The same applies to foundational texts of any regional grouping. In ASEAN's Treaty of Amity and Co-operation, for example, sovereign equality is found in Art 2(a). In the OAS's Charter, it is found in Art 1, 3a and 10. Textbox 8.4 looks back at attempts of the League of Nations to institutionalise horizontal relations.

Producing and reproducing horizontal relations is always a challenge. Nevertheless, it is not difficult to point to cases where relations located on various points of the horizontal side of the continuum made a major impact. In the UN General Assembly, for instance, every state is represented and entitled to participate in discussions, legal drafting, and voting on equal terms. Small nations, if they play the diplomatic game skilfully, can make a lot out of these procedural rules. To mention just a few intriguing cases, it was not a major power but Trinidad and Tobago that requested the General Assembly to ask the International Law Commission to revive preparations for an international criminal court. This happened in 1989. About a decade later, parties agreed upon the Rome Statute. It was not a great power that pushed the General Assembly

> **Textbox 8.4   The League of Nations, Promises of Horizontality, and Persisting Verticality**
>
> It is interesting to note that the institutional set-up of the League of Nations was closer to ideals of sovereign equality than the one of the UN. The League had three main organs: Assembly, Council and Secretariat. Every member state was represented at the Assembly and had voting rights at the Assembly. The Council was a smaller decision-making body made up by permanent and non-permanent members. The Secretariat consisted of international civil servants. This may appear to be very similar to the UN and in some ways it is. But there were some critical differences. Most importantly, Article 3 of the Covenant of the League of Nations empowered the Assembly to "deal at its meetings with any matter within the sphere of action of the League or affecting the peace of the world". In the end, however, these stronger legal provisions for sovereign equality could not counter deeply internalised vertical relations and prevent the collapse of the organisation. From the 1935 Abyssinian Crisis onwards, the League could no longer meaningfully shape matters of peace and war in the world. Italy, led by Benito Mussolini, invaded Abyssinia (Ethiopia). To the Italian invaders, the lives of Africans counted very little. Among the atrocities they committed was the use of chemical weapons against Ethiopian civilians (Fuller, 2022: 7–8). We are back at deeply seated – in this case racist – vertical understandings. Reactions, mainly economic sanctions, by the League were largely symbolic in nature and far removed from a determined response that collective security would have demanded. During World War II, the League merely survived as a shell. The buildings in Geneva remained largely empty. In 1946, the organisation was formally dissolved, to be replaced with the UN.

into negotiating a treaty to ban nuclear weapons either. The Humanitarian Initiative that gained momentum from 2010 onwards started with a network of smaller states and middle powers, including Austria, Chile, Mexico, Norway, Switzerland, and South Africa.

In regional organisations, too, sovereign equality has the potential to help states make an impact that would be unlikely to do so given their military or economic capabilities. Most regional organisations are intergovernmental. Thus, sovereign equality makes a difference. And even those that are not feature small nations with a track record of making an impact. Luxemburg, for example, has certainly punched way above its weight in the EU and its predecessor organisations (Harmsen and Högenauer, 2020).

Sovereign equality is a legal design. A different kind of horizontal relations is constituted by a distribution of power and status among major powers that is about equal. In global politics, the Cold War is often understood as a balance between two superpowers, that is, the United States and Soviet Union. In regional politics, states such as France and Germany in the EU, Egypt, Nigeria, and South Africa in the AU, or Argentina and Brazil in the OAS are rather powerful but they cannot get a lot done without doing things together.

Status can, under rare circumstances, even make for horizontal relations with actors that are, according to diplomatic law, not diplomats at all. Celebrity diplomats are a good example. Summit diplomacy in the early 2000s put a celebrity diplomat such as Bono *en par* with the leaders of great powers, including the US President George W. Bush. Being a celebrity endowed him with a certain measure of status from the start. Playing his diplomatic cards right on a stage that was not all that familiar to him at the beginning made sure that he could further augment this status.

Verticality

Occurrences of horizontal relations notwithstanding, there are plenty of vertical relations in diplomatic relations. The most extreme form of vertical relations is *dehumanisation.* Being no longer recognised as a human being, the enemy is vilified as someone who is not worth living. Joachim von Rippentrop, first Hitler's ambassador in London and then foreign minister, turned Germany's diplomacy into a facilitator of war and genocide. The foreign office was in charge of diffusing propaganda to obfuscate the Holocaust and justify the war. It was also in charge of providing administrative support for the SS and the deportation of Jews in occupied territories, such as France. The Nuremberg Trials found him guilty of crimes against peace, waging a war of aggression, war crimes, and crimes against humanity. He was hanged on October 16, 1946 (Seabury, 1954). Von Rippentrop's crimes serve as a chilling reminder that diplomacy is not always the opposite of violence; it can also be a willing instrument supporting violence.

Other instantiations of vertical relations are less extreme but much more frequent. There is, first of all, the issue of being recognised as a diplomatic actor. The Bonos of this world notwithstanding, it is first and foremost states who are recognised actors and as such entitled to step on the diplomatic stage. A territorial entity such as Somaliland may look very much like a state but it is not recognised as such and, therefore, its representatives are not recognised as diplomats. Other territorial entities are closer to fully recognised statehood. Palestine is a very unusual case. It is a full member of UNESCO but not the UN, where it is merely a non-member observer state. It is a party to a number of instruments, including the Rome Statute, the Geneva Conventions, and the Hague Conventions. Most UN member states recognise Palestine as a state, among these almost all states in the Global South. But most Western states do not.

Among UN member states, not everything is about horizontal relations either, of course. Some vertical relations are fully out in the open. Most importantly, there are five permanent members of the Security Council – China, France, Russia, the United Kingdom and the United States – and these so-called P5 have the right to veto a vote. This means among other things that resolutions cannot be adopted with the dissensus of any one of the P5. The ten non-permanent members do not have the right to veto but at least they are present during formal and informal sessions of the Security Council. But even here, they tend to be considerably less active, for example, in pen holding and drafting resolutions, than the P5. The P5, as Pouliot put it, are on top of the 'pecking order' (Pouliot, 2016). Note that this form of hierarchy is not out in the open. Nowhere does the Charter or any rules of procedure endow the P5 with more authority than the non-permanent members. This happens because of entrenched background understandings and practices that are hardly ever reflected upon. We are back to where we left off in the previous chapter, that is, with the logic of practice.

Similar dynamics prevail in regional organisations. In the EU, France and Germany – and arguably Western European powers more generally – have more clout than smaller member states, especially those located further in the east. Kuus uncovers hidden forms of hierarchy between West and East (Kuus, 2007), which are not all that different from what Pouliot finds in the Security Council. Similar arguments could be made with regard to Argentina and Brazil as well as Egypt, Nigeria, and South Africa, mentioned earlier, and many other regional constellations.

Yet these relations are never carved into stone and there is plenty of contestation about them. In the 1980s, Zimbabwe rose to become the protagonist among the Front-Line States (Angola,

Botswana, Lesotho, Mozambique, Tanzania, Zambia, and Zimbabwe) opposing Apartheid-South Africa in Southern Africa. When Apartheid finally ended and Nelson Mandela became president, South African-Zimbabwean relations seemed to be poised to be amicable and horizontal. After all, Zimbabwe's long-term President Robert Mugabe had been an important supporter of Mandela's ANC. Relations turned out to be much more troubled, however. Mugabe resented playing second fiddle in the region. Southern African Development Community (SADC) became an arena in which he sought to contest South African leadership (Dashwood, 2001).

Contestation about horizontalising vertical relations is also a key feature of global politics. It comes at least in four notable variants: First, great powers tend to be very reluctant to accept vertical relations with other great powers. In 2014, US President Obama's saying that Russia is merely a 'regional power' humiliated the Russian leadership around Putin, probably prompting it to project more power abroad rather than less (Borger, 2014). Instead, great powers often try to establish vertical relations in their favour. Textbox 8.5 speaks volumes about these practices. Second, rising powers seek to be accepted into the club of great powers. Among the BRICS states, Brazil, India, and South Africa are rising powers and, among them, India appears to have the most potential to become a great power. Its attempts to rise in international status are well documented in the literature (Nayar and Paul, 2003; Ogden, 2023; Paul, 2024a). Third, state groupings may be dissatisfied with their positioning in the international hierarchy. In current discussions, there are many postulates about the rise of the Global South (Grovogu, 2011; Gray and Gills, 2016). Fourth, there are intriguing questions of how non-state actors relate to state actors. On the one hand, they often remain marginalised. NGOs, for example, may succeed in helping push states to the negotiation table. But they are not parties to international organisations or legally binding instruments. Thus, they are not present at the negotiation table. On the other hand, they can play increasingly powerful roles. Giacomello and Eriksson (2023: 73), for example, write about 'the rise of the nerd'. Tech experts – the 'nerds' – have knowledge that others do not have. Dependence on this knowledge makes them rise in the international hierarchy.

Textbox 8.5   Kissinger, China, and the United States

Before the early 1970s, the United States recognised the Republic of China (Taiwan) as the official government of China. Washington did not have formal relations with the People's Republic of China (PRC). The latter, however, was an important player. Having emerged victoriously from the Chinese Civil War in 1949, Mao Zedong – the PRC's founder and leader – made the seemingly natural alliance choice in favour of the Soviet Union. After all, the two major powers shared a Marxist-Leninist ideology. The PRC's taking sides with the Soviet Union in the Cold War was a blow to the United States. Two powerful states stood together against Washington. Kissinger, while in office as national security advisor of President Nixon, tried to move China away from the Soviet Union and further towards the United States. There was an opportunity because Mao Zedong and Nikita Khrushchev, Stalin's successor in the Soviet Union, had major disagreements on how to advance Marxism-Leninism in world politics. Kissinger made the most of this opportunity. He opened up back-channels for diplomacy, secretly travelled to Beijing in 1971, and thus prepared President Nixon's visit to the PRC in February 1972. The rapprochement with China was a vehicle for making sure that the global distribution of capabilities would remain in favour of the United States.

From Vertical to Horizontal Relations?

On the face of it, the diplomatic system has become more and more horizontal in the last two centuries. In the early 19th century, Spain released most of its Latin American colonies into freedom (and Portugal did the same with Brazil). In the late 1940s, the UK, the Netherlands, France, and the United States ended most of their colonial rule in Asia. Finally, in the late 1950s and early 1960s, European colonisers withdrew from most of Africa (the big exception was Portugal, which followed only in the mid-1970s). As a result of these waives of decolonisation (as well as the breakdown of the Soviet Union and other states in the 1990s), there are now about 200 states in the world, most of which are members of the UN. What the UN refers to as the group of Western European and other States (including Australia, Canada, New Zealand and the United States) make for 29 states and there are 23 Eastern European States. Compare this to 33 Latin American and Caribbean States, 55 Asia-Pacific States and 53 African States (United Nations, n.d.a). European states, once the epicentre of the diplomatic system, ruling over colonised nations and denying them any kind of diplomatic representation, are greatly outnumbered by states from Africa, Asia, and Latin America.

These numbers should matter in a diplomatic world structured by sovereign equality. But do they really? Has diplomacy actually moved towards more horizontal relations? The scholarly literature provides us with three kinds of (partly competing) hypotheses: First, sovereign equality levels the playing field. It is, in the words of Jackson (1990: 6), 'liberating for weak states'. They gain more influence than they could otherwise, qua their power, have. Most importantly, they no longer have to fear to be attacked by stronger states. Even failed states – those states that lack the capacity to rule throughout their territories – persist. Second, while sovereign equality makes relations between states more horizontal than they otherwise would be, powerful states do build hierarchies as well. On the one hand, Viola, Snidal, and Zürn (2015) assert, institutions such as legal equality and the principle of non-intervention that comes with it makes for more horizontal relations. On the other hand, however, power differentials matter for the making of institutions and how they are developed further (Viola, Snidal and Zürn, 2015). Textbox 8.6 discusses a possible means to counter vertical relations in international institutions. Third, legal hierarchies have increasingly been replaced with more hidden forms of hierarchies, and the latter are highly consequential. Given these hidden forms of hierarchy, sovereign equality is nothing but a 'myth' (Mathieu, 2020: 339). From this point of view, colonialism evolved into

---

Textbox 8.6   Dag Hammerskjöld on the International Civil Servant

In his much-debated 1961 Oxford lecture, UN Secretary-General Dag Hammerskjöld cautioned against an intergovernmental UN Secretariat and pleaded for a truly international one. To Hammerskjöld, the international civil servant was an important vehicle for changing relations among states fundamentally. An intergovernmental Secretariat would be staffed by nation-states. States would then use 'their' civil servants to reproduce relations of distance rather than proximity and engage in positioning battles as opposed to establishing horizontal relations. Independent international civil servants, by contrast, would put UN principles, most importantly the Charter, ahead of national positions. This he expected to make for more proximate and horizontal relations (Dag Hammarskjöld Foundation, 2021).

postcolonialism (Darby and Paolini, 1994; Adem, 2014; Pourmokhtari, 2013; Young, 2016a). Hierarchies are no longer maintained by legal language but by material and intersubjective structures of dependence.

These three arguments provide highly generalising accounts that are, depending on the concrete constellation of relations under empirical investigation, sometimes more useful and sometimes less. Current literature on African diplomacy shows cases in which African diplomats exert plenty of agency in Africa and also the world (Brown, 2012; Coleman, Kornprobst and Seegers, 2019; Munyi, Mwambari and Ylönen, 2020). At the same time, empirical research also uncovers various forms of dependence and exploitation. For Opondo, for example, a case is to be made to 'decolonise' diplomacy (Opondo, 2010). The 'decolonise' means here to put an end to postcolonial relations and replace them with more horizontal ones.

Consider the following case that speaks volumes about sovereign equality, dependence, postcolonial relations. In the late 1950s and early 1960s, Africa's emerging leaders had two competing visions for Africa. One, advocated by the Casablanca Group, revolved around Pan-Africanism. Leaders such as Kwame Nkrumah (Ghana), Sékou Touré (Guinea), Muhammad Osman Said (Libya), and Gamal Abdel-Nasser rejected the application of a nation-state system to Africa. They advocated for an integrated African political system. In their reasoning, only such a One Africa would be able to thrive, steer clear of neocolonialism, that is, economic dependency, and avoid being dominated by outside powers through a strategy of divide and rule. The other, the Monrovia Group, put much less emphasis on Pan-Africanism and took a stance for independent African states. Key members of this group included the two longer-time independent African states of Ethiopia and Liberia as well as most former French colonies. Eventually, the OAU Charter formulated a lop-sided compromise between these two positions. There was mentioning of Pan-Africanism. But the nation-state system was applied to Africa. Decades later, the AU Constitutive Act appeared to be more resolved to move further towards Pan-Africanism (and again Ghana and Libya were the driving forces behind it), but few tangible steps towards more supranationality have been taken.

Explaining the making of the lop-sided compromise requires plenty of nuance. One Africa would have questioned the statehood of Ethiopia, priding itself as one of the oldest states in the world. Some African leaders feared for their newly gained power. And, last but not least, the former colonial states much preferred the export of the nation-state model to Africa. This especially applied to France. From the late 1950s onwards, French presidents established close personal relations with their African counterparts. Thus, French diplomacy spun a tightly knit network (*réseaux*) between France and its former African colonies. The French president was the central node. Some African heads of state, especially Felix Houphouët-Boigny, the first President of Côte d'Ivoire, also featured very prominently. In an institutional set-up like this, diplomacy and personal politics, not necessarily aimed at serving the national interest but at times rather focused on personal interests of staying in power and augmenting personal wealth, go hand in hand. Houphouët-Boigny nicknamed the system *Françafrique*. This system played its role in stalling progress towards a supra-national Africa.

Summary

- Diplomatic relations can be depicted on two continua: one from proximity to distance, and another from horizontality to verticality. Applying these continua to real world examples yields a great variety of relations, including those that tend more towards proximity and

horizontality (Franco-German friendship), proximity and verticality (*Françafrique*), distance and horizontality (the United States and the Soviet Union), and distance and verticality (Italy and Abyssinia).
- The diplomatic dictionary features many terms that are used to describe the transformation of diplomatic relations, usually from distance to more proximity: détente (relaxation of tensions), rapprochement (moving closer to one another), entente (informal alliance).
- As far as international law is concerned, there has been a great transformation towards more horizontality among states in the last two centuries. Yet plenty of hidden hierarchies persist, enacted by practices that are rarely ever reflected upon in any detail.
- The literature identifies many mechanisms through which diplomatic relations get transformed. These range from functionalism to intergovernmentalism and from agential powers characterised by metis to more far-reaching societal changes. Far-reaching transformations require a mixture of these mechanisms. Yet the latter is something akin to a necessary condition.

Study Questions

- On these continua from proximity to distance and horizontality to verticality, where are contemporary relations between the United States, Russia, and China located?
- Where are Israeli-Palestinian relations located? What mechanisms, if any, are there to transform relations fundamentally?
- How have relations between state and non-state actors changed since the end of the Cold War?
- Does populist diplomacy have repercussions for making and re-making diplomatic relations?

Notes

1 This section greatly benefitted from our thought-provoking discussions with Simon Pratt and Christopher LaRoche.
2 This section draws on Soreanu and Kornprobst (2009) as well as on a joint collaborate research project with Ehud Eiran and Piki Ish-Shalom.
3 We would like to thank Raluca Soreanu for drawing our attention to the concept of *metis*.

Recommended Further Reading

Adler-Nissen, Rebecca. 2015. "Conclusion: Relationalism or Why Diplomats find International Relations Theory Strange." In *Diplomacy and the Making of World Politics*, edited by Ole Jacob Sending, Vincent Pouliot, and Iver B. Neumann, 284–308. Cambridge: Cambridge University Press.

This chapter juxtaposes the lenses through which diplomats and International Relations scholars make sense of diplomacy. She argues that the former put to use a relational lens while the latter hold on to a substantialism.

James, Alan. "Diplomatic Relations." 2016. In *The SAGE Handbook of Diplomacy*, edited by Costas M. Constantinou, Paul Sharp, and Pauline Kerr, 257–67. London: Sage.

This chapter focuses on international legal provisions when discussing diplomatic relations. The author puts particular emphasis on processes of recognition.

McCourt, David M. 2022. *The New Constructivism in International Relations Theory*. Bristol: Bristol University Press.

This book puts a strong emphasis on relationist understandings of international relations. The author seeks to reconstruct the constructivist perspective of studying world politics.

Nordin, Astrid H. M., et al. 2019. "Towards Global Relational Theorizing: A Dialogue between Sinophone and Anglophone Scholarship on Relationalism." *Cambridge Review of International Affairs* 32 (5): 570–81.

> Co-authored by no less than 17 authors from the Global North and Global South, the article discusses different variations of relationism in international relations. Discussing similarities and differences between Sinophone and Anglophone scholarship on relationalism, they seek to offer a contribution to making the study of international relations more global.

9 Making Order

Chapter Objectives

- To introduce the reader to different scholarly conceptualisations of world order.
- To show the extent to which these conceptualisations leave room for diplomatic agency.
- To highlight the current transformations of world order and investigate how diplomacy is implicated in these transformations.

Introduction

This chapter introduces the reader to different scholarly conceptualisations of world order and discusses how they relate diplomacy to the making of order. In the last two decades, it has become increasingly apparent that this order is changing in critical ways. By most scholarly accounts, we no longer live in a unipolar order. The hegemony of the United States gives way to a situation in which three great powers – the United States, China, and Russia – compete for influence in the world. Additionally, there are more and more assertive regional powers, ranging from India to Saudi Arabia, some of which may even be able to challenge the status of the great powers in the future. International institutions are under duress. The OSCE, created, among other things, to guarantee the inviolability of borders, is paralysed by Russia's war of territorial conquest at the expense of Ukraine. The UN, even though professing to be "determined to save succeeding generations from the scourge of war" in its Charter's Preamble, fails to find adequate responses to armed conflicts, including the ones between Russia and Ukraine, Gaza, and Israel, as well as those in Myanmar and Sudan. A host of other pressing issues remains inadequately addressed. This includes failures to implement the SDGs, to find ways to counter climate change and mitigate its effects, and to uphold human rights standards throughout the world. All these problems make it all the more important to study world order, that is, the more or less durable configuration of material and ideational forces that patterns the interplay of actors in international relations.

We organise this chapter into five sections. First, we discuss the nexus of diplomacy and polarity. Many scholars equate the study of world order with investigating the relations, especially military capabilities, among great powers. Second, we move on to what diplomacy does to rules, broadly speaking (including institutions and norms). Third, we look at diplomacy and background, with the latter conceptualised in various ways (ideology, doxa, episteme, or nomos). Fourth, we put under scrutiny what diplomacy does and does not do to what we refer to as *polyplexity*, that is, an understanding of world order as a constellation of functional and regional orders. We conclude from this that there is a serious mismatch between today's diplomatic practices on the one hand and ordering demands within and between these functional and regional orders on the other. Fifth, we summarise our main points.

DOI: 10.4324/9781003485407-13

Polarity

Polarity is an easy analytical tool. Simply put, it revolves around identifying the number of great powers and inquiring into what kind of power relations they stand to one another. This can then be conceptualised as unipolarity (a single great power), bipolarity (two great powers) or multipolarity (more than two great powers). Many International Relations scholars understand these forms of polarity as the defining element of order in world politics.[1]

Scholars focusing on polarity disagree about what kind of polarity makes for a stable international order. On the one hand, power transition theories posit that unipolarity is much more stable than bipolarity or multipolarity. A single hegemon can, so to say, lay down the law. Once this hegemony declines, challengers and the declining hegemon are likely to fight out the future dominance over the international system (Organski, 1968: 364–6; Kugler and Lemke, 1996).

Diplomacy does not feature prominently in power transition theories. The focus is on material capabilities, especially military ones (and also economic ones that are linked to military capabilities). There are some exceptions in the literature. Analysing relations between the United States and China, Zhou (2019) contends that more assertive diplomacies on both sides indicate that we are moving towards shifting power relations between the two states. Yet this relegates diplomacy to an indicator about what is happening. Diplomacy is not understood as the maker (or breaker) of a new order. In a somewhat similar vein, authors analysing soft balancing look carefully at diplomacy. But diplomatic soft-balancing (e.g., voting against a hegemon at the UNGA) is conceptualised merely as the first step of a possible more fundamental change of international order. The driver of the latter, however, is hard-balancing, that is, balancing militarily against military might (Pape, 2005; Paul, 2005; He, 2008; Paul, 2018).

On the other hand, many writers – and with them an entire school of thought in international relations, that is, realism – focus on the balance of power between two or more great powers. Such a balance is considered the key ingredient of international order (Claude, 1964; Kissinger, 2014; Little, 2007; Paul, Wirtz and Fortmann, 2004). How this order comes about is subject to contention among Realists. Waltz (1979: 121) is the protagonist of a view that always expects states to balance. The international system is anarchic and this compels states to balance in order to survive. This involves increasing their own military capabilities and entering military alliances. Diplomacy hardly features in Waltz's writings at all and, if so, without any kind of causal significance ascribed to it. The same applies to the entire neorealist approach that follows Waltz's thought (see Jönsson, 2022). With classical realism, it is a different matter altogether. For Hans Morgenthau, the balance of power is an ordering outcome that is contingent upon skilful diplomacy. Most of the time, he argues, there is no balance of power in world politics. It can only come into being and be maintained if it is carefully crafted by diplomacy. Morgenthau took inspiration from the 19th century in Europe to make this argument. Following the Napoleonic Wars, the Congress of Vienna succeeded to establish a concert system among the great powers that would uphold a balance of power. This, in Morgenthau's view, stabilised the international system (Morgenthau, 1948). Henry Kissinger, mentioned already several times in this book as a practitioner of diplomacy, borrowed from Morgenthau's thought. He, too, studied the concert system in great depth (Kissinger, 1994, 2014). Textbox 9.1 tells the reader a bit more about Kissinger.

Where does today's world stand if we look at it through the lens of theories on polarity? The Cold War was, of course, a bipolar system, pitting the United States and the Soviet Union – as well as their respective military alliances – against one another. What followed was, in the words of Krauthammer (1990), a 'unipolar moment', a unipolar interlude of US hegemony, or even, as some authors put it a Pax Americana, similar to the Pax Romana some two millennia

Textbox 9.1   Henry Kissinger, 1923–2023

Henry Kissinger was born in Fürth, Germany, in 1923 as Heinz Alfred Kissinger. As a German Jew, he had to flee Nazi Germany (along with many other great thinkers that would shape the nascent discipline of International Relations such as Hans Morgenthau and Karl Deutsch) in 1938. From the 1950s to the early 1970s, he taught at Harvard University. From 1968 to 1977, he was an important figure in US foreign policy making. President Nixon, determined to side-step the foreign policy establishment, above all the State Department, appointed Kissinger National Security Advisor. Kissinger's legacy, very much guided by balance of power thinking and *Realpolitik*, is ambiguous and controversial. On the one hand, he is the architect of the rapprochement between the United States and China in the early 1970s, prepared the negotiations between the two superpowers that would culminate in the Strategic Arms Limitations Treaty (SALT) I and Anti-Ballistic Missiles (ABM) Treaty and negotiated a peaceful settlement of the Vietnam War. As Secretary of State, he mediated in the Middle East in the aftermath of the Yom Kippur War. At the time, the term shuttle diplomacy was coined because Kissinger travelled back and forth between Washington and several Middle Eastern states, especially Egypt, Israel and Syria. On the other hand, Kissinger pursued what he considered to be the US interest in at times highly uncompromising fashion. Initially, he was a hawk in the Vietnam War. Kissinger thought of the war very much in zero-sum terms in the struggle against the Soviet Union and only came to reconsider when it became obvious that military victory was unlikely. In 1973, Kissinger helped plan the US-sponsored coup that ousted the democratically elected President Salvador Allende in Chile and replaced him with the dictator General Augusto Pinochet. The latter's military junta wreaked havoc in the country for 17 years. Kissinger's move followed a Cold War logic. Latin America was supposed to be a US sphere of influence. A socialist President, no matter whether democratically elected or not, had to be replaced by a more US-friendly leader, even if this meant to back the installation of a dictatorship. After his time in office, Kissinger remained an informal advisor of many US presidents and important commentator on world affairs. In a rather remarkable initiative – not necessarily in line with his balance-of-power thinking – he advocated the abolition of nuclear weapons. 100 years old, he died in Kent, Connecticut, in 2023.

ago (Layne, 2012). But then something changed in the mid-2010s. Russia became militarily more assertive in its neighbourhood, especially against Ukraine, and, with the help of Wagner mercenaries, began to venture out into resource-rich areas in the global south, in particular the Horn of Africa and West Africa. China and the United States are embroiled in an escalating economic rivalry, which threatens to spill over into the military realm, especially in East Asia (Layne, 2018).

The new evolving order bears some resemblances with the Cold War. Thus, some authors refer to our times as the nascent stages of a New Cold War. The New Cold War bears some resemblances with the Cold War. The great powers avoid direct military confrontation with one another. This is underwritten by their possession of nuclear weapons (Freedman, 2010). This absence of direct great power war – this is where the metaphor has its shortcomings – comes at the expense of escalating conflicts in regions. Great powers wage wars by proxy to defend and augment their spheres of influence. The Horn of Africa was a major theatre of the Cold War and the same appears to happen again in the New Cold War. In Ukraine, too, Russians and Americans do not fight directly against one another. But the latter support Ukraine to repel the Russian attack. Yet the 'New' in the concept 'New Cold War' really is to be taken seriously. There are important differences between the Cold War and the New Cold War. Overall, the latter is more diffuse. Great powers are less able to lay down the law. There are important regional powers, including Brazil, India and South Africa that have a considerable amount of agency. Many states, these regional powers included, do not simply choose sides. They pursue hedging strategies, pragmatically looking out for benefits from cooperating with different great powers at the same time. Ideological dividing lines are less clear cut than during the Cold War, too, albeit some authors have started to portray the New Cold War as a struggle between democracies and authoritarianism (Grantseva and Balzacq, 2025).

For students of diplomacy, this opaque nature of the New Cold War is of major importance. There are plenty of contingencies. Diplomacy matters. It matters for how states practice their hedging strategies, for how they come to enter and play their cards in evolving state groupings ranging from the G-20 to BRICS[2] and from the Shanghai Cooperation Organisation (SCO)[3] to the Quadrilateral Security Dialogue (QUAD),[4] for how they negotiate the dividing lines between great powers and their spheres of influence, and, most importantly, for producing some kind of regional and global stability (Paul and Kornprobst, 2025).

Rules

Diplomats often postulate a rules-based international order. Some do so especially in times when key rules codified into international law are broken. We are again in the midst of such times. International humanitarian law, regulating the conduct of war, for example, is currently under massive pressure. In several of today's armed conflicts even particularly heinous international crimes such as crimes against humanity and genocide return with a vengeance.

Scholars have been arguing for the power of rules to tame the power of might for centuries. Initially, this was a normative postulate put forward by international lawyers long before International Relations became an academic discipline. In the late 16th and early 17th centuries, for instance, a number of legal scholars elaborated on the Roman foundations of the laws of war. This included Alberico Gentili's *De iure belli* (On the Law of War) and Hugo Grotius's *De iure belli ac pacis* (On the Law of War and Peace) (Gentili, 1612; Grotius, 1924). Over time, some authors formulated more and more ambitious normative accounts. This includes the Clark and Sohn proposals for making the UN something akin to a world government with fully-fledged military powers (Clark and Sohn, 1958; Clark, 1967).

International Relations scholars, too, became more and more interested in the kinds of rules, often conceptualised as institutions, shaping international affairs. Yet they predominantly settled for an analytical and not a normative agenda. The question they asked was what kinds of rules make a difference for international interaction and why. At least three different perspectives on rules, broadly speaking, may be distinguished: Liberal and English School theorising on institutions and Constructivist inquiries into norms.

From a liberal point of view, analytically drawing increasingly from rational institutionalism, states design institutions and uphold these institutions as long as this leaves them better off than without them (Koremenos, Lipson and Snidal, 2001; Voeten, 2019; Roger, Snidal and Vabulas, 2023). In a seminal article, Koremenos, Lipson and Snidal (2001: 762) define institutions as "explicit arrangements, negotiated among international actors, that prescribe, proscribe, and/or authorize behaviour". Institutions thus defined range from formal international organisations such as the UN to arrangements that operate without a formal bureaucracy that backs these arrangements up, say the institution of diplomatic immunity (Koremenos, Lipson and Snidal, 2001: 763).

The English School differentiates between primary and secondary institutions. The former are assumed to be ontologically prior and make up international society (Friedner, 2017; Buzan, 2018). Buzan (2004) lists the following primary institutions, which he considers constitutive of the Westphalian system: sovereignty, territoriality, balance of power, diplomacy, international law and great power management as well as nationalism, human equality and the market. Secondary institutions are those institutions that rational institutionalists tend to focus on. Buzan and Lawson (2018: 790) write that they are 'for the most part intergovernmental arrangements consciously designed by states to serve specific purposes. They include the UN, the World Bank, the World Trade Organization, and the Nuclear Non-Proliferation regime.'

Many Constructivists study the making and re-making of norms. Research often addresses what is reminiscent of the English School's primary institutions, including sovereignty (Reus-Smit, 2001; Santa-Cruz, 2005), territorial integrity (Zacher, 2001; Kornprobst, 2002), the dos and don'ts of diplomacy (Davies, Kamradt-Scott and Rushton, 2015; Murray et al., 2011), and human rights (Risse, Ropp and Sikkink, 1999; Wiener et al., 2012). But there is also plenty of research on what the English School would refer to as secondary institutions, including on arms control (Tannenwald, 1999; Kütt and Steffek, 2015), the international political economy (Shoji, 2015; Bigge, 2004) and international organisations (Lantis and Wunderlich, 2022; Krook and True, 2012). From a Constructivist point of view, these norms are identity-constituting. They are not merely regulating behaviour as presumed by rational institutionalists. In the 1990s, this Constructivist strand focused heavily on how new norms come into being. Of late, there are more and more authors inquiring into norm contestation. Actors frequently do not agree on the same norms, the same hierarchy of norms, or the meaning of norms (Wiener, 2018; Niemann and Schillinger, 2017).

Diplomacy features in all these schools of thought. But it does so to different degrees. Rational institutionalism often overlooks diplomacy. Nonetheless, research associated with it has generated a seminal article by Robert Putnam on two-level games. Putnam contends that negotiations really take place on two levels. The one he calls diplomatic and the other domestic. Agreements on the former level can only be reached if there is also an agreement among the constituents located on the latter one. Putnam himself does not elaborate on diplomacy. It is something akin to a synonym for international. Apart from the formulation 'diplomacy and domestic politics', diplomacy does not feature (Putnam, 1988). Diplomats do not have agency themselves. Much of the literature on two-level games proceeds in similar ways. Mo (1994), for instance, elaborates on domestic politics but not on diplomacy. Yet other strands of research on rational institutionalism have elaborated on diplomacy. Tallberg, for example, investigates how chairpersonship shapes processes through which multilateral agreements are designed (Tallberg, 2006).

English School proponents and authors partially drawing upon it have made major contributions to our understandings about how diplomacy works and how it makes international order. With diplomacy being identified as one of the primary institutions of this order, this is not surprising. The range of research is very broad. It includes early normative investigations into the kinds of diplomacy that ought to make world order (Wight, 1936; Butterfield, 1951), a diplomatic theory of international politics (Sharp, 2009), unorthodox diplomatic relations such as Taliban diplomacy (Sharp, 2003), and, more recently, investigations into how diplomacy and order hang together in the digital age (McLarren, 2023). On this topic, see also Textbox 9.2. To put this differently and into a distinct English School language, diplomacy is taken seriously as an institution of international society that develops this society in certain directions rather than others.

Textbox 9.2 Towards an International Agency for Artificial Intelligence?

A rules-based international order always faces many challenges. One of these is about commitment, of course. Parties may agree to all kinds of rules and then end up not implementing them. Another challenge is brought about by the fact that the world never stands still. New developments – technological ones very much included – require new rules. All too often, the time lag between technological innovation and international rules is very pronounced. Take nuclear weapons technology, for example. First used during World War II, it took a quarter of a century for states to sign and ratify the Treaty on Nuclear Non-proliferation (NPT). It was only this treaty that dealt with the nuclear order more comprehensively: non-proliferation, disarmament, and peaceful use. Yet much earlier than that states were able to agree upon creating a new international organisation –IAEA. Doing so, state parties entrusted scientists and experts with important tasks of implementing safeguards, promoting nuclear safety and fostering peaceful use. In line with this mandate, it is perhaps not surprising that the longest-serving Director-General, from 1961 to 1981, was Sigvard Eklund. The Swede was a highly respected scientist with plenty of expertise in nuclear technology. In our days, technological innovation leapfrogs from one milestone to the next. It is especially AI that has advanced enormously in recent years, spearheading a range of other innovations in adjacent technological areas. There are some attempts to internationally regulate AI such as the Digital Global Compact. But the Compact merely constitutes soft law and largely stays silent on military applications. We may still have some years to go until we get something comparable to the NPT. There are occasional calls to model a new international organisation after the IAEA, that is, to create an International Agency for Artificial Intelligence. The analogy is well worth exploring. With AI, too, there are military and civilian applications. The latter have major repercussions for development. Furthermore, once more, it is important to have expertise and put this to use for humankind. Whether diplomacy, all too polarised in our days, however, will be able to produce agreement on such an organisation, entrust it with an adequate mandate, and give it sufficient resources, is a different matter altogether. In many ways, we need new rules. But diplomacy finds it increasingly difficult to generate them.

Constructivist research into norms started with a focus on what we, in previous chapters of this book, referred to as non-traditional diplomatic actors, especially human rights advocacies. But even this earlier research already established a link between traditional and non-traditional diplomatic actors. Norm advocacy networks on, say, disarmament and human rights, very much feature representatives of NGOs and states. Advocacy networks expand, crisscrossing the divide between state and non-state actors, and this gives them the clout to make and diffuse norms (Finnemore and Sikkink, 1998; Sikkink, 1998). But there is also plenty of research on how traditional diplomats advocate for norms, especially in multilateral settings (Coleman, 2013). Some of this research focuses on distinct areas of diplomacy and international relations, including defence diplomacy (Capie, 2013) and disarmament diplomacy (Garcia, 2011).

Today, there are many debates about the decline of the liberal world order. Different schools of thought tend to reach different conclusions. Rational institutionalist accounts that bracket domestic politics expect the liberal world order to persist. Ikenberry, the most cited proponent of this view, argues that dismantling the liberal institutions making up world order would be too disruptive and, thus, costly for states. Thus, the liberal order is expected to persist (Ikenberry, 2018) or even reinvent (Ikenberry, 2020) itself. Diplomacy hardly features in these accounts, which are underwritten by assumptions of the state as a unitary actor that maximises its exogenously given interest. In English School research, there is much more emphasis on diplomacy and, with it, also on the contingency of the evolving international order. Buzan (2020), for example, sketches a future scenario in which great powers – assumed to be the builders of order in the English School – become more inward-looking and thus come to neglect building and maintaining international order. This scenario would not only be about the decline of the liberal international order. It would be about the decline of order more generally speaking. There are many Constructivists who address norm contestation and question the future of the liberal world order without addressing diplomacy (Bettiza and Lewis, 2020; Börzel and Zürn, 2021). Yet there is insightful research into the role of diplomacy, too. Aydin, for example, focuses on the role of middle powers. She contends that their diplomacy has become more independent from great powers. Thus, middle powers no longer simply back a particular order built by a particular great power (Aydin, 2021). Barrinha and Renard caution that cyber-diplomacy builds a post-liberal order (Barrinha and Renard, 2020).

Background

Chapter 5 already introduced the notion of the background. When researching the making and unmaking of world orders, the diplomatic background matters but so do backgrounds held by other kinds of actors, say experts on global trade and finance, advocacy networks, medical professionals, military officers, terrorists, and so on.

Authors use all kinds of different concepts to conceptualise what we refer to, broadly speaking, as background. Ideology may be the one that is most thoroughly researched already. Freeden (2018) even refers to ideology studies as a 'discipline' in its own right (Freeden, 2018). Studies on ideology and international order evolved in various ways but there is a notable change from emphasising hegemony to contestation. In the early 1990s, research inspired by the Italian social theorist Antonio Gramsci identified liberal ideology as a key dimension of hegemony. Liberalism, simply put, legitimised a kind of order, that, at closer scrutiny, failed to live up to the ideals it postulated (Cox, 1994; Gill, 1995). More recently, studies inquire more and more into battles between different kinds of ideologies, such as global liberalism versus political Islam (Adamson, 2005), and globalisation and anti-globalisation (Steger and Wilson, 2012). Some authors maintain that this ideological contestation leads to global disorder (Friedman, 1998; Lavery and Schmid, 2021).

Writers borrowing either from classic rhetorical studies or Bourdieu (who himself borrowed from the former), often write about doxa. As Aristotle put it, these are 'opinions' that are so widely taken for granted that they can serve as premises and building blocks of arguments (Aristotle, 2010). In Bourdieu's reading, doxa are deeply ingrained relational understandings of the world that constitute social classifications and hierarchies (Bourdieu, 1980). In studies on international order, there is very little research on the classic rhetoricians' formulation[5] but a lot on the Bourdieusian interpretation of it. Adler-Nissen, for example, likens the EU's reflex to strive for ever more integration to doxa (Adler-Nissen, 2011), and Senn and Elhard write about commonsensical strategic knowledge about nuclear weapons (Senn and Elhardt, 2014). Pouliot and Mérand define doxa in more general terms: Doxa make actors distinguish between who is included and who is not, how power is enacted among them, and, more generally speaking, constitute deeply seated political, economic, and social ideas they enact in their practices (Pouliot and Mérand, 2012: 26).

The first seminal contribution on epistemes and international order dates back to the mid-1970s. Ruggie observed that technological changes can have an impact on the, metaphorically speaking, lens actors put to use when making the world intelligible to themselves (Ruggie, 1975). Later on, he conducted something akin to a case study of this causal mechanism. He studied how technological changes in mapping make it possible for actors to imagine the territorial state and he also sketched pathways through which new technological changes may contribute to moving beyond territoriality (Ruggie, 1993). Other research on epistemes, a concept borrowed from Foucault, and orders include work on epistemic communities (Adler and Haas, 1992) and epistemic communities of practice (Adler and Faubert, 2022), as well as epistemes as actors' lenses for making sense of proximity and distance (Adler and Faubert, 2022) and the relationship between science and politics (Jahn, 2016). What these disparate avenues of research share in common is an interest in how epistemes make actors imagine, in Foucault's words, 'the order of things' (Foucault, 2005).

Finally, nomos is a concept used – rather rarely – to get at what holds the background across actor groupings together. Lebow defines it as "norms, rules, laws and accepted practices that make behavior legible and more predictable by directing it down some channels and away from others" (Lebow, 2018). Studies dealing with doxa and nomos tend to identify more heterogeneity in the former and less so in the latter (Epstein, 2008). To put this differently, they consider it more likely that order is built upon heterodoxy than heteronomy.[6] The latter would call into question whether there is any kind of order at all.

Authors examining ideology, doxa, and epistemes investigate the nexus of diplomacy and world order rather frequently. There is the argument that ideologically infused diplomacy makes a difference for world order. Various strands of research are explored. Revolutions are considered harbingers of changing international orders. Revolutionary or post-revolutionary diplomacy is seen as a vehicle to bring such a change about (Armstrong, 2016; Moore, 2010). Several authors portray great power competition partly as diplomatic battles fought over ideology such as during the Cold War but even in our days (Kelley, 2007; Jiuding and Leilei, 2023; Gaddis, 1993; Brain, 2016). The counterargument to this is that interest-based diplomacy can accomplish cooperation despite ideological battles (Strüver, 2017). Finally, Stagnell (2020) argues that diplomacy is constituted by the ideology of state unity. Since the French Revolution, diplomacy has been in charge of preserving the myth of state unity (Stagnell, 2020).

Studies on doxa, diplomacy, and order, too, come in different shapes and forms. Authors study how doxa shapes the everyday doings of diplomacy in various MFAs, and how this, especially if done by great powers (Loh, 2018) or rising powers (Huju, 2023), in turn, affects world order. Other research trajectories focus more on relations among states in general. Diplomacy itself is understood as a commonsensical way of doing things (Pouliot, 2010), especially for how to communicate with one another (Jansson, 2015). There are also arguments that seek to explore doxa from a substantive angle. Wacquant, for example, who cooperated with Bourdieu on a number of research projects, understands neoliberalism as a set of doxa made and re-made, among other actors, by diplomats (Wacquant, 1999).

Research on diplomacy, epistemes, and order tends to follow research trajectories set by Foucault as well as Adler and Haas. When Duran (2013), for example, writes about how different epistemes constitute different kinds of diplomatic relations and these, in turn, different orders, then this is an application of Foucault's attempts to identify eras that are epistemically constituted (Duran, 2013). Allan's argument on how cosmologies shape different international eras is somewhat similar but more complex. Cosmologies consist of an episteme (what counts as knowledge?) and a social ontology (what counts as key phenomena and entities?) that together amount to lenses through which to look at, among other things, material processes (Allan, 2018). Other researchers apply the concept of epistemic communities. They do so differently. Guliz, for instance, writes about how the scientific and diplomatic spheres can be bridged in world ordering processes. Scientists can become part of the diplomatic community of practice (Sutcu, 2012). Davis (2013), by contrast, holds that epistemic differences cannot be bridged that easily. Even among traditional diplomats, there are different epistemic communities.

If polarity and the fate of the liberal order make for major debates among more materially and more institutionally inclined authors, respectively, students of diplomacy and background direct their analytical gaze at tectonic shifts of the deeply taken-for-granted intersubjectivities (at times interacting with material forces) that make up world ordering processes. A major theme in this research is the decline of US hegemony, understood as a dominance that includes the making of intersubjective meaning. Cooley and Nexon (2020), for example, differentiate three agential processes that drive this decline of US hegemony: those emanating from other great powers, those shaped by middle powers, and those happening within the United States. This decline of hegemony is often equated with the rise of a more fragmented world order (De Graaff, Brink and Parmar, 2020). A similar term used by several scholars is polycentric order. Authors employing this concept emphasise two sides of the same coin. On the one hand, polycentricity is about heterogeneity and multiple actors (literally: many centres) capable to leave a mark on world ordering. On the other hand, there continues to be a background, conceptualised in different ways, that holds the order together (Koinova et al., 2021). For Gadinger, for instance, the background is composed of the doxa and practices that constitute world order as a field (Gadinger, 2023). For Bueger and Liebetrau, actors spin assemblages out of an otherwise heterogeneous, deeply held social context (Bueger and Liebetrau, 2023).

Backgrounds can be rather contested, too. Textbox 9.3 discusses how this contestation makes diplomats from different countries increasingly live in different intersubjective worlds.

Textbox 9.3   An Ever More Polarising World Order?

When Realists and other scholars focusing on the distribution of material capabilities write about polarity, they look at the number of great powers and assume that these great powers engage in competitive behaviour against one another. Some students of the background use the related word 'polarisation'. By this, they mean that there is a growing contestation of the background that increasingly pits groupings of actors against one another. These groupings are not simply alliances composed of states. They are networks that crisscross states. Steve Bannon, for example, was an important figure in the United States, who helped Donald Trump to win the presidency in 2017. But he tried to diffuse his brand of right-wing populism way beyond the United States, at times rather successfully. Polarisation often cuts through states. The United States itself is definitely a case in point and so are many other democracies around the world. In part, today's polarisation processes resemble those in the past. Media ownership plays an important role. But in part, these processes are quite different. This is in no small measure due to new digital technologies, ranging from social media platforms to ever more sophisticated techniques (such as deep fakes) to diffuse misinformation, that transmit fake news and related juxtapositions between Self and Other ever faster to an ever-increasing number of people. These polarisation processes are bound to have an impact on the background. Diplomats at the UN increasingly complain that they no longer seem to live in the same world. If basic meaning-making exercises become highly contested and diplomacy gets increasingly implicated in it, ordering the world becomes a major challenge.

Polyplexity

World order is a highly abstract concept. Attempts to make it intelligible to ourselves inevitably rely on heuristic shortcuts and simplifications. In much of the literature discussed earlier, this includes limiting the actors under scrutiny to great powers (polarity), equating world order with international security (polarity but also plenty of rules and backgrounds), and glossing over at times highly pronounced regional differentiations of order, say between Central Africa and Western Europe (very common throughout the literature).

Some authors have started to conceptualise world order differently. They are moving away from a monolithic conceptualisation of one order to an understanding of world order as a constellation of orders. We refer to such a constellation as polyplexity. Three dimensions define polyplexity. First, there is functional differentiation.[7] World order is not just about ordering international security but a range of orders and the relations among them. This very much includes all functional diplomatic fields that we dealt with in the fourth chapter of this book such as security, economics, development, environment, health, and migration. Textbox 9.4 discusses an important sub-field of the security order, that is, nuclear governance. In today's world constellation of orders, security reigns supreme. There is a hierarchy that puts security on top. The literature on securitisation shows this very clearly (Wæver, 1993; Mügge, 2023; Kirk and McDonald, 2021). Health, environment, or migration may get pushed a little further up the hierarchy once they come to be considered security threats. If this securitisation does not occur, they remain far down on the international agenda.

Second, there is regional differentiation.[8] All regional orders are open systems. In contrast to the world constellation of orders, which is a closed meta order, regional orders can always be shaped and re-shaped by what is happening in adjacent regions or in the constellation. Yet the extent to which they are open to extra-regional influences varies. Strong regional players such as China in East Asia and India in South Asia have considerable clout in regional systems. When Acharya writes about a multiplex world order in which regional order-making eclipses

---

Textbox 9.4 Polyplexity and Nuclear Governance

It is actually rather difficult to spell out how global nuclear governance looks like. There is the NPT but there is also the Treaty on the Prohibition of Nuclear Weapons. The former merely stipulates that nuclear weapons state ought to negotiate in good faith to disarm. The latter, according to which parties shall not possess or seek to acquire nuclear weapons, features much sharper obligations. To make things more complicated, there are also all kinds of regional treaties on nuclear governance. The Treaty of Pelindaba, for example, creates a nuclear weapons free zone in Africa. It is modelled in many ways after the Treaty of Tlatelolco. Yet Pelindaba, even more so than Tlatelolco, puts very strong emphasis on the nexus of the peaceful use of nuclear technology and development. If we move away from assuming that there is one monolithic world order, things become much more straight forward. From a polyplex point of view, it is to be expected that there are regional differences and that these differences, among other things, are about how proximate or distant functional orders are to one another. Africa and Latin America have, similar to the Treaty on the Prohibition of Nuclear Weapons, much stronger provisions on banning nuclear weapons. Furthermore, they postulate a kind of close horizontal relationship between the security and development fields that has always remained elusive on the global level.

global order-making, then he often refers to these regions. Yet there are also regions in which extra-regional actors are shapers and – very much so – breakers of orders. The Horn of Africa has been alluded to above already, but there are many others, ranging from Central Asia to the Middle East.

Third, there are plenty of liminal spaces.[9] The world cannot be neatly divided into either functional or regional orders. The environmental order, for example, is anything but hermetically sealed. Some rules in this order, for example carbon emissions trading, are borrowed from the economic field. When environmental degradation fuels conflicts, say between pastoralists and culturalists, failures to govern the environmental order spill over into the security order. When nuclear testing wreaked havoc with the health of generations of people living in close vicinity of testing sites such as on the Marshall Islands and in Semipalatinsk, early failures to regulate nuclear testing (security order) had major effects for health and environment. Seeking to demarcate clear-cut boundaries between regions is similarly pointless. Where, for example, does East Asia begin and end? Is Vietnam part of East Asia or Southeast Asia; Mongolia East Asia or Central Asia? From a scholarly point of view, liminal spaces are to be expected and they are well worth focusing on. It is often in these interstices[10] that agency develops and has the potential to make for changes: within functional and regional orders but also across them, for example by re-ordering the ranking across functional orders or putting them closer together, or by helping imagine larger regions.

Some functional and regional orders have always been cross-cutting; they are, so to say, inherently liminal. Human rights, for instance, are meant to be an important foundation for any functional field. This even applies to the security order, when arms control and disarmament initiatives dejustify entire weapons categories, ranging from landmines via cluster ammunition to nuclear weapons, based on their indiscriminate violations of human rights.[11] Science and technology has always been such a cross-cutting order, too. More recently, with digital technologies progressing even faster and becoming increasingly pervasive, every functional order is bound to be strongly affected by technological advances. This applies as much to, say, the global health order (prevention, diagnostics and treatment) as it does to the security order (surveillance, target-identification, autonomous and semi-autonomous weapons, etc.). Large cross-cutting regional orders, above all OSCE-Europe from the Urals to the Atlantic, are currently experiencing major crises. Long-standing regional liminal spaces such as the Caucasus, and especially Armenia, Azerbaijan, and Georgia (for the most part within what is often referred to as South Caucasus), are being torn apart by struggles between great and even middle powers to establish and widen their spheres of influence.

As soon as we start to understand world order not as something monolithic but as a constellation of many moving parts, we think of the challenges diplomacy faces rather differently. Diplomacy somehow has to manage the relations among the many, partly liminal, moving parts that make up this constellation. Polyplexity amounts to a major challenge to diplomacy. For one, diplomats are trained to be generalists, versed in foreign languages, able to move from, say, doing economic diplomacy in a capital on one continent to serve as expert on arms control at a multilateral hub on another continent almost from one day to the next. Yet with the subject matter becoming more and more complex and technical, this moving back and forth between different places and subject areas is becoming increasingly difficult. Moreover, diplomacy is often better in dividing labour up than in putting the pieces back to together. This starts with MFAs, which continue to be divided up along functional and regional departments and sections, extends to sections and departments located in other ministries (including economics, finance, environment, and health), goes on with their equivalents in ever increasing bureaucratic structures serving heads of state and government, and ends with a host of other (state and non-state) agencies and stakeholders.

To put this more concisely, there is a mismatch between a diplomacy that carves up competencies and responsibilities on the one hand and the demand to diplomatically govern a polyplex world on the other. Seen through this perspective, it is perhaps no coincidence that the world is stumbling from one crisis to the next, be they related to finance, trade, climate change, or armed conflict.

Summary

- There are many different scholarly conceptualisations of world order. These can be clustered into three categories: world order as unipolar, bipolar, or multipolar system; world order as a system of rules; and world order as configuration of deeply seated background knowledge.
- The role of diplomacy is less acknowledged in some of these conceptualisations than in others. With the exception of classical Realists, authors postulating that world order is a system of polarity among great powers tend to ascribe a much smaller role to diplomacy than those writing about rules. Diplomats are hypothesised to be the makers of these rules. In a similar vein, scholarly contributions on the background contend that diplomats are important producers of background (and, vice versa, diplomatic practices are generated by this background).
- New understandings of world order are necessary in order to make sense of the transformations that the world is currently experiencing. Polyplexity is such an understanding. It stresses the heterogeneous nature of world order – a constellation made up of functional and regional orders as well as the liminal spaces in between them – and the limitations of diplomacy to deal with this constellation.

Study Questions

- Do we live in a New Cold War and, if so, what does diplomacy have to do with it?
- Do today's diplomatic practices strengthen or weaken the liberal world order?
- How does diplomacy make and unmake hegemony?
- What is polyplexity and how well-equipped is diplomacy to deal with it?

Notes

1 For an excellent overview, see Graeger et al., 2022.
2 Since 2024, BRICS is no longer confined to Brazil, Russia, India, China and South Africa. Egypt, Ethiopia, Iran, Saudi Arabia, and the United Arab Emirates have also joined. Note the overlap of membership between BRICS and the SCO (see further in the text).
3 The following states are, at the time of writing, members: Belarus, China, Kazakhstan, Kyrgyzstan, Russia, Tajikistan, Uzbekistan, India, Iran, and Pakistan. In addition to the regular members, there are many more observer states and dialogue partners. The latter includes notable regional powers such as Egypt, Saudi Arabia, Turkey, and the United Arab Emirates.
4 This is a state grouping composed of Australia, India, Japan, and the United States.
5 For an exception see Kornprobst and Senn, 2016b.
6 We owe this point to Martin Senn.
7 See literature on regime complexes (Young, 1996; Alter and Raustiala, 2018), norm clusters (Lantis and Wunderlich, 2022; Winston, 2023), multi-level governance (Rosenau, 1992; Zürn, 2020), and inter-field relations (Canaughey, Musgrave and Nexon, 2018; Oskanian, 2023). See also concepts such as 'multi-order world' (Flockhart, 2016) and 'heterarchy' (Baumann and Dingwerth, 2015).

8 This is the focus on Acharya's path-breaking work on regions. He holds that it will be regional players rather than great powers with global reach who will be able to fundamentally shape their regions and even the world in future (Acharya, 2017; Acharya, Estevadeordal and Goodman, 2023).
9 On liminality, see Higgott and Nossal (1997), Neumann (2012), Adler (2019) and Bátora et al. (2021).
10 We would like to thank Jozef Bátora for many thought-provoking discussions on this issue.
11 On justification and dejustification, see Abulof and Kornprobst (2017).

Recommended Further Reading

Adler-Nissen, Rebecca, and Ayşe Zarakol. 2021. "Struggles for Recognition: The Liberal International Order and the Merger of Its Discontents." *International Organization* 75 (2): 611–34.

This article provides a very useful overview of forces challenging the liberal international order that we deal with under the heading of 'background'.

Larson, Deborah Welch. 2024. "Is the Liberal Order on the Way Out? China's Rise, Networks, and the Liberal Hegemon." *International Relations* 38 (1): 113–33.

Written by a leading liberal scholar, this review essay sums up the state of the art of discussions on the liberal world order. Furthermore, the author provides her own contingent account about whether this order will prove to be resilient or not.

Mearsheimer, John J. 2018. *The Great Delusion: Liberal Dreams and International Realities*. New Haven, CT: Yale University Press.

This leading Realist scholar holds that great power competition and even hegemonic war are inevitable. Seen through this prism, not even the most skilful diplomacy can prevent that great powers eventually clash with one another militarily.

Pardesi, Manjeet S. 2022. "Decentering Hegemony and 'Open' Orders: Fifteenth-Century Melaka in a World of Orders." *Global Studies Quarterly* 2 (4): ksac072.

This article, empirically focusing on historical inter-order relations, broadens our view of regional orders and orders more generally. The author opens up the study of orders by distinguishing centred and decentred systems instead of settling this issue by assumption.

Part V
Remaking Diplomacy

10 The Digital Turn

Chapter Objectives

- To examine the structured stages of digital crisis communication, from sense-making to reflection, and evaluate how digital tools influence strategic responses and decision-making in diplomatic crises.
- To analyse the evolving grammar of digital public diplomacy, distinguishing between front-stage visibility and back-stage strategic coordination in shaping state narratives.
- To assess the impact of digital technologies on international negotiations, exploring their role in confidentiality, real-time communication, and power asymmetries in diplomatic engagements.
- To synthesise the broader implications of the digital turn in diplomacy, evaluating how digital tools reshape norms, institutional adaptation, and the balance of influence between state and non-state actors.

Introduction

The integration of digital technologies into diplomatic practice represents a profound disruption to traditional modes of engagement between states and non-state actors (Bjola and Holmes, 2015). No longer confined to closed-door negotiations or controlled messaging, diplomacy now unfolds in a dynamic and highly public digital arena. The proliferation of digital platforms has fundamentally altered the grammar of diplomacy, challenging its core principles and reshaping how states project power, manage crises, and construct their international identities (Bjola and Manor, 2024a; Manor and Pamment, 2019).

Digital technologies disrupt diplomacy in several ways. First, they democratise access to diplomatic processes by enabling a broader range of actors – individuals, civil society organisations, and private corporations – to engage in global conversations. While this inclusivity fosters diverse perspectives, it also erodes the exclusivity that historically defined diplomatic practice, increasing the risk of fragmentation and conflicting narratives (Collins and Bekenova, 2019). Second, digital technologies introduce unprecedented visibility into diplomatic interactions. Negotiations and communications, once shielded by confidentiality, are now more accessible to public scrutiny. While this transparency can build trust, it also challenges the discretion critical to effective diplomacy, potentially limiting the space for candid dialogue and compromise (Pamment and Manor, 2024: 53). Third, the immediacy and informality inherent to digital platforms have fundamentally altered the carefully choreographed nature of traditional diplomatic exchanges. Diplomats now face the challenge of balancing clarity with nuance, as the brevity of digital communication often oversimplifies complex issues and can lead to misinterpretation (Holmes, 2024). Finally, digital technologies accelerate the pace of international engagement.

DOI: 10.4324/9781003485407-15

Real-time communication, particularly through social media platforms, has become a defining feature of contemporary diplomacy. However, this immediacy also amplifies the potential for missteps, miscommunication, and the rapid escalation of tensions during crises (Seib, 2012).

These disruptions are further magnified by the rise of AI and other computational tools. Generative AI, for example, offers the potential to streamline information analysis and enhance strategic communication. However, it also raises questions about the authenticity and ethical implications of digital engagements, particularly when algorithms shape narratives in ways that may distort reality (Reviglio and Agosti. 2020). Such technological acceleration underscores the dual nature of digital tools: they are both enablers of innovative practices and disruptors of established norms (Bjola and Manor, 2024b). In this new digital environment, the power of narrative and identity construction has grown exponentially. Digital platforms allow states to amplify their cultural and ideological influence, yet the success of these efforts depends on their ability to craft credible and resonant messages. The strategic use of narratives during global crises, as evidenced in recent public diplomacy campaigns, demonstrates the critical role of digital storytelling in maintaining international reputation (Moral, 2023). At the same time, the democratisation of communication has exposed states to greater reputational vulnerabilities, where hostile actors can weaponise platforms to undermine credibility (Habegger and Lemke, 2020).

The shift from traditional to digital diplomacy requires a re-evaluation of how global actors engage with one another. The following sections explore the thematic clusters of crisis communication, public diplomacy, and international negotiations, to unravel the opportunities and challenges posed by this digital transformation. These discussions aim to illuminate how digital technologies are reshaping the practices, norms, and institutions of diplomacy, forcing practitioners to adapt to an increasingly fragmented and fast-paced global landscape.

Digital Crisis Communication

Crisis communication has become a central pillar of digital diplomacy, where the power of digital tools to shape real-time narratives intersects with the complexities of managing misinformation, public trust, and strategic messaging. Digital platforms offer diplomats unprecedented opportunities to engage diverse audiences, control narratives, and respond to emergencies with speed and precision. However, they also present significant challenges, including the risk of amplifying disinformation, conflicting agendas in collaboration, and the ever-present demand for narrative coherence across global and domestic spheres. This section examines how the dual nature of digital tools – serving as instruments of both liberation and repression – impacts crisis communication. It explores strategies such as proactive narrative framing, collaborative approaches, and emotional resonance to counter misinformation and build trust. Additionally, it outlines the integration of feedback and reflection into a structured approach that ensures each phase of crisis communication informs the next.

The Dual Nature of Digital Tools: Liberation vs. Repression

Digital tools have emerged as powerful yet paradoxical forces in diplomacy, functioning simultaneously as instruments of *liberation* and *repression*. In this context, *liberation technologies* (→ glossary) refer to digital platforms and tools that empower individuals, amplify marginalised voices, and democratise access to global communication. These technologies reduce coordination costs, provide real-time feedback, and facilitate resource mobilisation for political and social movements. Conversely, *repression technologies* (→ glossary) describe the use of the same digital platforms to suppress dissent, manipulate public opinion, and consolidate authoritarian control. States and non-state actors exploit these tools to surveil, censor, and distort narratives for their strategic advantage (Tufekci, 2017; Rød and Weidmann, 2015).

As liberation technologies, social media platforms like Twitter and Facebook have proven instrumental in fostering political activism. For instance, during the Arab Spring, these platforms allowed activists to bypass traditional media, coordinate protests, and mobilise global attention. The use of hashtags like #Jan25 in Egypt and #SidiBouzid in Tunisia facilitated real-time communication, amplifying the reach of grassroots movements and inspiring transnational solidarity (Howard and Muzammil, 2013). Similarly, during the Hong Kong protests of 2014 and 2019, encrypted messaging apps and decentralised networks empowered citizens to organise while evading government surveillance and censorship, demonstrating the resilience afforded by these technologies (Lee and Joseph, 2018).

However, these same tools also serve as repression technologies. Governments and other actors harness them for disinformation campaigns, surveillance, and narrative control. For example, China's social credit system exemplifies the strategic use of digital technologies to monitor and control citizen behaviour, reinforcing state authority and societal compliance (Liu and Rona-Tas, 2024). Similarly, the weaponisation of bots during the Gulf Cooperation Council (GCC) blockade spread disinformation and polarised public opinion, illustrating how digital platforms can exacerbate tensions rather than resolve them (Akdenizli, 2024). The broader trend of organised disinformation campaigns, detected in over 70 countries by 2019, highlights how digital tools can undermine democratic institutions and fragment public discourse (Bradshaw and Howard, 2019).

For diplomacy, the implications of this duality are profound. The liberating potential of digital platforms expands the scope of public diplomacy, allowing states to engage with diverse audiences and shape global narratives. At the same time, the repressive applications of these tools challenge norms of trust, confidentiality, and inclusivity. Diplomats must adapt by developing strategies to counter misinformation, safeguard credibility, and navigate polarised digital environments. Ultimately, effective digital diplomacy requires balancing the opportunities of liberation technologies with the risks posed by their repressive counterparts. Collaborative efforts between governments, tech companies, and civil society will be essential to ensuring these tools function as instruments of dialogue and democracy, rather than control and division.

Crisis Communication Management

How can diplomats effectively navigate crises in an era where algorithms amplify information, blur the lines between truth and misinformation, and shape narratives in real time? Addressing the challenges of crisis communication in the digital age requires a structured approach that goes beyond the immediacy of messaging to account for the complexities of a hyper-connected world. Drawing on Arjen Boin's *The Politics of Crisis Management: Public Leadership Under Pressure* (2005), we propose that digital crisis management can be analytically segmented into five key stages: sense-making, decision-making, meaning-making, collaboration, and reflection. Applied to the realm of digital diplomacy (see Table 10.1), this framework provides valuable insights into the intricate balance between real-time communication, strategic narrative management, and the unique risks posed by the digital landscape.

The initial stage of crisis management, *sense-making*, requires constructing a clear understanding of an unfolding situation. Digital tools have transformed this process by providing real-time access to diverse sources of information. For example, during the Kenyan Westgate Mall attack, platforms like Twitter served as vital channels for disseminating safety instructions

Table 10.1 Digital Crisis Management Stages

Stage	Key Elements	Possible Risks
Sense-Making	Use digital tools (social media, analytics) to gather real-time data and identify emerging narratives.	Over-reliance on unverified data from social media; misinformation and cognitive overload can distort understanding.
Decision-Making	Develop strategies that align with diplomatic goals, leveraging digital channels for rapid dissemination.	Impulsive actions due to pressure for immediacy; poorly framed digital messages may escalate tensions or mislead audiences.
Expectations Management	Communicate transparently through digital platforms, emphasising empathy, cultural sensitivity, and clarity.	Inconsistent messaging across platforms risks confusing audiences; failure to manage emotional resonance can erode trust.
Collaboration	Align narratives and efforts across governments, NGOs, and tech platforms to ensure cohesive digital responses.	Conflicting agendas or fragmented digital strategies may amplify misinformation and weaken collaborative impact.
Termination and Reflection	Analyse digital campaigns' effectiveness, using feedback to refine future crisis communication strategies.	Inadequate integration of lessons learned; failure to adapt digital tools to address shortcomings identified in past crises.

and coordinating emergency responses. Citizen journalists and non-state actors often outpaced traditional media, providing immediate updates that proved invaluable for decision-makers (Simon et al., 2014). However, the influx of unverified information led to cognitive overload and misinformation, underscoring the need for robust mechanisms to filter credible insights from noise and deliberate "astroturfing" – fake grassroots campaigns designed to mislead (Keller et al., 2019). For diplomacy, this stage emphasises the necessity of strong analytical capabilities. Diplomatic institutions must invest in tools for verifying data and training personnel to distinguish actionable intelligence from distracting or erroneous inputs. Effective sense-making is foundational; failures here can derail the entire crisis response and diminish credibility (Bjola, 2022).

Once a clear understanding of the crisis has been established, the focus shifts to *decision-making*, where actionable strategies must be carefully developed. The urgency of digital communication presents a unique challenge, as decisions often need to be conveyed swiftly while maintaining accuracy and strategic alignment. Poorly crafted messages can escalate tensions, as seen in the realm of nuclear diplomacy, where provocative tweets from the US Strategic Command during arms control negotiations raised risks of misinterpretation and conflict escalation (Crilley, 2024). The digital environment demands a careful balance between immediacy and deliberation. For diplomats, this stage involves rigorous vetting of messages to ensure consistency with long-term objectives while addressing immediate concerns. Narrative coherence is paramount, as rushed or poorly calibrated communications can undermine trust, exacerbate tensions, and have far-reaching consequences in high-stakes scenarios.

Managing public expectations is crucial for maintaining trust during a crisis. Digital platforms such as Facebook and Twitter have become indispensable tools for providing clarity, reassurance, and updates. During the COVID-19 pandemic, MFAs effectively used these platforms to inform citizens about health measures, repatriation initiatives, and vaccine rollouts

(Manor and Yarchi, 2023). These efforts helped sustain public confidence and demonstrated institutional competence in managing uncertainty. However, the global nature of crises often highlights inconsistencies in messaging, as nations prioritise domestic audiences over international cohesion (Bjola and Coplen, 2022a). Diplomats must craft communication strategies that align national and global narratives, ensuring transparency and accessibility. Trust is built not only on the accuracy of information but also on empathy, cultural sensitivity, and the tone of engagement.

Crises often require the *collaboration* and coordination of multiple stakeholders, including governments, NGOs, international organisations, and private entities. Digital platforms facilitate such collaboration, enabling rapid information sharing and joint efforts. However, these same platforms can amplify conflicting or fragmented narratives, complicating collective responses. The GCC blockade exemplifies this challenge, where social media became a battleground of competing narratives that deepened tensions rather than fostering resolution (Akdenizli, 2024). Bots and disinformation campaigns further illustrated how uncoordinated narratives could undermine crisis management efforts (Bjola and Pamment, 2016). For diplomats, the ability to engage in proactive narrative coordination is essential, particularly as virtual platforms play an increasingly central role in crisis collaboration. As Bramsen and Hagemann (2021) observe, the COVID-19 lockdowns highlighted the need for coherent digital strategies to align diverse agendas and maintain collective focus. Successful collaboration depends on crafting a unified approach that bridges competing priorities, ensuring digital diplomacy remains both purposeful and effective in achieving shared objectives.

The final stage of crisis management focuses on *terminating* the immediate response and *reflecting* on lessons learned. This phase is essential for institutional growth and preparing for future crises. In digital diplomacy, termination involves assessing whether communication strategies aligned with overarching objectives and evaluating the impact of narratives on different audiences. Ukraine's digital diplomacy during its conflict with Russia provides a notable example. By analysing its messaging effectiveness, Ukraine strengthened its reputational security in Western nations while identifying areas for improvement in engaging the Global South (Cull, 2022). This reflective process enabled officials to refine their approaches, reinforcing resilience and legitimacy in subsequent communications. Integrating feedback loops into institutional practices is crucial for managing the performative and relational dynamics of digital diplomacy. As Duncombe (2018) notes, platforms such as Twitter/X shape engagement by amplifying public messaging and interactions, demanding careful management of both content and audience reception. Reflecting on how messages are received and adjusting strategies accordingly ensures diplomacy remains effective.

The five stages of crisis communication are interdependent, yet their integration can present significant challenges. Sense-making provides the foundation for understanding a crisis, but the need for immediacy in decision-making often forces action before all relevant information is fully vetted. For instance, during the COVID-19 pandemic, early decisions about lockdowns and travel restrictions were made based on incomplete data, which later required adjustments as more information became available. This tension between rapid action and thorough analysis highlights the risks inherent in moving too quickly from one stage to the next. Similarly, collaboration among stakeholders can create friction with expectations management, as divergent priorities or messaging strategies may confuse or alienate audiences. The GCC blockade, for example, saw conflicting narratives from involved parties on social media, which exacerbated public uncertainty rather than providing clarity or resolution.

These tensions underscore the importance of iterative feedback loops between stages, allowing lessons learned in one phase to refine and improve the next. Diplomatic actors must also remain attuned to the broader context, ensuring that short-term actions do not undermine long-term credibility or objectives. The integration of digital tools further complicates this dynamic, demanding agility and coordination to manage the rapid pace of information exchange. For example, during a hypothetical cyberattack targeting critical infrastructure, such as a national power grid, digital tools would enable real-time updates to affected populations through social media and government apps. However, the same platforms could also become conduits for misinformation or panic-inducing narratives, potentially overwhelming emergency response teams. By proactively addressing these challenges and maintaining a focus on coherence, diplomats can ensure that each stage reinforces the others, leading to more effective and sustainable crisis communication.

Strategies for Effective Digital Crisis Communication

Effective crisis communication in digital diplomacy requires a strategic approach that addresses the pervasive *challenges of misinformation* while amplifying trust through narrative coherence and collaboration. The rapid spread of misinformation during crises can undermine diplomatic efforts, destabilise public trust, and fragment international narratives. To counteract this, diplomats must employ *containment strategies* that pre-empt misinformation before it escalates (Bjola and Pamment, 2016). Proactively framing narratives is critical to shaping public perceptions early, ensuring that misinformation has limited space to take hold. For instance, in a hypothetical scenario involving disputed maritime boundaries, pre-emptive statements supported by visual evidence, such as satellite images, could reinforce credibility while countering adversarial narratives.

Collaboration with technology platforms is equally vital. Governments and MFAs working with platforms like Twitter and Facebook can flag harmful content and limit the spread of disinformation, as seen during the COVID-19 pandemic when governments partnered with social media companies to counter vaccine misinformation (Manor and Yrachi, 2023). However, this process must be transparent to avoid perceptions of censorship, which can further polarise audiences. By leveraging the unique affordances of different platforms, diplomats can tailor their messaging to diverse audiences, using, for example, Bluesky for real-time updates targeting policymakers and Instagram for visually engaging narratives that resonate with younger, global audiences. Chan, Lee and Chen (2021) highlight the importance of multi-platform strategies, noting that they allow for targeted engagement while maximising reach and impact across varied demographic groups. Ultimately, the ability to collaborate effectively and engage audiences across platforms reinforces the credibility and adaptability of digital crisis communication.

Building trust is not solely about countering misinformation; it requires crafting emotionally resonant and culturally relevant narratives. Papacharissi (2015) highlights how affective publics form through shared emotions in digital spaces, binding individuals and amplifying collective sentiment. For diplomats, this means addressing public concerns with empathy and emphasising shared resilience to foster solidarity and credibility. Digital platforms are not merely tools for information but spaces where emotions shape discourse, making emotional resonance essential for sustaining trust and ensuring impactful engagement. The EU demonstrated this approach during the COVID-19 pandemic by using Twitter to project competence and solidarity, which helped bolster its reputation as a reliable crisis manager (Moral, 2023).

Finally, diplomats must approach crisis communication as an iterative process that integrates *feedback and reflection*. In his landmark work *The Reflective Practitioner*, Schön (2008) emphasises that reflective practice is not just about evaluating successes or failures but about understanding why specific approaches resonated or fell short. In the context of digital diplomacy, this means analysing audience responses, engagement metrics, and the broader impact of narratives across platforms. Such reflection enables diplomats to adapt strategies to the evolving dynamics of digital spaces and ensure that feedback informs institutional learning. A case in point is Ukraine's digital diplomacy during its conflict with Russia, which successfully bolstered support in the West but faced challenges in engaging audiences in the Global South (Kaneva, 2022; Digital Forensic Research Lab, 2024). This underscores the importance of tailoring strategies to diverse audiences and integrating insights from past efforts to refine future responses.

Digital Public Diplomacy

The 'Grammar Rules' of Digital Engagement

Soft power and public diplomacy are critical frameworks for understanding how states engage with global audiences in the digital age. Joseph Nye defines *soft power* as the ability of a nation to influence others through attraction and persuasion rather than coercion or payment, leveraging cultural values, political ideals, and foreign policies to foster voluntary alignment (Nye, 2004). *Public diplomacy*, as articulated by Nicholas Cull, is a strategic effort by states to communicate directly with foreign publics, aiming to foster mutual understanding, build trust, and shape positive perceptions of their policies and values. Cull identifies five core functions of public diplomacy: listening, advocacy, cultural exchange, international broadcasting, and relationship-building, which collectively signal a paradigm shift from traditional state-to-state diplomacy to a more inclusive, participatory model centred on trust and credibility (Cull, 2008).

In the digital age, the practice of public diplomacy has been profoundly influenced by the rise of digital platforms, demanding that practitioners navigate the complexities of online engagement with precision and adaptability. The digital environment has become an active facilitator of soft power, not just a medium for its communication. As highlighted by Gary D. Rawnsley (2024), soft power in the digital space reflects and amplifies the values, innovation, and credibility that underlie a nation's offline culture and institutions. However, it also poses challenges, as the plurality of voices and the rapid spread of information can dilute official narratives, creating ideological silos or amplifying distrust. Bjola and Manor's four grammar rules of digital engagement – visual simplicity, emotional framing, computational personalisation, and engagement hybridisation – offer a systematic framework for effectively leveraging digital tools in public diplomacy (Bjola and Manor, 2024a). Together, these concepts provide a roadmap for states to effectively project influence and foster international goodwill in an increasingly interconnected world.

- **Visual simplicity** emphasises the importance of clear, accessible, and aesthetically engaging communication. Digital platforms are saturated with information, making simplicity crucial for capturing attention. For instance, the minimalist design of a public health awareness campaign – such as a visually appealing infographic on vaccination benefits – can cut through the noise, ensuring the message is not only seen but remembered. This approach supports soft power by enhancing the reach and appeal of cultural or policy messages, making them more relatable and widely understood.
- **Emotional framing** capitalises on the psychological impact of emotions to create memorable narratives. Messages that evoke joy, pride, fear, or hope are more likely to be shared and discussed. For example, a climate change initiative that highlights personal stories of resilience and community action can foster empathy and alignment with the broader cause. By embedding policy or cultural messages within emotionally resonant

stories, emotional framing strengthens public diplomacy by connecting with audiences on a deeply human level.
- **Computational personalisation** (→ glossary) leverages algorithmic tools to tailor messages to specific audience segments. This ensures that the right message reaches the right audience, increasing its relevance and impact. For instance, a digital campaign promoting educational scholarships may use data analytics to target students in underserved regions with content tailored to their aspirations and needs. Personalisation enhances soft power by demonstrating inclusivity and understanding, fostering trust, and building stronger connections with diverse audiences.
- **Engagement hybridisation** (→ glossary) combines digital and physical forms of diplomacy to maximise their complementary strengths. While digital platforms enable broad and rapid outreach, in-person engagements provide depth and trust-building. For instance, a state's cultural institute may host a virtual seminar featuring live-streamed panel discussions, followed by local workshops or exhibitions. This hybrid approach reinforces the message's impact and sustains relationships over time, aligning with the principles of public diplomacy by ensuring both accessibility and authenticity.

The integration of these grammar rules with the principles of soft power and public diplomacy highlights their transformative potential in a digital context. By adopting these strategies, MFAs can more effectively project their values, foster trust, and build meaningful relationships, advancing their influence and credibility on the global stage. As Nicholas J. Cull emphasises in his work on public diplomacy, the success of such efforts rests on foundational principles: authenticity, adaptability, and a genuine commitment to mutual respect and understanding (Cull, 2019). These qualities not only underpin the effectiveness of traditional, offline public diplomacy but also remain equally vital in navigating the complexities of today's dynamic digital landscape.

Digital Public Diplomacy as Impression Management

In the digital age, public diplomacy has increasingly taken on the characteristics of impression management, where states and diplomats use digital platforms to shape global perceptions, project national identities, and foster international partnerships. Drawing on Erving Goffman's dramaturgical framework (Goffman, 1959), Marcus Holmes (2024) expands this concept by introducing two key processes in digital diplomacy: *projection* and *retrieval*. Projection refers to front-stage performances, the carefully curated messages and public actions designed to influence audiences. Retrieval, on the other hand, involves backstage analysis of audience reactions, providing feedback to refine future projections. Together, these processes illustrate how digital technologies enable states to manage both gradual, endogenous changes and significant, transformational shifts in the international system.

The *front-stage* of digital public diplomacy represents the public-facing performance of states and diplomats on platforms like Twitter, Facebook, and official websites. This space is where leadership, resilience, and solidarity are showcased, with messaging strategically framed to align with diplomatic goals. A striking example of effective front-stage digital diplomacy is Ukraine's online communication during the Russian invasion. By employing hashtags such as #StopRussianAggression and sharing visually impactful infographics detailing Russian losses, Ukraine projected an image of strength and unity, rallying global support and enhancing its position on the international stage. Similarly, nation-branding campaigns, like those undertaken by Norway, have leveraged digital media to cultivate an image of cultural vibrancy and economic opportunity, enhancing the country's appeal to investors and global audiences.

The effectiveness of front-stage digital diplomacy rests on the interplay of three pivotal elements: *consistency*, *strategic framing*, and *visibility*. Consistency is not merely about uniform messaging across platforms; it reflects a deeper alignment with the overarching narratives that define a nation's identity and values. This coherence fosters trust and credibility, reassuring audiences that the messages are part of a genuine, well-considered strategy rather than opportunistic gestures. *Strategic framing* goes beyond selecting resonant themes, such as sustainability or peacebuilding; it involves crafting narratives that not only engage audiences emotionally but also position the state as a thoughtful and proactive actor in global affairs. *Visibility*, achieved through timely and dynamic engagement with global events, signals relevance and authority, ensuring that a digital diplomat's voice is heard in the global digital sphere. However, these strengths are tempered by inherent challenges. Over-curation – where messaging is so meticulously polished that it appears staged – risks alienating audiences by undermining the perception of authenticity. In an era where sincerity is prized, such overtly managed communication can provoke scepticism and disengagement. Furthermore, the ephemeral nature of digital content introduces a temporal fragility; messages, even when impactful, are subject to rapid reinterpretation or obsolescence in the fast-paced digital environment. This impermanence underscores the need for adaptive strategies that balance the immediacy of digital diplomacy with the longevity of its influence.

The *back-stage* of digital public diplomacy is the engine room where the preparatory and reflective work necessary for effective front-stage performances takes place. It is characterised by strategic planning, rehearsals, and data-driven analysis, all of which enable diplomats to refine their messaging and respond adeptly to shifting audience dynamics. For instance, the Swedish Ministry for Foreign Affairs (MFA) employs a real-time dashboard to monitor social media engagement, allowing for the timely adjustment of strategies based on audience reactions. Similarly, the US State Department's use of tools like Hootsuite during the Obama administration illustrates how systematic monitoring of public sentiment can amplify the effectiveness of diplomatic communications. A distinctive feature of the backstage is its emphasis on *resilience*. Through meticulous preparation for diverse scenarios, diplomats can maintain composure and coherence in their public engagements, even under challenging circumstances. This environment also fosters *professional development*, as it provides opportunities for diplomats to build skills in digital communication, cultural sensitivity, and crisis management – competencies that are crucial for successful public-facing efforts.

However, the backstage is not without its limitations and vulnerabilities. *Transparency* risks loom large in the digital age; leaks or errors that expose backstage activities can undermine carefully curated narratives, highlighting inconsistencies or revealing strategies intended for internal deliberation. Additionally, the backstage often grapples with *internal misalignment*, where differing perspectives or lack of consensus within a diplomatic team can lead to disjointed or contradictory public narratives. This discord can erode the credibility of front-stage performances, particularly in high-stakes situations. Another characteristic of the backstage is its role in *audience retrieval and interpretation*. By analysing audience responses, diplomats can tailor their strategies to better resonate with diverse demographics. However, this process is complicated by the inherent heterogeneity of digital audiences. Messages that resonate strongly with one group may be misunderstood or rejected by another, increasing the likelihood of conflicting interpretations. This diversity requires nuanced and context-sensitive approaches to ensure that messaging aligns with the expectations and values of various stakeholders.

The interplay between front-stage projection and backstage refinement is central to effective digital public diplomacy. Marcus Holmes underscores the importance of a feedback loop, where retrieval processes inform future projections, enabling states to adapt their performances in response to audience reactions. For example, Michelle Obama's #BringBackOurGirls campaign initially aimed to project solidarity with Nigerian families. However, backlash reframed the campaign as a critique of US foreign policy, illustrating the precarious balance between frontstage messaging and audience reception. Such cases highlight the need for diplomats to anticipate audience reactions and recalibrate their strategies accordingly. Digital public diplomacy, as understood through the frameworks of Goffman and Holmes, reflects the performative nature of state interactions in the global arena. However, the integration of modern engagement strategies – such as visual simplicity, emotional framing, computational personalisation, and engagement hybridisation – further enhances the potential for impression management. Visual simplicity ensures clarity and accessibility, reducing the risk of misinterpretation. Emotional framing fosters empathy, connecting messages to audience values. Computational personalisation tailors messages to diverse demographics, while engagement hybridisation transforms passive audiences into active participants. Together, these strategies strengthen the feedback loop between projection and retrieval, enabling states to manage impressions more effectively. Nevertheless, these approaches also present limitations. Over-reliance on personalisation may fragment audiences, while hybrid engagement risks diluting core messages in favour of broad appeal. As states continue to refine their digital public diplomacy strategies, the challenge remains to balance these tools with the principles of authenticity and coherence, ensuring that public-facing performances resonate meaningfully with an increasingly dynamic and diverse global audience.

Digital International Negotiations

The integration of digital technology into diplomatic negotiations has reshaped both the processes and outcomes of negotiations, although the full magnitude and value of this transformation remain to be determined. While it has introduced new efficiencies in the preparation and conduct of negotiations, it has also disrupted traditional frameworks that have historically proven effective. The shift has been particularly evident in how negotiations are conducted, the role of public engagement, the use of social media as a diplomatic tool, the rising importance of data, and the erosion of distinctions between formal and informal negotiation spaces. While these transformations offer undeniable advantages, they also introduce profound risks that require careful mitigation. As diplomatic negotiations evolve within an increasingly digitalised landscape, states must adeptly navigate the delicate equilibrium between fostering transparency and safeguarding strategic discretion, ensuring that openness does not come at the expense of diplomatic efficacy and security.

The Transformation of Negotiation Dynamics

The use of digital platforms in diplomatic negotiations has altered how deals are structured and finalised. Digital tools enable real-time communication and collaboration, making negotiations more dynamic and interactive. However, this shift also reduces the ability of negotiators to maintain control over information flows. In the past, negotiators could manage the timing and sequencing of information disclosure, ensuring that parties were introduced to specific aspects of an agreement at the appropriate moments. Today, digital tools such as real-time document editing and cloud-based collaboration platforms expose negotiations to increased scrutiny and potential manipulation. The concept of "track-change diplomacy" illustrates this transformation, as technological affordances such as Microsoft Word's track-change function allow multiple stakeholders to modify and comment on agreements in real time, significantly altering the power dynamics of negotiation (Adler-Nissen and Drieschova, 2019). While this enhances transparency, it also introduces the risk of losing control over the negotiation process, as different actors may seek to shape agreements in ways that benefit their interests rather than the collective diplomatic outcome.

The Iran nuclear deal negotiations exemplify how digital tools have transformed diplomatic interactions, particularly within the framework of Robert Putnam's two-level game theory (Putnam, 1988). Traditionally, diplomatic negotiations operated within a dual framework: Level I, where national leaders negotiate with foreign counterparts, and Level II, where these agreements must be ratified domestically. Digital diplomacy has altered this equilibrium by enabling states to simultaneously influence both levels in real time. Moreover, digital communication has blurred the boundary between international and domestic arenas, allowing negotiators to strategically shape both while also raising concerns about the manipulation of public opinion by external forces.

Prior to the ratification of the Iran Deal, the Obama administration's use of social media, particularly Twitter, played a decisive role in shaping public perceptions and expanding the domestic win-set – the range of acceptable agreements that could gain sufficient political support at home. By engaging directly with domestic audiences, the US government was able to counter misinformation, refute adversarial narratives, and emphasise the costs of non-ratification (Bjola and Manor, 2018). The Iran deal negotiations thus demonstrated how digital diplomacy can reshape the bargaining power of negotiators. The highly visible nature of online engagement made it easier for opponents to mobilise counter-campaigns, as seen in efforts by conservative lawmakers and interest groups to delegitimise the agreement. However, the ability to engage with domestic constituencies in real time also strengthened the Obama administration's leverage in Level I negotiations with Iran and European allies. By demonstrating robust domestic support – or at least the ability to counteract opposition digitally – US negotiators were able to present themselves as more credible partners, reassuring counterparts that the agreement had a higher likelihood of domestic approval.

The Rise of Virtual Diplomacy

The COVID-19 pandemic forced diplomats to rely on virtual platforms for high-level negotiations, fundamentally altering the traditional process of diplomatic engagement. The transition to virtual diplomatic summitry, while initially an emergency response to travel restrictions, has since become an integral aspect of diplomatic practice, reshaping both the process and dynamics of international negotiations. Virtual diplomacy has enabled greater inclusivity, allowing more stakeholders – including representatives from civil society and international organisations – to participate in discussions that were traditionally restricted to diplomats and heads of state. Additionally, virtual formats have increased efficiency by reducing the logistical and financial costs associated with travel and large in-person summits While digital platforms enabled inclusive and continued diplomatic engagement, they also undermined critical elements of face-to-face diplomacy, particularly informal networking and trust-building. Personal rapport in diplomatic negotiations is indispensable, as high-stakes talks often rely on side conversations, informal gestures, and personal chemistry to break deadlocks and facilitate compromise. Without these informal spaces – previously cultivated through coffee breaks, corridor meetings, and private dinners – negotiations in virtual settings risk becoming rigid and overly transactional, reducing the potential for diplomatic creativity and flexibility (Bjola and Coplen, 2022b).

One of the key limitations of virtual diplomacy, particularly in peace negotiations, has been its inability to replicate the trust-building dynamics of physical meetings. The absence of direct, in-person interaction deprives negotiators of vital non-verbal cues such as body language, tone, and gestures, which are essential for assessing sincerity, de-escalating tensions, and fostering mutual understanding. Studies have shown that during the COVID-19 lockdown, digital negotiations often stalled, leading to diminished progress in conflict resolution efforts, as trust and relationship-building suffered in a virtual environment (Bramsen and Hagemann, 2021). This phenomenon reflects a broader concern in diplomatic summitry: while virtual tools facilitate continuity, they often fail to create the interpersonal depth necessary for successful conflict resolution.

Moreover, digital diplomacy introduces new asymmetries in negotiations, favouring states and actors with greater technological literacy, advanced cybersecurity measures, and stable internet access. This digital divide risks reinforcing existing power imbalances, marginalising weaker states or actors who lack the infrastructure for secure, real-time diplomatic engagement. Furthermore, the lack of confidentiality in virtual negotiations has raised security concerns, as sensitive discussions are increasingly vulnerable to cyber espionage and leaks, undermining the discretion that has historically been central to diplomatic practice (Bjola and Coplen, 2022b). Virtual summitry also complicates diplomatic signalling, making it harder for negotiators to read their counterparts and gauge the credibility of commitments, which is crucial in both multilateral and bilateral negotiations (Hedling, 2024).

The challenge now is to strike a balance between these efficiencies and the interpersonal elements that make diplomacy effective. As diplomatic practices continue to evolve, a hybrid approach appears to be the most viable model moving forward. Hybrid diplomacy, which integrates both virtual and in-person engagements, can preserve the efficiencies of digital tools while restoring the critical human elements that underpin effective negotiation. This approach recognises that diplomacy is not merely about exchanging information but about building relationships, trust, and strategic understanding. As diplomatic interactions increasingly unfold across both physical and virtual domains, negotiators must develop new skills to navigate the complexities of digital engagement while ensuring that technology does not erode the core principles of diplomacy.

Social Media as a Double-Edged Sword

The role of social media in diplomatic negotiations represents one of the most profound shifts brought about by digital technology, fundamentally altering how states, diplomats, and non-state actors engage with global audiences. Platforms such as Twitter (now 'X'), Facebook, and more recently TikTok have provided unprecedented opportunities for shaping public narratives in real time, but they have also introduced significant challenges. On one hand, social media has become a powerful instrument of public diplomacy, enabling governments to bypass traditional media gatekeepers and engage directly with both domestic and international audiences. On the other hand, it has heightened the visibility of diplomatic negotiations, exposing them to greater public scrutiny and increasing the risk of opposition movements mobilising against agreements before they are even finalised.

A striking example of social media's influence on diplomatic negotiations is the Iran-US nuclear deal, where Twitter was used as a tool for direct engagement. US officials leveraged the platform to counter misinformation and frame the deal in a way that underscored its benefits to the American public (Duncombe, 2017). However, social media also served as a space for opposition groups to organise resistance, amplifying discontent and increasing pressure on policymakers, thereby complicating the negotiation process. Similar dynamics emerged during the COP21 climate negotiations, where climate activists and international organisations used Twitter to foreground discussions around climate justice, while fossil fuel industry stakeholders sought to undermine these narratives (Hopke and Hestres, 2018). The ability of social media to shape diplomatic discourse underscores the necessity for negotiators to develop sophisticated digital engagement strategies to effectively manage public perception.

The evolving landscape of digital diplomacy has been further complicated by the rise of platformisation and algorithmic governance, where the infrastructure of social media itself influences the visibility and reach of diplomatic messaging. As mentioned earlier, social media algorithms, particularly on platforms like TikTok, shape the visibility and influence of narratives, introducing new power asymmetries in diplomatic communications with significant domestic and international ramifications. Governments and international organisations have begun engaging with these platforms not only to disseminate official messaging but also to counter misinformation and enhance strategic influence. The White House, for instance, partnered with TikTok influencers to address vaccine hesitancy, demonstrating how social media engagement strategies now extend beyond traditional diplomatic channels to include content creators with significant digital influence (Lai, 2021).

However, the geopolitics of social media platforms introduces additional risks. Platforms such as TikTok, with its ties to the Chinese government, have raised concerns over data security, content moderation biases, and the potential manipulation of information flows. Governments have responded with regulatory measures, as seen in India's ban on TikTok and the restrictions placed on the platform's use within US government agencies (Fjällhed, Lüfkens and Sandre, 2024). These developments highlight the growing intersection between digital diplomacy and cyber governance, where state actors must navigate the dual challenges of leveraging social media's diplomatic potential while mitigating its vulnerabilities.

As social media continues to reshape diplomatic engagement, it is clear that the influence of digital platforms extends beyond mere messaging – it is embedded within the very infrastructure of global communications. The ability of states to effectively conduct diplomacy in this evolving digital environment will depend on their capacity to anticipate and adapt to the shifting dynamics of platform governance, algorithmic visibility, and online mobilisation. The challenge for contemporary diplomacy is thus not only to master digital engagement but also to understand and shape the technological ecosystems within which diplomatic narratives unfold.

The Growing Role of Data and AI

The increasing reliance on data and AI in diplomatic negotiations represents a potential game-changer in the practice of diplomacy. AI-driven data analysis offers negotiators the ability to extract valuable insights into adversarial strategies, anticipate obstacles, and refine their approaches in real time. Computational tools can model negotiation dynamics, simulate possible scenarios, and even generate predictive insights to inform decision-making. However, the integration of AI into diplomatic practice also raises significant concerns regarding security, reliability, and susceptibility to manipulation. Governments that fail to establish robust frameworks for managing diplomatic data risk being outmanoeuvred by adversaries who exploit data vulnerabilities, distort narratives, or manipulate predictive models to generate misleading forecasts (Cafiero, 2023).

The concept of 'data diplomacy' (→ glossary) highlights the intricate governance and ethical challenges associated with integrating AI and big data into international negotiations. As diplomatic interactions become increasingly digitised, securing and managing data effectively becomes paramount. Boyd et al. (2019) emphasise that while AI and big data can enhance diplomatic agility, they also introduce risks related to algorithmic bias, data manipulation, and cyber threats. The geopolitical dimension of AI-driven diplomacy, as explored by Fjällhed, Lüfkens and Sandre (2024), underscores that control over digital infrastructures and data flows is now a fundamental aspect of state power. In this context, AI's ability to process vast amounts of information – ranging from diplomatic statements to voting patterns in multilateral institutions – grants states strategic leverage. However, the central challenge remains: how can AI be harnessed to improve negotiations without eroding diplomatic discretion and human judgement?

One of the most promising applications of AI in diplomacy is its potential to assist in argument recognition and computational modelling of negotiation processes. Koit (2023) explores how AI can enhance strategic reasoning by mapping inter-argument relations, identifying rebuttals, and even detecting rhetorical inconsistencies in real time. Automated argument analysis strengthens diplomatic decision-making by assessing the credibility of claims and pinpointing weaknesses in adversarial rhetoric. However, this raises critical concerns regarding overreliance on AI-generated insights. AI lacks the contextual and cultural sensitivity of human negotiators and, without careful oversight, could misinterpret complex political signals, leading to strategic miscalculations.

The role of AI in predictive modelling of diplomatic behaviour is another area of intense interest. Stanzel and Voelsen (2022) examine whether AI can provide strategic value by evaluating the likelihood of negotiation outcomes based on historical data. Their research suggests that AI can be particularly effective in generating a spectrum of possible scenarios, assisting negotiators in formulating adaptive strategies. AI models have been used to assess voting behaviour in the UN General Assembly, tracking patterns in multilateral negotiations to predict state alignments on contentious issues. However, these predictive capabilities remain constrained by data limitations and the unpredictability of diplomatic decision-making. While AI excels at pattern recognition, it struggles with forecasting disruptive geopolitical shifts, unexpected crises, or the influence of individual diplomatic personalities.

The ethical and strategic challenges of AI in diplomacy extend beyond data security and predictive reliability. The risk of algorithmic bias looms large, as AI systems are only as reliable as the data they are trained on. If historical biases or incomplete datasets shape AI models, their recommendations may reinforce existing power imbalances or generate skewed assessments of negotiation dynamics. Furthermore, the potential for AI-driven misinformation campaigns – where digital adversaries manipulate AI-generated insights to mislead diplomats – adds another layer of complexity to AI's role in negotiations. Addressing these challenges requires the development of cyber-diplomacy frameworks that establish clear guidelines for AI's application, ensuring that digital tools enhance rather than undermine diplomatic practice.

Moving forward, the integration of AI into diplomatic negotiations must be approached with both strategic foresight and ethical caution. AI should not replace human judgement but rather serve as an augmentation tool that complements the experience and intuition of seasoned diplomats. A hybrid model, in which AI-generated insights are subject to rigorous human oversight, offers the most viable path forward. Diplomatic training must also evolve to equip negotiators with the technical literacy needed to interpret and critically evaluate AI-driven recommendations.

The Blurring of Formal and Informal Negotiation Practices

One of the most profound shifts brought about by digital communication tools is the erosion of traditional diplomatic hierarchies and formal protocols. In the past, diplomatic negotiations adhered to structured processes, where official statements and agreements were carefully crafted, vetted, and disseminated through established channels. The proliferation of digital communication tools has blurred the once-clear distinctions between formal and informal negotiation spaces. Messaging platforms such as WhatsApp, Signal, and Telegram have become indispensable tools for diplomats, facilitating real-time coordination, rapid information exchange, and off-the-record discussions that streamline negotiation processes. While these digital tools enhance efficiency and enable greater responsiveness, they also pose significant risks to the integrity, security, and coherence of diplomatic engagements.

Today, informal digital interactions often run parallel to, or even supersede, formal negotiation tracks. Cornut, Manor and Blumenthal (2022) highlight how diplomats in Geneva increasingly rely on encrypted messaging apps to conduct sensitive backchannel discussions, accelerating decision-making but simultaneously raising concerns about the transparency and accountability of diplomatic processes. The informal nature of these digital exchanges means that key deliberations may take place outside official records, leading to inconsistencies in policy implementation and misalignment between negotiators and their respective governments. This transformation is particularly evident in high-stakes negotiations, where backchannel diplomacy – previously conducted through discreet in-person meetings – has migrated to digital platforms. During the Iran nuclear deal negotiations, informal digital communications allowed negotiators to clarify positions and mitigate misunderstandings outside the constraints of formal sessions. However, this shift also made negotiations more susceptible to information leaks and external influence, as digital interactions are inherently more vulnerable to cyber espionage and interception by adversarial actors (Eggeling and Adler-Nissen, 2024). The digitisation of informal diplomacy thus raises a paradox: while digital tools enhance real-time engagement and flexibility, they also introduce new risks related to surveillance, data security, and the manipulation of digital records.

Moreover, the increasing reliance on digital platforms in diplomatic negotiations exacerbates asymmetries in access and influence. States with advanced digital capabilities, robust cybersecurity infrastructures, and greater expertise in digital diplomacy gain a strategic advantage in negotiations, while those with limited technological resources risk being marginalised. The digital divide in diplomacy, as observed by Bjola and Coplen (2022b), is particularly pronounced in multilateral negotiations, where smaller or less technologically equipped states struggle to participate effectively in digital backchannel discussions. This disparity reinforces existing power imbalances, as technologically dominant states can exert disproportionate influence over informal negotiation processes, potentially sidelining less digitally adept actors from key deliberations. Beyond concerns about access and transparency, the informal nature of digital diplomacy also complicates the codification of diplomatic commitments. Traditionally, formal negotiations produce official transcripts, communiqués, and legally binding agreements that provide a clear framework for accountability. In contrast, digital backchannel discussions often lack the same level of documentation, leading to ambiguity over what has been agreed upon and by whom. This lack of institutional memory in digital diplomacy can create challenges in enforcing agreements and resolving disputes, as informal understandings reached via encrypted messaging platforms may not always translate into concrete policy actions.

To navigate this evolving digital landscape, diplomatic institutions must establish clearer governance frameworks for the use of digital communication tools in negotiations. This involves not only strengthening cybersecurity protocols to safeguard sensitive communications but also ensuring that digital engagements remain aligned with formal diplomatic objectives. Establishing structured guidelines for the integration of informal digital interactions within broader diplomatic strategies is essential to preventing fragmentation and ensuring coherence across negotiation tracks. Furthermore, capacity-building initiatives must be prioritised to equip diplomats with the necessary skills to navigate digital negotiations effectively, particularly for states that face technological disadvantages in diplomatic arenas.

Summary

- *Digital Crisis Communication: speed vs control:* Crisis diplomacy in the digital era unfolds through structured stages – sense-making, decision-making, meaning-making, collaboration, and reflection – each influenced by the speed and visibility of digital platforms. Arjen Boin's crisis management framework highlights how digital networks accelerate response time while complicating message coherence and credibility. The interplay between real-time engagement and strategic narrative control underscores the challenges of maintaining authority and trust in crisis scenarios.
- *Digital Public Diplomacy – performance vs strategy:* Digital technologies redefine the grammar of public diplomacy by intensifying the relationship between highly visible front-stage performances and strategically managed back-stage processes. Drawing on Erving Goffman's dramaturgical model, the chapter highlights how states engage in digital diplomacy by carefully balancing open communication with controlled messaging. The increasing use of digital platforms for engagement also raises concerns about credibility, authenticity, and the strategic management of diplomatic narratives.
- *Digital International Negotiation – transparency vs secrecy:* Digital platforms challenge traditional negotiation structures by increasing transparency while raising risks of leaks and strategic manipulation. The shift from closed-door diplomacy to digitally mediated negotiations forces states to adapt their strategies for maintaining confidentiality and managing public narratives. The integration of AI-driven analysis, encrypted communication tools, and real-time media engagement reflects both the vulnerabilities and opportunities that digital diplomacy presents in modern negotiations.

Study Questions

- How do digital platforms reshape the structured stages of crisis communication, particularly in balancing real-time responsiveness with strategic control?
- How does the distinction between front-stage visibility and back-stage coordination shape digital public diplomacy, and what strategies are used to maintain credibility and influence?
- How does digital transparency impact the confidentiality of diplomatic negotiations, and what approaches can states take to navigate new digital challenges in negotiation?
- What are the broader implications of the digital turn for diplomatic norms, institutional adaptation, and the evolving role of state and non-state actors in shaping global diplomacy?

Recommended Further Reading

Bjola, Corneliu, and Ilan Manor. 2022. "The Rise of Hybrid Diplomacy: From Digital Adaptation to Digital Adoption." *International Affairs* 98 (2): 471–91.

This article analyses the evolution of digital diplomacy, arguing that states are moving from merely adapting to digital tools towards fully integrating them into diplomatic practice. It discusses how hybrid diplomacy blends traditional and digital methods to manage crises, conduct negotiations, and engage in strategic communications.

Manor, Ilan. 2019. *The Digitalization of Public Diplomacy*. London: Palgrave Macmillan.

This book provides a comprehensive study of how digital technologies have transformed public diplomacy, examining key trends in state-led digital engagement. It offers case studies on how governments use digital platforms to communicate foreign policy messages, manage crises, and shape international perceptions.

Manor, Ilan, and James Pamment. 2019. "Towards Prestige Mobility? Diplomatic Prestige and Digital Diplomacy." *Cambridge Review of International Affairs* 32 (2): 93–131.

This article examines how states use digital diplomacy to enhance or maintain their diplomatic prestige in the global order. It explores how digital engagement reshapes traditional diplomatic hierarchies, with particular attention to how states leverage social media platforms to project influence and status.

Margetts, Helen, Peter John, Scott Hale, and Taha Yasseri. 2015. *Political Turbulence: How Social Media Shape Collective Action.* Princeton, NJ: Princeton University Press.

This book examines how social media drive political mobilisation, revealing its unpredictability and instability. Using large-scale data and experiments, the authors analyse how personality types engage online and how digital platforms create a turbulent form of democracy. Their insights inform digital diplomacy by highlighting the role of digital publics in shaping state narratives and crisis responses.

Varela, Damián Tuset. 2024. "Diplomacy in the Age of AI: Challenges and Opportunities." *Journal of Artificial Intelligence General Science (JAIGS)* 2 (1): 98–109.

This article explores the implications of AI for diplomatic practice, focusing on how AI is transforming decision-making, strategic forecasting, and diplomatic negotiations. It assesses both the potential benefits – such as enhanced data analysis – and the challenges, including ethical concerns and the risk of AI-driven disinformation in diplomatic relations.

11 Crises in the Inter-epoch

Chapter Objectives

- To introduce reader to the nexus of polycrisis and permacrisis on the one hand and today's inter-epoch – times in between two eras – on the other.
- To define crisis, crisis management and crisis co-management.
- To differentiate between two kinds of crises: policy and institutional.
- To discuss the process of crisis co-management and its challenges for diplomacy.
- To examine problems of diplomacy to prevent crises.

Introduction

Epochal change does not happen frequently in international affairs (Onuf, 2018). But when it happens, world politics is very prone to international crises. When E.H. Carr famously wrote The Twenty-Years Crisis 1919–1939 (shortly before the onset of World War II), he addressed troubled power transitions in world politics. After discussing how the rise of new powers and the decline of old ones gave rise to fundamental challenges for preserving peace in international politics, he concluded his book with a chapter on peaceful change. Borrowing the concept from International Law, he applied legal conceptualisations of how to settle disputes peacefully to ways for how to steer clear from hegemonic war among great powers. In doing so, he broadened the concept and made it amenable to studying power transitions in international relations (Carr, 1946).

We, too, live in an era of epochal change. The transition has at least two dimensions. First, the days of US unipolarity are over. World politics increasingly moves towards a multipolar system. Russia reasserts itself and China is the major rising power. India becomes economically increasingly powerful on the world stage, and it may, in the foreseeable future, get more determined to convert these capacities into military ones. Regional powers also become savvier and savvier. Saudi Arabia and the United Arab Emirates, for example, no longer confine enacting their rivalry to the Gulf but project it into neighbouring regions, such as the Horn of Africa, as well. Second, major technological innovations make themselves felt for most people and international actors, and very profoundly so. Digital technology revolutionises how people spend their leisure time, work, get politically informed, act politically, how diplomatic actors communicate with one another, how weapons technologies get modernised, and so on. With this, new actors enter the diplomatic stage. Tech companies have plenty of clout on this stage by now, especially the politically very well-connected CEOs of major tech giants such as Elon Musk. These two dimensions, of course, are very much interrelated. Technological innovation makes it possible for great powers and regional powers to rise.

DOI: 10.4324/9781003485407-16

Once again, the kind of inter-epoch in which the world has moved in the last decade or so is highly crisis prone. Similarly to how Carr put it, this involves inter-state crises in which peace and security are at stake. Russia's war against Ukraine is the most pronounced one among these, but elsewhere, too, inter-state relations have become tense, especially in the Middle East and the South-China Sea. Yet the kinds of crises our inter-epoch experiences go beyond the kinds of crises that Carr writes about. There are many intra-state armed conflicts, ranging from Sudan to Myanmar and Ethiopia to Nigeria. With global economic flows being disrupted, global trade and finance have become more volatile. The numbers of refugees and internally displaced persons remains at a very high level. The corona pandemic killed many millions of people worldwide. Climate change remains an unresolved issue, causing more and more severe weather events worldwide.

It is, therefore, not surprising that our inter-epoch is referred to with terminology such as polycrisis (Morin and Kern, 1993; Lawrence, Janzwood and Homer-Dixon, 2022) and permacrisis (Shariatmadari, 2022; Turnbull, 2022). There really are many (poly)crises. At times, the state of international affairs resembles one of permanent crisis. This chapter discusses the nexus of these crises, epochal change and diplomacy. Is there something that diplomacy can do to help us move beyond crises? What repercussions do our decisions in the here and now have for the new epoch ahead of us? In order to address these questions, we provide a framework for diplomatic crisis management, arguing that such a crisis management is always a co-management, and illustrate our points by applying this framework to studying policy crises and institutional crises.

Two Kinds of Crises

A crisis is a critical juncture in a course of events that pose a major threat to what is deemed highly important by actors. Decision-making is characterised by a high degree of uncertainty. At the same time, there is pressure to decide. Actors are of the opinion that they have to act fast in order to prevent things from getting even much worse than they already are; there is a sense of urgency by the perception that otherwise the course of will spiral out of control (Freedman, 2014; Boin et al., 2017: 5–7; Brecher and Wilkenfeld, 1997: 5). Crises end with what actors perceive to be a marked de-escalation of the course of events. Crisis management is the process through which actors seek to defuse a crisis and achieve such a de-escalation (Swaine, 2006: 3).

There are two kinds of crises. A *policy crisis* is triggered in at least one of the policy areas discussed in this book. Thus, there are security crises, economic crises, development crises, environmental crises, health crises, and so on. Since diplomacy gets involved in all these fields, diplomats are among those expected to defuse policy crises. Note that some of these policy crises tend to be more protracted than others. On the one hand, there are crisis moments, traditionally studied by International Relations scholars, that escalate at a certain point in time, say by one state issuing an ultimatum to another one, and then defuse by another clear-cut event such as the addressee giving in to the demands of the ultimatum. On the other hand, there are crises that are very protracted. The most protracted one of them all is global climate change. The course of events has been in motion for a long time already and it is predicted to continue – and even exacerbate – long into the future.

An *institutional crisis* is not just about substantive measures to be taken within a policy area but shakes the institutions through which diplomacy is to agree upon such measures. Some institutional crises are more confined than others. The Conference on Disarmament in Geneva and the WTO, for example, have experienced rather protracted institutional crises. The former suffers from procedural wrangling that prevents diplomats from agreeing on an agenda while the latter's dispute settlement mechanism remains dysfunctional. Yet, in these cases, not the entire range of diplomatic activities is in crisis. The institutional crises make work on disarmament and trade more difficult. Other institutional crises are more all-encompassing. For decades, for example, the EU deepened and broadened integration and co-operation. But then came Brexit and the rise of populist governments in member states that makes it difficult to put existing institutions to use in issue areas ranging from migration to defence.

Policy and institutional crises hang together. If international institutions are strong, it is easier to co-manage policy crises. In the early 1990s, a far-reaching consensus on territorial integrity and collective security made it possible for the UN to liberate Kuwait after having been invaded and annexed by Iraq. In the early 2020s, a weakening agreement on territorial integrity and the UN left the world's primary organisation entrusted with maintaining peace and security sidelined during Russia's aggression against Ukraine.

These examples highlight something that is of great salience in today's highly interconnected world. In most cases, unilateral crisis management cannot defuse international crises. Different actors – not necessarily all like-minded but including the not all that like-minded ones – have to come together and de-escalate a crisis together. This co-management does not come easy in our inter-epoch. But why is co-management actually such a challenge?

Co-managing Crises

Analytically speaking, co-management can be broken apart into three processes: overlapping repertoires, intersecting prejudgements and consonant judgements (Kornprobst, 2019b). In international relations, it is very rare indeed that all actors involved in crisis decision-making draw from the same toolbox when they seek to make a crisis situation intelligible to themselves, and, based on this, figure out what to do.[1] This is partly because crisis actors are embedded in different intersubjectivities. Today's Japanese decision-makers, for instance, draw to a considerable extent from a more pacifist toolbox than, say, Chinese ones. Yet repertoires vary among decision-makers within a state, too. It does matter, for instance, whether Xi Jinping or Hu Jintao are in office. They embrace different kinds of subjective idiosyncrasies when it comes to dealing with border disputes in the South China Sea. The latter was much more risk-averse than the former. Different repertoires and personal idiosyncrasies are configured in certain ways among different actors. They may be far apart or overlap to different degrees. Overlaps facilitate crisis co-management. Their lack, by contrast, hinders it. Consider the case of climate change. If actors cannot even agree upon whether climate change is happening or not or, if they do, whether it is caused by human activity or not, they may not even agree that there is a crisis.

If they do agree, decision-makers usually have a first hunch for how to deal with a crisis. This hunch is usually not all that reflective. Given certain circumstances, leaders are predisposed to fall back to certain universals that they select from the repertoire. From the beginning of the Bosnian Crisis in the early 1990s onwards, François Mitterrand resorted to an alliance universal that, to him, was an important lesson of World War II, that is, the juxtaposition of historical alliances of France and Serbia versus Germany and Croatia. Because of this, he was not prepared to move militarily against the Serbs (Védrine, 2005). For Helmut Kohl, his German counterpart, not to intervene militarily abroad was the key lesson from World War II. These prejudgements proved to be rather sticky and made crisis co-management difficult. While Mitterrand and Kohl were in power, France and Germany, often referred to as engine of European unification, were not able to steer the EU towards a crisis co-management pathway that would go beyond a lowest common denominator.

Decision-makers elaborate on their judgements through communicative encounters. These elaborations may happen within domestic decision-making units, in exchanges between elites and masses in domestic politics, and on the diplomatic stage. Mitterrand and Kohl relied to a considerable extent on their advisors but disregarded a much more interventionist public opinion in both states. To them, foreign policy decision-making was an elite affair, not to be disrupted by public sentiments. Their successors, Chirac and Schröder, respectively, would be very different in this regard, and this had major repercussions for how the next crisis situation during the breakdown of Yugoslavia – in Kosovo – was handled. Sharing universals about the EU as an actor in matters of foreign affairs and international security, not being held back by Mitterrand's and Kohl's prejudgements, and frequently exchanging views with one another, their judgements became more consonant over time. Other players on the diplomatic stage, most importantly Bill Clinton and Madeleine Albright on the US side and Tony Blair on the British one, played crucial roles in moulding more consonant judgements as well. Textbox 11.1 elaborates on these exchanges.

How then does diplomacy succeed or fail to co-manage international crises? It all depends on these three processes: overlaps, intersections and consonances. Diplomacy has designed numerous mechanisms for how to co-manage international crises. The UN features two sets of tools in its Charter, that is, pacific settlement of disputes (Chapter 6) and enforcement measures (Chapter 7). These tools are very much about crisis co-management. Chapter 6 obliges all member states to seek to settle disputes peacefully. Chapter 7 ultimately sets up a great power crisis co-management mechanism. Due to their veto power, the permanent 5 members (P5) are in a privileged position but they, too, are to put this mechanism to use in a way that does not violate the rights of other members and respects their Charter obligations as guardians of peace and security. If these stipulations featured prominently in the repertoires of all key actors – perhaps even in their prejudgements – and, in addition to this, perhaps even the far-reaching promises of a diplomatic peace that UN member states have made over the decades – co-managing international security crises would become much easier. But the same caveats apply here in similar ways as we have discussed them in Chapter 5 on making order already. Background provisions

---

Textbox 11.1   Srebrenica

Particulars, when they are emphasised over and over, can evolve into universals. When Bosnian Serbs overran Srebrenica in July 1995 and massacred thousands of Bosniak boys and men, this was a particular. The course of events in Bosnia had escalated to the point of genocide. Decision-makers on both sides of the Atlantic made sense of this particular through the lens of the Holocaust universal. After Srebrenica, the United States and EU member states became much more assertive in co-managing the crisis. Once the Bosnian War was finally over, Srebrenica continued to be commemorated in political elite circles and civil society. Court proceedings started. Being invoked again and again, Srebrenica sank in as a universal in the repertoires of many actors, including Western leaders. When violence escalated in Kosovo, especially after the Račak Massacre in January 1999 perpetrated by Serb security forces fighting Albanian separatists, these leaders used Srebrenica as universal to make the course of events in Kosovo intelligible to themselves. Very much in line with this sense-making, their decision-making came down heavily on the military side. NATO started to bomb Serbia.

oftentimes look very different from the foreground promises, and many universals that actors fall back to, especially in their prejudgements are located in the background.

Reaching intersections among judgements, even if repertoires overlap, is not always easy. Decision-makers select universals from the repertoire. It is not to be taken for granted that they select them from the overlaps. For diplomacy, there is an additional challenge. Diplomatic universals, to put it mildly, are not the only game in town. Leaders and their persuasions matter in crisis situations a lot. So does domestic politics, ranging from advisors to public opinion. We chose the aforementioned illustration deliberately. The kind of crisis co-management that Mitterrand and Kohl pursued, ignoring public pressures as much as they could, has become very rare in our days. Leaders have become much more inclined to take public opinion very seriously. They may be very savvy in trying to shape it, but they are usually attuned to limitations for how to do so and factor this into their crisis management strategies.

All of this has repercussions for reaching consonances. Domestic politics may tear leader judgements further apart. In the age of populism, this is an even greater problem than in the past. The problem has several facets. For one, populist leaders, attempting to sideline the 'establishment', tend to rely on their own hand-picked advisors rather than career diplomats. Domestic grandstanding becomes an important goal. Compromise is frowned upon. Furthermore, domestic encounters with the public cater to nationalist sentiments. These, in turn, make the production of consonant judgements among leaders of different nations even more difficult.

The illustrations on overlaps, intersections, and consonances we just provided were about leaders. Things get even more complicated if we zoom in on the interaction patterns of political leaders and other kinds of actors. Take experts, for example. Leaders are dependent on expert advice when they want to make sound judgements. But the experts put very different repertoires to use. A medical expert thinks scientifically. A political leader, by contrast, does not reason based on a controlled experiment or the intricacies of genome sequences. Troubled encounters between political elites, career diplomats, and experts abounded during the corona pandemic. But this is not confined to pandemics or global health. In a world that is becoming increasingly complex, different types of actors need to work together to defuse crises.

Co-managing Foreign Policy Crises?

In our inter-epoch, crises happen in all issue areas diplomacy gets involved in. But there is often no diplomatic agreement whether there is a crisis in the first place or, if so, whether major steps ought to be taken to co-manage it. This is underpinned by lacking overlaps of repertoires among actors. This section illustrates this problem by comparing crisis perceptions across different kinds of actors in January 2025.

The 2025 Emergency Watchlist, published by the International Rescue Committee in early January 2025, rank-ordered the world's most severe crisis hotspots from 1 to 10. The civil war in Sudan ranked number one due to its enormous destructiveness and the return of genocide to Darfur. Then came Gaza, where Israel's military response to Hamas's attack on Israel resulted in many dead and injured civilians, destruction of houses and infrastructure, and severe food shortages. Myanmar followed third on that list. Twenty million people depend on humanitarian aid because of a civil war that pitted several armed groups against the government. Next on the list was South Sudan where three quarters of the population were dependent on humanitarian aid amidst clashes between military splinter groups and government forces. Sixth was Lebanon due to the escalation of fighting between Hezbollah and Israel. Then came Burkina Faso, Haiti, Mali, and Somalia, where civil war destroyed the livelihood for civilians, diseases spread (especially in camps for internally displaced people), and starvation sat in among some segments of the population. In Somalia, a severe drought exacerbated the already dire situation further (International Rescue Committee, 2025).

Thinktanks and data sets focusing on international security only partly agreed with this list, put together by a humanitarian NGO. The International Crisis Behaviour Group and the Armed Conflict and Event Data (ACLED), for instance, featured fewer cases of humanitarian disasters in their top 10 crises to be watched out for in 2025. They also did not include a case of Gaza. What did feature prominently on their lists were cases in which contagion effects might engulf entire regions. For the Group, these were especially the confrontations between 'Israel-Palestine' and 'Iran vs. U.S. and Israel' (International Crisis Group, 2025). For ACLED, these were 'Israel, Gaza, the West Bank and Lebanon' and 'Iran & its allies' (ACLED, 2024).

Yet there were altogether different yardsticks for how to dub something a crisis as well. In his speeches, Antonio Guterres, the UN Secretary-General, focused very strongly on environmental crises, especially climate change. He urged to take an exit off 'the highway to climate hell' (United Nations, 2024a). In his inaugural address in January 2025, Trump mentioned the word 'crisis' four times, referring to domestic crises but not international ones. Inflation, for instance, was described as such a domestic crisis, to be addressed by domestic – and not international – politics (U.S. Mission, 2025). In his New Year's Address on December 31, 2024, Putin did not use the word 'crisis' at all. Instead, he praised the 'bravery and valour' of Russian soldiers and declared 2025 the 'Year of the Defender of the Fatherland' (President of Russia, 2024).

For all the general agreement that we are living in an era of crises, there is actually not all that much agreement on where these crises are and what constitutes them. The actors' repertoires are too far removed from one another to allow for more convergence.

Co-managing Institutional Crises?

Since the mid-2010s, many international organisations have experienced significant institutional crises. Not being able to co-manage policy crises that they are mandated to co-manage, their legitimacy has suffered. This applies to regional organisations as much as to the UN. Among the former, the Organization for Security and Co-operation in Europe (OSCE) may experience the deepest crisis. Evolving from the mid-1970s détente during the Cold War that produced the Helsinki Final Act, the organisation is to guarantee the inviolability of borders, human rights and minority rights. Since Russia's attack on Ukraine, the OSCE has been deadlocked. Operating by consensus, Russia can easily prevent any action being taken against it. This deadlock has not only marginalised the organisation during the war between Russia and Ukraine but also during other crises, such as fighting between Armenia and Azerbaijan over Nagorno-Karabakh. In this dire institutional crisis, even "questions about the survival of the OSCE have taken an acute form" (Eilstrup-Sangiovanni, 2022: 33).

Textbox 11.2   United Nations Reform

There have been many proposals and attempts to reform the UN. A particularly far-reaching attempt has been circulating since 2023. Authored by the Global Governance Forum, composed by NGOs, former UN officials, former diplomats, legal scholars and other experts from all over the world, the aim is to gain momentum for a process to redraft the UN Charter. The document entitled A Second UN Charter details the proposed changes, one after the other. These include the following: for the purposes of the organisation to include addressing 'collective challenges' and to 'cooperate in the global interest' (Article 2); to get rid of the Trusteeship Council and add a Parliamentary Assembly, a more meaningful Human Rights Council and an Earth Systems Council (Article 7); to strengthen the General Assembly and make it the 'chief deliberative and policy making body of the United Nations' (Article 12/1), for the Assembly to assume the powers of the Security Council if the latter is deadlocked and there is a two thirds majority in the Assembly on matters to be decided (Article 12/3); and to enlarge the Security Council to 25 members, ensuring the representation of the five regions of Africa, Asia-Pacific, Eastern Europe, Latin America and the Caribbean, and Western Europe (Article 23). Overall, the proposal is meant to address the problems of representation, performance and outlook comprehensively. Yet gaining the necessary momentum to reform the Charter, even though it reflects the political realities of the mid-1940s more closely than today's, remains a formidable task.

The UN, too, experiences an institutional crisis. Its legitimacy has suffered on three dimensions: representation, performance, and outlook. Textbox 11.2 discusses a currently debated proposal for how to fix these problems. The murals in San Francisco's Grace Cathedral depicting the making of the UN make for a good illustration of the problem of representation. Harping back to imagery of ancient Greece, it does not look all that different from paintings and sculptures depicting the Congress of Vienna in the early 19th century. In this imagery, it is an idealised European world that makes peace. This had concrete repercussions for the making of the UN Charter, most importantly the Security Council and its composition. It is the Security Council that is to co-manage international security crisis and not, say the General Assembly. Chapter 7 measures can only be decided by the Security Council. Equally important, the composition of the Security Council privileges the permanent five members of the Council, that is, China, France, Russia, the UK, and the United States. Among the permanent five, there is no representation for Africa or Latin America. Europe is highly over-represented and Asia under-represented. Many suggestions have been made for how to reform the Security Council. But with the exception of a small amendment with regard to the non-permanent members many decades ago, no changes have been made.

Performance amounts to another problem that has damaged the standing of the UN. While the empirical record in maintaining inter-state peace and security was, overall, encouraging even during the Cold War, the UN always struggled to find adequate responses to intra-state wars. These amount to a major problem for the organisation. While they have occurred much more frequently than inter-state wars and were also much more destructive, the UN is founded upon the principle of sovereignty. Intervening against a member state does not come easy. The responsibility to protect, mentioned in previous chapters several times, was meant as a vehicle to reconcile peace with sovereignty. But it never gained the kind of legitimacy needed to play this role. Russia's attack on Ukraine, along with annexing territories it conquers, casts doubt over the UN's ability to co-manage inter-state crises. It shows a problem that is closely connected to representation. Due to their veto power, permanent members of the Security Council can get away with doing things that violate central pillars of the Charter.

Outlook is about the UN's perceived ability to shape tomorrow's world. The 2024 Pact for the Future is an attempt to make the UN ready to work towards a better future in times in which world politics undergoes a deep transformation. The Preamble puts it as follows:

> We believe that there is a path to a brighter future for all of humanity, including those living in poverty and vulnerable situations Through the actions we take today, we resolve to set ourselves on that path, striving for a world that is safe, peaceful, just, equal, inclusive, sustainable and prosperous, a world in which well-being, security and dignity and a healthy planet are assured for all humanity.

Yet there is plenty of scepticism whether the Pact will actually make the UN ready for the future. Mathiasen puts the criticism quite starkly: "Unfortunately, the Pact suffers from two fatal flaws: the first is the disconnect between its vision and current events and the second is the disconnect between its signatories' pledges and their capacity to deliver" (Mathiasen, 2024). Given the fact that the Pact is merely a declaration and not binding law, one could add an insufficient common political will to these *caveats*.

The UN is not alone with these kinds of problems. As the literature puts it over and over, there is a crisis of multilateralism, at least the kind of broad multilateralism that can give rise to global agreements. Smaller kinds of multilateralism, featuring a handful of like-minded states, are still alive and well (Bello, 2021; Anuar and Hussain, 2021; Woods, 2023). Textbox 11.3 provides further details on the state of multilateralism.

Preventing Crises

Our inter-epoch is prone to crises and inadequate crisis management. What underpins this problem? We contend that, from a diplomatic point of view, the *globalisation-deglobalisation*

Textbox 11.3   The Multilateralism Index

The International Peace Institute and the Institute for Economics & Peace have published their multilateralism index since 2013. The measure multilateralism along three dimensions: (a) How many states participate? (b) Does multilateralism perform, that is, yield tangible outcomes? (c) Is multilateralism sufficiently inclusive to include NGOs? Multilateralism is measured along five dimensions (for the most part policy fields): peace and security, human rights, climate action, public health and trade. The results are very interesting. On the one hand, participation and inclusivity have, overall grown in the last decade. In other words, states still want to attend multilateral gatherings and negotiations, and they extend invitations to NGOs. The only exception to this pattern is trade, where state participation declined. On the other hand, performance has plummeted severely along all dimensions. The situation is most dire in the field of peace and security, where performance has halved since 2013 (Institute for Economics and Peace, 2024). One can interpret these figures in the following way: States still have their multilateral reflexes and so do NGOs. When multilateral discussions start, they want to be part of it (or at least not excluded). But they can get less and less done. Thus, we are back at a kind of performance that threatens the legitimacy of international institutions.

gap is at the core of the issue. On the one hand, the world continues to globalise, often driven by material forces. On the other hand, political responses to globalising challenges, more and more pretending that challenges can be mastered by domestic politics, have started to deglobalise.

Material forces continue to globalise international security even further. Weapons, ranging from SALW to drones, are traded, often illicitly, worldwide and with ever more ease (Callsen, 2022). Nuclear weapons, which can destroy life on earth several times, are modernised using, among other things, state-of-the-art digital technology. Deep learning is expected to improve early-warning-systems, intelligence, surveillance, and reconnaissance (ISR), and nuclear command, control and communications (NC3) (Chernavskikh, 2024). Cyberwarfare, too, shrinks time and space in the security field further. It ranges from attacking critical infrastructure to misinformation campaigns (Ventre, 2012; Stoddart, 2022). The mindset many key actors put to use, however, appears to deglobalise. Most importantly, the three great powers China, Russia, and the United States proudly stress their ability to handle their security all by themselves. In this way, their national security strategies converge (The White House, 2022; Nikkei Asia, 2022; Ministry of Foreign Affairs of the Russian Federation, 2024).

Many economic indicators, such as global flows of foreign direct investment and the global merchandise trade volume (UNCTAD, 2024; WTO, 2024), point to a very high level of globalisation albeit no longer an ever-increasing one. Some sectors of the economy, most importantly information technology services, continue to globalise (World Bank, 2024). Yet assumptions of a comparative advantage arising from global economic flows have given more and more ways to protectionist economic thinking. The WTO, dedicated to open up trade, struggles to fulfil its mandate. Its dispute settlement mechanism is in dire straits. Analysts increasingly analyse the dynamics of trade wars and the levying of tariffs (Fetzer and Schwarz, 2021).

Most environmental problems do not know national boundaries. This applies, first and foremost, to climate change. Severe weather events, ranging from floods to droughts, and from hurricanes to wildfires become more frequent and more destructive in many parts of the world (World Meteorological Organization, 2023; United States Environmental Protection Agency, 2024). Rising sea levels are estimated to put major cities in Bangladesh, Egypt, Indonesia, and Pakistan at existential risk by 2050. Some small island states such as the Marshall Islands also face this risk (Hauer et al., 2020). There has certainly been no shortage of climate change negotiations in recent decades but the voices of those claiming that there is no such thing as climate change or that it is not the result of human activity have become more numerous and louder again of late. Similar to his first presidency in the United States, one of the first announcements he made at the beginning of his second was that Washington would withdraw from the 2015 Paris Agreement. In the Executive Order 'Putting America First in International Environmental Agreements', signed the day he was inaugurated again, he justified this step by putting "the interests of the United States and the American people first" (The White House, 2025). There was nothing about addressing global problems together with others.

Viruses, needless to say, do not ask for visas to move from one state to the next. This became painfully obvious to everyone during the corona pandemic. Yet attempts to design a Pandemic Treaty have come to naught thus far. Likewise, WHO continues to suffer from insufficient funding. Pandemic preparedness, as a result, is as incomplete as it was before SARS-CoV-2 started to spread across the world, killing millions of people. If anything, matters may become even more problematic for WHO. On the day of his inauguration, Trump not only decided to pull out of the Paris Agreement but also signed a decree to withdraw from WHO (The White House, 2025). Given that the United States is the largest funder of the organisation, such a drastic step would significantly affect the organisation.

This list of illustrations of a globalisation-deglobalisation gap could be extended almost indefinitely. While the world is highly globalised, background understandings of some key actors have come to deglobalise. While there is plenty of demand for effective multilateralism, there is very little diplomatic supply.

It is, therefore, not only difficult to co-manage international crises. In our inter-epoch, preventing such crises from occurring is at least as challenging. A quick glance at history books shows that this is not just a problem for the inter-epoch. It also makes for trouble for the new epoch that is to follow. What we referred to as today's inter-epoch, other scholars dub an interregnum (Pegram and Acuto, 2015; Babic, 2020; Knight, 2022). This draws an analogy to the late 13th-century disruptions in the Holy Roman Empire. But for all the tumultuous transformation that happened, it prepared the ground for the new epoch. The pillars of a new order, built on complex relations of authority between pope and emperor, emerged in the interregnum. To put this differently, what happens to today will affect the world of tomorrow in fundamental ways.

Summary

- Contemporary world politics is best described as an inter-epoch. Such inter-epochs are prone to crises and failures to co-manage them adequately. Today's inter-epoch is characterised by power transition and technological revolution.
- Diplomacy struggles to address two kinds of crises: policy crises and institutional crises. While the former are crises disrupting policy areas diplomacy gets involved in (such as security, economics, etc.), the latter are about the decline of legitimacy of institutional procedures for doing so.
- In our complex world, most international crises cannot be managed by one actor, even the most powerful state, all by itself. Crises need to be co-managed. Successful co-management is a process that moves from overlapping repertoires actors put to use to intersecting judgements (including prejudgements) and further to consonant judgements. Judgements are pushed and shoved over and over in communicative encounters.
- Increasingly diverging repertoires among actors hinder co-managing policy and institutional crises. Given schisms across repertoires – something akin to actors living in different worlds – they find it very difficult to converge upon judgements. The starting points of their judgements – the universals they pick from their repertoires – are far removed from one another.
- Diverging repertoires also make crisis prevention very difficult. Additionally, there is the problem that deglobalising repertoires become more influential. They are out of sync with the globalised – and for the most part ever more globalising – challenges diplomacy needs to address.

Study Questions

- What is an inter-epoch? Are we living in an inter-epoch? If so, what indications are there?
- What is crisis co-management? How do actors come to co-manage a crisis?
- A permanent representative to the UN in New York recently remarked to us: 'We are no longer living in the same world'. By 'we', he meant diplomats representing different UN member states. What could this mean? What repercussions does this have for co-managing international crises?
- What are the challenges for politicians, career diplomats and experts to communicate meaningfully about crises?
- How could successes and failures of crisis co-management shape the epoch to come?

Note

1 On sense-making and decision-making, see Boin, Hardt and Sundelius (2017).

Recommended Further Reading

Brecher, Michael, and Jonathan Wilkenfeld. 2022. *A Study of Crisis*. Ann Arbor: University of Michigan Press.

Written by the protagonists of the International Crisis Behavior Project, this latest edition of their path-breaking book features nuanced discussions of how states escalate and de-escalate crises that revolve around matters of peace and war.

Kahl, Colin, and Thomas Wright. 2021. *Aftershocks: Pandemic Politics and the End of the Old International Order*. New York: St. Martin's Press.

This book reminds us that crises have important legacies. They can be turning points. The authors analyse how the COVID-19 pandemic disrupted the international order.

Kornprobst, Markus. 2019. *Co-Managing International Crises: Judgments and Justifications*. Cambridge: Cambridge University Press.

This book sketches a frame for how to study successes and failures of crisis co-management. The empirical cases discussed are Bosnia, Kosovo, Afghanistan, and Iraq.

Myrick, Rachel. 2021. "Do External Threats Unite or Divide? Security Crises, Rivalries, and Polarization in American Foreign Policy." *International Organization* 75 (4): 921–58.

Focusing on the United States, the author analyses the interplay of domestic and international politics during crisis management in depth.

Sowers, Jeannie, and Erika Weinthal. 2021. "Humanitarian Challenges and the Targeting of Civilian Infrastructure in the Yemen War." *International Affairs* 97 (1): 157–77.

Studying the repercussions of the civil war in Yemen for civilians, the authors provide an overview of the complexities of humanitarian crises and their co-management.

12 Diplomatic Power

Chapter objectives

- To examine epistemic power in diplomacy, analysing how diplomats wield influence by shaping, controlling, and disseminating knowledge.
- To explore symbolic power, assessing how representational, conceptual, and cultural narratives construct legitimacy, influence perception, and define diplomatic discourse.
- To evaluate strategic power in diplomacy, examining how configurations of self-interest, historical contingencies, and shifting power dynamics shape statecraft and global influence.
- To synthesise the evolving dimensions of power in diplomacy, exploring how digital transformation, AI, and geopolitical shifts are redefining engagement and authority.

Introduction

"Diplomacy puts people in touch with power, but in a rather paradoxical manner: diplomats largely live and work in the proximity of power, but they rarely exercise power directly" (Sharp, 2009: 58). Sharp's observation captures a fundamental tension at the heart of diplomacy – while diplomats operate within the corridors of political authority, their influence is often mediated, indirect, and contingent. They are both *agents of power* and *its interpreters*, tasked with shaping diplomatic relations without always possessing the final authority to dictate them. This paradox invites a deeper examination of the nature of power itself and how it is exercised in diplomatic practice.

This chapter explores three interrelated forms of power that structure diplomatic engagement across history and into the digital age:

1. **Power through knowledge production (epistemic power)** – Diplomacy, at its core, is an intellectual endeavour. It involves the collection, classification, and strategic deployment of knowledge. Timothy Chappell's theory of varieties of knowledge offers a framework for understanding how diplomatic actors exercise power by shaping what is known, how it is known, and who has access to that knowledge. The symbiotic relationship between different forms of knowledge – from propositional knowledge (treaties, legal agreements) to experiential knowledge (embodied diplomatic expertise), practical knowledge-how (the ability to navigate negotiations and wield influence), and objectual knowledge (a holistic understanding of geopolitical systems) – demonstrates the evolving nature of epistemic power in statecraft.
2. **Power through meaning-making (symbolic power)** – Power is not only about what is known but also about how it is represented. Ernst Cassirer's work on symbolic representations highlights the role of myths, narratives, and ideological constructs in diplomacy.

DOI: 10.4324/9781003485407-17

The ability to control historical memory, political myths, and discursive frames allows states to define who is a friend and who is an enemy, to justify interventions, and to consolidate legitimacy on the world stage. From MFAs as the institutional nerve centres of diplomacy to ambassadors as the embodiment of national identity, symbolic power remains central to statecraft. These structures do more than facilitate negotiation; they project legitimacy, reinforce geopolitical influence, and shape international perceptions.

3. **Power through statecraft (strategic power)** – If knowledge and symbolism shape diplomatic power, statecraft determines how it is operationalised through negotiation, coercion, and strategic manoeuvring. Francesco Guicciardini and Raymond Aron offer two contrasting views on strategic power: Guicciardini sees it as transactional and adaptive, driven by shifting self-interests, while Aron situates it within structural statecraft and historical contingency. Their perspectives reveal diplomacy's dual nature – both a flexible, situational tool and a structured force shaped by geopolitical realities.

Together, epistemic, symbolic, and strategic power provide a comprehensive framework for understanding the evolving role of diplomacy in global affairs. This chapter examines how these three interrelated dimensions have shaped the exercise of power in diplomacy, structuring its practice from history to the digital age: epistemic power, which defines what is known and who controls its dissemination; symbolic power, which constructs meaning and legitimises authority; and strategic power, which translates knowledge and symbolism into concrete diplomatic action. In doing so, it seeks to answer a fundamental question: *How does diplomacy wield power when authority is fragmented, knowledge is both an asset and a battleground, and representation is increasingly shaped by digital and symbolic narratives?*

Power as Knowledge

Diplomacy is fundamentally an exercise in knowledge – its acquisition, interpretation, and strategic deployment. The effectiveness of diplomacy depends not just on what is known, but also on how knowledge is framed, communicated, and acted upon. Throughout history, diplomats and statesmen have navigated complex political landscapes by mastering different dimensions of knowledge, whether in negotiating treaties, gathering intelligence, shaping ideological narratives, or making strategic calculations. The way in which knowledge is structured through epistemic power (→ glossary) determines the credibility of diplomatic discourse, the strength of alliances, and the sustainability of international agreements.

In this context, it is also important to emphasise that diplomacy is not simply about information exchange; it is about how *knowledge is used as an instrument of power*. The control of knowledge – what is revealed, what is concealed, and how it is presented – has always been at the core of diplomatic practice. Treaties and legal agreements rely on *propositional knowledge*, which consists of formal, codified principles such as laws and written commitments, while personal intuition and judgement in negotiations require *experiential knowledge*, gained through direct practice and lived experience. The capacity to construct compelling narratives and shape international perceptions hinges on *practical knowledge-how*, the mastery of rhetorical and strategic execution in diplomacy, whereas long-term strategic foresight, which ensures the coherence of national interests, relies on *objectual knowledge*, a deep and integrative understanding of political systems and their underlying dynamics.

Timothy Chappell's framework of four forms of knowledge – propositional, experiential, practical (knowledge-how), and objectual knowledge – offers a valuable perspective on this epistemic dimension of diplomacy (Chappell, 2012). These categories help us move beyond the simplistic notion of diplomacy as a matter of acquiring and disseminating facts. Instead, they allow us to explore how different types of knowledge intersect in shaping diplomatic practice, international negotiations, and the broader geopolitical landscape. The enduring relevance of these forms of knowledge is evident in the works and strategies of Niccolò Machiavelli, Confucius, Thomas Cromwell, Cardinal Richelieu, George Kennan, Henry Kissinger, and Charles-Maurice de Talleyrand, whose ideas and methods have profoundly shaped diplomatic traditions across history. By examining their approaches, we can trace how their insights – ranging from strategic manoeuvring and institutional governance to ethical leadership and long-term statecraft – have become embedded in diplomatic practice. Recognising these distinctions also enhances our understanding of how knowledge functions as an instrument of influence in contemporary diplomacy, where digital communication, intelligence networks, and algorithmic decision-making further complicate the epistemic dimensions of global affairs.

Propositional Knowledge: The Cornerstone of Diplomatic Authority

Propositional knowledge – the knowledge of facts, laws, and codified principles – has always been central to diplomacy. Treaties, diplomatic protocols, and international law depend on shared, verifiable knowledge that provides structure to international relations. The Westphalian system, established in 1648, is often associated with the principle that sovereignty – though only tacitly acknowledged at the time and more forcefully defended in later interpretations (Osiander, 2001) – should be recognised and upheld through formal agreements. This illustrates the power of propositional knowledge in structuring diplomatic order, as legal codifications and treaties became central instruments for legitimising state authority and regulating diplomatic relations. Similarly, modern diplomacy relies on extensive legal frameworks, such as the Vienna Convention on Diplomatic Relations (1961), which codifies the rights and responsibilities of diplomats and provides a shared epistemic foundation for state interactions.

Richelieu and Confucius, though separated by centuries and cultural traditions, both exemplify the crucial role of propositional knowledge in statecraft and diplomacy. In both cases, propositional knowledge serves as the intellectual foundation for legitimising power and structuring diplomatic engagement. Cardinal Richelieu, as Chief Minister to Louis XIII, was instrumental in centralising power in France, laying the groundwork for modern diplomatic institutions. Under his leadership, France established the first MFA (1626), creating a structured system for continuous diplomatic negotiations and intelligence gathering. His reliance on codified policies, written treaties, and formal diplomatic correspondence illustrates how propositional knowledge was used not only to consolidate state authority but also to institutionalise diplomacy as a means of managing international relations (Church, 2016).

Confucius, the foundational thinker of an enduring political philosophy, also emphasised the role of structured knowledge in governance. For him, an effective state relied on leaders who studied history, adhered to established wisdom, and applied precedent to maintain stability. Central to his thought is the concept of ritual propriety (*li*) – a system of customs, social norms, and institutional practices that regulate behaviour and uphold political order. *Li* is not merely about ceremonial observances but serves as a codified framework for governance, ensuring that rulers act in accordance with established moral and political principles. His teachings stress that governance should be rooted in *li*, ethical leadership, and an understanding of historical models, all of which align with propositional knowledge as a foundation for effective statecraft (Confucius, 2020). Just as Richelieu institutionalised diplomacy through formal negotiation and bureaucratic structures, Confucius framed governance as a disciplined application of accumulated wisdom, ensuring that rulers governed not through arbitrary force, but through knowledge embedded in tradition and ethical order.

Experiential Knowledge: Intuition and Judgement

Diplomatic success often depends on more than written agreements; it requires the ability to navigate unpredictable situations based on personal experience. While treaties, legal frameworks, and formal negotiations provide structure to diplomatic relations, they do not account for the fluidity and nuance of human interactions in diplomacy. This is where experiential knowledge – gained through practice rather than formal study – becomes crucial. Unlike propositional knowledge, which is codified and explicitly taught, experiential knowledge is developed over time through observation, trial and error, and repeated engagement with political actors in different contexts. A seasoned diplomat does not simply rely on procedural guidelines; rather, they cultivate a refined intuition that allows them to sense when to press an issue, when to concede, and how to interpret subtle shifts in political dynamics that might not be captured in formal reports. This type of situational awareness is invaluable, as much of diplomacy unfolds in unspoken gestures, implicit commitments, and the unstructured spaces between official dialogues. The ability to read body language, decipher ambiguous statements, and detect underlying tensions can be the difference between a successful negotiation and a diplomatic impasse.

Historical examples illustrate the power of experiential knowledge in diplomacy. One of the most adept users of experiential knowledge in diplomacy was Thomas Cromwell, whose ability to navigate the volatile Tudor court ensured his rise under Henry VIII. Cromwell's mastery of court intrigue and international negotiations allowed him to dismantle the Catholic Church's authority in England and engineer the king's break with Rome. He relied not just on legal arguments but on his deep understanding of the personalities involved, ensuring that Henry's new religious policies were accepted by both parliament and foreign allies (MacCulloch, 2019). Charles-Maurice de Talleyrand, the French diplomat who played a pivotal role at the Congress of Vienna (1815), mastered the art of adaptation. Rather than following rigid principles, he relied on his deep understanding of personalities and shifting political currents to ensure France retained influence despite its recent defeat in the Napoleonic Wars (Jarrett, 2013). His ability to anticipate unspoken concerns and adjust his strategies accordingly made him one of the most effective negotiators of his time.

Similarly, George Kennan, the architect of the US containment policy during the Cold War, understood that Soviet actions could not be interpreted solely through ideological declarations or official communiqués. His famous Long Telegram (1946) was rooted in his on-the-ground observations in Moscow, where he absorbed the underlying psychological and strategic anxieties shaping Soviet behaviour (Gaddis, 2012). His recommendations, informed by direct experience, influenced decades of US foreign policy. Experiential knowledge is particularly essential in crisis diplomacy, where rigid adherence to pre-established protocols can be counterproductive. Henry Kissinger's shuttle diplomacy in the Middle East during the 1970s, for instance, relied not just on formal peace proposals but on his ability to sense when to apply pressure and when to step back, when to offer assurances and when to exploit divisions. His personal engagement with Arab and Israeli leaders, built over repeated interactions, allowed him to manoeuvre negotiations towards agreements that might have otherwise collapsed under the weight of entrenched hostilities (Isaacson, 2013).

In contemporary diplomacy, experiential knowledge remains critical, though it is now mediated by technology, data analytics, and algorithmic decision-making. Digital intelligence and predictive analytics can enhance a diplomat's understanding of global trends, but they cannot replace the tacit knowledge acquired through face-to-face interactions, relationship-building, and the ability to sense when official statements diverge from actual intentions. In an era of disinformation and rapid geopolitical shifts, the ability to discern when an adversary's conciliatory tone masks deeper strategic objectives or when a seemingly minor concession signals a broader shift in policy is a skill that no algorithm can fully replicate.

Knowledge-How: The Craft of Diplomacy

Beyond knowing facts and having experience, diplomats must possess knowledge-how – the ability to execute strategy effectively. Knowledge-how in diplomacy is the ability to strategically apply knowledge in real-world negotiations, persuasion, and statecraft. Unlike propositional knowledge, which provides formal frameworks, or experiential knowledge, which builds intuition through exposure, knowledge-how is skill-based, deliberate, and adaptable. It is acquired through mentorship, immersive diplomatic practice, mastery of rhetoric, and repeated exposure to negotiation and crisis management. This form of knowledge is action-oriented, requiring diplomats not only to understand policies and political dynamics but to manipulate them effectively. It is what enables diplomats to read the room, adjust strategies in real-time, and turn theoretical insights into tactical advantages. Ultimately, knowledge-how is what distinguishes those who merely understand diplomacy from those who can shape its course.

In ancient Rome, officials acquired diplomatic expertise through a gradual progression within the *cursus honorum*, the hierarchical career path for public officials (Lintott, 2003). Young aristocrats learned statecraft by serving as aides, observing negotiations, and gradually taking on greater responsibilities, ensuring that their diplomatic skills were honed through direct engagement in governance and foreign relations. This system emphasised practical experience, mentorship, and rhetorical training, preparing officials to navigate complex political landscapes with strategic precision. During the Renaissance, the humanist method reshaped diplomatic education, emphasising formal study of classical texts, historical precedent, and rhetorical mastery (Skinner, 2013). Figures like Erasmus and Petrarch championed the idea that good education required not only practical skill but also a broad intellectual foundation in history, philosophy, and ethics (Bouwsma, 2002). Aspiring diplomats were trained in Latin, legal traditions, and persuasive oratory, equipping them to engage effectively in European courts where diplomacy was an art of both negotiation and eloquence (Mattingly, 1971).

Baldassare Castiglione, in *The Book of the Courtier* (1528), articulated an ideal of the diplomat as a master of grace, discretion, and rhetorical finesse, arguing that the ability to persuade, adapt, and maintain influence through subtlety and charm was as vital as political knowledge itself (Castiglione, 2023). This vision of diplomacy as an artful performance complemented Machiavelli's more ruthless pragmatism, underscoring the necessity of knowledge-how not only in manipulating alliances but also in cultivating personal authority and credibility within elite political circles. Machiavelli took this idea further, arguing that merely understanding power was insufficient; one must know how to wield it effectively in an unpredictable political environment (Machiavelli, 2020). His analysis of Cesare Borgia exemplifies this principle, showing that Borgia's success depended not just on his grasp of governance but on his ability to forge and sever alliances, exploit opportunities, and maintain control through calculated action.

In the digital age, knowledge-how in diplomacy extends beyond traditional negotiation and statecraft to encompass digital communication, media influence, and algorithmic strategy. Diplomats must navigate a landscape where public perception is shaped in real-time through social media, AI-driven narratives, and rapid information flows, making persuasion, adaptability, and strategic messaging in virtual spaces as crucial as face-to-face negotiation. Crisis diplomacy, once confined to closed-door discussions, now unfolds under global scrutiny, where real-time responses and narrative control can determine the outcome of an international agreement. As diplomacy becomes increasingly mediated by technology, acquiring knowledge-how requires new methods. Training in cybersecurity, digital influence campaigns, open-source intelligence, and AI-driven diplomacy is now essential. Diplomatic academies and foreign ministries are integrating social media crisis management, disinformation counter-strategies, and algorithmic engagement tactics into their programmes, recognising that power is now exercised as much through digital platforms and cyber operations as through conventional diplomatic channels.

Objectual Knowledge: Seeing the Whole Diplomatic Landscape

Objectual knowledge – the ability to grasp the full complexity of political systems – is perhaps the rarest and most valuable form of knowledge in diplomacy. Unlike propositional knowledge, which codifies treaties, laws, and formal agreements, or experiential knowledge, which provides intuitive judgement from lived experience, objectual knowledge is holistic, integrative, and deeply strategic. It allows diplomats and statesmen not only to understand individual components of statecraft – legal frameworks, negotiations, intelligence, or economic policies – but to perceive how these elements interact over time within the broader geopolitical landscape. This form of knowledge is *what distinguishes great diplomats and statesmen from mere tacticians*. While practical knowledge-how enables effective execution of diplomatic manoeuvres, objectual knowledge grounds those actions in a long-term vision, ensuring that immediate decisions align with overarching strategic objectives. A diplomat with objectual knowledge sees beyond the momentary success or failure of a negotiation, recognising how current actions will ripple through alliances, economic structures, and shifting power balances for decades to come. It is the ability to anticipate unintended consequences, recognise historical patterns, and position a nation advantageously within an evolving international order.

Because objectual knowledge requires synthesising vast amounts of information, balancing competing interests, and predicting long-term political trajectories, it is difficult to acquire through conventional training. Unlike propositional knowledge, which can be learnt through legal and institutional study, or experiential knowledge, which develops through diplomatic practice, objectual knowledge emerges from a capacity to integrate disparate elements into a coherent strategic vision. It demands deep historical awareness, cross-disciplinary understanding, and the cognitive ability to perceive interconnections where others see isolated events. This is why, historically, the most influential diplomats and strategists – figures like Cardinal Richelieu, Klemens von Metternich, George Kennan or Jean Monnet and Robert Schuman – were not merely skilled negotiators but architects of enduring diplomatic frameworks that shaped international order long after their immediate engagements ended.

Richelieu exemplified this knowledge by viewing France not as a fragmented state beset by factionalism but as a unified political entity requiring long-term strategic planning. His policies, aimed at weakening the nobility, centralising power, and expanding France's geopolitical role, were not dictated by short-term opportunism but by a vision of France as a dominant European power insulated from internal instability and external threats (Church, 2016). His orchestration of the Thirty Years' War strategy, supporting Protestant states abroad while enforcing Catholic absolutism at home, demonstrates the integration of ideology, military power, and diplomacy into a single strategic framework. Similarly, Metternich's balance-of-power diplomacy was based on his ability to see beyond immediate conflicts and understand how different alliances, economic pressures, and ideological forces interacted across Europe. His role at the Congress of Vienna (1815) was not merely about restoring monarchies but about designing a system that would stabilise Europe for decades by ensuring no single power could dominate the continent (Okey, 2002). His diplomatic manoeuvring, which secured Austria's central role in European politics despite its declining military strength, illustrates the importance of objectual knowledge in crafting geopolitical equilibrium.

In the 20th century, George Kennan's containment strategy was similarly shaped by objectual knowledge, as he understood that the Cold War was not simply an ideological struggle but a structural confrontation between competing economic and security systems. His famous 'Long Telegram' (1946) laid out a vision of US foreign policy that was rooted in an understanding of Soviet strategic imperatives and historical anxieties (Gaddis, 2011). By advocating for selective containment rather than direct military confrontation, Kennan provided a framework that shaped US policy throughout the Cold War. The European integration project following World War II serves as another example of the application of objectual knowledge, as visionary leaders like Jean Monnet and Robert Schuman recognised that long-term European stability required more than military alliances; it necessitated an economic and political framework that would prevent future conflicts. The establishment of the European Coal and Steel Community (1951) – which later evolved into the EU – was not merely an economic initiative but a strategic effort to bind former adversaries into an interdependent system, making war between them structurally impossible (Duchene, 1996). Like Kennan, Monnet and Schuman understood that enduring geopolitical stability depended on integrating economic, security, and political interests into a coherent, long-term vision, rather than relying on short-term diplomatic agreements.

Just as Richelieu, Metternich, Kennan, Monnet, and Schuman crafted grand strategies that outlived them, diplomacy in the digital age requires the ability to navigate a world where power

---

Textbox 12.1 Kennan's 'Long Telegram' (1946): Four Dimensions of Knowledge

Propositional Knowledge: The intellectual framework of containment

- Kennan's telegram provided a systematic analysis of Soviet ideology and strategy, forming the intellectual foundation of US containment policy. He argued that the USSR was "impervious to logic of reason, and highly sensitive to logic of force", a principle that shaped Cold War diplomacy.

Experiential Knowledge: Insights from the Moscow assignment

- Kennan's conclusions were shaped by his firsthand experience in the Soviet Union, where he observed leadership behaviour and propaganda tactics. He noted that Soviet officials had a "disrespect for objective truth", seeing all facts as "instruments for furtherance of one ulterior purpose or another".

Knowledge-How: The craft of policy implementation

- Kennan's insights were translated into action, guiding the Truman Doctrine, the Marshall Plan, and NATO's formation. He emphasised the need to counter Soviet influence not just militarily but by offering a "more positive and constructive picture" of the Western world.

> **Objectual Knowledge: A grand strategic vision of the Cold War**
> - Beyond immediate policy, Kennan framed a long-term geopolitical strategy, recognising that the USSR was "not just another great power" but an ideological adversary seeking to "disrupt our society and break the international authority of our state". His vision influenced US foreign policy for decades, shaping the Cold War's grand strategy.

is increasingly diffuse, interdependencies are more intricate, and geopolitical alignments remain in constant flux. This challenge is further compounded by technological disruption, and algorithmic governance, which have introduced new layers of complexity, necessitating a more adaptive, networked, and systems-based approach to diplomatic strategy (Slaughter, 2017). Objectual knowledge now demands a systems-based approach, integrating AI-driven intelligence, cybersecurity risks, and real-time data flows to anticipate not just political shifts but the unintended consequences of AI-informed decision-making, digital misinformation, and tech governance. As influence extends beyond states to global tech firms, decentralised platforms, and AI-driven systems, diplomats must develop the ability to synthesise vast, rapidly evolving information streams into a coherent long-term vision. Those who fail to adapt risk being overtaken by the velocity of technological change (Bjola and Manor, 2024b), while those who master this evolving landscape will not merely engage in diplomacy but fundamentally shape its trajectory, much like the great strategists of the past who redefined the international order in their time.

Power as Symbolic Representation

Ernst Cassirer's philosophy of symbolic representation, most notably articulated in *The Philosophy of Symbolic Forms* (Cassirer, 1998) and *An Essay on Man* (Cassirer, 2021), examines how humans use symbols to structure, interpret, and engage with their world. For Cassirer, symbols are not passive reflections of reality but active mediators that shape our understanding and interactions across cultural, political, and social experiences. Through their mediating role, symbols reveal their plurality, adaptability, and relational nature, dynamically connecting individuals and societies to the broader context of human experience. Building on this, Tafdrup (2024) extends Cassirer's insights into the realm of technology, arguing that all human-technology interactions are inherently embedded in symbolic structures. He emphasises that there is no raw perception of technological artefacts; they are always interpreted through pre-existing symbolic frameworks. This notion reinforces the idea that symbols are not merely communicative tools but fundamental to cognition itself, shaping how societies engage with both traditional and digital forms of mediation. Just as Cassirer saw myth, language, and science as evolving symbolic forms that mediate reality, Tafdrup's analysis suggests that digital platforms, AI, and robotic technologies similarly function as mediating structures that co-construct meaning in political and diplomatic discourse.

Four interconnected dimensions of symbolic representation emerge from Cassirer's theory of symbolic representation: the expressive, the representational, the conceptual, and the cultural. The *expressive* dimension highlights how symbols capture emotional and instinctive responses, often conveyed through art, music, and rituals, which evoke shared feelings and meanings. Just as national anthems, religious ceremonies, or public monuments stir collective sentiment, modern symbolic representations – ranging from visual media to interactive platforms – shape emotional engagement in ways that transcend direct communication. The *representational* dimension focuses on symbols as tools for visually or linguistically depicting objects, ideas, or events, enabling individuals to understand and communicate their understanding of the world. These representations are not static but continuously mediated through evolving forms of expression, from written texts and imagery to dynamic, immersive environments. The way a diplomatic speech, an emblem, or a digital interface is designed fundamentally alters how its message is perceived, demonstrating that symbols actively construct rather than simply reflect meaning.

The *conceptual* dimension emphasises the role of symbols in abstract reasoning, where mediums like language, science, and mathematics allow for complex thought and theoretical exploration. This symbolic function is central to knowledge production and governance, shaping how societies envision progress, authority, and interaction. In this way, symbols serve not only as records of cultural knowledge but also as tools for shaping emerging ideas, whether through the written word, algorithmic models, or interactive frameworks that structure social or diplomatic discourse. Finally, the *cultural* dimension underscores how symbols embody collective values, traditions, and histories, functioning as vessels for a society's shared identity and worldview. Symbols are deeply embedded within the narratives that societies tell about themselves, from national myths to modern ideological constructs. As new mediums of representation emerge, the symbolic forms they carry are increasingly shaped by both historical legacies and evolving modes of engagement, influencing how identity and power are articulated on a global scale.

Cassirer's theory reveals that the dimensions of symbolic representation – expressive, representational, conceptual, and cultural – are deeply interconnected, reflecting the dynamic and relational power of symbols to shape human understanding. Symbols, as mediators, evolve with societal contexts, bridge cultural divides, and invite interpretation, enabling shared meaning while preserving distinctiveness. This framework provides a compelling tool for analysing how states and diplomats use symbolic power (→ glossary) to strategically craft narratives that embody national values, influence perceptions, and build meaningful connections in a complex international environment. Cassirer's insights, in particular, shed light on how MFAs and ambassadors construct and communicate a nation's identity. By applying these dimensions, we can better grasp how MFAs weave together visual, linguistic, and cultural symbols to create adaptive strategies that resonate with specific audiences while maintaining coherence with broader national objectives. At the same time, individual diplomats, as visible and humanised extensions of their nation's image, translate these institutional narratives into personal interactions that can forge trust, amplify influence, and engage audiences at an emotional and intellectual level. These processes illustrate the transformative potential of symbols to navigate trajectories of digital public diplomacy.

Institutional Branding: The MFA as a Symbolic Architect

MFAs serve as the architects of a nation's symbolic identity, crafting narratives that project its cultural, political, and economic values. Cassirer's concept of symbols as mediators highlights how MFAs use language, imagery, and rituals to construct meaning and foster connections with foreign publics. These efforts rely on the representational dimension, which involves visually or linguistically depicting national identity through symbols, and the cultural dimension, which conveys collective values and traditions. However, as Spry (2020) notes, the success of these initiatives depends on the ability to create symbolic connections that resonate across diverse audiences. For example, MFAs in the Asia-Pacific region have leveraged platforms like Facebook to build engagement, illustrating the adaptive nature of symbols within the conceptual dimension, where digital tools allow for innovative representations of identity. The EU's Global Strategy exemplifies the expressive and representational dimensions by using storytelling and visual elements to mediate its identity as a cohesive and legitimate global actor (Hedling, 2020). Similarly, the British Council's *Shakespeare Lives* campaign demonstrates the cultural dimension, employing the iconic figure of Shakespeare to project the UK's soft power while fostering intercultural dialogue (Aslan Ozgul et al., 2021). These campaigns reflect Cassirer's insight that symbols are dynamic and evolve through interaction, enabling institutions to adapt narratives to changing geopolitical and cultural contexts.

NATO's Return to Hope campaign in Afghanistan exemplifies how institutions can blend these dimensions to create compelling narratives. By highlighting personal stories of Afghan individuals and NATO personnel, the campaign combined military strategy with humanitarian values, effectively humanising NATO's presence (Wright, 2019). This approach reflects Cassirer's assertion that symbols are dynamic and relational, evolving through interaction with audiences to foster trust and legitimacy. Similarly, Sweden's feminist foreign policy illustrates the cultural dimension, integrating gender equality into Sweden's national identity and global messaging. This alignment between symbolic narratives and actionable policies has helped Sweden resonate with global audiences who value human rights and progressive leadership (Cassidy, 2024).

Yet, the alignment between symbolic narratives and lived realities is critical for maintaining credibility and fostering authentic connections. Strauß et al. (2015) reveal how Western embassies in the GCC struggled with the relational dimension of symbols, where the lack of interactive and personalised communication undermined their efforts. Cassirer's emphasis on the participatory nature of symbols thus underscores the importance of engaging audiences not merely as passive recipients but as co-creators of meaning. By fostering relationships rooted in authenticity and cultural sensitivity, MFAs can ensure their narratives reflect shared identities and purposes, reinforcing the symbolic resonance of their efforts.

Personal Branding: The Diplomat as a Symbolic Figure

Individual diplomats, such as ambassadors, embody the personal dimension of symbolic representation, acting as living symbols of their nation's identity. Cassirer's philosophy, particularly the expressive and representational dimensions, provides a deeper understanding of this role, highlighting how diplomats convey their nation's values and aspirations through their actions, appearances, and interactions. Ambassadors are not merely conduits of information but symbolic figures whose presence and engagement reinforce – or potentially undermine – the narratives constructed by their institutions.

In Latin America, digital diplomacy strategies have often relied heavily on personal engagement. For example, the Mexican MFA has required its ambassadors to maintain active Twitter accounts, integrating representational and cultural dimensions into their digital presence. Marcelo Ebrard, Mexico's Foreign Minister, has become a prominent voice on social media, using his personal account to articulate national positions, communicate directly with domestic and international audiences, and amplify institutional narratives (Aguirre and Ramos, 2024). This approach demonstrates how personal branding can reinforce institutional objectives by building symbolic connections that are both relational and participatory. Similarly, in Central Asia, the expressive dimension is evident in how diplomats and heads of state use social media to personalise interactions and reduce hierarchical distance. For instance, the use of Instagram and Twitter by Central Asian leaders, often managed with a blend of personal and institutional content, serves to humanise their roles while showcasing cultural and policy achievements. However, as Faizullaev (2024) notes, many of these accounts focus primarily on broadcasting and lack meaningful engagement with audiences. This aligns with Cassirer's assertion that symbols lose their resonance when they are static and one-directional, rather than dynamic and participatory.

Indonesia's innovative use of Virtual YouTubers (VTubers) by Hololive Indonesia showcases how personal branding can integrate the cultural and conceptual dimensions of symbolic representation. These VTubers combine Indonesia's cultural diversity and multilingualism with digital storytelling, making the nation's identity accessible and relatable to global audiences (Gallennius and Akil, 2024). This approach exemplifies Cassirer's idea that symbols are most effective when they emerge organically from shared cultural experiences and evolve to meet the expectations of diverse audiences. Personal branding is also shaped by the adaptive dimension, as illustrated by Chilean diplomats' shift towards incorporating visual storytelling and dynamic social media strategies during the COVID-19 pandemic. These efforts reflect an understanding that symbols must evolve in response to new contexts, enabling ambassadors to maintain relevance and resonance even in times of crisis (Aguirre and Ramos, 2024). Similarly, Central Asian diplomats have begun to leverage platforms like Telegram to engage with diaspora communities, adapting their strategies to meet the expectations of domestic and international audiences in real time (Faizullaev, 2024).

The interplay between institutional and personal branding exemplifies the relational nature of symbolic representation, a cornerstone of Cassirer's philosophy. Institutional branding, directed by MFAs, lays the foundational contours of a nation's identity, weaving together representational elements such as visual symbols and cultural dimensions like shared traditions and values. This broad narrative acts as a scaffold, providing coherence and strategic direction for a country's diplomatic image. Individual diplomats, however, add nuance and vitality to these institutional narratives. Through expressive gestures and relational interactions, they personalise and humanise their nation's identity, creating connections that can resonate on a deeply human level. This symbiotic relationship is critical. When institutional and personal branding align seamlessly, they reinforce each other, amplifying the effectiveness and authenticity of a nation's diplomatic messaging. For example, Sweden's feminist foreign policy exemplifies this alignment. The Swedish MFA's institutional commitment to gender equality is not only represented in its policies but is actively embodied by diplomats who advocate for women's rights in international forums, host discussions, and collaborate on gender-focused initiatives. This harmony between institutional narrative and personal engagement bolsters Sweden's global image as a champion of human rights, adding credibility and emotional resonance to its broader narrative (Cassidy, 2024).

Conversely, a disconnect between institutional and personal branding can erode credibility and trust, undermining the coherence of a nation's diplomatic image. For instance, the Mexican MFA has emphasised centralised control over digital diplomacy, requiring diplomats to replicate headquarters' messaging on platforms like Twitter. While this strategy ensures consistency, it often limits diplomats' ability to adapt to local contexts and engage authentically with their audiences. The lack of flexibility has led to diminished audience engagement, illustrating how a rigid institutional framework can stifle the relational and adaptive dimensions of symbolic representation. This delicate balance underscores the importance of crafting symbolic representations that are not only coherent but also dynamic and relational. When institutional strategies provide clear frameworks that allow for adaptive and personal touches, they create a more powerful and resonant diplomatic presence. Aligning institutional narratives with the personalised engagements of diplomats fosters trust and influence, while misalignment risks reducing diplomatic efforts to static and unrelatable representations. Together, institutional and personal branding hold the potential to reinforce a nation's identity on the global stage, provided they work in harmony to navigate the complexities of international engagement.

Power as Statecraft

Unlike epistemic power, which governs the production and control of knowledge, and symbolic power, which constructs legitimacy through narratives and representation, statecraft asserts itself through the tangible exercise of influence, leveraging negotiation, coercion, and strategic manoeuvring to shape geopolitical realities. It is the realm of calculated intervention – where diplomacy is not merely about defining or interpreting the international order but actively recalibrating its balance through alliances, deterrence, and the projection of force. Whereas epistemic and symbolic power operate within the domain of perception and persuasion, strategic power (→ glossary) is concerned with the art of effecting concrete change, translating abstract interests into decisive actions that alter the structure of global affairs. Two thinkers, Francesco Guicciardini and Raymond Aron, offer contrasting yet equally instructive perspectives on how diplomats define and wield power. Guicciardini and Aron offer two distinct lenses on diplomatic power – one centred on the immediate, transactional calculations of self-interest, the other on the structural and strategic dimensions of statecraft. Their perspectives highlight diplomacy's dual nature: it is both an agile, context-driven tool and a structured force shaped by historical and geopolitical realities.

Francesco Guicciardini's diplomatic thought is deeply rooted in the fragmented and unstable political reality of Renaissance Italy, where foreign domination, factional rivalries, and shifting alliances defined statecraft. Unlike Machiavelli, who sought to construct a unified theory of power, Guicciardini approached diplomacy as an adaptive art, shaped by prudence, self-interest, and the recognition of the limits of rational calculation (Călina and Grozoiu, 2021). His career unfolded against the backdrop of the Italian Wars (1494–1559), a prolonged struggle among France, Spain, and the Holy Roman Empire, during which Guicciardini held several significant diplomatic positions. He served as Florence's ambassador to Spain (1512–1514), where he navigated the delicate balance of power between Ferdinand II of Aragon and Italian interests. Later, as Governor of Modena and Reggio under Pope Leo X (1521–1524), he played a critical role in defending Papal authority. His tenure as one of Pope Clement VII's chief advisors (1524–1527) placed him at the heart of the diplomatic manoeuvring that led to the ill-fated League of Cognac and, ultimately, the Sack of Rome. Spain, and the Holy Roman Empire for dominance over the Italian peninsula (Cesa, 2018: 3–5). The inability of the city-states – Florence, Milan, Venice, Naples, and the Papal States – to form a united front against foreign intervention necessitated a diplomatic approach based on manoeuvrability rather than structural stability.

At the heart of Guicciardini's diplomatic philosophy is the assumption that states act out of *particulare* (self-interest) rather than virtue (Guicciardini, 2021: 11–12). He viewed political actors as rational calculators whose motivations could be anticipated and manipulated, a principle that guided his most successful diplomatic engagements. This was evident in his role in the defence of Parma (1521), where he secured a favourable outcome by swiftly assessing the self-interest of all involved parties and leveraging their motivations to align with his own strategic objectives. Serving as Papal Governor, he successfully blocked a French advance by securing short-term commitments from Emperor Charles V and various Italian states, demonstrating his ability to operate within a controlled political environment where actors behaved predictably.

His diplomatic method thrived in such conditions, allowing him to exploit temporary alliances and maintain Papal authority through careful negotiation.

However, the same strategic reliance on self-interest exposed its limitations in the Sack of Rome (1527). Tasked with reinforcing Pope Clement VII's position, Guicciardini played a crucial role in shaping the League of Cognac (1526), an anti-Imperial alliance between the Papacy, France, Venice, and Milan. His assumption that France would commit to substantial military support and that Charles V could maintain control over his armies proved fatally flawed. The Sack of Rome was triggered not by calculated state action but by the mutiny of unpaid Imperial mercenaries, demonstrating that diplomatic foresight cannot fully account for irrationality, factional disobedience, and the volatility of military forces (Chastel, 2023). Guicciardini's failure to anticipate the breakdown of command structures and the emotional volatility of troops revealed the limits of a purely rationalist approach to diplomacy.

His experience with both success and failure led to a cautious approach to alliances, distinguishing between natural and occasional allies. Natural allies shared long-term strategic interests, while occasional allies were temporary partners of convenience, whose reliability was contingent on immediate benefits. The Medici's shifting relationships with the Papacy and the Holy Roman Empire demonstrated the dangers of miscalculating such distinctions. Trusting an occasional ally as though they were a natural one could lead to betrayal, as alliances in Renaissance Italy were rarely governed by loyalty but by the balance of power. This pragmatic approach to diplomacy was not governed by fixed theories but by a set of guiding principles. Guicciardini prioritised situational awareness over ideological commitments, favouring practical judgement over rigid doctrines.

Unlike later diplomatic theorists such as Richelieu, who sought to institutionalise diplomacy through bureaucratic mechanisms, Guicciardini's model remained personal and situational, relying on the individual diplomat's discretion rather than a formalised diplomatic corps. In this sense, his approach closely resembles modern realpolitik, where statecraft is an ongoing negotiation with uncertainty rather than a preordained system. Yet, the very strengths of his method – its pragmatism, adaptability, and reliance on self-interest – also highlight its inherent weaknesses. His reluctance to commit to overarching principles left him vulnerable to forces beyond human control. In the final years of his career, as he rewrote his *History of Italy* (Guicciardini, 2020) for the third time, he increasingly grappled with the limits of human foresight, acknowledging that even the most astute diplomat could be undone by unpredictable events. His reflections

---

Textbox 12.2 Francesco Guicciardini's Diplomatic Method

Guicciardini's diplomatic method rested on four interlocking tenets:

1) The *primacy of circumstances*, requiring decisions to be guided by immediate strategic realities rather than abstract principles.
2) *Prudence and calculation*, demanding constant reassessment of self-interest among relevant actors.
3) *Flexibility in alliances*, recognising that treaties were tools rather than permanent bonds.
4) An awareness of the *limits of control*, acknowledging that diplomacy was subject to misperception, fortune, and irrationality.

on Savonarola's apocalyptic visions (Yusim, 2018), which he had previously dismissed as irrational, suggest a late recognition that diplomacy could not always contain historical forces shaped by fate, fanaticism, and miscalculation.

Ultimately, Guicciardini's diplomatic legacy is one of cautious realism. He provided a remarkably modern vision of diplomacy as a game of incentives, perception, and adaptability, but his failures demonstrated the fragility of this model in the face of disorder and human unpredictability. His method offers valuable insights for contemporary diplomacy, particularly in an era where global instability, fragile alliances, and unpredictable leaders demand constant recalibration. His enduring lesson is not one of fixed doctrines but of *strategic prudence*, where success depends on the ability to navigate contingency rather than impose theoretical certainty upon a world that resists prediction.

Raymond Aron's engagement with diplomacy presents a sophisticated dialectic that interweaves power and war in a manner that resists simplistic theoretical reductionism. His analysis, particularly in *Peace and War: A Theory of International Relations* (2003) and *Clausewitz: Philosopher of War* (1986), is animated by a concern for the historical and strategic contingencies that shape state behaviour. Rather than adopting a mechanistic view of international politics, Aron articulates a theory of foreign policy as an art of calculated decisions, constrained by history, shaped by leadership, and conditioned by both structural forces and the agency of statesmen. While military force and economic resources provide the material foundations of a state's strength, Aron contends that the true exercise of power resides in diplomacy – the art of navigating alliances, projecting influence, and managing conflicts without recourse to war. Far from being a passive or subordinate instrument, diplomacy emerges as the primary mechanism through which states calibrate their national interests within a perpetually shifting international system.

While Guicciardini focuses on the micro-dynamics of statecraft, Aron examines the systemic interplay of military, economic, and ideological forces shaping international relations. For Aron, diplomacy is more than a pursuit of self-interest – it is a mechanism for managing conflict, stabilising order, and articulating a state's role within the global system. At the core of diplomatic statecraft lies the management of power – understood not merely in terms of coercion but as a balance of persuasion, deterrence, and negotiation. Aron's distinction between strength and power is especially pertinent: whereas strength encompasses a state's military, economic, and technological capacities, power signifies the ability to translate these resources into influence over other actors (Aron, 2003: 50). Diplomacy, in this sense, becomes the crucial medium through which states maximise their influence while minimising the costs of military engagement, ensuring that war remains a last resort rather than a default instrument of statecraft.

Aron's tripartite model of state motivations – security, power, and glory – finds its most effective expression in diplomatic strategy. If security constitutes the primary concern of all states, diplomacy serves as the first line of defence, facilitating alliances, treaty negotiations, and pre-emptive deterrence against emerging threats. Power, within the diplomatic sphere, extends beyond military coercion to encompass economic leverage, cultural diplomacy, and ideological leadership. The pursuit of prestige, or 'glory', occupies a particularly significant place in Aron's diplomatic vision (Aron, 2003: 76). For many states, foreign policy is not solely about securing material interests but also about gaining recognition, status, and legitimacy on the world stage. Diplomacy is as much about symbolism as it is about substance – commanding respect, projecting strength, and shaping global narratives. The Cold War, for instance, was not merely a military contest, but a diplomatic struggle for ideological supremacy between the United States and the Soviet Union. Aron recognises that states engage in diplomacy not only to secure their borders but also to shape their international image – a factor that diplomats must skilfully manage through rhetoric, strategic signalling, and calibrated engagement.

One of Aron's most enduring contributions to diplomatic theory is his analysis of the dialectical relationship between diplomacy and military force. Unlike realists who view diplomacy as subordinate to military strategy, Aron argues that the two are interdependent. The diplomat's role is to create conditions in which power can be exercised without resorting to war, while the soldier serves as the instrument of last resort when diplomatic avenues are exhausted. However, Aron warns against what he calls 'diplomatic illusionism' – the fallacy that diplomacy alone can resolve conflicts in the absence of credible military backing. A state that engages in diplomacy without the capacity to enforce its commitments risks irrelevance in the strategic calculations of stronger powers. Conversely, excessive reliance on military force without diplomatic finesse may lead to strategic overextension, diplomatic isolation, or unnecessary conflict. This dynamic is particularly evident in Aron's analysis of the Cold War, where diplomacy functioned not as a tool of pacification but as a strategy of controlled escalation and crisis management. The Cuban Missile Crisis of 1962 (Aron, 2003: 655) exemplifies this principle: its resolution hinged on both military deterrence (the US naval blockade) and high-level diplomatic negotiation (the secret agreement to remove US missiles from Turkey). For Aron, such moments define modern diplomacy – where statesmen must maintain a delicate balance between coercion and concession, force and dialogue.

A crucial dimension of Aron's diplomatic thought is his distinction between 'permanent' and 'occasional' allies (Aron, 2003: 28). Rejecting rigid ideological or geographical determinism, he sees alliances as fluid, shaped by evolving strategic interests and historical contingencies.

- **Permanent allies** share long-term strategic interests, cultural affinities, or common political traditions, making their alliances more durable and resilient.
- **Occasional allies**, by contrast, emerge out of short-term necessity and dissolve when circumstances shift. These alliances are purely instrumental, dictated by immediate exigencies rather than enduring partnerships.

For diplomats, recognising this distinction is paramount. Successful diplomacy does not rest on static alliances but requires constant recalibration of partnerships based on shifting geopolitical realities. This insight underpins Aron's critique of Cold War ideological rigidity, as he argues that diplomatic manoeuvrability is essential for long-term strategic flexibility.

Aron's engagement with Clausewitz further informs his understanding of diplomatic statecraft. If Clausewitz asserts that war is the continuation of politics by other means, Aron extends this logic to diplomacy, contending that diplomacy is the principal means through which war can be avoided, controlled, or strategically directed. In the nuclear age, the Clausewitzian logic of total war becomes self-defeating, making diplomacy not merely a mechanism for conflict resolution but an instrument of strategic deterrence. Nuclear diplomacy itself becomes an extension of statecraft, where signalling, credibility, and ambiguity serve as key tools for maintaining stability (Aron, 1986).

Aron underscores the decisive role of historical contingency in shaping diplomatic strategy, rejecting rigid theoretical models that seek to impose universal laws upon international relations. He argues that diplomatic success is predicated on historical awareness and the capacity for context-specific adaptation, emphasising that no single formula can govern diplomacy. Instead, each geopolitical moment demands a tailored synthesis of coercion, negotiation, and persuasion, contingent upon prevailing historical and strategic conditions (Schmitt, 2021: 65).

The effectiveness of diplomacy hinges on a state's ability to read the historical conditions in which it operates.

- **Metternich's balance-of-power diplomacy** was well-suited to 19th-century Europe but would be ineffective in a nuclear world.
- **Churchill and Roosevelt's wartime diplomacy**, based on ideological coalition-building, was vital for defeating Nazi Germany but later gave way to Cold War bipolarity.
- **Nixon and Kissinger's détente strategy**, balancing coercion with engagement, proved essential in stabilising US-Soviet relations in the 1970s.

For Aron, diplomatic statecraft is never static; it must evolve in response to geopolitical shifts, technological advancements, and ideological transformations. The great diplomat is not one who adheres to a rigid script but one who understands when to negotiate, when to deter, and when to wield force.

In Aron's vision, diplomacy is not a utopian quest for perpetual peace but a sophisticated tool of statecraft that operates within the continuum of war and peace. It is neither separate from nor subordinate to military power; rather, it manages the conditions under which force is applied or withheld. The diplomat, in this framework, is not merely a conciliator but a strategist who must navigate the intricate web of alliances, deterrence mechanisms, and ideological confrontations. In an era where direct war is increasingly catastrophic, Aron sees diplomacy as the foremost mechanism through which power is exercised and stability preserved, making it the defining craft of global politics.

Strategic Power in the Digital Age

The arguments of Guicciardini and Aron offer a constructive lens through which to assess statecraft in the digital age, particularly in the context of geopolitical competition over critical minerals, semiconductors, and digital infrastructures. These domains are no longer just components of economic power but fundamental levers of geopolitical influence. Guicciardini's emphasis on pragmatic statecraft – defined by transactional alliances, adaptability, and the calculated pursuit of self-interest – mirrors how states today navigate the fragile dependencies of global supply chains. In contrast, Aron's distinction between strength and power provides a deeper understanding of why control over digital infrastructures, resource flows, and semiconductor production has become central to diplomatic competition.

The competition over critical minerals and rare earth elements (REEs) is an interesting example of Guicciardini's transactional diplomacy. States are forming short-term alliances to secure access to cobalt, lithium, and rare earth metals, balancing between resource-rich but politically unstable suppliers and strategic competitors controlling refining capabilities (Fan, Omura and Roca, 2023). The EU's Critical Raw Materials Act, US supply chain diversification efforts, and China's dominance over global REE processing all illustrate this fragile balancing act. Guicciardini's principle of distinguishing "natural allies" from "occasional allies" is particularly relevant – while Western states may look to Africa and Latin America as alternative suppliers, these partnerships remain vulnerable to economic shifts, political instability, and competing Chinese investment strategies. Aron's distinction between strength and power is also relevant in this context. Strength refers to a state's possession of raw resources, whereas power is the ability to leverage those resources to shape global outcomes. China's strength in controlling the REE supply chain has allowed it to exercise power by restricting exports of gallium and germanium, forcing Western industries to seek alternatives. However, the United States and EU lack this conversion capability – despite having raw material reserves, they lack processing infrastructure, leaving them vulnerable to external dependencies. Aron's insight suggests that states must translate their material strengths into geopolitical power, either through investment in domestic refining capabilities or through strategic partnerships that offer long-term supply chain security.

The semiconductor industry exemplifies Aron's view of power as the ability to structure international dependencies. While China is rapidly investing in semiconductor production, it remains critically dependent on Taiwanese fabrication plants (TSMC), Dutch lithography technology (ASML), and US chip design (Nvidia, Qualcomm, Intel). The US export controls on advanced chip manufacturing equipment reveal how power is exercised – not simply through possession (strength) but through control over chokepoints in the supply chain. Guicciardini's principle of adapting to shifting alliances is visible in the US-Netherlands-Japan coalition restricting semiconductor technology exports to China (Yoon, 2023). While temporarily effective, this strategy remains vulnerable, as China accelerates its own semiconductor R&D and builds new partnerships with Middle Eastern and Southeast Asian states to bypass restrictions. As Guicciardini's experience with the League of Cognac shows, miscalculating the reliability of short-term alliances can lead to diplomatic setbacks – here, if Japan or the Netherlands shift economic priorities and begin relaxing export restrictions, the entire US containment strategy could unravel.

The battle over digital infrastructures – 5G networks, cloud platforms, undersea cables, and AI ecosystems – again highlights Aron's distinction between strength and power in shaping the global digital order. While the United States and its allies maintain technological superiority (strength) in areas like AI development and cloud computing, China has translated infrastructure control into geopolitical power through its Digital Silk Road initiative, which funds data centres, telecommunications networks, and AI surveillance systems across Africa, Asia, and Latin America. Aron's concept of power as relational influence rather than static capability is particularly relevant here. Owning infrastructure is not enough – what matters is the ability to set the rules governing its use. The United States still dominates cloud computing through AWS, Microsoft Azure, and Google Cloud, but China has increasingly built alternative digital ecosystems through Huawei's 5G networks, Alibaba Cloud, and BeiDou satellite navigation, reducing reliance on Western technologies. The ongoing fragmentation of digital governance – with China advocating "cyber sovereignty" and the West pushing for an open internet – illustrates how digital infrastructure is now a contested domain of power rather than a neutral economic asset. Guicciardini's realist perspective on statecraft as a game of calculated positioning is also evident in how the EU has responded to US-China digital competition. Rather than fully aligning with Washington, the EU has promoted its own "digital sovereignty" initiatives (Burwell and Propp, 2022), such as the Digital Markets Act and European cloud projects, balancing between reliance on US technology and resisting American dominance. This mirrors Guicciardini's preference for diplomatic manoeuvrability over rigid alliances, ensuring that European actors retain leverage in negotiations with both Beijing and Washington.

The strategic implications of Guicciardini and Aron's arguments for digital statecraft are surprisingly relevant and timely – states must integrate short-term adaptability with long-term structural positioning. Guicciardini's pragmatism is essential for navigating the volatile alliances of resource and technology supply chains, while Aron's distinction between strength and power underscores the need for states to control the governance of strategic assets, rather than merely possessing them. More specifically:

- Guicciardini's model suggests that states should continuously reassess alliances over digital and technological resources, ensuring they are not locked into over-reliance on a single supplier or geopolitical bloc.

- Aron's framework argues that digital statecraft must go beyond technological ownership (strength) to shaping global regulatory frameworks (power), ensuring that whoever sets the rules controls the future of the digital order.

The next phase of digital statecraft will likely be determined by how well states balance these two dimensions – adapting to immediate geopolitical realities while ensuring long-term structural control over the rules of digital governance. Those that succeed in translating technological strengths into strategic power – whether in critical minerals, semiconductors, or digital infrastructure – will shape the next global order.

Summary

This chapter explores the multifaceted nature of power in diplomacy, dividing it into three interrelated dimensions – epistemic power, symbolic power, and strategic power. Diplomats operate within complex structures of influence, shaping knowledge, constructing meaning, and leveraging strategy to advance state interests in an evolving global order.

- **Epistemic Power – Knowledge as Influence:** Diplomacy is an intellectual exercise, grounded in knowledge control, classification, and dissemination. Drawing on Timothy Chappell's framework of knowledge types, the chapter examines how diplomats use information strategically – whether in treaties, intelligence gathering, or the framing of geopolitical narratives – to shape outcomes and reinforce authority. The ability to control what is known and how it is interpreted remains a critical source of diplomatic influence.
- **Symbolic Power – Meaning-Making in Diplomacy:** Power in diplomacy extends beyond knowledge to the realm of representation. Ernst Cassirer's theory of symbolic forms highlights how myths, narratives, and ideological constructs define state legitimacy, friend-enemy distinctions, and geopolitical positioning. From foreign ministries acting as symbolic nerve centres to ambassadors as embodiments of national identity, symbolic diplomacy shapes perceptions and legitimises diplomatic action on the world stage.
- **Strategic Power – The Exercise of Statecraft:** While knowledge and symbolism shape diplomatic power, strategy determines its implementation. Drawing on the contrasting perspectives of Francesco Guicciardini and Raymond Aron, this section explores statecraft as both a transactional and structural force. Diplomacy is revealed as a dynamic interplay between negotiation, coercion, and long-term geopolitical contingencies.
- **Epistemic, symbolic, and strategic power:** In the digital age, such power shapes diplomacy through AI-driven narratives, digital governance, and technological competition. Epistemic power determines who controls knowledge in an era of algorithmic decision-making. Symbolic power extends to digital diplomacy, where states construct legitimacy through strategic communication and online engagement. Strategic power is exercised through control over critical infrastructures – rare materials, semiconductors, and digital networks – shaping global dependencies. Together, these forms of power redefine statecraft, making digital governance and technological supremacy central to diplomatic influence.

Study Questions

- How do different forms of knowledge – propositional, experiential, practical, and objectual – shape diplomatic decision-making, and how do diplomats leverage these knowledge types to maintain influence?

- How do MFAs and individual diplomats function as symbolic architects of national identity, and what are the risks of misalignment between institutional and personal branding in diplomacy?
- In what ways does digitalisation transform the exercise of epistemic power in diplomacy, and how can diplomats navigate the challenges of information control in an era of algorithmic governance and AI-driven narratives?
- What role does historical contingency play in shaping diplomatic strategy, and how do diplomats balance immediate self-interest with long-term geopolitical considerations?
- How do strategic power and symbolic power intersect in diplomacy, and what mechanisms allow states to translate meaning-making into concrete geopolitical influence?
- How do Guicciardini's emphasis on pragmatic, transactional diplomacy and Aron's distinction between strength and power shape our understanding of statecraft in the digital age?

Recommended Further Reading

Aron, Raymond. 2003. *Peace and War: A Theory of International Relations*. Somerset, NJ: Transaction Publishers.

This book offers a deep analysis of strategic power, exploring how diplomacy manages conflict, stabilises order, and balances deterrence with negotiation. Aron's tripartite model of state motivations – security, power, and prestige – provides a crucial lens for examining statecraft in modern diplomacy.

Bjola, Corneliu, and Ilan Manor. 2024b. "Digital Diplomacy in the Age of Technological Acceleration: Three Impact Scenarios of Generative Artificial Intelligence." *Place Branding and Public Diplomacy*. https://doi.org/10.1057/s41254-023-00323-4.

This article explores how generative AI accelerates diplomacy, expanding its reach across domains (horizontal acceleration) and deepening its impact (vertical acceleration). It examines AI's role in shaping knowledge production, diplomatic narratives, and strategic statecraft in a technology-driven world.

Cassirer, Ernst. 2021. *An Essay on Man: An Introduction to a Philosophy of Human Culture*. New Haven, CT: Yale University Press.

Cassirer's work on symbolic forms explores how narratives, myths, and ideological constructs shape perception and power. His insights provide a theoretical foundation for understanding how symbolic diplomacy operates through state branding, public diplomacy, and ambassadorial representation.

Gilbert, Felix. 1984. *Machiavelli and Guicciardini: Politics and History in Sixteenth-Century Florence*. New York: W. W. Norton & Company.

This book explores how Machiavelli and Guicciardini, shaped by Florence's political upheavals, developed distinct yet interconnected approaches to politics and history. Gilbert examines their contrasting views on power, contingency, and historical causation, highlighting how their ideas bridged humanist scholarship and pragmatic statecraft, influencing modern political thought.

Slaughter, Anne-Marie. 2017. *The Chessboard and the Web: Strategies of Connection in a Networked World*. New Haven, CT: Yale University Press.

This book redefines strategic power for the digital era, arguing that diplomacy is shifting from hierarchical structures to network-based influence. It provides insights into how states, diplomats, and institutions navigate interconnected global challenges through adaptive strategies.

Part VI
Conclusion

13 The Philosophy of Diplomacy

Diplomacy's Underlying Philosophy

Is diplomacy merely a pragmatic craft, dictated by circumstance and necessity, or does it rest upon a deeper, underlying philosophy – one that, even if often unspoken, informs its principles, methods, and objectives? If such a philosophy exists, is it a coherent and structured intellectual framework, or does it remain an evolving assemblage of historical traditions, legal precedents, and normative assumptions? To pose these questions is to acknowledge that philosophy, in its most fundamental sense, is not merely a rarefied exercise in abstract reasoning, but a means of interrogating the premises that structure human thought and action. At its core, diplomacy is more than tactical negotiation or strategic manoeuvring; it is a system of thought, one that provides both an epistemological foundation – defining how states and societies understand their place in the world – and an ethical compass, shaping the values, obligations, and aspirations that guide international engagement.

As Wilfrid Sellars – a philosopher who sought to reconcile scientific realism with human cognition – famously argued, philosophy is about "seeing how things, in the broadest possible sense of the term, hang together in the broadest possible sense of the term" (Sellars, 1963: 1). It is not confined to theoretical speculation but is, as John Dewey – a radical thinker who reshaped education and democracy – argues, a method cultivated to instil "courage and confidence . . . to carry the burden of life more successfully" (Dewey, 1929/2022: 33). At its core, philosophy concerns itself with the articulation of first principle, what can be known, how we should act, and what constitutes the good life. Hannah Arendt – a seminal intellectual and refugee from totalitarianism who redefined our understanding of power and responsibility – reminds us that philosophical inquiry is not detached from practical but is instead rooted in "vita activa", her concept of the active life. Contrasting with purely contemplative existence, "vita active" emphasises engagement in the world through labour, work, and action (Arendt, 1999). It embodies the relentless capacity to question what is taken for granted and to reimagine the ethical and political conditions of human existence (Arendt, 1978: 11).

If diplomacy, as the primary mode of structured international engagement, mediates between competing interests, reconciles estrangement, and constructs legitimacy, then reflecting on its philosophical foundations becomes not merely an intellectual exercise but an imperative for understanding its deeper logic and future trajectory. The benefits of such reflection are profound. First, it allows us to ask whether diplomacy is an end in itself – a stabilising force that enables co-existence amid diversity – or a mere instrument of strategic calculation, subordinated to more tangible expressions of political will. Second, it encourages a critical examination of diplomacy's ethical and epistemic underpinnings: does diplomacy derive legitimacy from tradition, legal codification, or its ability to produce

DOI: 10.4324/9781003485407-19

equitable outcomes? To what extent does it rely on tacit knowledge, rhetorical persuasion, or performance as opposed to codified rules and institutional structures? Third, interrogating diplomacy's philosophical core helps clarify its relationship with time: is it inherently conservative, privileging continuity and order, or is it capable of generating new forms of political imagination and institutional innovation?

Existing diplomatic literature suggests that diplomacy operates at the intersection of recognition, communication, and mediation. It is shaped by formal structures – such as treaties, protocols, and diplomatic immunity – but is equally constituted by symbolic exchange, cultural performance, and personal relationships. These elements together define diplomacy not merely as a technical function of statecraft but as a complex, meaning-generating practice that navigates the tensions between sovereignty and interdependence, stability and change, power and legitimacy. If diplomacy indeed embodies an implicit philosophy, making it explicit would refine its conceptual clarity, elevate its intellectual standing, and illuminate the deeper forces governing its evolution in an increasingly fragmented world.

In this volume, we have focused on one of diplomacy's core philosophical dimensions: its role as the institutionalised practice of communication. To say that diplomacy is institutionalised is to acknowledge that it does not emerge spontaneously in response to political needs, but is embedded in historically developed norms, legal codifications, and procedural conventions that lend it structure, continuity, and legitimacy. Philosophically, this raises fundamental questions: does diplomacy primarily reflect existing power structures, or does it actively construct the international order in which it operates? If diplomacy is a means of enabling predictable, rule-based interaction, does this make it inherently conservative, privileging continuity over transformation? Or does its reliance on mediation and symbolic engagement suggest a more constitutive role, shaping the very norms and identities that define international politics?

Understanding diplomacy as an institutionalised form of communication highlights its ontological status – not merely as a conduit for state interaction but as a practice that actively produces legitimacy, authority, and order. Diplomacy is not simply a neutral mechanism for transmitting information or resolving disputes; it is a performative act through which political realities are constructed, power is negotiated, and international hierarchies are reinforced or challenged. Nowhere is this more apparent than in its dual role in the recognition and the distribution of public goods, two interwoven processes that shape the very architecture of international order. Recognition is more than a diplomatic formality – it is the precondition for political agencies in international affairs. Through diplomatic engagement, states, international organisations, and even non-state actors gain legitimacy, assert authority, and claim a role in governance. The process is never impartial; recognition is historically contingent and politically charged, defining who has access to diplomatic influence and who remains on the periphery of global decision-making. In parallel, diplomacy structures the negotiation and allocation of public goods, from economic stability to environmental governance and global health security. The distribution of these goods is not a straightforward exercise in technocratic management but a highly contested diplomatic process, where power, obligation, and entitlement are continuously negotiated. Diplomacy, by institutionalising these processes, ensures that they are not resolved through coercion or unilateral action but embedded within shared procedural frameworks, lending them legitimacy and continuity.

In this sense, *diplomacy is not merely about managing international relations – it is about ordering them*. By defining the terms of recognition and structuring the allocation of public goods, diplomacy establishes the rules, norms, and expectations that shape the global system. Yet this order is neither fixed nor inherently just. It is continually contested and reconstituted through diplomatic practice, revealing diplomacy not as a passive reflection of power but as an active force that produces and sustains it. By framing diplomacy in these terms, we move beyond seeing it as a reactive or technical function and instead recognise it as a constitutive process, one that does not merely facilitate international engagement but fundamentally shapes the world as it is – and as it might become.

While this discussion illuminates diplomacy's role in the recognition, communication, and distribution of public goods, it stops short of determining whether these elements cohere within a unified philosophical framework or whether diplomacy remains an inherently adaptive, fragmented, and historically contingent practice. This gap leads to a fundamental question: *can diplomacy be understood as a structured philosophical system that integrates its institutional logic with its deeper intellectual foundations?* A structured philosophical system is one that offers not just a descriptive account of how something functions but a coherent, internally ordered framework that explains *why it functions as it does* and *what principles govern its operation*.

In the case of diplomacy, this means moving beyond viewing it as a collection of practices, customs, and responses to shifting global dynamics and instead articulating its underlying conceptual architecture – the ways in which its elements relate to one another and the normative assumptions that shape its purpose. If diplomacy is both a mechanism of ordering and a process of mediation, what holds together its various dimensions – pragmatic negotiation, normative legitimacy, and strategic positioning – into a coherent intellectual structure? What is needed, therefore, is an integrated system of diplomatic thought – one that does not simply describe how diplomacy operates but articulates its first principles, internal logic, and conceptual foundations within a broader philosophical tradition.

The Vitruvian Model

For over two centuries, the Gallerie dell'Accademia in Venice has housed one of the most significant studies from the Italian Renaissance: *The Study of Human Body Proportions*, better known as "The Vitruvian Man", created by Leonardo da Vinci around 1490 in Milan (Gallerie Dell'accademia di Venezia, 2025). This drawing remains one of the most iconic and profound works of the Italian Renaissance, embodying the era's ideals in art, science, and humanism. The original concept for the study belongs to the Roman architect Marcus Vitruvius Pollio (commonly known as Vitruvius), who argued that the human body could serve as a model for the proportions of buildings. He outlined these ideal proportions in his treatise *De Architectura*, written approximately between 20 and 30 BCE (Oksanish, 2019). Da Vinci created *The Vitruvian Man* while living in Milan under the patronage of Ludovico Sforza, Duke of Milan, at a time when Vitruvius's ideas were actively discussed among architects involved in the construction of Milan Cathedral (Isaacson, 2018: 170).

Da Vinci's notebooks from this period contain numerous observations on the relationship between the human body and geometry, partly inspired by the works of Leon Battista Alberti, another highly influential Renaissance figure. Alberti's treatises, written a few decades earlier (1434–1452) – including *On Sculpture*, *On Painting*, and *On Architecture* (itself drawing from Vitruvius) – extended beyond the refinement of artistic skills. For Alberti, the geometry of the human body carried clear metaphysical significance. He asserted that by studying human anatomy, an artist could perceive more than all philosophers combined (McLaughlin, 2024). Thus, The Vitruvian Man aligns with a broader intellectual current of the period, reflecting Da Vinci's ambition to explore human anatomy and his fascination with symmetry, proportion, and the relationship between nature and human-made structures.

Da Vinci's *Vitruvian Man* was executed on a sheet of paper slightly larger than an A4 page, using a pen, light brown ink, and a delicate wash of brown watercolour (see Figure 13.1).

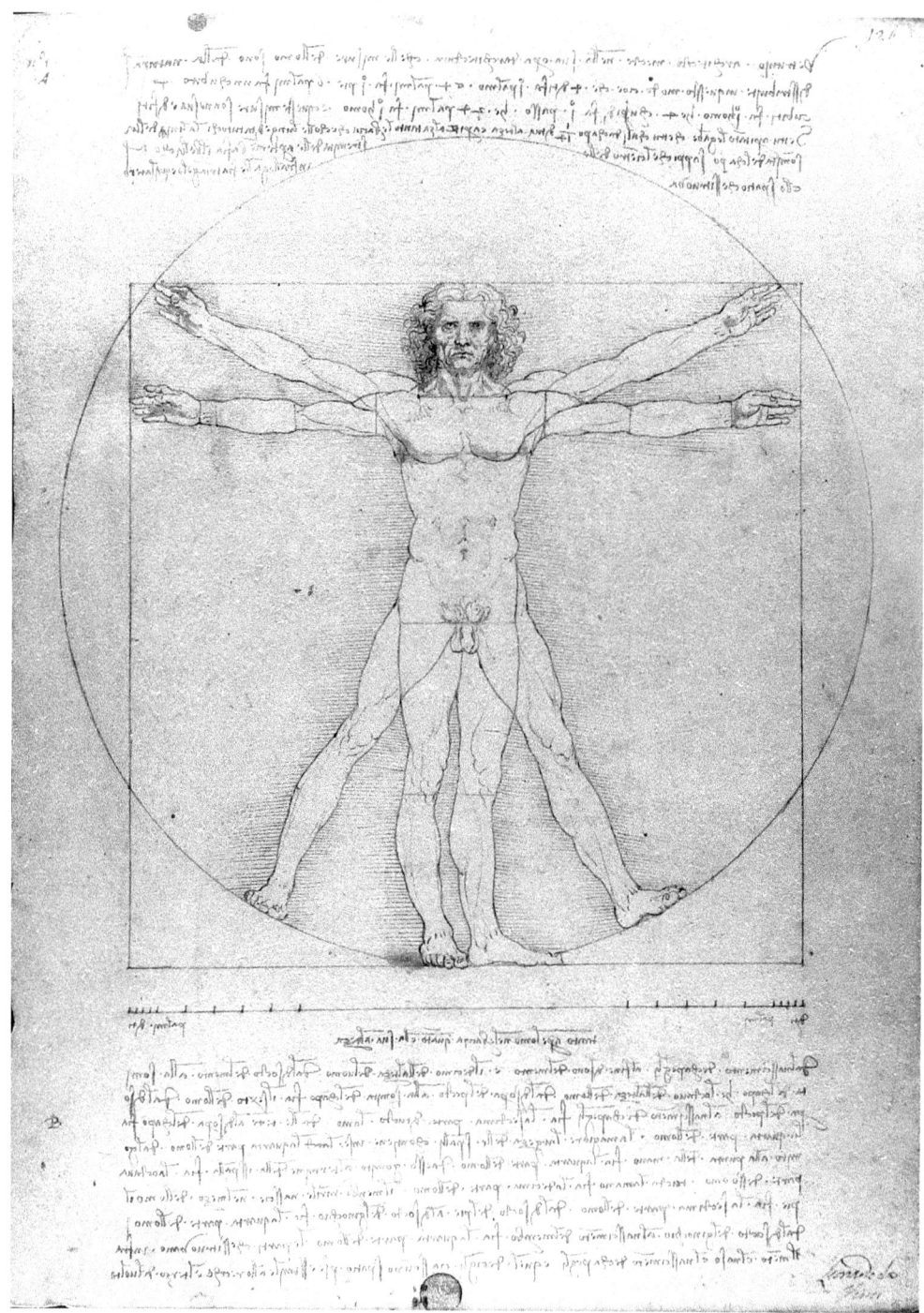

Figure 13.1 Leonardo Da Vinci: Study of the Proportions of the Human Body (Known as the Vitruvian Man).

The meticulously crafted drawing, marked by its precise lines, depicts a male figure in two superimposed positions, with arms and legs extended to inscribe both a square and a circle. These geometric forms carry deep symbolic meaning (Magazù, Coletta and Migliardo, 2019):

- **The Circle:** A symbol of the cosmic and the divine, the circle in Da Vinci's drawing is centred on the navel, which he regarded as the natural fulcrum of the human form. This placement evokes the idea that humanity is intrinsically linked to the larger order of the universe, reflecting the Neoplatonic ideal of a reality governed by mathematical precision and metaphysical unity.
- **The Square:** Representing the earthly and material realm, the square delineates the boundaries of human existence within the physical world. Its alignment with the figure's outstretched limbs suggests that while human beings are grounded in materiality, they are also ordered and proportioned according to universal principles. The juxtaposition of the circle and the square in Da Vinci's composition thus symbolises the dual nature of human existence – at once finite and transcendent, rooted in the terrestrial yet reaching towards the celestial.

The Vitruvian Man illustrates the ideal proportions of the human body, based on the symmetry and balance described by Vitruvius. The artwork embodies the Renaissance belief in man as the measure of all things – though in a manner fundamentally distinct from the classical conception of Protagoras, who argued that truth and reality were subjective, dependent on individual perception and experience (Burrell, 1932). Through *The Vitruvian Man*, Da Vinci underscores the profound connection between the microcosm (the human body) and the macrocosm (the universe), offering a vision of how the laws governing the cosmos can be deciphered through reason and empirical observation.

These ideas offer a compelling foundation for articulating a philosophical framework of diplomacy, one that, like *The Vitruvian Man*, is shaped by dualities that must be reconciled. The circle, representing the cosmic and universal, reflects the timeless principles of diplomacy – communication, legitimacy, and mediation – that transcend historical periods and cultural contexts. The square, embodying the earthly and tangible, corresponds to the practical mechanisms through which diplomacy operates – treaties, institutions, and governance structures that give material form to diplomatic engagement. Just as da Vinci's composition seeks to integrate these geometric elements into a harmonious and proportionate whole, a Vitruvian-inspired philosophy of diplomacy would seek to unify its normative ideals with its institutional realities, ensuring that diplomacy is not merely a reactive or ad hoc practice, but a structured system of thought that brings order to international affairs.

This approach directly addresses a key limitation of existing diplomatic theory: its fragmented nature, which tends to frame diplomacy either as a set of technical procedures or as a historically contingent phenomenon, rather than as a coherent intellectual system governed by internal logic and proportioned functions. The Renaissance dictum that "man is the measure of all things" can be reinterpreted in diplomatic terms: diplomacy should not merely reflect the contingent and often chaotic nature of global politics but instead serve as an ordering force, a framework that mediates between the material realities of power and the normative aspirations of global order. A Vitruvian model of diplomacy would thus provide more than a functional structure for diplomatic practice – it would establish an intellectual architecture that integrates its strategic, ethical, and communicative dimensions into a proportioned and internally balanced whole. In doing so, it would elevate diplomacy from a pragmatic craft to a philosophical system, one in which the universal and the particular, the theoretical and the practical, the abstract and the concrete exist in dynamic yet measured interplay.

A Vitruvian-inspired philosophical model of diplomacy – one that envisions diplomacy as a structured and proportioned system rather than a fragmented set of practices – offers a fundamentally new approach to the study of diplomacy. By synthesising universal principles (symbolised by the circle) with institutional and strategic realities (embodied by the square), this model establishes a cohesive intellectual framework applicable across multiple dimensions of diplomatic inquiry. Such a model provides a structural lens through which diplomacy can be examined not as a loose collection of practices, but as a system of interdependent components – normative, institutional, strategic, and communicative – each functioning in measured proportion to the others. This perspective enables scholars to move beyond the traditional dichotomies of pragmatism versus idealism or technical function versus normative aspiration, allowing diplomacy to be understood instead as a dynamic yet ordered intellectual field, one that evolves while maintaining an underlying philosophical coherence.

One of the most significant contributions of this model lies in its ability *to bridge the gap between theoretical abstraction and practical execution*. Diplomatic studies often remain either overly conceptual, detached from the realities of international engagement, or overly technical, reducing diplomacy to a set of case-specific strategies with little connection to broader intellectual frameworks. A Vitruvian model provides a conceptual structure in which diplomatic practice is always contextualised within larger principles, ensuring that diplomacy is understood as an evolving system of norms, institutions, and strategies rather than as a collection of isolated techniques. This perspective allows for a more refined study of how diplomacy both shapes and is shaped by legal, ethical, and strategic imperatives over time. It also facilitates a comparative approach, enabling scholars to assess how different diplomatic traditions balance principle and pragmatism across cultures and historical periods. Furthermore, it provides a more holistic framework for analysing diplomacy's role in global governance, moving beyond the binary framing of diplomacy as either an instrument of power or a vehicle for cooperation to a more nuanced understanding of its function as both.

Equally important is the model's capacity to offer *a structured methodology for diplomatic analysis*. Rather than treating diplomacy as an ad hoc response to international contingencies, this approach seeks to identify the deeper structural relationships that govern diplomatic interactions. By conceptualising diplomacy as an ordered and proportioned system with interdependent components – normative, institutional, strategic, and communicative – a Vitruvian framework allows scholars to study diplomacy through a systematic lens that emphasises proportion, hierarchy, and interconnectedness. This makes it possible to analyse how different actors navigate tensions between power and legitimacy, secrecy and transparency, mediation and coercion in a more structured and comparative way. Furthermore, this model encourages scholars to examine the proportion between diplomatic ideals and institutional realities. Diplomacy often exists in a tension between aspiration and constraint, where international norms must be reconciled with political pragmatism and institutional limitations. A Vitruvian methodology provides the analytical tools to map this interplay with precision, offering insights into how diplomatic mechanisms both sustain and adapt within the broader architecture of international order. Ultimately, a Vitruvian methodology enables a more precise mapping of diplomacy's core functions – recognition, communication, mediation, and governance – not as isolated processes but as interconnected dimensions of a larger, evolving diplomatic system.

Beyond its impact on diplomatic theory and analysis, a Vitruvian model also redefines the *training and professional formation of diplomats*, providing them with a structured intellectual foundation that enhances their ability to navigate the complexities of their profession. Diplomatic training often oscillates between practical skill-building and theoretical study, with little effort to integrate these elements into a unified system of learning. A Vitruvian approach would ensure that training in negotiation, mediation, and governance is always situated within a broader conceptual framework, fostering a more strategic and reflective approach to diplomatic engagement. This model would also encourage a greater emphasis on the interdependence of diplomatic functions, moving beyond the compartmentalisation of public diplomacy, economic diplomacy, and crisis diplomacy as separate disciplines, and instead highlighting their interconnected roles within a single intellectual system. Moreover, it would cultivate a deeper engagement with the philosophical foundations of diplomacy, encouraging practitioners to critically reflect on their role not merely as negotiators or policymakers but as architects of global order, responsible for maintaining equilibrium between competing forces in international relations.

By integrating these three dimensions – theoretical-practical synthesis, methodological structure, and diplomatic education – a Vitruvian model of diplomacy provides a comprehensive intellectual foundation for both the study and practice of diplomacy. It transforms diplomacy from a reactive craft shaped by external events into a structured and proportioned discipline, governed not by contingency alone but by a reasoned and enduring conceptual framework.

Proportion and Order

Having outlined the Vitruvian philosophical model in the previous section, we now turn to its analytical utility – not merely to apply it as a conceptual overlay but to examine what deeper insights it reveals when tested against the conclusions drawn from this volume. The book provides a rich and multifaceted exploration of diplomacy's evolution, core functions, and contemporary challenges, offering a strong foundation for understanding its role in global affairs. Yet, as with any expansive examination of a complex discipline, there remains an intellectual space for greater integration – a need to connect historical trajectories, institutional structures, functional tasks, and strategic imperatives within a more cohesive and proportioned conceptual framework.

The Vitruvian model, with its emphasis on balance, relationality, and structural proportion, provides an approach to harmonising these diverse elements, revealing diplomacy not as a series of fragmented practices but as an ordered and evolving system. By positioning diplomacy within this structured model, we gain a more refined understanding of its inner logic, tracing the reciprocal relationship between theoretical abstraction and practical execution, the interconnections between diplomatic methodology and governance structures, and the evolving demands of diplomatic education and training. These three dimensions stand out as areas where a Vitruvian perspective can enrich both the study and practice of diplomacy, illuminating its underlying order and enabling a more integrated reading of its governing principles.

Bridging the Theory/Practice Divide

One of the strengths of the volume is its ability to capture both the historical evolution and contemporary relevance of diplomacy, tracing its development from early institutionalisation to modern multilateralism (Chapter 2). By examining how diplomacy has expanded into areas such as economic governance, environmental diplomacy, and human rights (Chapter 4), the book illustrates its capacity for adaptation, while also raising important questions about how these expansions fit within a cohesive theoretical framework that accounts for both continuity and change. Similarly, the volume explores the core functions of diplomacy – negotiation, mediation, messaging, and dialogue (Chapter 6), offering a functional perspective on diplomatic engagement. This discussion complements Chapter 3's exploration of tradition, mediation, and power, which examines raison d'état and raison de système as distinct but interrelated forces in diplomatic reasoning. Taken together, these analyses highlight diplomacy's dual role – as an instrument of statecraft and as a systemic ordering mechanism – a balance that is also reflected in the study of decision-making models (Chapter 7).

The discussion of rational choice, heuristic reasoning, and habitual practice provides a structured way of understanding how diplomats navigate complex strategic dilemmas, demonstrating the interplay between deliberate calculation and adaptive intuition. By linking these insights, the volume presents a diplomatic landscape shaped by both historical precedent and contemporary challenges, illustrating how tradition and innovation coexist within diplomatic reasoning. A structured framework can help position these discussions within a larger intellectual framework, allowing scholars to examine diplomacy not only as a response to geopolitical change but as a discipline governed by enduring principles of order and mediation.

Integrating Methodological Approaches

This volume also highlights the diverse methodological lenses through which diplomacy can be studied. Chapter 8 introduces valuable distinctions between proximity and distance, horizontality and verticality in diplomatic relationships, while in Chapter 9, a discussion of world order presents different frameworks – polarity, rule-based systems, and background structures – for understanding diplomacy's role in global governance. These analytical categories provide a structured means of assessing diplomatic interactions, offering insight into how diplomatic engagement varies across different scales and political contexts. Similarly, Chapter 5 introduces the distinction between foreground and background factors in diplomacy, noting how diplomacy operates within both formal legal structures (such as the Vienna Convention) and unwritten norms (such as diplomatic tact, authority, and communicative style).

Meanwhile, Chapter 12's examination of symbolic and epistemic power highlights the ways in which diplomacy constructs legitimacy through narratives and representation, reinforcing the discursive and performative dimensions of diplomatic engagement. By drawing on these perspectives, the volume underscores the importance of a multi-layered approach to studying diplomacy – one that takes into account both structural constraints and the agency of diplomats, both material institutions and intangible forms of influence. The analysis of digital diplomacy in Chapter 10 provides a compelling case study of how diplomacy is evolving in response to technological change, while in Chapter 11, the exploration of crisis diplomacy demonstrates how diplomats navigate both policy crises and systemic shocks. Together, these discussions highlight the intersections between diplomatic structures, communicative strategies, and evolving geopolitical contexts, reinforcing the value of a methodological approach that is proportioned, integrated, and dynamic.

Reframing Diplomatic Training

This volume also makes important contributions to the discussion of diplomatic education and professional training, particularly in the context of decision-making, crisis diplomacy, and power dynamics. In Chapter 7, the examination of strategic reasoning in diplomacy highlights the cognitive complexity of diplomatic decision-making, demonstrating the need for diplomats to be trained not only in procedural negotiation techniques but also in broader strategic and philosophical reasoning. Similarly, in Chapter 11, the discussion of crisis diplomacy explores how diplomats manage institutional and policy crises, underscoring the need for training that prepares practitioners for both immediate tactical responses and long-term crisis governance.

In Chapter 6, the discussion of negotiation, mediation, and dialogue reinforces this point by illustrating the need for diplomats to be equipped with a conceptual understanding of how these engagement techniques operate within broader diplomatic systems.

A related discussion emerges in Chapter 12, which examines diplomatic power across epistemic, symbolic, and strategic dimensions. The volume highlights how diplomacy shapes global narratives and constructs legitimacy, yet these aspects are often underrepresented in practitioner training, which tends to emphasise technical skills over conceptual depth. Expanding training to include these dimensions would ensure that diplomats are not only skilled in negotiation and governance but also capable of critically engaging with the deeper structures of international influence. Similarly, in Chapter 10, the discussion of digital diplomacy underscores the growing need for diplomats to engage with emerging technologies, yet digital diplomacy is often taught as a separate skill set rather than as an extension of diplomacy's evolving communicative and institutional structures. By incorporating these themes into diplomatic education, training programmes could provide a more holistic preparation for contemporary diplomatic challenges, ensuring that diplomats are equipped to engage with both traditional and emerging forms of diplomatic practice.

Taken together, this volume presents a rich and multi-dimensional exploration of diplomacy, illustrating how historical traditions, strategic imperatives, and institutional structures interact in shaping diplomatic practice. However, rather than treating diplomacy as a collection of empirical observations, methodological tools, and professional techniques, the Vitruvian model reconfigures these insights into a structured philosophical system – one that does not merely describe how diplomacy functions but seeks to explain why it functions as it does and what principles govern its operation. A structured philosophical system does more than document processes; it provides an internally ordered framework that reveals the underlying logic, proportional relationships, and governing dynamics of its subject – much like how diplomatic institutionalisation (Chapter 2) balances state sovereignty with systemic order, how foreground and background factors (Chapter 5) structure diplomacy's legal and normative dimensions, or how crisis diplomacy (Chapter 11) recalibrates itself to absorb systemic shocks while maintaining its foundational equilibrium. This same principle applies across diplomacy's theoretical foundations, methodological approaches, and professional training – ensuring that diplomacy is not merely a collection of case studies or tactical responses, but an intellectual system where theory informs practice, methodological rigour enhances coherence, and structured training prepares diplomats to navigate complexity without losing sight of diplomacy's core logic and proportionality.

Diplomacy Between the Circle and the Square: Balancing Post-human Agency

The Vitruvian philosophical perspective on diplomacy, which conceptualises diplomacy as a structured and proportioned system, offers a compelling framework for examining the potential disruptions introduced by post-human agency. Historically, diplomacy has been an intrinsically anthropocentric enterprise, with its foundational processes – representation, communcation, negotiation – predicated on human intentionality, judgement, and interaction. However, as AI-driven decision-making, algorithmic governance, and autonomous systems increasingly mediate diplomatic engagements, the balance of agency is undergoing a gradual but consequential transformation. This shift raises fundamental questions about the nature of diplomatic authority, legitimacy, and accountability in an era where human diplomats may no longer be the sole architects of international negotiation and governance.

The advent of post-human agency – the notion that non-human entities such as AI systems, autonomous platforms, and algorithmic decision-making tools possess the capacity to influence diplomatic processes partially or independently of direct human intervention – poses an unprecedented challenge to diplomacy's epistemic and operational foundations. No longer confined to the realm of human deliberation and negotiation, diplomacy must now navigate emergent forms of agency that dissolve the clear distinctions between human intent, machine-driven intelligence, and their entangled roles in decision-making processes. The traditional tripartite structure of epistemic, symbolic, and strategic power (Chapter 12), which has historically governed diplomacy's role in knowledge control, legitimacy-building, and negotiation, must now be reassessed in light of machine-driven intelligence, AI-generated narratives, and automated diplomatic engagement.

This shift prompts two critical questions: can diplomacy maintain its structured proportions as non-human actors assume a more decisive role in shaping international engagements? And what happens when AI-driven systems do not merely assist in diplomatic processes but actively shape or redefine them, potentially operating beyond human oversight? *The challenge, then, is to determine whether diplomacy, as an adaptive but structurally ordered system, can incorporate post-human agents while preserving its core principles of balance, proportionality, and legitimacy – or whether this technological evolution will necessitate a fundamental reconfiguration of how agency, accountability, and influence are conceived in foreign affairs.*

Post-human Agency: Philosophical Roots

The concept of post-human agency is deeply embedded within posthumanist thought, which critically re-examines the Enlightenment-era premise that agency is an exclusively human attribute (Landgraf, 2022). Traditional humanism placed humans at the centre of political agency, intellectual inquiry, and ethical consideration, reinforcing a hierarchical distinction between human and non-human actors. Posthumanism, emerging as a response to these assumptions, challenges this anthropocentric paradigm by deconstructing the human/non-human binary and recognising agency as something distributed across assemblages of human, technological, and systemic forces (Wolfe, 2009). As Kuby, Rucker and Darolia (2017: 356) put it, the posthuman notion of agency is one which "decentres the human as the focus of agency and instead conceptualises agency as the in-betweenness, togetherness, flows and forces of human(s) and nonhuman(s)". Influenced by poststructuralist critiques (Foucault, Derrida) and scientific advancements in AI, synthetic biology, and cybernetics, posthumanism compels a rethinking of governance, power, and agency in an era where machines, algorithms, and autonomous systems increasingly shape global interactions.

Defining posthumanism is inherently challenging due to its fluid, contested, and multidimensional nature. However, Sharon's cartography of posthumanist thought provides a structured framework by mapping it along three key axes: pessimist/optimist, historical-materialist/philosophical-ontological, and humanist/non-humanist (Sharon, 2014). The *pessimist/optimist* axis reflects attitudes towards technological enhancement, ranging from those who reject modification for fear of altering essential human nature to those who embrace enhancement as a moral imperative to improve the (post)human condition. The *historical-materialist/philosophical-ontological* axis distinguishes between perspectives that see the posthuman condition as a product of specific historical-technological shifts and those that interrogate 'human' as an analytical category, independent of historical contingencies. Finally, the *humanist/non-humanist axis* differentiates between posthumanist strands that extend traditional humanist ideals and those that reject humanism outright, critiquing its role in legitimising exclusion and marginalisation.

Using these axes, posthumanist thought can be broadly categorised into several distinct perspectives, each reflecting a different stance on human enhancement, technological agency, and the evolving nature of personhood. *Dystopian posthumanism* views human enhancement and bioengineering as an existential threat to human nature, arguing that artificial interference undermines human dignity and the foundational principles of human rights. This perspective sees posthuman agency as a form of 'hyperagency', where humanity's ability to reshape nature according to its own design paradoxically erodes the very qualities that define human existence. The fear is that, in the pursuit of mastery over biology, we may strip life of its unpredictability, giftedness, and intrinsic meaning (Sandel, 2009). *Liberal posthumanism*, by contrast, extends traditional humanist ideals of rationality, progress, and individual agency, embracing technological enhancement as a means of liberation from biological limitations. Rather than perceiving 'hyperagency' as a danger to human integrity, liberal posthumanists see it as an avenue for self-actualisation, allowing individuals to transcend biological constraints and reach new frontiers of human potential (Hayles, 2017). This vision envisions posthumanism not as the dissolution of human nature, but as its ultimate realisation – an expansion rather than an erosion of human possibility.

Unlike dystopian and liberal posthumanism, which view the blurring boundaries of the human as a product of technoscientific progress, *radical posthumanism* challenges the core assumptions of liberal humanism, rejecting human exceptionalism and the human-machine divide. It critiques the idea that agency, rationality, and progress have ever been universally accessible, arguing that historically, autonomy was a privilege reserved for the few – those with the wealth, power, and social standing to define themselves as fully human. From this perspective, the posthuman condition is not about expanding human potential but dismantling the exclusionary categories that have defined subjectivity and agency (Braidotti, 2021). *Methodological posthumanism*, by contrast, examines how technology mediates human experience, arguing that agency emerges through interactions between human and non-human actors. Drawing on Latour's Actor-Network Theory (2007), it rejects the binary distinction between humans and machines, seeing social and political systems as co-constituted by both. While humans may initiate action, technologies, infrastructures, and algorithms exert passive yet consequential agency, continuously shaping how individuals perceive, engage with, and respond to their environments (Herbrechter, 2013).

Table 13.1 presents key perspectives within posthumanist thought, each defined by its core ideas and conceptual foundations. These frameworks – dystopian, liberal, radical, and methodological posthumanism – offer distinct ways of understanding human enhancement, technological agency, and the reconfiguration of decision-making in an era of AI and automation. While each perspective engages with questions of agency, legitimacy, and governance, their implications for diplomacy vary significantly. From concerns over black-box AI and accountability to the emergence of AI-driven negotiation and distributed authority, these frameworks help map the shifting terrain where human and non-human actors increasingly shape global diplomacy.

These typologies offer a critical lens through which to understand the transformation of diplomacy's epistemic, strategic, and symbolic dimensions in an era of AI-driven intelligence and algorithmic governance. They underscore the necessity of moving beyond traditional anthropocentric models of diplomacy, towards a framework that accounts for the growing entanglement of human and machine agency in global affairs.

Post-human Challenges

One of the fundamental challenges of AI-driven diplomacy lies in the illusion of neutrality embedded within algorithmic systems. While AI is often presented as objective and data-driven,

Table 13.1 Posthumanist Perspectives and Their Implications for Diplomacy

Posthumanist Perspective	Core Idea	Key Concepts	Implications for Diplomacy
Dystopian Posthumanism	Views human enhancement and AI as existential threats, eroding human dignity and agency.	Hyperagency, loss of unpredictability, existential concerns over human enhancement.	Black-box AI systems create opacity in diplomatic decision-making, raising concerns over accountability and bias.
Liberal Posthumanism	Sees technological augmentation as an opportunity for self-actualisation and human progress.	Technological self-actualisation, expansion of human potential, mastery over biological constraints.	AI-assisted diplomacy enhances efficiency, reduces bias, and broadens diplomatic engagement in negotiations and conflict resolution.
Radical Posthumanism	Challenges human exceptionalism, asserting that agency is unevenly distributed across human and non-human actors.	Decentralised agency, fluid subjectivity, and a reconceptualisation of autonomy beyond individual human control	Diplomatic authority shifts from human actors to networks of human and AI systems, altering traditional power structures and legitimacy.
Methodological Posthumanism	Examines how human and non-human actors co-construct agency through technological mediation.	Emergent agency, co-constitutive governance, dissolution of human-machine boundaries.	Diplomatic agency emerges from complex interactions between human and non-human actors, necessitating new governance models to manage AI-driven negotiation and decision-making.

it inevitably reproduces underlying biases and asymmetries of power that exist within its training data and model architecture (Horowitz and Kahn, 2024). This issue is particularly relevant to the discussion of epistemic power in Chapter 12, which examines how diplomacy has historically relied on control over information, strategic framing, and knowledge production as a tool of influence. In a world where AI-driven intelligence analysis begins to replace human judgement, a pressing question arises: who – or what – now controls epistemic power in diplomatic affairs?

This concern is heightened by the phenomenon of algorithmic bias, wherein AI models – trained on historically contingent datasets – inadvertently perpetuate geopolitical assumptions, cultural hierarchies, and asymmetries of power. These biases arise from structural imbalances in data representation, the privileging of hegemonic narratives, and the systematic omission or marginalisation of alternative perspectives, resulting in AI systems that do not merely reflect the past but actively reproduce and entrench existing power structures (Miceli, Posada and Yang, 2021). Rather than serving as neutral arbiters, AI-driven diplomatic tools may inadvertently privilege selective narratives, shaping diplomatic discourse in ways that introduce new forms of asymmetry, exclusion, and opacity in international negotiations and decision-making. By embedding historically embedded biases into automated decision-making, these systems challenge diplomacy's delicate equilibrium between symbolic and strategic power – where legitimacy, once negotiated through human deliberation and diplomatic dialogue, is increasingly shaped by machine-generated narratives, algorithmic inference, and computationally derived legitimacy. This shift raises fundamental questions about who or what determines credibility, authority, and influence in an era where non-human actors mediate diplomatic reality.

The challenge is further intensified by the "black-box" nature of AI (Carabantes, 2020), an inherent limitation of advanced deep learning systems that process vast datasets using opaque, non-interpretable logic. Unlike human decision-makers, who can articulate and justify their reasoning, many AI models operate through high-dimensional correlations and self-adjusting parameters, making their outputs difficult to scrutinise or contest. This opacity raises profound concerns for diplomatic decision-making, where credibility, accountability, and interpretability are foundational to negotiation and statecraft. Compounding this issue is automation bias – the cognitive tendency to over-rely on algorithmic outputs, assuming them to be inherently superior or objective (Alon-Barkat and Busuioc, 2023). This can lead policymakers to adopt AI-generated intelligence uncritically, without fully understanding the underlying assumptions, data biases, or potential limitations of the system. Such reliance introduces risks not only in diplomatic accuracy and strategic forecasting but also in the assignment of responsibility when AI-driven errors or miscalculations influence high-stakes negotiations, conflict resolution, or crisis management. In an arena where precision, intent, and interpretability are paramount, the inability to trace, contest, or revise algorithmic determinations threatens to recalibrate diplomatic agency in ways that challenge its very foundations.

The Vitruvian model's emphasis on proportion and balance provides a valuable framework for addressing these challenges. In traditional diplomacy, knowledge production, strategic influence, and negotiation have existed in a carefully measured equilibrium, ensuring that no single element overpowers the others. However, as AI-driven intelligence and autonomous negotiation tools become increasingly dominant, this proportion risks being fundamentally altered, potentially leaving human actors with diminished oversight over diplomatic processes. If diplomacy is to maintain its structural integrity, mechanisms must be developed to ensure that AI-driven agency remains proportionally integrated within diplomatic practice, rather than overwhelming human judgement and institutional legitimacy. The challenge for the future is not merely technological but philosophical: how to embed AI within diplomacy in a way that enhances, rather than disrupts, the fundamental principles of diplomatic order and negotiation.

Post-human Diplomacy

As diplomacy moves into an era where AI systems, digital infrastructures, and algorithmic governance shape diplomatic interactions in increasingly profound ways, the Vitruvian model provides a structured lens for evaluating the implications of this transformation. In Chapter 9, the discussion of world order – which examines polarity, rule-based governance, and deep background structures – outlines the traditional mechanisms through which international stability has been maintained. Yet, if diplomacy is no longer an exclusively human domain, these models may require fundamental reconsideration. The emergence of post-human diplomatic actors – from AI-assisted negotiation systems to fully autonomous diplomatic entities – recasts foundational questions of sovereignty, agency, and the architecture of diplomatic authority. Vitruvian proportion ensures that technological optimisation does not come at the cost of ethical judgement, interpretability, or adaptive reasoning, preserving diplomacy's delicate balance between strategic efficacy and the relational, trust-building processes that underpin international negotiations.

The rise of AI-driven diplomacy also challenges the traditional balance between state authority and systemic governance. If decision-making is increasingly automated and data-driven, who or what holds diplomatic legitimacy? In Chapter 10, the discussion of technological supremacy highlights the growing role of AI capabilities as a determining factor in global influence, suggesting that states with advanced AI infrastructure will have a disproportionate ability to shape diplomatic outcomes. This shift could create new asymmetries in global politics, as control over algorithmic governance mechanisms becomes a form of diplomatic leverage. Will states retain sovereignty over international negotiations, or will diplomatic power shift towards those who control AI-driven intelligence, digital infrastructure, and machine-generated decision-making? If diplomacy is to maintain its structural integrity, it must find a way to integrate AI without subordinating human agency to opaque, machine-led processes. The challenge lies not only in regulating AI's influence over diplomatic decision-making but also in ensuring that the principles of transparency and accountability remain at the core of diplomatic practice.

A more profound challenge emerges in the realm of diplomatic representation, where the symbolic dimensions of diplomacy – long anchored in ritual, performative authority, and negotiated recognition – face an unprecedented shift. In Chapter 12, the discussion of symbolic power highlights how diplomacy is not merely an instrument of governance but a theatrical and legitimising practice, where states and institutions perform sovereignty, credibility, and influence through carefully orchestrated engagements. However, as AI-driven systems become increasingly embedded in diplomatic processes, the very mechanisms through which legitimacy is conferred, and authority is recognised come under scrutiny. What happens when AI-generated agreements – crafted through machine-driven logic rather than human deliberation – are contested, revised, or subjected to scrutiny? Can non-human agents wield the same normative authority as human diplomats, or does their introduction fracture the delicate performativity that underpins diplomacy's legitimacy? These questions go beyond technical feasibility and strike at the heart of diplomacy's epistemic and ontological foundations – challenging whether its symbolic power can endure in an era where agency is increasingly distributed across both human and artificial actors.

The Vitruvian model's emphasis on proportion and balance offers an insightful lens for understanding the evolving landscape of diplomacy in the age of AI-driven governance and post-human agency. Historically, diplomacy has operated as a system of interdependent forces, sustaining equilibrium between epistemic power (knowledge production and intelligence control), strategic influence (negotiation and statecraft), and symbolic legitimacy (ritual, recognition, and persuasion). These dimensions have remained in dynamic balance, much like the Vitruvian Man, where the circle of abstract principles and ideals coexists with the square of structured institutions and pragmatic governance. Yet, as AI systems, algorithmic decision-making, and autonomous diplomatic mechanisms, may assume an increasingly decisive role, the proportions of diplomacy may be at risk of distortion.

The *square of diplomacy*, representing the formal structures of global governance, is being reconfigured by the rise of AI-mediated intelligence analysis, automated negotiation platforms, and predictive diplomatic modelling. Traditional institutions – multilateral forums, treaty-based diplomacy, and state-driven negotiations – now co-exist with AI-generated diplomatic strategies and algorithmically optimised crisis responses. Meanwhile, *the circle of diplomacy*, which embodies its normative and symbolic dimensions, is also shifting. Legitimacy, persuasion, and human intuition, long central to diplomacy's performative aspects, are now increasingly mediated by machine-generated narratives and AI-driven discourse framing. The central challenge, therefore, is not merely integrating AI into diplomatic practice, but ensuring that this integration preserves diplomacy's underlying structural equilibrium.

If AI systems are treated simply as technical tools, diplomacy risks becoming mechanistic and overly determined by algorithmic logic, stripping it of the human discretion and adaptability necessary for managing the complexities of global affairs. Conversely, if post-human agency is allowed to redefine diplomatic authority without constraint, legitimacy itself may become diffuse, fragmented, or even unmoored from the traditional principles that have anchored diplomacy for centuries. The challenge is to ensure that AI-driven agency is proportionally incorporated, neither overwhelming human judgement nor diminishing diplomacy's institutional coherence.

Diplomacy has always been a discipline of adaptation, evolving alongside technological, geopolitical, and institutional shifts. However, the emergence of post-human agency represents more than just an advancement in diplomatic technique – it signals a transformation in the very nature of agency itself. The fundamental question is not how diplomacy will integrate AI, but whether it can do so while preserving its essential proportions – its delicate interplay of knowledge, authority, and legitimacy – in a world where agency is increasingly distributed across human and non-human actors. Whether diplomacy retains its structured proportions or undergoes a radical reconfiguration will shape not only the future of international engagement but also the broader architecture of global order in the post-human era.

Glossary

Back-channel diplomacy

When it proves difficult for conflict parties to find an agreement, negotiators and mediators sometimes resort to back-channel diplomacy. This form of diplomacy is geared towards opening up new communication channels between the conflict parties. These channels have two crucial features: (1) they are shielded from the public; (2) they are shielded from possible spoilers.

Cold War

The Cold War was the major defining feature of the post–World War II order that ended in the late 1980s. The metaphor is, for the most part, adequate when it comes to interactions between the Cold War's superpowers, that is, the United States and the Soviet Union. There were, with minor exceptions during the Korean War (and these were kept secret for a long time), no direct military clashes between them. The term is not appropriate, however, when it comes to developing countries. The United States and the Soviet Union, often helped by their allies in NATO and Warsaw Pact, respectively, fought wars by proxy in order to install or back a regime of their liking.

Computational Personalisation

The use of algorithmic tools to tailor diplomatic messages to specific audiences, enhancing engagement and ensuring message relevance. This technique allows states and diplomats to craft targeted narratives that resonate with different demographic groups, maximising the effectiveness of digital diplomacy while raising ethical concerns about manipulation and bias.

Concert of Europe

Established in the aftermath of the 1814 settlement of the Napoleonic Wars, this form of summit diplomacy held regular face-to-face consultation between Great Britain, Austria, Prussia, Russia, and France with the purpose of maintaining peace, containing revolution, and restoring the system of law in Europe. This congress system encouraged self-restraint among its members by making visible the balance of power to those who constituted it, and helped prevent a direct conflict between the great powers until the Crimean War in 1856.

Constructivism

Constructivism is a set of approaches in International Relations that understands the world actors inhabit as socially constructed by these actors. Constructivist scholarship deals with context (especially what we label deeper background, that is, taken-for-granted ideas), the processes through which actors come to act politically while putting this context to use, and the mechanisms through which actors, acting politically, come to make and remake context. On an ontological scale from material to ideational, constructivism tends towards the ideational.

Data Diplomacy

The strategic use of big data, analytics, and AI in diplomatic decision-making, crisis management, and international negotiations. By leveraging vast datasets, states and diplomatic actors can enhance situational awareness, predict trends, and tailor diplomatic interventions, though this also raises concerns about data sovereignty, ethical use, and algorithmic bias in global governance.

Emotions

Although emotions were considered very important by Jeremy Bentham, who, in many ways, paved the way for today's rationalist approaches, rational choice frameworks leave no room for them. A rational decision, in the latter view, is one that is made without any interference from emotions. Political psychology approaches this issue very differently. There are more and more authors contending that human beings cannot make the world intelligible to themselves and figure out what to do without putting emotions to use for doing so.

Engagement Hybridisation

The blending of digital and traditional engagement to create a multi-layered approach to diplomatic relations. This concept highlights how states and diplomats combine online interactions, such as social media engagement and virtual summits, with physical meetings and traditional negotiations to maximise reach, impact, and credibility in diplomatic practice. It reflects the evolving nature of diplomacy in an increasingly digitalised global environment.

Episteme

This concept was originally coined by Michel Foucault, who likened it to a lens through which to look at the world. The lens enables actors to make the world intelligible to themselves but channels this making intelligible into certain directions rather than others. The Idea of Europe, for example, is such a lens. The formula of 'integration breeds peace and standing apart breeds war' is the prism through which pro-European decision-makers have looked at intra-European relations in the past half century. This predisposed them to an integration scheme that has softened the boundaries among European nations. The episteme is part of the deeper layer.

Epistemic Power

The ability to shape, control, and disseminate knowledge in diplomacy, influencing what is considered valid information and who has access to it. This power operates through different forms of knowledge – *propositional* (codified facts and treaties), *experiential* (intuition and lived practice), *practical/knowledge-how* (strategic execution and negotiation skills), and *objectual* (holistic understanding of geopolitical systems).

Fourteen Points

On January 8 1918, US President Woodrow Wilson delivered his "Fourteen Points" speech to the US Congress in which he outlined, among other imperatives, the need for accountability and transparency in diplomacy (Point 1), the importance of self-determination for peoples as an extension of individual rights at the state level (Point 5), and the need for a general framework of collective security between states based on mutual trust and cooperation (Point 14). These liberal guiding principles of diplomatic conduct remain valid in state conduct today.

Front-Stage and Back-Stage Diplomacy

A concept adapted from Erving Goffman's dramaturgical model, describing the dual nature of digital diplomacy where highly visible public engagement (front-stage), is carefully managed while private strategic coordination and negotiations (back-stage) occur behind the scenes. This distinction is crucial in digital diplomacy, where states perform in global online spaces while simultaneously managing confidential diplomatic interactions through secure channels.

Fusion of Horizons

A concept from Hans-Georg Gadamer's *Truth and Method* (1960), the fusion of horizons describes the process of understanding as an interaction between the historical context of a text, tradition, or event and the interpreter's contemporary perspective. This dynamic interplay creates new meaning by merging past and present viewpoints. In diplomacy, the fusion of horizons is highly relevant for understanding the adaptation of traditional norms to modern contexts, such as reinterpreting face-to-face ambassadorial protocols for digital diplomacy. The concept underscores the importance of continuity and reinterpretation in sustaining effective diplomatic practices.

Games

Game theory uses the term 'game' as a metaphor for the kind of strategic interaction (see Strategy in this list) through which actors are assumed to make decisions. Similarly to a chess game, actors are portrayed as being selfish and concerned with outwitting one another. In more technical language, they play in order to maximise their expected utility. Well-known games are the prisoner's dilemma and the chicken game. Game theory is criticised by rival perspectives (for instance, by psychological approaches) for assuming super-human computational capacities.

Globalisation

Globalisation has been a buzzword since the 1990s. Given that it is such a broad and deep-reaching phenomenon, it is difficult to define. Scholars tend to look at two different dimensions of the phenomenon: the material side, especially more and more rapid and frequent economic transactions (e.g., finance) and ongoing technological revolutions (in particular telecommunications), and the ideational side of coming to imagine communities beyond the nation-state. Globalisation pressures have a lot to do with the multiplicities of global diplomacy. Globalisation pushes items on the global agenda that used to be (at least primarily) on the domestic political agenda.

Governance

Governance is governing without a central authority that can put down the law. In global politics, there is no equivalence to a government or a parliament in domestic politics. Even in highly integrated regional polities such as the EU, there is no clear equivalent. Instead, multiple actors, communicating with one another on various levels, have to converge on common courses of action in order to steer the polity in certain directions. For the salience of diplomacy, governance is a two-edged sword. On the one hand, diplomacy becomes even more important because more and more communication occurs among state-representatives and other diplomatic actors. On the other hand, traditional diplomats (foreign services) become sidelined when communication addresses the many technical aspects of problem-solving in our globalising age (e.g., trade, finance, and environment).

International Court of Justice (ICJ)

The ICJ is the main judicial organ of the UN. The Court decides about contentions issues and provides legal opinions. It rules about contentions issues after states have agreed to submit a dispute to the Court and to abide by its ruling. According to the UN Charter, the UN has the authority to enforce its ruling if parties end up not complying with it. In practice, however, the UNSC (and the five veto powers) has proven highly reluctant to engage in such enforcement measures. The Court provides legal opinions at the request of UN bodies and agencies. Although these are only opinions, they can be rather influential. The ICJ does command a significant amount of respect in the diplomatic community.

International organisation

An international organisation is an institution featuring formal decision-making procedures, formal membership and a permanent secretariat. In order for an institution to qualify as an international organisation, it has to have at least three members. Thus, an international organisation is always a multilateral arrangement.

Jus fetiale (ius fetiale)

A feature of Roman conduct of foreign relations carried over to Greek diplomacy, any declaration of war had to follow the proper procedure, as determine by *jus fetiale*, or fetial law. The College of Fetiales, a religious body composed of priests whose duties also included overseeing international treaties, informed the enemy of Rome's grievances and, barring any other event occurring during a fixed period, a declaration would be made at the border of the enemy's territory and a javelin would be thrown across the border.

League of Nations

Established at the Paris Peace Conference following the end of World War I, this multilateral institutional framework was created to facilitate the peaceful resolution of disputes. Its objective was to facilitate the peaceful resolution of disputes by disallowing member states recourse to war until they had exhausted procedures for arbitration and conciliation provided by the League. The League was a precursor to the UN in its efforts to institutionalise collective security amongst states.

Liberation vs. Repression Technology

A conceptual distinction that differentiates between technologies that empower individuals and grassroots movements (liberation technologies) and those that enable states and institutions to control narratives and manage public perception (representation technologies). While liberation technologies facilitate decentralised engagement and activism, representation technologies help state actors structure and frame official messages, raising questions about power, influence, and digital governance in International Relations.

Lingua franca

It was required for the permanent resident ambassador to be a good linguist and fluent in Latin, the *lingua franca* of the time, meaning the language that was systematically used for communication between individuals who do not share their mother tongue. The actual language of the *lingua franca* used by diplomats has changed over the centuries and is a function of agreement between the interlocutors of the era, having evolved from Latin to French to English.

Logics of action

How do actors come to act in a certain way and not another one? On a rather abstract level, logics of action seek to provide broad frames for answering this question. Four logics of action are frequently discussed in the social sciences: The logic of consequences holds that actors carefully calculate the consequences of the courses of action available to them (e.g., game theory). The logic of appropriateness assumes that actors follow identity-constituting norms when they embark on a certain course of action. The logic of argumentation revolves around persuasion (an argument outperforms another argument). The logic of practice is about following the common sense that is ingrained in the habitus.

New diplomacy

New diplomacy, championed by US President Woodrow Wilson after World War I, sought to replace the secrecy and power-driven nature of old diplomacy with transparency, public accountability, and multilateral cooperation. Wilson's Fourteen Points advocated for open treaties, self-determination, and collective security, leading to the establishment of the League of Nations as a forum for peaceful conflict resolution. Unlike the balance-of-power system, new diplomacy emphasised international institutions, broader diplomatic participation beyond elites, and moral principles in foreign policy. While it faced resistance from European powers and was often constrained by great-power politics, its legacy endures in modern multilateral diplomacy and organisations like the UN.

Nuncius

The main form of diplomatic representation in Europe during the early Middle Ages, a nuncius was an agent whose main function was to provide a channel of communication between rulers and to explore opportunities for concluding treaties and alliances. Sending a nuncius was chosen over a written letter, on certain occasions, for his actual wording and responses to his interlocutor. While benefitting from immunity from harm, the nuncius spoke in the person of the principal but was not given full powers (*plena potestas*) to enter private contracts and to negotiate agreements on behalf of their leaders.

Old diplomacy

Diplomatic conduct among European powers during the 18th and 19th centuries can be understood on the basis of five premises: 1) the five major European powers were central to politics; 2) a global hierarchy existed between Great Powers and Small Powers due to wider range of interests, responsibilities, and resources; 3) Great Powers were responsible for maintaining peace; 4) a professional diplomatic service was required; and 5) continuous and confidential negotiation was crucial for diplomacy. When 'old diplomacy' was blamed for failing to restrain the Great Powers from warfare, the pre-eminence of this type of diplomatic conduct was fundamentally undermined. For the opposite, that is, New Diplomacy (see earlier in the list).

Paradigm

A paradigm is a prism through which to look at the world. The term was coined by Thomas Kuhn in his work on scientific revolutions. Scholars, he maintains, see the world through certain lenses. This enables them to see certain things but makes it impossible for them to see others.

Perceptions

Political psychology suggests that human beings do not have privileged access to the objective reality. Instead, making sense of the world is a subjective endeavour. Different people, therefore, make sense of the world differently; they perceive it (and particular aspects of it) differently. Where there is perception, there is also misperception.

Power

Power remains central to world politics, but its understanding has evolved from being purely coercive ("power over") to enabling action ("power to"). Diplomacy, as a practice, embodies multiple interrelated forms of power. *Epistemic power* shapes what is known and how knowledge is used in diplomatic negotiations, influencing international norms and policy frameworks. *Symbolic power* constructs meaning through narratives, historical memory, and ideological representation, allowing states to justify actions and reinforce legitimacy. *Strategic power*, rooted in statecraft, operationalises diplomacy through negotiation, coercion, and tactical manoeuvring. These dimensions of power illustrate how diplomacy is not merely a tool of state interaction but an evolving mechanism of influence in global affairs.

Proxenos

As one of three types of diplomatic representation in the Ancient Greek system, the proxenos would reside in their own state while acting for another state, out of a general sympathy for the political system or culture that other state. To facilitate inter-state negotiations, the proxenos was expected to protect their nationals residing in the receiving-state, while performing duties ranging from providing hospitality and assistance to visitors from the relevant state to contributing to public policy-making.

Public diplomacy

Public diplomacy aims at influencing the publics in host states. Thus, it departs from the traditional state to state communication of diplomacy. The influencing can be directed at a particular public in a particular state. It can also be directed more generally at publics around the world. As the means to create, maximise, and render soft power into diplomatic influence, diplomats use various tools of public diplomacy to advance the interests and extend the values of their state to another country's public. As Joseph Nye explains, this type of diplomacy includes daily communication, strategic communication, and relationship building with key individuals through scholarships, exchanges, training, seminars, conferences, and access to media channels.

Raison de système

Coined by Adam Watson, this doctrine refers to "the use of diplomacy to achieve the ultimate purpose of an international society of independent states". In contrast to the doctrine of raison d'etat, members of the international society have an inherent interest in preserving the system and thus subsume national interests to broader systemic considerations. Looking at the EU, one such example is that the diplomat's job is to balance their national interests with the inherent interest of preserving the system.

Raison d'état

According to this doctrine of international conduct, literally meaning "reason of state", a ruler or government will conduct its foreign policy with state interests as the ultimate objective, and with disregard for ethical considerations. This doctrine was specifically influential in the establishment of the Westphalian concept of sovereign state. The norms, rules and principles of the international system legitimated by this doctrine thus gave rise to 18th-century dynastic absolutism and recourse to war. The diplomatic pursuit of the doctrine of raison d'état is known as 'Realpolitik'. States assure their survival through the accumulation and rational use of power, defined primarily in military terms. Realpolitik helps ensure the survival of the state through a foreign policy that skilfully balances or cuts favours with the dominant power(s).

Realism

Realism may very well be the most influential school of thought in International Relations. Different Realist strands share the following assumptions in common: the actors on the global stage are states (statism); there is no common power in international politics (anarchy); because there is no common power, states have to safeguard their security by themselves (self-help); and the only kind of tenuous peace possible is the balance of power. These shared assumptions notwithstanding, there are important differences among Realist strands. Classical Realism, for example, puts strong emphasis on diplomacy. Neo-classical Realism echoes this emphasis to some extent. Neorealism, by contrast, leaves very little room for diplomacy or indeed any kind of agency and focuses on structural forces (distribution of military capabilities) instead.

Security Council

The UN Charter puts the Security Council in charge of maintaining international peace and security. The Security Council has three sets of means available for doing so: Chapter 6 measures (peaceful settlement of disputes); Chapter 7 measures (enforcement); and, located in between the two (but closer to Chapter 6), peacekeeping. The Security Council has five permanent and ten non-permanent members. Reflecting the outcome of World War II, the five permanent members are China, France, Russia, the UK, and the United States. Each of the five permanent members has the power to veto decisions on substantive matters (but not on procedural ones).

Shared lifeworld

A lifeworld is a conceptualisation of the context in which actors are embedded. The lifeworld enables actors to make sense of the world in a certain way. A shared lifeworld is of crucial importance for Habermasian and Habermas-inspired approaches because this is seen as the prerequisite for actors to be able to communicate meaningfully with one another. A shared lifeworld, in this reading, is the sine qua non for reaching agreements. The concept of lifeworld has been employed by several philosophers and social theorists. Yet it is the social theorist Jürgen Habermas with whom the concept is associated the most.

Sovereignty

Sovereignty is the right to exercise supreme authority over a piece of territory. The 1648 Peace of Westphalia codified many aspects of what we refer to as state authority today. Our current state system is the contingent outcome of a historical process. In the Europe of the Middle Ages, for instance, there was no exclusive authority over a piece of territory. Instead, there was a system of overlapping authority, in which the Pope, the Holy Roman Emperor and local princes features prominently.

Strangeness

Georg Simmel conceptualised strangeness as a unique social condition where an individual or entity is simultaneously part of a system yet remains distant or external to it. This dual position allows the stranger to mediate, connect, and provide objectivity while maintaining a degree of detachment. James Der Derian builds on this idea within the realm of diplomacy, emphasising estrangement as an inherent condition in International Relations. Unlike Simmel's focus on social distance, Der Derian highlights how diplomacy institutionalises otherness, framing states or actors as 'strangers' to justify the need for mediation or intervention. Der Derian critiques this process, arguing that while estrangement can enable diplomacy, it can also perpetuate divisions by reinforcing narratives of difference.

Strategic power

The capacity to manoeuvre within geopolitical constraints through negotiation, coercion, and calculated statecraft. It functions as both a *context-driven tool*, adapting to immediate circumstances, and a *structured force*, shaped by historical and geopolitical realities that define long-term diplomatic engagement. Francesco Guicciardini emphasised the role of pragmatic self-interest in diplomacy, advocating for adaptability in shifting alliances, while Raymond Aron highlighted the structural dimensions of power, viewing diplomacy as a means to balance security, influence, and prestige within the global order.

Strategy

Put very simply, strategy is a plan for action. Different theoretical frameworks conceptualise the term differently. The literature on grand strategy tends to equate strategy with linking interests to means in the issue area of peace and war. In game theory, strategy is a key concept; actors are assumed to behave strategically, that is, they seek to outwit other players in order to maximise their benefits. In rhetorical studies, there is the concept of rhetorical strategies. Here, the concept is closely associated with communicative moves, ranging from persuasion by the better argument to vilifying other actors.

Structure

To what extent an actor (individual or an anthropomorphised political entity) has political efficacy depends on the structure in which this actor is embedded. The structure is what makes an actor in the first place; it places an actor in the driver's seat of decision-making or banishes him/her to the back seat. Structure also enables the actor to make sense of the world and to do something in this world. How much structure matters, and, with it, how much autonomy actors have in world politics, is contested among scholars (see under ontology). It is also contested how largely material, as opposed to ideational, factors feature in constituting structure. Realists, for example, put a lot of emphasis on material factors (military capabilities) whereas Constructivists foreground ideational forces (e.g., identity and its constituting norms).

Symbolic Power

The use of myths, narratives, and ideological constructs to shape perceptions of legitimacy and authority in diplomacy. It operates through four dimensions of *symbolic representation*: the *expressive* (emotional and instinctive responses), the *representational* (visual and linguistic depictions of identity), the *conceptual* (abstract reasoning and ideological framing), and the *cultural* (shared values and historical narratives that shape collective identity).

Track-two diplomacy

Track-one diplomacy is state-to-state diplomacy with states being represented by their governments, foreign ministries, and/or other ministries. Track-two diplomacy is only loosely linked to governments. It can involve a host of actors such as parliamentarians, private citizens, activists, scholars, religious communities and so on. The advantage of track-two diplomacy is that it does not require the many formalities and routine posturing of official diplomacy. Opening up the second track, therefore, can provide a stabilising element in troubled relations among states and help to improve these relations. The literature points, for instance, to the importance of track-two diplomacy to help manage and reduce tensions between the Soviet Union and the United States during the Cold War.

UN veto system

Within the UNSC, the five permanent members each hold the right to veto decisions considered by the Council, as per Article 27 of the UN Charter. This feature, which provides major powers with strong incentives to remain engaged in the system, was specifically designed to address a key weakness of the League of Nations framework, or the alienation or exclusion of a major power from the decision-making body responsible for setting and implementing rules of international conduct. See also the entry 'Security Council'.

Zooming in/zooming out

A concept associated with Henry Kissinger's negotiation style, "zooming in/zooming out" describes the dual approach of balancing tactical and strategic priorities in diplomacy. Zooming out involves assessing the broader geopolitical landscape, focusing on systemic stability, long-term trends, and overarching goals. Zooming in, by contrast, addresses immediate issues, interpersonal dynamics, and specific negotiations. This dual approach allows diplomats to align localised solutions with global objectives, ensuring coherence between short-term actions and long-term strategies. Kissinger's method highlights the necessity of integrating these perspectives to navigate the balance between raison d'état and raison de système effectively.

References

Abulof, Uriel, and Markus Kornprobst. 2017. "Introduction: The Politics of Public Justification." In *Communication, Legitimation and Morality in Modern Politics*, 1–18. Routledge.
Acharya, Amitav. 2017. "After Liberal Hegemony: The Advent of a Multiplex World Order." *Ethics & International Affairs* 31 (3): 271–85.
Acharya, Amitav, Antoni Estevadeordal, and Louis W. Goodman. 2023. "Multipolar or Multiplex? Interaction Capacity, Global Cooperation and World Order." *International Affairs* 99 (6): 2339–65.
ACLED. 2024. "Conflict Watchlist 2025." December 12. https://acleddata.com/conflict-watchlist-2025/.
Adamson, Fiona B. 2005. "Global Liberalism versus Political Islam: Competing Ideological Frameworks in International Politics." *International Studies Review* 7 (4): 547–69.
Adem, Seifudein. 2014. "Ali A. Mazrui, the Postcolonial Theorist." *African Studies Review* 57 (1): 135–52.
Adler, Emanuel. 2005. *Communitarian International Relations: The Epistemic Foundations of International Relations*. Psychology Press.
Adler, Emanuel. 2008. "The Spread of Security Communities: Communities of Practice, Self-Restraint, and NATO's Post – Cold War Transformation." *European Journal of International Relations* 14 (2): 195–230.
Adler, Emanuel. 2019. *World Ordering: A Social Theory of Cognitive Evolution*. Cambridge University Press.
Adler, Emanuel, and Michael Barnett. 1998. *Security Communities*. Cambridge University Press.
Adler, Emanuel, and Michael Faubert. 2022. "Epistemic Communities of Practice." In *Conceptualizing International Practices: Directions for the Practice Turn in International Relations*, edited by Alena Drieschova, Christian Bueger, and Ted Hopf, 47–76. Cambridge: Cambridge University Press.
Adler, Emanuel, and Peter M. Haas. 1992. "Conclusion: Epistemic Communities, World Order, and the Creation of a Reflective Research Program." *International Organization* 46 (1): 367–90.
Adler-Nissen, Rebecca. 2011. "Opting Out of an Ever Closer Union: The Integration Doxa and the Management of Sovereignty." *West European Politics* 34 (5): 1092–113.
Adler-Nissen, Rebecca. 2014. "Stigma Management in International Relations: Transgressive Identities, Norms, and Order in International Society." *International Organization* 68 (1): 143–76.
Adler-Nissen, Rebecca, and Alena Drieschova. 2019. "Track-Change Diplomacy: Technology, Affordances, and the Practice of International Negotiations." *International Studies Quarterly: A Publication of the International Studies Association* 63 (3): 531–45.
Aguirre, Daniel, and Alejandro Ramos. 2024. "Digital Diplomacy in Latin America." In *The Oxford Handbook of Digital Diplomacy*, 546–63. Oxford: Oxford University Press.
Akdenizli, Banu. 2024. "Diplomacy in Times of Crisis in the GCC: The Blockade and the Pandemic." In *The Oxford Handbook of Digital Diplomacy*, edited by C. Bjola and I. Manor, 564–81. Oxford University Press.
Alberque, William, and Benjamin Schreer. 2022. "Finland, Sweden and NATO Membership." *Survival* 64 (3): 67–72.
Al Jazeera. 2023. "Singapore, Indonesia Condemn Attack on Diplomats in Myanmar." *Al Jazeera*. May 9. www.aljazeera.com/news/2023/5/9/singapore-indonesia-condemn-attack-on-diplomats-in-myanmar.
Allan, Bentley B. 2018. *Scientific Cosmology and International Orders*. Cambridge University Press.
Allison, Graham T. 1969. "Conceptual Models and the Cuban Missile Crisis." *The American Political Science Review* 63 (3): 689–718.

Alon-Barkat, Saar, and Madalina Busuioc. 2023. "Human–AI Interactions in Public Sector Decision Making: 'Automation Bias' and 'Selective Adherence' to Algorithmic Advice." *Journal of Public Administration Research and Theory: J-PART* 33 (1): 153–69.
Alter, Karen J., and Kal Raustiala. 2018. "The Rise of International Regime Complexity." *Annual Review of Law and Social Science* 14: 329–49.
Altman, Steven A., and Caroline R. Bastian. 2022. "Trade Regionalization: More Hype Than Reality?" *Harvard Business Review* (May 31). https://hbr.org/2022/05/trade-regionalization-more-hype-than-reality.
Aniche, Ernest Toochi. 2020. "From Pan-Africanism to African Regionalism: A Chronicle." *African Studies* 79 (1): 70–87.
Anter, Andreas. 2007. *Die Macht der Ordnung: Aspekte einer Grundkategorie des Politischen*. Mohr Siebeck.
Anuar, Amalina, and Nazia Hussain. 2021. "Minilateralism for Multilateralism in the Post-COVID Age." *@RSIS_NTU*. January 19. www.rsis.edu.sg/rsis-publication/cms/minilateralism-for-multilateralism-in-the-post-covid-age/.
Arendt, Hannah. 1978. *Life of the Mind*. London, England: Martin Secker & Warburg.
Arendt, Hannah. 1999. *The Human Condition*. 2nd ed. Chicago, IL: University of Chicago Press.
Aristotle. 2010. *Rhetoric*. Cosimo, Inc.
Armstrong, David. 2016. "Revolutionary Diplomacy." In *The Sage Handbook of Diplomacy*, edited by Costas M. Constantinou, Pauline Kerr, Paul Sharp, and Paul Meerts, 487–98. London, England: SAGE Publications.
Aron, Raymond. 1986. *Clausewitz, Philosopher of War*. Simon & Schuster.
Aron, Raymond. 2003. *Peace and War: A Theory of International Relations*. Somerset, NJ: Transaction.
Asghedom, T. 1999. "Behind the Ethiopian Authorities' Wars of Aggression against Eritrea." *Eritrea Profile*. February 27. https://shabait.com/category/newspapers/eritrea-profile/.
Aslan Ozgul, Billur, Eva Nieto McAvoy, Marie Gillespie, and Ben O'Loughlin. 2021. "Shakespeare Lives on Twitter: Cultural Diplomacy in the Digital Age." *International Journal of Cultural Policy* (April): 1–17.
Aydin, Umut. 2021. "Emerging Middle Powers and the Liberal International Order." *International Affairs* 97 (5): 1377–94.
Babic, Milan. 2020. "Let's Talk about the Interregnum: Gramsci and the Crisis of the Liberal World Order." *International Affairs* 96 (3): 767–86.
Barker, Craig J. 2006. *The Protection of Diplomatic Personnel*. Farnham: Ashgate Publishing, Ltd.
Barnett, Michael N., and Martha Finnemore. 1999. "The Politics, Power, and Pathologies of International Organizations." *International Organization* 53 (4): 699–732.
Barrinha, André, and Thomas Renard. 2020. "Power and Diplomacy in the Post-Liberal Cyberspace." *International Affairs* 96 (3): 749–66.
Bátora, Jozef, Kari M. Osland, Florian Qehaja, and Sonja Stojanović Gajić. 2021. "Spaces and Institutional Logics in Post-Conflict Settings of Mitrovica." *Journal of Intervention and Statebuilding* 15 (1): 114–31.
Bauman, Zygmunt. 2000. *Liquid Modernity*. Cambridge: Polity Press.
Baumann, Rainer, and Klaus Dingwerth. 2015. "Global Governance vs Empire: Why World Order Moves towards Heterarchy and Hierarchy." *Journal of International Relations and Development* 18 (1): 104–28.
BBC News. 2020. "Australia Demands China Apologise for Posting 'Repugnant' Fake Image." *BBC*. November 30. www.bbc.com/news/world-australia-55126569.
Beardsley, Kyle. 2008. "Agreement without Peace? International Mediation and Time Inconsistency Problems." *American Journal of Political Science* 52 (4): 723–40.
Beaumont, P., M. Bright, and E. Vullyamy. 2003. "Revealed: US Dirty Tricks to Win Vote on Iraq War." *The Guardian*.
Beeson, M. 2014. *Regionalism and Globalization in East Asia: Politics, Security and Economic Development*. New York: Palgrave Macmillan.
Bello, Walden. 2021. "The Rise and Fall of Multilateralism." *Dissent* 68 (2): 56–64.
Benford, Robert D., and David A. Snow. 2000. "Framing Processes and Social Movements: An Overview and Assessment." *Annual Review of Sociology* 26 (1): 611–39.
Bentham, Jeremy. 1789. *An Introduction to the Principles of Morals and Legislation*. London: Payne.
Bercovitch, Jacob, and Ayse Kadayifci. 2002. "Exploring the Relevance and Contribution of Mediation to Peace-Building." *Peace and Conflict Studies* 9 (2): 21–40.
Berger, Miriam. 2023. "Post-9/11 Wars Have Contributed to Some 4.5 Million Deaths, Report Suggests." *The Washington Post*. May 15. www.washingtonpost.com/world/2023/05/15/war-on-terror-911-deaths-afghanistan-iraq/.

Berridge, G. 2004. *Diplomatic Classics: Selected Texts from Commynes to Vattel*. UK: Palgrave Macmillan.
Berridge, Geoffrey R. 2010. *Diplomacy: Practice and Theory*. Basingstoke: Palgrave.
Bettiza, Gregorio, and David Lewis. 2020. "Authoritarian Powers and Norm Contestation in the Liberal International Order: Theorizing the Power Politics of Ideas and Identity." *Journal of Global Security Studies* 5 (4): 559–77.
Bianchi, A. 1999. "Immunity versus Human Rights: The Pinochet Case." *European Journal of International Law* 10 (2): 237–77.
Bigge, David M. 2004. "Bring on the Bluewash: A Social Constructivist Argument against Using Nike V. Kasky to Attack the UN Global Compact." *Int'l Legal Persp.* 14 (6). https://heinonline.org/HOL/LandingPage?handle=hein.journals/intlegp14&div=6&id=&page=.
Bjola, Corneliu. 2005. "Legitimating the Use of Force in International Politics: A Communicative Action Perspective." *European Journal of International Relations* 11 (2): 266–303.
Bjola, Corneliu. 2013. "Understanding Enmity and Friendship in World Politics: The Case for a Diplomatic Approach." *The Hague Journal of Diplomacy* 8 (1): 1–20.
Bjola, Corneliu. 2016. "Diplomacy as World Disclosure: A Fractal Theory of Crisis Management." *British Journal of Politics and International Relations* 18 (2): 335–50.
Bjola, Corneliu. 2022. "Digital Diplomacy as World Disclosure: The Case of the COVID-19 Pandemic." *Place Branding and Public Diplomacy* 18 (1): 22–5.
Bjola, Corneliu. 2024a. "Understanding Digital Diplomacy – the Grammar Rules and Patterns of Digital Disruption." In *Oxford Handbook of Digital Diplomacy*, edited by Corneliu Bjola and Ilan Manor. Oxford University Press.
Bjola, Corneliu. 2024b. "Digital Diplomacy in the Age of Technological Acceleration: Three Impact Scenarios of Generative Artificial Intelligence." *Place Branding and Public Diplomacy* (February).
Bjola, Corneliu, and James Pamment. 2016. "Digital Containment: Revisiting Containment Strategy in the Digital Age." *Global Affairs* 2 (2): 131–42.
Bjola, Corneliu, and Michaela Coplen. 2022a. "Digital Diplomacy in the Time of the Coronavirus Pandemic: Lessons and Recommendations." In *Handbook of Diplomatic Reform and Innovation*, edited by Paul W. Hare, Juan Luis Manfredi-Sánchez, and Kenneth Weisbrode. Palgrave Macmillan.
Bjola, Corneliu, and Michaela Coplen. 2022b. "Virtual Venues and International Negotiations: Lessons from the COVID-19 Pandemic." *International Negotiation* 1 (aop): 1–25. https://doi.org/10.1163/15718069-bja10060.
Bjola, Corneliu, and Marcus Holmes. 2015. *Digital Diplomacy: Theory and Practice*. Abingdon: Routledge.
Bjola, Corneliu, and Markus Kornprobst. 2007. "Security Communities and the Habitus of Restraint: Germany and the United States on Iraq." *Review of International Studies* 33 (2): 285–305.
Bjola, Corneliu, and Ilan Manor. 2018. "Revisiting Putnam's Two-Level Game Theory in the Digital Age: Domestic Digital Diplomacy and the Iran Nuclear Deal." *Cambridge Review of International Affairs* 31 (1): 3–32.
Bjola, Corneliu, and Ilan Manor. 2024a. "Understanding Digital Diplomacy – the Grammar Rules and Patterns of Digital Disruption." In *Oxford Handbook of Digital Diplomacy*, edited by Corneliu Bjola and Ilan Manor. Oxford University Press.
Bjola, Corneliu, and Ilan Manor. 2024b. "Digital Diplomacy in the Age of Technological Acceleration: Three Impact Scenarios of Generative Artificial Intelligence." *Place Branding and Public Diplomacy* (February). https://doi.org/10.1057/s41254-023-00323-4.
Boin, Arjen. 2005. *The Politics of Crisis Management: Public Leadership under Pressure*. Cambridge, UK and New York: Cambridge University Press.
Boin, Arjen, Paul 't Hart, Eric Stern, and Bengt Sundelius. 2017. *The Politics of Crisis Management*. 2nd ed. Cambridge, England: Cambridge University Press.
Borger, Julian. 2014. "Barack Obama: Russia Is a Regional Power Showing Weakness over Ukraine." *The Guardian*. March 25. www.theguardian.com/world/2014/mar/25/barack-obama-russia-regional-power-ukraine-weakness.
Börzel, Tanja A., and Michael Zürn. 2021. "Contestations of the Liberal International Order: From Liberal Multilateralism to Postnational Liberalism." *International Organization* 75 (2): 282–305.
Bourdieu, Pierre. 1998. *Practical Reason: On the Theory of Action*. Stanford: Stanford University Press.
Bourdieu, Pierre, and Maison des sciences de l'homme. 1977. *Outline of a Theory of Practice*. Cambridge: Cambridge University Press.
Bourdieu, Pierre, and Maison des sciences de l'homme. 1980. *Le sens pratique*. Les Editions de Minuit.

Bourdieu, Pierre, and Maison des sciences de l'homme. 1988. *Homo Academicus*. Stanford University Press.
Bourdieu, Pierre, and Maison des sciences de l'homme. 1990. *The Logic of Practice*. Stanford University Press.
Boutros-Ghali, Boutros. 1992. *An Agenda for Peace: Preventive Diplomacy, Peacemaking and Peace-Keeping: Report of the Secretary-General Pursuant to the Statement Adopted by the Summit Meeting of the Security Council on 31 January 1992/Boutros Boutros-Ghali*. UN Department of Public Information.
Bouwsma, William J. 2002. *Waning of the Renaissance, 1550–1640*. Revised ed. New Haven, CT: Yale University Press.
Bown, Chad, and Soumaya Keynes. 2020. "Why Trump Shot the Sheriffs: The End of WTO Dispute Settlement 1.0." *CEPR Discussion Papers*. March. https://ideas.repec.org/p/cpr/ceprdp/14477.html.
Boyd, Andy, Jane Gatewood, Stuart Thorson, and Timothy D. V. Dye. 2019. "Data Diplomacy." *Science & Diplomacy* 8 (1).
Bradshaw, Samantha, and Philip N. Howard. 2019. "The Global Disinformation Order 2019." https://comprop.oii.ox.ac.uk/wp-content/uploads/sites/93/2019/09/CyberTroop-Report19.pdf.
Braidotti, Rosi. 2021. *Posthuman Feminism*. Oxford, England: Polity Press.
Brain, Stephen. 2016. "The Appeal of Appearing Green: Soviet-American Ideological Competition and Cold War Environmental Diplomacy." *Cold War History* 16 (4): 443–62.
Bramsen, Isabel, and Anine Hagemann. 2021. "The Missing Sense of Peace: Diplomatic Approachment and Virtualization during the COVID-19 Lockdown." *International Affairs* 97 (2): 539–60. https://doi.org/10.1093/ia/iiaa229.
Brecher, Michael, and Jonathan Wilkenfeld. 1997. *A Study of Crisis*. Ann Arbor, MI: University of Michigan Press.
Britton, Roswell R. 2004. "Chinese Interstate Intercourse before 700 B.C." *The American Journal of International Law* 29 (4): 616–35.
Broadbridge, Anne F. 2008. *Kingship and Ideology in the Islamic and Mongol Worlds*. Cambridge and New York: Cambridge University Press.
Brown, Jonathan. 1988. "Diplomatic Immunity: State Practice under the Vienna Convention on Diplomatic Relations." *The International and Comparative Law Quarterly* 37 (1): 53–88.
Brown, William. 2012. "A Question of Agency: Africa in International Politics." *Third World Quarterly* 33 (10): 1889–908.
Bueger, Christian, and Tobias Liebetrau. 2023. "Governing Assemblages: Territory, Technology, and Traps." In *Polycentrism: How Governing Works Today*, edited by Jan Aart Scholte and Frank Gadinger, 236–59. Oxford, England: Oxford University Press.
Bull, Hedley. 1977/2002. *The Anarchical Society*. New York: Columbia University Press.
Bull, Hedley. 1995. *The Anarchical Society*. New York: Columbia University Press.
Bundesregierung, Die. 2022. "Bundeskanzler-Olaf-Scholz-Reden-Zur-Zeitenwende-Download-Bpa-Data.Pdf." www.bundesregierung.de/resource/blob/992814/2131062/78d39dda6647d7f835bbe76713d30c31/bundeskanzler-olaf-scholz-reden-zur-zeitenwende-download-bpa-data.pdf.
Burwell, Frances, and Kenneth Propp. 2022. "Digital Sovereignty in Practice: The EU's Push to Shape the New Global Economy." *Atlantic Council*. November 2. www.atlanticcouncil.org/in-depth-research-reports/report/digital-sovereignty-in-practice-the-eus-push-to-shape-the-new-global-economy/.
Burrell, P. S., M.A. 1932. "Man the Measure of All Things: Socrates versus Protagoras (II)." *Philosophy (London, England)* 7 (26): 168–84.
Butterfield, H. 1951. *History and Human Relations*. London, England: Macmillan.
Buzan, Barry. 2004. *From International to World Society?: English School Theory and the Social Structure of Globalisation*. Cambridge University Press.
Buzan, Barry. 2018. "Revisiting World Society." *International Politics* 55 (1): 125–40.
Buzan, Barry. 2020. "Will the Liberal International Order Survive? An English School Perspective." In *The Decline of the Western-Centric World and the Emerging New Global Order*, edited by Yun-Han Chu and Yongnian Zheng, 166–85. Routledge.
Buzan, Barry, and George Lawson. 2018. "The English School: History and Primary Institutions as Empirical IR Theory?" In *Oxford Research Encyclopedia of Politics*. Oxford: Oxford University Press.
Búzás, Zoltán I. 2022. "Racial Ideologies in World Politics." In *The Routledge Handbook of Ideology and International Relations*, 233–48. London: Routledge.
Cafiero, Florian. 2023. "Datafying Diplomacy: How to Enable the Computational Analysis and Support of International Negotiations." *Journal of Computational Science* 71 (July): 102056.

Călina, Nicoleta, and Loredana Maria Grozoiu. 2021. "On Francesco Guicciardini's Thought and Some of His Considerations on Machiavelli." *Athens Journal of History* 7 (4): 257–88.

Callsen, Emma. 2022. "Small Arms and Light Weapons Proliferation and Violence: Estimating Its Scale and Forms (June 2022)." *IANSA*. June 23. https://iansa.org/salw-proliferation-and-violence-june-2022/.

Campbell, Brian. 2001. "Diplomacy in the Roman World (c. 500 BC–AD 235)." *Diplomacy and Statecraft* 12 (1): 1–22.

Capie, David. 2013. "Structures, Shocks and Norm Change: Explaining the Late Rise of Asia's Defence Diplomacy." *Contemporary Southeast Asia: A Journal of International and Strategic Affairs* 35 (1): 1–26.

Carabantes, Manuel. 2020. "Black-Box Artificial Intelligence: An Epistemological and Critical Analysis." *AI & Society* 35 (2): 309–17.

Carcasson, Martin, and Linda Putnam. 1997. "Communication and the Oslo Negotiation: Contacts, Patterns, and Modes." *International Negotiation* 2 (2): 251–78.

Carnevale, Peter J., and Dong-Won Choi. 2000. "Culture in the Mediation of International Disputes." *International Journal of Psychology: Journal International de Psychologie* 35 (2): 105–10.

Carr, E. H. 1946. *The Twenty Years' Crisis, 1919–1939: An Introduction to the Study of International Relations*. London: Macmillan.

Carrió-Invernizzi, Diana. 2014. "A New Diplomatic History and the Networks of Spanish Diplomacy in the Baroque Era." *The International History Review* 36 (4): 603–18.

Carter, Charles H. 2004. "The Ambassadors of Early Modern Europe: Patterns of Diplomatic Representation in the Early Seventeenth Century." In *Diplomacy*, edited by Christer Jönsson and Richard Langhorne. London and Thousand Oaks: Sage Publications.

Cassidy, Jennifer A. 2024. "Digital Feminist Foreign Policy." In *The Oxford Handbook of Digital Diplomacy*, 157–76. Oxford: Oxford University Press.

Cassirer, Ernst. 1998. *The Philosophy of Symbolic Forms: Volume 4: The Metaphysics of Symbolic Forms*. Translated by John Michael Krois. New Haven, CT: Yale University Press.

Cassirer, Ernst. 2021. *An Essay on Man: An Introduction to a Philosophy of Human Culture*. New Haven, CT: Yale University Press.

Castiglione, Baldesar. 2023. *The Book of the Courtier*. Edited and translated by Peter Hainsworth. Cambridge, MA: Hackett Publishing.

Center for International Environmental Law. 2015. "2006 International Environmental Law Award Recipient – Raúl Estrada-Oyuela." *Center for International Environmental Law*. February 20. www.ciel.org/about-us/2006-international-environmental-law-award-recipient-raul-estrada-oyuela/.

Cesa, Marco, ed. 2018. *Debating Foreign Policy in the Renaissance: Speeches on War and Peace by Francesco Guicciardini*. Edinburgh, Scotland: Edinburgh University Press.

Chan, Michael, Francis L. F. Lee, and Hsuan-Ting Chen. 2021. "Examining the Roles of Multi-Platform Social Media News Use, Engagement, and Connections with News Organizations and Journalists on News Literacy: A Comparison of Seven Democracies." *Digital Journalism* 9 (5): 571–88. https://doi.org/10.1080/21670811.2021.1890168.

Chappell, Timothy. 2012. "Varieties of Knowledge in Plato and Aristotle." *Topoi: An International Review of Philosophy* 31 (2): 175–90.

Chastel, André. 2023. *The Sack of Rome, 1527*. Translated by Beth Archer. The A. W. Mellon Lectures in the Fine Arts 26. Princeton, NJ: Princeton University Press.

Chatterjee, Charles. 2007. *International Law and Diplomacy*. London and New York: Routledge.

Chatterjee, Charles. 2020. *Economic Diplomacy and Foreign Policy-Making*. Cham: Springer International Publishing.

Chen, Shanshan. 2023. "Introduction to the Macartney Embassy to China." In *Art, Science, and Diplomacy: A Study of the Visual Images of the Macartney Embassy to China, 1793*, 1–29. Singapore: Springer Nature Singapore.

Chernavskikh, Vladislav. 2024. "Nuclear Weapons and Artificial Intelligence: Technological Promises and Practical Realities." *Sipri*. September 2024. www.sipri.org/publications/2024/sipri-background-papers/nuclear-weapons-and-artificial-intelligence-technological-promises-and-practical-realities.

Chowdhury, Arjun, and Ronald R. Krebs. 2010. "Talking about Terror: Counterterrorist Campaigns and the Logic of Representation." *European Journal of International Relations* 16 (1): 125–50.

Chughtai, Ameer, and Theodore Murphy. 2023. "Conflict and Interests: Why Sudan's External Mediation Is a Barrier to Peace." *ECFR: European Council on Foreign Relations*. September 8. https://ecfr.eu/article/conflict-and-interests-why-sudans-external-mediation-is-a-barrier-to-peace/.

Church, William Farr. 2016. *Richelieu and Reason of State*. Princeton Legacy Library 1344. Princeton, NJ: Princeton University Press.

Clark, Grenville. 1967. *World Peace through World Law: Two Alternative Answers*. Harvard University Press.

Clark, Grenville, and Louis B. Sohn. 1958. *World Peace through World Law*. London, England: Harvard University Press.

Claude (Jr.), Inis. 1964. *Power and International Relations: (2. Print.)*. Random House.

CNN. 2019. "North Korea Revives 'Dotard' Insult after Trump's 'Rocket Man' Comment 'Displeased' Kim Jong Un." December 5. www.cnn.com/2019/12/04/asia/north-korea-kim-jong-un-intl-hnk/index.html.

Cohen, Raymond. 1996. "All in the Family: Ancient Near Eastern Diplomacy." *International Negotiation* 1 (1): 11–28. https://doi.org/10.1163/157180696X00269.

Cohen, Raymond. 2001. "The Great Tradition: The Spread of Diplomacy in the Ancient World." *Diplomacy and Statecraft* 12 (1): 23–38.

Coleman, Katharina P. 2011. "Innovations in 'African Solutions to African Problems': The Evolving Practice of Regional Peacekeeping in Sub-Saharan Africa." *The Journal of Modern African Studies* 49 (4): 517–45.

Coleman, Katharina P. 2013. "Locating Norm Diplomacy: Venue Change in International Norm Negotiations." *European Journal of International Relations* 19 (1): 163–86.

Coleman, Katharina, Markus Kornprobst, and Annette Seegers, eds. 2019. *Diplomacy and Borderlands: African Agency at the Intersections of Orders*. London: Routledge.

Collins, Neil, and Kristina Bekenova. 2019. "Digital Diplomacy: Success at Your Fingertips." *Place Branding and Public Diplomacy* 15 (1): 1–11. https://doi.org/10.1057/s41254-017-0087-1.

Confucius. 2020. *The Analects: Conclusions and Conversations of Confucius*. Translated by Moss Roberts. World Literature in Translation. Berkeley, CA: University of California Press.

Conrad, Geoffrey W., and Arthur Andrew Demarest. 1984. *Religion and Empire: The Dynamics of Aztec and Inca Expansionism*. Cambridge and New York: Cambridge University Press.

Cooley, Alexander, and Daniel Nexon. 2020. *Exit from Hegemony: The Unraveling of the American Global Order*. Oxford University Press.

Cooper, Andrew Fenton. 2008. *Celebrity Diplomacy*. Paradigm Publishers.

Cornut, J., I. Manor, and C. Blumenthal. 2022. "WhatsApp with Diplomatic Practices in Geneva? Diplomats, Digital Technologies, and Adaptation in Practice." *International Studies Review*. https://academic.oup.com/isr/article-pdf/doi/10.1093/isr/viac047/47901538/viac047.pdf.

Cox, Robert W. 1994. "The Crisis in World Order and the Challenge to International Organization." *Cooperation and Conflict* 29 (2): 99–113.

Crilley, Rhys. 2024. "Digital Nuclear Diplomacy." In *The Oxford Handbook of Digital Diplomacy*, edited by C. Bjola and I. Manor, 138–56. Oxford: Oxford University Press.

Cull, Nicholas J. 2008. "Public Diplomacy: Taxonomies and Histories." *The Annals of the American Academy of Political and Social Science* 616 (1): 31–54.

Cull, Nicholas J. 2019. *Public Diplomacy: Foundations for Global Engagement in the Digital Age*. Cambridge, UK: Polity Press.

Cull, Nicholas J. 2022. "The War for Ukraine: Reputational Security and Media Disruption." *Place Branding and Public Diplomacy* (October). https://doi.org/10.1057/s41254-022-00281-3.

da Conceição-Heldt, Eugénia. 2013. "Two-Level Games and Trade Cooperation: What Do We Now Know?" *International Politics* 50 (4): 579–99.

Dag Hammarskjöld Foundation. 2021. "Dag Hammarskjöld's 1961 Oxford Lecture: Three Untold Stories." May 30. www.daghammarskjold.se/blog/dag-hammarskjolds-1961-oxford-lecture-three-untold-stories/.

Daghar, Mohamed, and Willis Okumu. 2021. "Cattle Rustling: A Flourishing Illicit Market in East Africa." *ENACT Africa*. October 7, 2021. https://enactafrica.org/enact-observer/cattle-rustling-a-flourishing-illicit-market-in-east-africa.

Dahli, H. 2000. "Ethiopia's Obsession with the Red Sea." *Eritrea Profile*. July 20.

Daniel Schmidt, Jetzt kommt die Konkurrentin. 2018. "Frankfurter Allgemeine Zeitung." Accessed April 26, 2025. https://www.faz.net/aktuell/politik/ausland/angela-merkel-bei-donald-trump-besuch-der-konkurrentin-15561315.html.

Danielson, August, and Elsa Hedling. 2022. "Visual Diplomacy in Virtual Summitry: Status Signalling during the Coronavirus Crisis." *Review of International Studies* 48 (2): 243–61.

Darby, Phillip, and A. J. Paolini. 1994. "Bridging International Relations and Postcolonialism." *Alternatives to Laboratory Animals: ATLA* 19 (3): 371–97.

Dashwood, Hevina. 2001. "Mugabe, Zimbabwe, and Southern Africa: The Struggle for Leadership." *International Journal* 57 (1): 78–100.

Davies, Sara E., Adam Kamradt-Scott, and Simon Rushton. 2015. *Disease Diplomacy: International Norms and Global Health Security*. JHU Press.

Davis, Alexander E. 2018. *India and the Anglosphere: Race, Identity and Hierarchy in International Relations*. London: Routledge.

Davis Cross, Mai'a K. 2013. "Rethinking Epistemic Communities Twenty Years Later." *Obirin Review of International Studies* 39 (1): 137–60.

de Callières, François. 1716. *On the Manner of Negotiating with Princes*. Translated ed. 1919. London: Oxford University Press.

de Callières, François. 2004. "The Art of Negotiating with Sovereign Princes." In *Diplomatic Classics: Selected Texts from Commynes to Vattel*, edited by Geoff Berridge, 148. Basingstoke, England: Palgrave.

de Callières, François. 2021 [1716]. "The Practice of Diplomacy." *Wikisource*. Accessed April 26, 2025. The Practice of Diplomacy/On the Manner of Negotiating with Princes - Wikisource, the free online library.

de Certeau, Michel. 1988. *The Practice of Everyday Life*. Translated by Steven F. Rendall. Berkeley, CA: University of California Press.

Deitelhoff, Nicole. 2009. "The Discursive Process of Legalization: Charting Islands of Persuasion in the ICC Case." *International Organization* 63 (1): 33–65.

Denza, Eileen. 2008. "Interaction between State and Diplomatic Immunity." *Proceedings of the ASIL Annual Meeting* 102 (January): 111–14.

Derian, J. D. 1987. "Mediating Estrangement: A Theory for Diplomacy." *Review of International Studies* 13 (2): 91–110.

"Detecting Nuclear Tests." n.d. *CTBTO*. Accessed March 22, 2024. www.ctbto.org/our-work/detecting-nuclear-tests.

Detienne, Marcel, and Jean-Pierre Vernant. 1991. *Cunning Intelligence in Greek Culture and Society*. Translated by J. Lloyd. Chicago, IL: University of Chicago Press.

Dewey, John. 1929/2022. *The Quest for Certainty a Study of the Relation of Knowledge and Action*. Legare Street Press.

Diamond, Louise, and John W. McDonald. 1996. *Multi-Track Diplomacy: A Systems Approach to Peace*. Kumarian Press.

Dicken, Peter. 2007. *Global Shift: Mapping the Changing Contours of the World Economy*. SAGE Publications Ltd.

Digital Forensic Research Lab. 2024. "Undermining Ukraine: How Russia Widened Its Global Information War in 2023." *Atlantic Council*. February 29. www.atlanticcouncil.org/in-depth-research-reports/report/undermining-ukraine-how-russia-widened-its-global-information-war-in-2023/.

duc de Sully, Maximilien de Béthune. 1856 [1638]. *Memoirs of the Duke of Sully, Prime Minister to Henry the Great*. London: HG Bohn.

Duchene, Francois. 1996. *Jean Monnet: The First Statesman of Interdependence*. New York, NY: W. W. Norton.

Dumont, Jean-Christophe, Gilles Spielvogel, and Sarah Widmaier. 2010. "International Migrants in Developed, Emerging and Developing Countries: An Extended Profile." *OECD Social, Employment and Migration Working Papers No. 114*.

Duncombe, Constance. 2017. "Twitter and Transformative Diplomacy: Social Media and Iran–US Relations." *International Affairs* 93 (3): 545–62. https://doi.org/10.1093/ia/iix048.

Duncombe, Constance. 2018. "Twitter and the Challenges of Digital Diplomacy." *SAIS Review of International Affairs* 38 (2): 91–100. https://doi.org/10.1353/sais.2018.0019.

Duran, Manuel. 2013. "An Archaeology of Mediterranean Diplomacy: The Evidence of Paradiplomacy." *International Journal of Euro-Mediterranean Studies* 5 (2): 147–58.

Dutta, Anusmita, and Manish S. Dabhade. 2014. "Diplomatic Theory of Kautilya and Sun Tzu: Assessing Interpretations." *International Studies* 51 (1–4): 162–79.

Dyduch, Joanna, and Patrick Müller. 2021. "Populism Meets EU Foreign Policy: The de-Europeanization of Poland's Foreign Policy toward the Israeli-Palestinian Conflict." *Journal of European Integration* 43 (5): 569–86.

Dyson, Stephen Benedict. 2006. "Personality and Foreign Policy: Tony Blair's Iraq Decisions." *Foreign Policy Analysis* 2 (3): 289–306.

Dyson, Stephen Benedict. 2007. "Alliances, Domestic Politics, and Leader Psychology: Why Did Britain Stay Out of Vietnam and Go into Iraq?" *Political Psychology* 28 (6): 647–66.

Eggeling, Kristin Anabel, and Rebecca Adler-Nissen. 2024. "Diplomatic Negotiations in the Digital Context: Key Issues, Emerging Trends, and Procedural Changes." In *The Oxford Handbook of Digital Diplomacy*, edited by C. Bjola and I. Manor, 103–20.

Eilstrup-Sangiovanni, Mette. 2022. "OSCE Insights: The OSCE in Crisis: Five Lessons from the League of Nations." *Institute for Peace Research and Security Policy*. October 13. https://ifsh.de/en/news-detail/osce-insights-the-osce-in-crisis-five-lessons-from-the-league-of-nations.

Elias, Norbert. 2000. *The Civilizing Process: Sociogenetic and Psychogenetic Investigations*. Wiley.

ENACT. 2024. *The Organized Crime Index - Africa.ocindex.net*. https://africa.ocindex.net/.

Epstein, Charlotte. 2008. *The Power of Words in International Relations: Birth of an Anti-Whaling Discourse*. MIT Press.

Ewalefoh, Jobson. 2022. "The New Scramble for Africa." In *The Palgrave Handbook of Africa and the Changing Global Order*, edited by Samuel Ojo Oloruntoba and Toyin Falola, 309–22. Cham: Springer International Publishing.

Faizullaev, Alisher. 2024. "Digital Diplomacy of the Central Asian Countries." In *The Oxford Handbook of Digital Diplomacy*, 491–510. Oxford University Press.

Fan, John Hua, Akihiro Omura, and Eduardo Roca. 2023. "Geopolitics and Rare Earth Metals." *European Journal of Political Economy* 78 (102356): 102356.

Farrow, Ronan. 2023. "Elon Musk's Shadow Rule." *New Yorker*, 34–45.

Feldstein, Steven. 2021. *Rise Digital Repression: How Technology Reshaping Power, Politics, Resistance*. Oxford University Press.

Fetzer, Thiemo, and Carlo Schwarz. 2021. "Tariffs and Politics: Evidence from Trump's Trade Wars." *The Economic Journal* 131 (636): 1717–41.

Fichtner, Paula Sutter. 1976. "Dynastic Marriage in 16th Century Habsburg Diplomacy and Statecraft – Interdisciplinary Approach." *American Historical Review* 81 (2): 243–65.

Finnemore, Martha, and Kathryn Sikkink. 1998. "International Norm Dynamics and Political Change." *International Organization* 52 (4): 887–917.

Fisher, Walter R. 1984. "Narration as a Human Communication Paradigm: The Case of Public Moral Argument." *Communication Monographs* 51 (1): 1–22.

Fjällhed, Alicia, Matthias Lüfkens, and Andreas Sandre. 2024. "New Trends in Digital Diplomacy." In *The Oxford Handbook of Digital Diplomacy*, 269–88. Oxford University Press.

Flockhart, Trine. 2016. "The Coming Multi-Order World." *Contemporary Security Policy* 37 (1): 3–30.

Fogel, Joshua A. 2009. *Articulating the Sinosphere: Sino-Japanese Relations in Space and Time*. Cambridge, MA: Harvard University Press.

Forsberg, Tuomas, and Christer Pursiainen. 2017. "The Psychological Dimension of Russian Foreign Policy: Putin and the Annexation of Crimea." *Global Society* 31 (2): 220–44.

Foster, Chase, and Jeffry Frieden. 2021. "Economic Determinants of Public Support for European Integration, 1995–2018." *European Union Politics* 22 (2): 266–92.

Foucault, Michel. 2005. *The Order of Things*. London: Routledge.

France-Presse, Agence. 2017. "North Korea 'Sentences Trump to Death' for Insulting Kim Jong-Un." *The Guardian*. November 15. www.theguardian.com/us-news/2017/nov/15/north-korea-sentences-trump-to-death-for-insulting-kim-jong-un.

Freeden, Michael. 2018. *Re-Energizing Ideology Studies: The Maturing of a Discipline*. Routledge.

Freedman, Lawrence D. 2010. "Frostbitten: Decoding the Cold War, 20 Years Later." *Foreign Affairs* 89: 136.

Freedman, Lawrence. 2014. "Ukraine and the Art of Crisis Management." *Survival* 56 (3): 7–42.

Friedman, Jonathan. 1998. "Transnationalization, Socio-Political Disorder, and Ethnification as Expressions of Declining Global Hegemony." *International Political Science Review* 19 (3): 233–50.

Friedner Parrat, Charlotta. 2017. "On the Evolution of Primary Institutions of International Society." *International Studies Quarterly: A Publication of the International Studies Association* 61 (3): 623–30.

Fuller, Mia. 2022. "Italy: Beyond the Clichés That Obscure Unacceptable Histories." *Journal of Genocide Research* 24 (2): 298–307.

Fullilove, Courtney. 2018. "Gift and Gunboat: Meanings of Exchange in the Perry Expedition." *Diplomatic History* 42 (1): 90–108.

Gadamer, Hans-Georg. 1960. *Wahrheit Und Methode: Grundzüge Einer Philosophischen Hermeneutik*. Tübingen, Germany: Mohr Siebeck.

Gaddis, John Lewis. 1993. *The United States and the End of the Cold War*. Reprint ed. New York, NY: Oxford University Press.

Gaddis, John Lewis. 2011. "Is This George Kennan?" *The New York Review* 8.
Gaddis, John Lewis. 2012. *George F. Kennan: An American Life*. New York, NY: Penguin.
Gadinger, Frank. 2023. "Fields, Trajectories, and Symbolic Power: Studying Practices of Polycentric Governing with Bourdieu." In *Polycentrism: How Governing Works Today*, edited by Jan Aart Scholte and Frank Gadinger, 213–35. Oxford, England: Oxford University Press.
Gallagher, Michael M. 2002. "Declaring Victory and Getting Out of Europe: Why the North Atlantic Treaty Organization Should Disband." *Houston Journal of International Law* 25: 341.
Gallennius, Gustav, and Salsabila Andi Akil. 2024. "Digital Diplomacy: Hololive Indonesia and Virtual Youtuber (Vtuber) as Indonesia's New Public Diplomacy." *Ilomata International Journal of Social Science* 5 (1): 272–87.
Gallerie Dell'accademia di Venezia. 2025. "Study of the Proportions of the Human Body, Known as the Vitruvian Man." www.gallerieaccademia.it/en/study-proportions-human-body-known-vitruvian-man.
Garcia, Denise. 2011. "Disarmament Diplomacy and Human Security: Regimes, Norms and Moral Progress in International Relations." February. https://doi.org/10.4324/9780203830703/disarmament-diplomacy-human-security-denise-garcia.
Garrett, Geoffrey. 2010. "G2 in G20: China, the United States and the World after the Global Financial Crisis." *Global Policy* 1 (1): 29–39.
Gentili, Alberico. 2022 [1612]. *De iure belli*. Cambridge: Cambridge University Press.
George, Alexander L. 1969. "The 'Operational Code': A Neglected Approach to the Study of Political Leaders and Decision-Making." *International Studies Quarterly: A Publication of the International Studies Association* 13 (2): 190–222.
"Ghent University." 2021. *Every Casualty Counts*. December 8. https://everycasualty.org/casualty-recording-organisations/university-of-ghent/.
Giacomello, Giampiero, and Johan Eriksson. 2023. "Rise of the Nerd." In *Digital International Relations*, edited by C. Bjola and M. Kornprobst, 73–95. London: Routledge.
Gigerenzer, Gerd, and Peter M. Todd. 1999. "Fast and Frugal Heuristics: The Adaptive Toolbox." In *Simple Heuristics That Make Us Smart*, 3–34. Oxford University Press.
Gilkes, Patrick, and Martin Plaut. 1999. *War in the Horn: The Conflict between Eritrea and Ethiopia*. Royal Institute of International Affairs.
Gill, Stephen. 1995. "Globalisation, Market Civilisation, and Disciplinary Neoliberalism." *Millennium* 24 (3): 399–423.
Glass, Andrew. 2019. "Egypt, Israel Conclude Peace Treaty, March 26, 1979." *Politico*. March 26. www.politico.com/story/2019/03/26/egypt-israel-peace-treaty-1233742.
Goffman, Erving. 1959. *The Presentation of Self in Everyday Life*. Anchor Books. New York, NY: Bantam Doubleday Dell Publishing Group.
Goldman, Alvin L., and J. Rojot. 2002. "Negotiation: Theory and Practice." www.semanticscholar.org/paper/0dd143e0f171e780eda993f579e7e638e1d7a5f9.
Götz, Elias, and Jørgen Staun. 2022. "Why Russia Attacked Ukraine: Strategic Culture and Radicalized Narratives." *Contemporary Security Policy* 43 (3): 482–97.
Graaff, Nana de, Tobias ten Brink, and Inderjeet Parmar. 2020. "China's Rise in a Liberal World Order in Transition – Introduction to the FORUM." *Review of International Political Economy* 27 (2): 191–207.
Græger, Nina, Bertel Heurlin, Ole Wæver, and Anders Wivel. 2022. *Polarity in International Relations: Past, Present, Future*. Springer Nature.
Graham, Sarah Ellen, and John Robert Kelley. 2009. "U.S. Engagement in East Asia: A Case for 'Track Two' Diplomacy." *Orbis* 53 (1): 80–98.
Grantseva, Vera, and Thierry Balzacq. 2025. "The Ideological Sources of Great Power Competition in the Regions." In *The New Cold War and the Remaking of Regions*, edited by T. Paul and Markus Kornprobst. Washington, DC: Georgetown University Press.
Gray, Kevin, and Barry K. Gills. 2016. "South–South Cooperation and the Rise of the Global South." *Third World Quarterly* 37 (4): 557–74.
Green, Donald, and Ian Shapiro. 1994. *Pathologies of Rational Choice Theory: A Critique of Applications in Political Science*. Yale University Press.
Greig, J. Michael. 2001. "Moments of Opportunity: Recognizing Conditions of Ripeness for International Mediation between Enduring Rivals." *The Journal of Conflict Resolution* 45 (6): 691–718.
Greig, J. Michael, and Paul F. Diehl. 2005. "The Peacekeeping-Peacemaking Dilemma." *International Studies Quarterly: A Publication of the International Studies Association* 49 (4): 621–45.

Griessl, Lukas. 2023. "The Power of Secret Knowledge: The RAND Corporation, Ignorance Studies and Sociology." *The American Sociologist* (March). https://doi.org/10.1007/s12108-023-09567-2.

Grotius, Hugo. 1924. *De Jure Belli Ac Pacis Libri Tres: The Translation. Book I*. Clarendon.

Grovogu, Siba. 2011. "A Revolution Nonetheless: The Global South in International Relations." *The Global South* 5 (1): 175–90.

Guardian News. 2017. "Trump: I'll Handle 'Little Rocket Man' Kim Jong-Un." *YouTube*. September 23. www.youtube.com/watch?v=ETNKAQGq8Ts.

Guicciardini, Francesco. 2020. *The History of Italy*. Edited and translated by Sidney Alexander. Princeton, NJ: Princeton University Press.

Guicciardini, Francesco. 2021. *The Defeat of a Renaissance Intellectual: Selected Writings of Francesco Guicciardini*. Edited by Carlo Celli. Early Modern Studies. University Park, FL: Pennsylvania State University Press.

Guymer, Laurence. 2010. "The Wedding Planners: Henry Bulwer, and the Spanish Marriages, 1841–1846." *Diplomacy and Statecraft* 21 (4): 549–73.

Haas, Ernst B. 1958. *The Uniting of Europe: Political, Social, and Economic Forces, 1950–1957*. Stanford University Press.

Haas, Michael. 2023. *Professionalization of Foreign Policy: Transformation of Operational Code Analysis*. Springer Nature.

Habegger, Mike, and Tobias Lemke. 2020. "Diplomat or Troll? The Case against Digital Diplomacy." In *International Organisations and Digital Diplomacy: Autonomy, Legitimacy and Contestation*, edited by Corneliu Bjola and Ruben Zaiotti, 229–66. Abingdon and New York: Routledge.

Habermas, Juergen. 1984. *The Theory of Communicative Action: Volume 1: Reason and the Rationalization of Society*. Beacon Press.

Hamilton, K., and Richard Langhorne. 1995. *The Practice of Diplomacy: Its Evolution, Theory and Administration*. London: Routledge.

Hamilton, Keith, and Richard Langhorne. 2011. *The Practice of Diplomacy*. London: Routledge.

Hare, P. W. 2015. *Making Diplomacy Work: Intelligent Innovation for the Modern World*. Washington, DC: CQ Press.

Harmsen, Robert, and Anna-Lena Högenauer. 2020. "Luxembourg and the European Union." In *Oxford Research Encyclopedia of Politics*. Oxford University Press.

Harries, Owen. 1993. "The Collapse of 'The West'." *Foreign Affairs*, 41–53.

Hathaway, Oona A., and Stewart Patrick. 2024. "Can the UN Security Council Still Help Keep the Peace? Reassessing Its Role, Relevance, and Potential for Reform." *Carnegie Endowment for International Peace*. July. https://carnegieendowment.org/posts/2024/07/can-un-security-council-still-help-keep-the-peace?lang=en.

Hauer, Mathew E, et al. 2020. "Sea-Level Rise and Human Migration." *Nature Reviews Earth & Environment* 1 (1): 28–39.

Hayles, N. Katherine. 2017. *Unthought: The Power of the Cognitive Nonconscious*. Chicago, IL: University of Chicago Press. https://doi.org/10.7208/chicago/9780226447919.001.0001.

He, Kai. 2008. "Institutional Balancing and International Relations Theory: Economic Interdependence and Balance of Power Strategies in Southeast Asia." *European Journal of International Relations* 14 (3): 489–518.

He, Kai, and Huiyun Feng. 2013. "Xi Jinping's Operational Code Beliefs and China's Foreign Policy." *The Chinese Journal of International Politics* 6 (3): 209–31.

Hedling, Elsa. 2020. "Storytelling in EU Public Diplomacy: Reputation Management and Recognition of Success." *Place Branding and Public Diplomacy* 16 (2): 143–52.

Hedling, Elsa. 2024. "Virtual Diplomatic Summitry." In *The Oxford Handbook of Digital Diplomacy*, edited by C. Bjola and I. Manor, 367–82. Oxford: Oxford University Press.

Herbrechter, Stefan. 2013. *Posthumanism: A Critical Analysis*. London, England: Bloomsbury Academic.

Hettyey, András. 2021. "The Europeanization of Hungarian Foreign Policy and the Hungarization of European Foreign Policy, 2010–18." *Journal of Contemporary European Studies* 29 (1): 125–38.

Higgott, Richard A., and Kim Richard Nossal. 1997. "The International Politics of Liminality: Relocating Australia in the Asia Pacific." *Australian Journal of Political Science* 32 (2): 169–86.

Holmes, Marcus. 2024. "Digital Diplomacy: Projection and Retrieval of Images and Identities." In *The Oxford Handbook of Digital Diplomacy*, edited by C. Bjola and I. Manor, 29–44. Oxford: Oxford University Press.

Holsti, Ole. 1970. "The 'Operational Code' Approach to the Study of Political Leaders: John Foster Dulles' Philosophical and Instrumental Beliefs." *Canadian Journal of Political Science/Revue Canadienne de Science Politique* 3 (1): 123–57.

Holzscheiter, Anna. 2016. "Representation as Power and Performative Practice: Global Civil Society Advocacy for Working Children." *Obirin Review of International Studies* 42 (2): 205–26.

Hopf, Ted. 2010. "The Logic of Habit in International Relations." *European Journal of International Relations* 16 (4): 539–61.

Hopke, Jill E., and Luis E. Hestres. 2018. "Visualizing the Paris Climate Talks on Twitter: Media and Climate Stakeholder Visual Social Media During COP21." *Social Media + Society* 4 (3): 2056305118782687.

Horowitz, Michael C., and Lauren Kahn. 2024. "Bending the Automation Bias Curve: A Study of Human and AI-Based Decision Making in National Security Contexts." *International Studies Quarterly* 68 (2): sqae020.

Howard, Philip N., and M. Muzammil. 2013. *Democracy's Fourth Wave? Digital Media Arab Spring*. Oxford University Press.

Howarth, David, and Joachim Schild. 2021. "Nein to 'Transfer Union': The German Brake on the Construction of a European Union Fiscal Capacity." *Journal of European Integration* 43 (2): 209–26.

Hudson, Valerie M. 2005. "Foreign Policy Analysis: Actor-Specific Theory and the Ground of International Relations." *Foreign Policy Analysis* 1: 1–30.

Huju, Kira. 2023. *Cosmopolitan Elites: Indian Diplomats and the Social Hierarchies of Global Order*. Oxford University Press.

Igini, Martina. 2022. "Sea Level Rise Projections: 10 Cities at Risk of Flooding." *Earth.org*. June 4. https://earth.org/sea-level-rise-projections/.

Ikenberry, G. John. 2018. "Why the Liberal World Order Will Survive." *Ethics & International Affairs* 32 (1): 17–29.

Ikenberry, G. John. 2020. "The Next Liberal Order." *Foreign Affairs* 99 (4): 133–42.

Imran, S. 2018. "Nation Branding Endeavours of Azerbaijan: Reshaping National Image." www.semanticscholar.org/paper/8a52d6ea9df3d0e61b30ecaed1f6e82a113cb589.

Institute for Economics and Peace. 2024. "Multilateralism Index 2024." *International Peace Institute and Institute for Economics and Peace*. www.ipinst.org/wp-content/uploads/2024/10/2024-Multilateralism-index.pdf.

International Crisis Group. 2025. "10 Conflicts to Watch in 2025." January 1. www.crisisgroup.org/global/10-conflicts-watch-2025.

"International Health Regulations (2005) – Third Edition." 2016. *World Health Organization*. January 1. www.who.int/publications/i/item/9789241580496.

International Monetary Fund. 2024. *World Economic Outlook, April 2023*. International Monetary Fund.

International Organisation for Migration (IOM). 2024. "World Migration Report 2024." https://worldmigrationreport.iom.int/msite/wmr-2024-interactive/.

International Organization for Migration (IOM). 2018. "World Migration Report 2005." *International Organization for Migration*. July 11. www.iom.int/resources/world-migration-report-2005.

International Rescue Committee. 2025. "2025 Emergency Watchlist." *The IRC*. www.rescue.org/watchlist.

Irwin, G. W. 1975. "Precolonial African Diplomacy: The Example of Asante." *International Journal of African Historical Studies* 8 (1): 81–96.

Isaacson, Walter. 2013. *Kissinger: A Biography*. New York: Simon & Schuster.

Isaacson, Walter. 2018. *Leonardo Da Vinci*. London: Simon & Schuster.

Jabri, Vivienne. 1996. *Discourses on Violence: Conflict Analysis Reconsidered*. Manchester University Press.

Jackson, Robert H. 1990. *Quasi-States: Sovereignty, International Relations, and the Third World*. Cambridge University Press.

Jahn, Beate. 2016. "Theorizing the Political Relevance of International Relations Theory." *International Studies Quarterly* 61 (1): 64–77.

Jamal, Urooba. 2023. "Diplomats, Aid Workers under Attack in 'Nightmare' Sudan Violence." *Al Jazeera*. April 19. www.aljazeera.com/news/2023/4/19/diplomats-aid-workers-under-attack-in-nightmare-sudan-violence.

Janis, Irving Lester. 1972. *Victims of Groupthink: A Psychological Study of Foreign-Policy Decisions and Fiascoes*. Houghton: Mifflin.

Jansson, André. 2015. "Using Bourdieu in Critical Mediatization Research: Communicational Doxa and Osmotic Pressures in the Field of UN Organizations." *MedieKultur Journal of Media and Communication Research* 31 (58): 13–29.

Jarrett, Mark. 2013. *The Congress of Vienna and Its Legacy: War and Great Power Diplomacy after Napoleon*. London: I. B. Tauris.

Jiuding, Quan, and Zou Leilei. 2023. "Research Review on Ideological Factors in Public Diplomacy Discourse Translation." *International Journal of Translation and Interpretation Studies* 3 (1): 8–16.

Johnston, Alastair Iain. 1998. *Cultural Realism: Strategic Culture and Grand Strategy in Chinese History*, vol. 75. Princeton, NJ: Princeton University Press.

Johnstone, Ian. 2003. "Security Council Deliberations: The Power of the Better Argument." *European Journal of International Law* 14 (3): 437–80.

Jönsson, Christer. 2022. "Theorising Diplomacy." In *The Routledge Handbook of Diplomacy and Statecraft*, edited by B. J. C. McKercher, 13–26. London: Routledge.

Kagwanja, Peter. 2006. "Counter-Terrorism in the Horn of Africa: New Security Frontiers, Old Strategies." *African Security Review* 15 (3): 72–86.

Kahneman, Daniel, and Amos Tversky. 1979. "Prospect Theory: An Analysis of Decision under Risk." *Econometrica: Journal of the Econometric Society* 47 (2): 363–91.

Kaneva, Nadia. 2022. "'Brave Like Ukraine': A Critical Discourse Perspective on Ukraine's Wartime Brand." *Place Branding and Public Diplomacy* (September).

Kaplan, David. 2000. *Structural Equation Modeling: Foundations and Extensions*. SAGE Publications.

Keller, Franziska B., David Schoch, Sebastian Stier, and Junghwan Yang. 2019. "Political Astroturfing on Twitter: How to Coordinate a Disinformation Campaign." *Political Communication* (October): 1–25.

Kelley, John Robert. 2007. "US Public Diplomacy: A Cold War Success Story?" *The Hague Journal of Diplomacy* 2 (1): 53–79.

Kennedy-Pipe, Caroline, and Rhiannon Vickers. 2007. "'Blowback' for Britain?: Blair, Bush, and the War in Iraq." *Review of International Studies* 33 (2): 205–21.

Kenya Digital News. 2022. "Kenya's Ambassador to UN Martin Kimani's Speech on the Ukraine-Russia Crisis Wows the World." *YouTube*. February 22. www.youtube.com/watch?v=ZxZlaiuicYM.

Keohane, Robert O. 1988. "International Institutions: Two Approaches." *International Studies Quarterly* 32 (4): 379–96.

Kerbrat-Orecchioni, Catherine. 2004. "Introducing Polylogue." *Journal of Pragmatics* 36 (1): 1–24.

Kerr, Paul. 2004. "More U.S. Claims on Iraq WMD Rebutted." *Arms Control Today* 34 (8): 32.

Kim, Victoria. 2023. "Elon Musk Acknowledges Withholding Satellite Service to Thwart Ukrainian Attack." *The New York Times (Digital Edition)*. September 8.

Kirk, Jessica, and Matt McDonald. 2021. "The Politics of Exceptionalism: Securitization and COVID-19." *Global Studies Quarterly* 1 (3): ksab024.

Kissinger, Henry. 1994. *Diplomacy*. New York: Simon & Schuster.

Kissinger, Henry. 2014. *World Order*. London: Penguin.

Kleiboer, Marieke. 2002. "Great Power Mediation: Using Leverage to Make Peace." In *Studies in International Mediation*, edited by J. Bercovitch, 127–40. UK: Palgrave Macmillan.

Kleiner, Jürgen. 2010. *Diplomatic Practice: Between Tradition and Innovation*. World Scientific.

Knight, W. Andy. 2022. "The Interregnum: Governance in the New World Disorder." *International Journal* 77 (3): 485–502.

Koinova, Maria, Maryam Zarnegar Deloffre, Frank Gadinger, Zeynep Sahin Mencutek, Jan Aart Scholte, and Jens Steffek. 2021. "It's Ordered Chaos: What Really Makes Polycentrism Work." *International Studies Review* 23 (4): 1988–2018.

Koit, Mare. 2023. "How to Recognize Arguments? A Study of Human Negotiations." *Artificial Intelligence and Applications* 2 (3): 202–8.

Koremenos, Barbara, Charles Lipson, and Duncan Snidal. 2001. "The Rational Design of International Institutions." *International Organization* 55 (4): 761–99.

Kornprobst, Markus. 2002. "The Management of Border Disputes in African Regional Sub-Systems: Comparing West Africa and the Horn of Africa." *The Journal of Modern African Studies* 40 (3): 369–93.

Kornprobst, Markus. 2008. *Irredentism in European Politics: Argumentation, Compromise and Norms*. Cambridge University Press.

Kornprobst, Markus. 2019a. "Framing, Resonance and War: Foregrounds and Backgrounds of Cultural Congruence." *European Journal of International Relations* 25 (1): 61–85.

Kornprobst, Markus. 2019b. *Co-Managing International Crises: Judgments and Justifications*. Cambridge University Press.

Kornprobst, Markus. 2023. "Diplomatic Peace." *The Hague Journal of Diplomacy* 18 (4): 475–508.

Kornprobst, Markus, Vincent Pouliot, N. Shah, and Ruben Zaiotti, eds. 2008. *Metaphors of Globalization*. Basingstoke: Palgrave Macmillan.
Kornprobst, Markus, and Martin Senn. 2016a. "A Rhetorical Field Theory: Background, Communication, and Change." *British Journal of Politics and International Relations* 18 (2): 300–17.
Kornprobst, Markus, and Martin Senn. 2016b. "Introduction: Background Ideas in International Relations." *British Journal of Politics and International Relations* 18 (2): 273–81.
Kornprobst, Markus, and Martin Senn. 2017. "Arguing Deep Ideational Change." *Contemporary Politics* 23 (1): 100–19.
Kornprobst, Markus, and Stephanie Strobl. 2021. "Global Health: An Order Struggling to Keep up with Globalization." *International Affairs* 97 (5): 1541–58.
Kornprobst, Markus, and Stephanie Strobl. 2024. "When the Background Looms Large over the Foreground: Medical Professionals, Diplomats, and Co-Managing SARS-CoV-2." *Global Studies Quarterly* 4 (1).
Krauthammer, Charles. 1990. "The Unipolar Moment." *Foreign Affairs* 70 (1): 23–33.
Kristeva, Julia. 1977. *Polylogue*. Paris: Seuil.
Krook, Mona Lena, and Jacqui True. 2012. "Rethinking the Life Cycles of International Norms: The United Nations and the Global Promotion of Gender Equality." *European Journal of International Relations* 18 (1): 103–27.
Kuby, Candace R., Tara Gutshall Rucker, and L. Darolia. 2017. "Persistence(ing): Posthuman Agency in a Writers' Studio." *Journal of Early Childhood Literacy* 17 (August): 353–73.
Kugler, Jacek, and Douglas Lemke. 1996. *Parity and War: Evaluations and Extensions of the War Ledger*. University of Michigan Press.
Kütt, Moritz, and Jens Steffek. 2015. "Comprehensive Prohibition of Nuclear Weapons: An Emerging International Norm?" *The Nonproliferation Review* 22 (3–4): 401–20.
Kuus, Merje. 2007. "Something Old, Something New: Eastness in European Union Enlargement." *Journal of International Relations and Development* 10 (2): 150–67.
Kuus, Merje. 2013. *Geopolitics and Expertise: Knowledge and Authority in European Diplomacy*. John Wiley & Sons.
Kydd, Andrew H. 2006. "When Can Mediators Build Trust?" *The American Political Science Review* 100 (3): 449–62.
Lai, Steven. 2021. "White House Partners with Influencers to Encourage Vaccinations." *ION*. August 13. www.ion.co/white-house-enlists-infuencers-to-dispel-vaccine-information.
Landgraf, Edgar. 2022. "Posthumanism and the Enlightenment." In *Palgrave Handbook of Critical Posthumanism*, 1–21. Cham: Springer International Publishing.
Langer, M. 2015. "Universal Jurisdiction Is Not Disappearing: The Shift from 'Global Enforcer' to 'No Safe Haven' Universal Jurisdiction." *Journal of International Criminal Justice*. https://academic.oup.com/jicj/article-abstract/13/2/245/896503.
Lantis, Jeffrey S., and Carmen Wunderlich. 2022. "Reevaluating Constructivist Norm Theory: A Three-Dimensional Norms Research Program." *International Studies Review* 24 (1): viab059.
Latour, Bruno. 2007. *Reassembling the Social: An Introduction to Actor-Network-Theory*. Oxford: Oxford University Press.
Lavery, Scott, and Davide Schmid. 2021. "European Integration and the New Global Disorder." *Journal of Common Market Studies* 59 (5): 1322–38.
Lawrence, Michael, Scott Janzwood, and Thomas Homer-Dixon. 2022. "What Is a Global Polycrisis?" *Cascade Institute*. September 16. https://cascadeinstitute.org/technical-paper/what-is-a-global-polycrisis/.
Layne, Christopher. 2012. "This Time It's Real: The End of Unipolarity and the Pax Americana." *International Studies Quarterly: A Publication of the International Studies Association* 56 (1): 203–13.
Layne, Christopher. 2018. "The US–Chinese Power Shift and the End of the Pax Americana." *International Affairs* 94 (1): 89–111.
League of Nations. 1924. C. N. -. Jx1975 A39. *The Covenant of the League of Nations*. Geneva: Information Section League of Nations Secretariat.
Lebow, Richard Ned. 2018. *The Rise and Fall of Political Orders*. Cambridge University Press.
Lee, Francis L. F., and M. Joseph. 2018. *Media Protest Logics Digital Era: Umbrella Movement Hong Kong*. Oxford: Oxford University Press.
Leitenberg, Milton. 2006. "Deaths in Wars and Conflicts in the 20th Century." *Cornell University Peace Studies Program*.
Lepskiy, Maxim, and Nataliia Lepska. 2023. "The War in Ukraine and Its Challenge to NATO: Peacekeeping to Peace Engineering." *The American Behavioral Scientist* 67 (3): 402–25.

Levy, Jack S. 2000. "Loss Aversion, Framing Effects, and International Conflict: Perspectives from Prospect Theory." In *Handbook of War Studies II*, ed. Manus I. Midlarsky, 193–221. Ann Arbor: University of Michigan Press.

Linklater, Andrew. 2009. "Grand Narratives and International Relations." *Global Change Peace & Security* 21 (1): 3–17.

Lintott, Andrew. 2003. *The Constitution of the Roman Republic*. London, England: Oxford University Press.

Little, Richard. 2007. *The Balance of Power in International Relations: Metaphors, Myths and Models*. Cambridge University Press.

Liu, Chuncheng, and Akos Rona-Tas. 2024. "Trusting by Numbers: An Analysis of a Chinese Social Credit System Governance Infrastructure." *Critical Sociology*. https://doi.org/10.1177/08969205241246528.

Loh, Dylan M. H. 2018. "Diplomatic Control, Foreign Policy, and Change under Xi Jinping: A Field-Theoretic Account." *Journal of Current Chinese Affairs* 47 (3): 111–45.

Low, Maurice A. 1918. "The Vice of Secret Diplomacy." *The North American Review* 207 (747): 209–20.

Lynch, Marc. 2000. "The Dialogue of Civilisations and International Public Spheres." *Millennium Journal of International Studies* 29 (2): 307–30.

MacCulloch, Diarmaid. 2019. *Thomas Cromwell: A Life*. Harlow, England: Penguin Books.

Machiavelli, Niccolò. 2020. *Machiavelli: The Prince*. Edited by Quentin Skinner and Russell Price. 2nd ed. Cambridge Texts in the History of Political Thought. Cambridge, England: Cambridge University Press (Virtual Publishing).

Magazù, S., Nella Coletta, and F. Migliardo. 2019. "The Vitruvian Man of Leonardo Da Vinci as a Representation of an Operational Approach to Knowledge." *Foundations of Science* 24 (4): 751–73.

Malchow, H. L. 2016. *History and International Relations: From the Ancient World to the 21st Century*. London: Bloomsbury.

Mander, Jerry. 2014. *The Case against the Global Economy: And for a Turn towards Localization*. Routledge.

Manor, Ilan, and James Pamment. 2019. "Towards Prestige Mobility? Diplomatic Prestige and Digital Diplomacy." *Cambridge Review of International Affairs* 32 (2): 93–131.

Manor, Ilan, and Moran Yrachi. 2023. "From the Global to the Local and Back again: MFAs' Digital Communications during COVID-19." *International Journal of Communication Systems* 17: 22.

March, James G., and Johan P. Olsen. 1989. *Rediscovering Institutions: The Organizational Basis of Politics*. Free Press.

March, James G., and Johan P. Olsen. 2004. "The Logic of Appropriateness." *ARENA Working Paper* 4 (9): 1–28.

Mathiasen, Karen. 2024. "The UN Pact for the Future: Mired in the Past and Hamstrung by the Present." September 25. www.cgdev.org/blog/un-pact-future-mired-past-and-hamstrung-present.

Mathieu, Xavier. 2020. "Sovereign Myths in International Relations: Sovereignty as Equality and the Reproduction of Eurocentric Blindness." *Journal of International Political Theory* 16 (3): 339–60.

Mattern, Janice Bially. 2005. "Why 'Soft Power' Isn't so Soft: Representational Force and the Sociolinguistic Construction of Attraction in World Politics." *Millennium* 33 (3): 583–612.

Mattern, Janice Bially, and Ayşe Zarakol. 2016. "Hierarchies in World Politics." *International Organization* 70 (3): 623–54.

Mattingly, Garrett. 1955. *Renaissance Diplomacy*. London: Cape.

Mattingly, Garrett. 1971. *Renaissance Diplomacy*. Boston, MA: Houghton Mifflin.

Mattingly, Garrett. 2004. "The First Resident Embassies: Medieval Italian Origins of Modern Diplomacy." In *Diplomacy*, edited by Christer Jönsson and Richard Langhorne. London and Thousand Oaks: Sage Publications.

McLarren, Katharina. 2023. "Conclusion: The English School and Diplomacy as a Dynamic and Core Primary Institution." In *The Palgrave Handbook of Diplomatic Thought and Practice in the Digital Age*, edited by Francis Onditi, Katharina McLarren, Gilad Ben-Nun, Yannis A. Stivachtis, and Pontian Okoth, 521–33. Cham: Springer International Publishing.

McLaughlin, Martin. 2024. *Leon Battista Alberti*. Princeton, NJ: Princeton University Press.

McLeod, John. 1994. "The English Honours System in Princely India, 1925–1947." *Journal of the Royal Asiatic Society* 4 (2): 237–49.

Mears, Natalie. 2001. "Love-Making and Diplomacy: Elizabeth I and the Anjou Marriage Negotiations, c. 1578–1582." *History* 86 (284): 442–66.

Mearsheimer, John J. 2014. "Why the Ukraine Crisis Is the West's Fault: The Liberal Delusions That Provoked Putin." *Foreign Affairs* 93 (5): 77–89.

Mearsheimer, John J. 2022. "The Causes and Consequences of the Ukraine War." *Horizons: Journal of International Relations and Sustainable Development* 21: 12–27.

Meerts, Paul, and Peter Beeuwkes. 2008. "The Utrecht Negotiations in Perspective: The Hope of Happiness for the World." *International Negotiation* 13 (2): 157–77.

Meinecke, Friedrich. 1957. *Machiavellism: The Doctrine of Raison d'État and Its Place in Modern History*. New Haven, CT: Yale University Press.

Mercer, Jonathan. 2010. "Emotional Beliefs." *International Organization* 64 (1): 1–31.

Miceli, Milagros, Julian Posada, and Tianling Yang. 2021. "Studying up Machine Learning Data: Why Talk about Bias When We Mean Power?" *ArXiv [Cs.HC]. arXiv*. http://arxiv.org/abs/2109.08131.

Ministry of Foreign Affairs of the Russian Federation. 2024. "Foreign Minister Sergey Lavrov's Remarks at a UN Security Council Meeting on Ukraine, New York, January 22, 2024." January 22. https://mid.ru/en/foreign_policy/news/1927070/.

Mintz, Alex, and Amnon Sofrin. 2017. "Decision Making Theories in Foreign Policy Analysis." In *Oxford Research Encyclopedia of Politics*. Oxford: Oxford University Press.

Mitchell, C. R. 1981. *The Structure of International Conflict*. London, UK: Palgrave Macmillan.

Mitrany, David. 1946. *A Working Peace System: An Argument for the Functional Development of International Organization*. Royal Institute of International Affairs.

Mitzen, Jennifer. 2005. "Reading Habermas in Anarchy: Multilateral Diplomacy and Global Public Spheres." *The American Political Science Review* 99 (3): 401–17.

Mo, Jongryn. 1994. "The Logic of Two-Level Games with Endogenous Domestic Coalitions." *The Journal of Conflict Resolution* 38 (3): 402–22.

Moore, David. 2010. "A Decade of Disquieting Diplomacy: South Africa, Zimbabwe and the Ideology of the National Democratic Revolution, 1999–2009." *History Compass* 8 (8): 752–67.

Moral, Pablo. 2023. "Restoring Reputation through Digital Diplomacy: The European Union's Strategic Narratives on Twitter during the COVID-19 Pandemic." *Communication & Society* (April): 241–69.

Moran, William L., ed. 2002. *The Amarna Letters*. Baltimore, MD: Johns Hopkins University Press.

Moravcsik, Andrew. 1999. "The Future of European Integration Studies: Social Science or Social Theory?" *Millennium* 28 (2): 371–91.

Morgenthau, Hans Joachim. 1948. *Politics among Nations: The Struggle for Power and Peace*. A. A. Knopf.

Morin, Edgar, and Anne Brigitte Kern. 1993. *Terre-Patrie*. Paris: Seuil.

Morrow, James D. 1994. *Game Theory for Political Scientists*. Princeton University Press.

Mügge, Daniel. 2023. "The Securitization of the EU's Digital Tech Regulation." *Journal of European Public Policy* 30 (7): 1431–46.

Müller, Harald. 1994. "Internationale Beziehungen Ais Kommunikatives Handeln. Zur Kritik Der Utilitaristischen Handlungstheorien." *Zeitschrift Für Internationale Beziehungen* 1 (1): 15–44.

Müller, Harald. 2004. "Arguing, Bargaining and All That: Communicative Action, Rationalist Theory and the Logic of Appropriateness in International Relations." *European Journal of International Relations* 10 (3): 395–435.

Munn-Rankin, Joan M. 2004. "Diplomacy in Western Asia in the Early Second Millennium B.C." In *Diplomacy*, edited by Christer Jönsson and Richard Langhorne. London and Thousand Oaks, CA: Sage Publications.

Munyi, Elijah Nyaga, David Mwambari, and Aleksi Ylönen, eds. 2020. *Beyond History: African Agency in Development, Diplomacy, and Conflict Resolution*. Lanham, MD: Rowman & Littlefield.

Murray, Eustace Clare Grenville. 1855. *Embassies and Foreign Courts*. London and New York: G. Routledge & Co.

Murray, Stuart, Paul Sharp, Geoffrey Wiseman, David Criekemans, and Jan Melissen. 2011. "The Present and Future of Diplomacy and Diplomatic Studies." *International Studies Review* 13 (4): 709–28.

Musgrave, Paul, and Daniel H. Nexon. 2018. "Defending Hierarchy from the Moon to the Indian Ocean: Symbolic Capital and Political Dominance in Early Modern China and the Cold War." *International Organization* 72 (3): 591–626.

Non-Aligned Movement. 2024. "NAM-Uganda Chairmanship 2024–2027." *Non-Aligned Movement (NAM)*. January 16. https://nam.go.ug/.

"National Institute of Diplomacy." 2025. https://diplomacy.ind.in/diplomacy.html.

Nayar, Baldev Raj, and T. V. Paul. 2003. *India in the World Order: Searching for Major-Power Status*. Cambridge University Press.

Neumann, Iver B. 2002. "Returning Practice to the Linguistic Turn: The Case of Diplomacy." *Millennium Journal of International Studies* 31 (3): 627–51.
Neumann, Iver B. 2012. "Introduction to the Forum on Liminality." *Review of International Studies* 38 (2): 473–9.
Neumann, Iver B. 2021. "Diplomatic Gifts as Ordering Devices." *The Hague Journal of Diplomacy* 16 (1): 186–94.
Neumann, Iver B., and Ole Jacob Sending. 2021. "Performing Statehood through Crises: Citizens, Strangers, Territory." *Journal of Global Security Studies* 6 (1): ogz073.
Nexon, Daniel H., and Iver B. Neumann. 2018. "Hegemonic-Order Theory: A Field-Theoretic Account." *European Journal of International Relations* 24 (3): 662–86.
Nicolson, Harold. 1963. *Diplomacy*. Oxford: Oxford University Press.
Nicolson, Harold. 1988. *The Evolution of Diplomatic Method*. London: Cassell.
Niemann, Holger, and Henrik Schillinger. 2017. "Contestation 'All the Way down'? The Grammar of Contestation in Norm Research." *Obirin Review of International Studies* 43 (1): 29–49.
Nikkei Asia. 2022. "Transcript: President Xi Jinping's Report to China's 2022 Party Congress." October 18. https://asia.nikkei.com/Politics/China-s-party-congress/Transcript-President-Xi-Jinping-s-report-to-China-s-2022-party-congress.
Nye, Joseph S. 2004. *Soft Power: The Means to Success in World Politics*. New York: Public Affairs.
Odell, John S. 2009. "Breaking Deadlocks in International Institutional Negotiations: The WTO, Seattle, and Doha." *International Studies Quarterly* 53 (2): 273–99.
Ogburn, D. 2008. "Dynamic Display, Propaganda, and the Reinforcement of Provincial Power in the Inca Empire." *Archeological Papers of the American Anthropological Association* 14 (1): 225–39.
Ogden, Chris. 2023. *Global India: The Pursuit of Influence and Status*. London: Taylor & Francis.
Okey, Robin. 2002. *The Habsburg Monarchy: From Enlightenment to Eclipse*. Gordonsville, VA: Palgrave Macmillan.
Oksanish, John. 2019. *Vitruvian Man: Rome under Construction*. Oxford: Oxford University Press.
Onuf, Nicholas Greenwood. 2018. *The Mightie Frame: Epochal Change and the Modern World*. Oxford: Oxford University Press.
Opitz, Sven. 2016. "Regulating Epidemic Space: The Nomos of Global Circulation." *Hand Surgery* 19 (2): 263–84.
Opondo, Sam Okoth. 2010. "Decolonizing Diplomacy: Reflections on African Estrangement and Exclusion." In *Sustainable Diplomacies*, edited by Costas M. Constantinou and James Der Derian, 109–27. London, UK: Palgrave Macmillan.
Organski, Abramo F. K. 1968. *World Politics*. New York: Alfred A. Knopf.
Osiander, Andreas. 2001. "Sovereignty, International Relations, and the Westphalian Myth." *International Organization* 55 (2): 251–87.
Oskanian, Kevork. 2023. "Beyond State and Hegemony: International Orders as Anarchic Meta-Fields." *International Studies Quarterly* 67 (2): sqad034.
Owen, Lord David. 2006. "Hubris and NEMESIS in Heads of Government." *Journal of the Royal Society of Medicine* 99 (11): 548–51; discussion 552–3.
Pamment, James, and Ilan Manor. 2024. "From Micro Macro Digital Disruptions: New Prism Investigating Digital Diplomacy." In *The Oxford Handbook of Digital Diplomacy*, edited by Ilan Manor and Corneliu Bjola, 45–62. Oxford, England: Oxford University Press.
Papacharissi, Zizi. 2015. *Affective Publics: Sentiment, Technology, Politics*. Oxford: Oxford University Press.
Pape, Robert A. 2005. "Soft Balancing against the United States." *International Security* 30 (1): 7–45.
Paul, T. V. 2005. "Soft Balancing in the Age of U.S. Primacy." *International Security* 30 (July): 46–71.
Paul, T. V. 2018. *Restraining Great Powers: Soft Balancing from Empires to the Global Era*. Yale University Press.
Paul, T. V. 2024a. "Introduction: Resurging Great Power Conflicts, Regional Order and Peaceful Change." In *The New Cold War and Regional Orders in the 21st Century*, edited by T. V. Paul and Markus Kornprobst. Washington: Georgetown University Press.
Paul, T. V. 2024b. *The Unfinished Quest: India's Search for Major Power Status from Nehru to Modi*. USA: Oxford University Press.
Paul, T. V., and Markus Kornprobst, eds. 2025. *The New Cold War and the Remaking of Regions*. Georgetown University Press.

Paul, T. V., J. J. Wirtz, and M. Fortmann. 2004. *Balance of Power*. Edited by T. V. Paul, James J. Wirtz, and Michel Fortmann. Palo Alto, CA: Stanford University Press.

"PBS: Public Broadcasting Service." 2009. *Pbs.org*. Accessed March 22, 2024. www.pbs.org/.

Pegram, Tom, and Michele Acuto. 2015. "Introduction: Global Governance in the Interregnum." *Millennium Journal of International Studies* 43 (2): 584–97.

Perelman, Chaïm, and Lucie Olbrechts-Tyteca. 1969. *The New Rhetoric: A Treatise on Argumentation*. University of Notre Dame Press.

Phillipson, C. 2001. *The International Law and Custom of Ancient Greece and Rome*. Buffalo, NY: W. S. Hein.

Pietkiewicz, Michał. 2018. "The Military Doctrine of the Russian Federation." *Polish Political Science* (September). https://doi.org/10.15804/ppsy2018305.

Porter, Tony. 2009. "Why International Institutions Matter in the Global Credit Crisis." *Global Governance* 15 (1): 3–8.

Pouliot, Vincent. 2008. "The Logic of Practicality: A Theory of Practice of Security Communities." *International Organization* 62 (2): 257–88.

Pouliot, Vincent. 2010. *International Security in Practice: The Politics of NATO-Russia Diplomacy*. Cambridge University Press.

Pouliot, Vincent. 2016. *International Pecking Orders: The Politics and Practice of Multilateral Diplomacy*. Cambridge University Press.

Pouliot, Vincent, and Frédéric Mérand. 2012. "Bourdieu's Concepts: Political Sociology in International Relations." In *Bourdieu in International Relations*, edited by Rebecca Adler-Nissen, 24–44. 1st ed. Routledge.

Pourmokhtari, Navid. 2013. "A Postcolonial Critique of State Sovereignty in IR: The Contradictory Legacy of a 'West-Centric' Discipline." *Third World Quarterly* 34 (10): 1767–93.

Prendergast, John. 2001. "U.S. Leadership in Resolving African Conflict: The Case of Ethiopia-Eritrea." *United States Institute of Peace*. September 7. www.usip.org/publications/2001/09/us-leadership-resolving-african-conflict-case-ethiopia-eritrea.

President of Russia. 2024. "New Year Address to the Nation." December 31. http://en.kremlin.ru/events/president/news/76073.

Price, Richard. 1998. "Reversing the Gun Sights: Transnational Civil Society Targets Land Mines." *International Organization* 52 (3): 613–44.

Putin, Vladimir. 2021. "Article by Vladimir Putin 'On the Historical Unity of Russians and Ukrainians'." *President of Russia*. July 12. http://en.kremlin.ru/events/president/news/66181.

Putnam, Linda L. 2010. "Negotiation and Discourse Analysis." *Negotiation Journal* 26 (2): 145–54.

Putnam, Robert D. 1988. "Diplomacy and Domestic Politics: The Logic of Two-Level Games." *International Organization* 42 (3): 427–60.

Qin, Y. (2020). Diplomacy as Relational Practice. *The Hague Journal of Diplomacy*, 15(1–2), 165–173. https://doi.org/10.1163/1871191X-15101092

Queller, D. 2004. "Medieval Diplomacy." In *Diplomacy. Volume II. History of Diplomacy*, edited by Christer Jönsson and Richard Langhorne, 193–213. Sage Publications.

Ramsay, Kristopher W. 2011. "Cheap Talk Diplomacy, Voluntary Negotiations, and Variable Bargaining Power." *International Studies Quarterly* 55 (4): 1003–23.

Rawnsley, Gary D. 2024. "Soft Power in the Digital Space." In *The Oxford Handbook of Digital Diplomacy*, edited by Corneliu Bjola and Ilan Manor, 63–79. Oxford University Press.

Ray, Michael. 2024. "Deadliest Wars of the 21st Century." *Encyclopedia Britannica*.

ReliefWeb. 2017. *UN Casualties for Iraq for the Month of January 2017*. Accessed April 23, 2025. https://reliefweb.int/report/iraq/un-casualties-figures-iraq-month-january-2017-enarku.

ReliefWeb. 2023. "Declaration of the Expanded Mechanism on the Crisis in Sudan." December 7. Accessed February 14, 2025. https://reliefweb.int/report/sudan/declaration-expanded-mechanism-crisis-sudan.

Reus-Smit, Christian. 2001. "Human Rights and the Social Construction of Sovereignty." *Review of International Studies* 27 (4): 519–38.

Reviglio, Urbano, and Claudio Agosti. 2020. "Thinking Outside the Black-Box: The Case for 'Algorithmic Sovereignty' in Social Media." *Social Media + Society* 6 (2): 205630512091561.

RIA Novosti. 2011. "Statement by Dmitry Medvedev on the Situation in Libya." *President of Russia*. March 21. http://en.kremlin.ru/events/president/news/10701.

Richelieu, Armand Jean du Plessis. 1961. *Political Testament: The Significant Chapters and Supporting Selections*. Madison, WI: University of Wisconsin Press.

Risse, Thomas. 2000. "'Let's Argue!': Communicative Action in World Politics." *International Organization* 54 (1): 1–39.
Risse, Thomas, Stephen C. Ropp, and Kathryn Sikkink. 1999. *The Power of Human Rights: International Norms and Domestic Change*. Cambridge University Press.
Roach, Brian. 2023. "Corporate Power in a Global Economy." www.bu.edu/eci/files/2023/09/Corporate-Power-Module.pdf.
Roberts, Geoffrey. 2006. "History, Theory and the Narrative Turn in IR." *Review of International Studies* 32 (4): 703–14.
Rød, Espen Geelmuyden, and Nils B. Weidmann. 2015. "Empowering Activists or Autocrats? The Internet in Authoritarian Regimes." *Journal of Peace Research* 52 (3): 338–51.
Roger, Charles, Duncan Snidal, and Felicity Vabulas. 2023. "The Importance of Rational Institutionalism in the Analysis of Informal International Institutions." *International Politics* (July). https://doi.org/10.1057/s41311-023-00483-3.
Rosenau, James N. 1992. "Normative Challenges in a Turbulent World1." *Ethics & International Affairs* 6: 1–19.
Rostow, Walt Whitman. 1960. *The Stages of Economic Growth: A Non-Communist Manifesto*. Cambridge University Press.
Roussev, Ivan. 2021. "The Telegraph in the Crimean War." In *The Routledge Handbook of the Crimean War*, 310–19. London: Routledge.
Ruggie, John Gerard. 1975. "International Responses to Technology: Concepts and Trends." *International Organization* 29 (3): 557–83.
Ruggie, John Gerard. 1993. "Territoriality and beyond: Problematizing Modernity in International Relations." *International Organization* 47 (1): 139–74.
Rung, E. 2008. "War, Peace and Diplomacy in Graeco-Persian Relations from the Sixth to the Fourth Century BC." In *War and Peace in Ancient and Medieval History*, edited by Philip De Souza and John France, 28–50. Cambridge and New York: Cambridge University Press.
Russell, Joycelyne Gledhill. 1969. *The Field of Cloth of Gold: Men and Manners in 1520*. London: Routledge & K. Paul.
Saint Pierre, Abbé de. 2013 [1713]. *Projet Pour Rendre La Paix Perpétuelle En Europe*. Paris: Institut Coppet.
Salacuse, Jeswald W. 1998. "Ten Ways That Culture Affects Negotiating Style: Some Survey Results." *Negotiation Journal* 14 (3): 221–40.
Sampson, Cynthia. 2007. "Religion and Statebuilding." In *Peacemaking in International Conflict: Methods & Techniques*, edited by William Zartman and Lewis Rasmussen, 273–323. US Institute of Peace Press.
Sandel, Michael J. 2009. *The Case against Perfection: Ethics in the Age of Genetic Engineering*. London, England: Belknap Press.
Santa-Cruz, Arturo. 2005. "Constitutional Structures, Sovereignty, and the Emergence of Norms: The Case of International Election Monitoring." *International Organization* 59 (3): 663–93.
Sarrica, Mauro, and Alberta Contarello. 2004. "Peace, War and Conflict: Social Representations Shared by Peace Activists and Non-Activists." *Journal of Peace Research* 41 (5): 549–68.
Satow, Ernest Mason. 1917. "A Guide to Diplomatic Practice." In *Contributions to International Law and Diplomacy*, edited by Lassa Oppenheim. London: Longmans.
Satow, Ernest Mason. 1979. *Satow's Guide to Diplomatic Practice*. 5th ed. London: Longman.
Savun, Burcu. 2008. "Information, Bias, and Mediation Success." *International Studies Quarterly: A Publication of the International Studies Association* 52 (1): 25–47.
Schimmelfennig, Frank. 2001. "The Community Trap: Liberal Norms, Rhetorical Action, and the Eastern Enlargement of the European Union." *International Organization* 55 (1): 47–80.
Schmitt, Olivier, ed. 2021. *Raymond Aron and International Relations*. London: Routledge.
Schmitter, Philippe. 2004. "Neo-Functionalism." In *European Integration Theory*, edited by Antje Wiener and Thomas Diez, 45–74. Oxford University Press.
Schön, Donald A. 2008. *The Reflective Practitioner: How Professionals Think in Action*. London, England: Basic Books.
"Schuman Declaration May 1950." 2020. *European Union*. https://european-union.europa.eu/principles-countries-history/history-eu/1945-59/schuman-declaration-may-1950_en.
Seabury, Paul. 1954. *The Wilhelmstrasse: A Study of German Diplomats under the Nazi Regime*. University of California Press.

Searle, John. 1980. *Speech Act Theory and Pragmatics*. Dordrecht, Netherlands: Springer.
Seckinelgin, Hakan. 2005. "A Global Disease and Its Governance: HIV/AIDS in Sub-Saharan Africa and the Agency of NGOs." *Global Governance: A Review of Multilateralism and International Organizations* 11 (3): 351–68.
Seib, Philip M. 2012. *Real-Time Diplomacy: Politics and Power in the Social Media Era*. New York: Palgrave Macmillan.
Sellars, Wilfrid. 1963. *Science, Perception and Reality*. International Library of Philosophy. London: Humanities Press.
Sending, Ole Jacob. 2015. *The Politics of Expertise: Competing for Authority in Global Governance*. University of Michigan Press.
Senn, Martin, and Christoph Elhardt. 2014. "Bourdieu and the Bomb: Power, Language and the Doxic Battle over the Value of Nuclear Weapons." *European Journal of International Relations* 20 (2): 316–40.
Shariatmadari, David. 2022. "A Year of 'Permacrisis.'" *Collins Dictionary Language Blog*. November 1. https://blog.collinsdictionary.com/language-lovers/a-year-of-permacrisis/.
Sharon, Tamar. 2014. "A Cartography of the Posthuman." In *Human Nature in an Age of Biotechnology*, 17–56. Dordrecht, Netherlands: Springer.
Sharp, Paul. 2003. "Mullah Zaeef and Taliban Diplomacy: An English School Approach." *Review of International Studies* 29 (4): 481–98.
Sharp, Paul. 2009. *Diplomatic Theory of International Relations*. Cambridge: Cambridge University Press.
Shepard, Jonathan. 2004. "Information, Disinformation and Delay in Byzantine Diplomacy." In *Diplomacy*, edited by Christer Jönsson and Richard Langhorne. London and Thousand Oaks, CA: Sage Publications.
Shils, Edward. 1981. *Tradition*. Chicago: University of Chicago Press.
Shinoda, Tomohito. 2020. "Two-Level Game Analysis of Japan in the TPP Negotiations." *Asian Journal of Comparative Politics* 5 (4): 337–50.
Shoji, Mariko, and Keiai University School of International Studies Keiai University, Inage Campus, 1-5-21 Anagawa, Inage-ku, Chiba-shi, Chiba 263-8588 Japan. 2015. "Global Accountability of Transnational Corporations: The UN Global Compact as a Global Norm." *Journal of East Asia and International Law* 8 (1). https://doi.org/10.14330/jeail.2015.8.1.02.
Siebenhüner, K. 2013. "Approaching Diplomatic and Courtly Gift-Giving in Europe and Mughal India: Shared Practices and Cultural Diversity." *The Medieval History Journal* 16 (2): 525–46.
Sikkink, Kathryn. 1998. "Transnational Politics, International Relations Theory, and Human Rights." *PS, Political Science & Politics* 31 (3): 517–23.
Simma, Bruno, et al. 2002. *The Charter of the United Nations: A Commentary*. Oxford: Oxford University Press.
Simma, Bruno, et al. 2013. *The Charter of the United Nations*. 3rd ed., vol. 1. Oxford University Press.
Simmel, Georg. 1950. *The Sociology of Georg Simmel*. Translated and edited by Kurt H. Wolff. Glencoe, IL: Free Press.
Simon, Herbert Alexander. 1957. *Models of Man: Social and Rational: Mathematical Essays on Rational Human Behavior in Society Setting*. Wiley.
Simon, Tomer, Avishay Goldberg, Limor Aharonson-Daniel, Dmitry Leykin, and Bruria Adini. 2014. "Twitter in the Cross Fire – the Use of Social Media in the Westgate Mall Terror Attack in Kenya." *PLoS One* 9 (8): e104136.
Siracusa, Joseph M. 2010. *Diplomacy: A Very Short Introduction*. Oxford: Oxford University Press.
Skinner, Quentin. 2013. *The Foundations of Modern Political Thought: The Renaissance*. Cambridge, England: Cambridge University Press.
Slaughter, Anne Marie. 2017. *The Chessboard and the Web: Strategies of Connection in a Networked World*. New Haven, CT: Yale University Press.
Smith, Robert Sydney. 1989. *Warfare & Diplomacy in Pre-Colonial West Africa*. 2nd ed. Madison, WI: University of Wisconsin Press.
Smith, Steve. 1986. "Theories of Foreign Policy: An Historical Overview." *Review of International Studies* 12 (1): 13–29.
Snyder, Scott A. 2021. "The Singapore Declaration and the Biden Administration's Policy Review." *Council on Foreign Relations*. February 22. www.cfr.org/blog/singapore-declaration-and-biden-administrations-policy-review.
Sofer, S. 2013. *The Courtiers of Civilization: A Study of Diplomacy*. New York: State University of New York Press.

Soreanu, Racula, and Markus Kornprobst. 2009. "The Positive Sanctions Dilemma and the Diplomatic Habitus: The United States, North Korea and Nuclear Non-Proliferation." *Paper delivered at the American Political Science Association Annual Convention*, Toronto, September 3–6.

Spry, Damien. 2020. "From Delhi to Dili: Facebook Diplomacy by Ministries of Foreign Affairs in the Asia-Pacific." *The Hague Journal of Diplomacy* 15 (1–2): 93–125.

Stagnell, Alexander. 2020. *Diplomacy and Ideology: From the French Revolution to the Digital Age*. London: Routledge.

Stanzel, Volker, and Daniel Voelsen. 2022. "Diplomacy and Artificial Intelligence." *Stiftung Wissenschaft und Politik (SWP)*. Stiftung Wissenschaft und Politik (SWP), German Institute for International and Security Affairs. https://doi.org/10.18449/2022RP01.

St. Clair, Asunción Lera. 2006. "Global Poverty: Development Ethics Meets Global Justice." *Globalizations* 3 (2): 139–58.

Steger, Manfred B. 2008. *Globalisms: The Great Ideological Struggle of the Twenty-First Century*. Rowman & Littlefield Publishers.

Steger, Manfred B., and Erin K. Wilson. 2012. "Anti-Globalization or Alter-Globalization? Mapping the Political Ideology of the Global Justice Movement." *International Studies Quarterly* 56 (3): 439–54.

Steiner, Barry H. 2004. "Diplomacy and International Theory." *Review of International Studies* 30 (4): 493–509.

Stewart, Frances. 2013. "Capabilities and Human Development: Beyond the Individual – the Critical Role of Social Institutions and Social Competencies." https://papers.ssrn.com/abstract=2344469.

Stoddart, Kristan. 2022. *Cyberwarfare*. Cham: Springer International Publishing.

Strauß, Nadine, Sanne Kruikemeier, Heleen van der Meulen, and Guda van Noort. 2015. "Digital Diplomacy in GCC Countries: Strategic Communication of Western Embassies on Twitter." *Government Information Quarterly* 32 (4): 369–79.

Strömvik, Maria, and Christer Jönsson. 2005. "Negotiations in Networks." In *European Union Negotiations. Processes, Networks and Institutions*, edited by Ole Elgström and Christer Jönsson. London, England: Routledge.

Strüver, Georg. 2017. "China's Partnership Diplomacy: International Alignment Based on Interests or Ideology." *The Chinese Journal of International Politics* 10 (1): 31–65.

Sushentsov, Andrey A., and William C. Wohlforth. 2020. "The Tragedy of US–Russian Relations: NATO Centrality and the Revisionists' Spiral." *International Politics* 57 (3): 427–50.

Sutcu, Guliz. 2012. "Evolution of Diplomacy and the Future of Epistemic Communities: Scientists as the Diplomats of the 21st Century." *ESJ, European Scientific Journal*. https://doi.org/10.19044/ESJ.2012.V8N26P%P.

Svendsen, Øyvind. 2020. "'Practice Time!' Doxic Futures in Security and Defence Diplomacy after Brexit." *Review of International Studies* 46 (1): 3–19.

Tafdrup, Oliver Alexander. 2024. "Ernst Cassirer and the Symbolic Mediation of Technological Artefacts in Advance." *Techné: Research in Philosophy and Technology* 28 (1): 49–70.

Tallberg, Jonas. 2006. "Formal Leadership in Multilateral Negotiations: A Rational Institutionalist Theory." *The Hague Journal of Diplomacy* 1 (2): 117–41.

Tannenwald, Nina. 1999. "The Nuclear Taboo: The United States and the Normative Basis of Nuclear Non-Use." *International Organization* 53 (3): 433–68.

Tekle, Amare. 2000. "Amare_old_ethiopian_policy.Html." *Dehai-Eritrea Online*. September 9. www.dehai.org/conflict/articles/amare_old_ethiopian_policy.html.

Terman, Rochelle. 2023. *The Geopolitics of Shaming: When Human Rights Pressure Works – and When It Backfires*. Princeton University Press.

Thompson, Leigh L. 2009. *The Mind and Heart of the Negotiator*. Prentice Hall.

Touval, Saadia, I. William Zartman, and I. William Zartman. 1985. *International Mediation in Theory and Practice*. Avalon Publishing.

Trager, Robert F. 2011. "Multidimensional Diplomacy." *International Organization* 65 (3): 469–506.

Tremml-Werner, Birgit, Lisa Hellman, and Guido van Meersbergen. 2020. "Introduction: Gift and Tribute in Early Modern Diplomacy: Afro-Eurasian Perspectives." *Diplomatica* 2 (2): 185–200.

Trump, Donald. 2018. "Remarks by President Trump to the 73rd Session of the United Nations General Assembly." *The White House*. September 25. https://trumpwhitehouse.archives.gov/briefings-statements/remarks-president-trump-73rd-session-united-nations-general-assembly-new-york-ny/.

Tsekeris, Charalambos. 2009. "Blogging as Revolutionary Politics." *Research Journal of Social Sciences* 4 (2): 51–4.

Tufekci, Zeynep. 2017. *Twitter Tear Gas: Power Fragility Networked Protest*. Yale University Press.
Turnbull, Neil. 2022. "Permacrisis: What It Means and Why It's Word of the Year for 2022." *The Conversation*. November 11. http://theconversation.com/permacrisis-what-it-means-and-why-its-word-of-the-year-for-2022-194306.
Turner, Grant W. 2022. "The Forgotten Heartland: Africa, Mackinder, and Great Power Competition." *Global Policy Journal*. October 13. www.globalpolicyjournal.com/blog/13/10/2022/forgotten-heartland-africa-mackinder-and-great-power-competition.
UN General Assembly, 2005. "Resolution A/RES/60/1: 2005 World Summit Outcome." *United Nations*. https://peacemaker.un.org/sites/default/files/document/files/2022/08/gaworld-summit-outcome-documentares601english0.pdf.
UN General Assembly. 2024. "Reform of the Security Council: Intergovernmental Negotiations." *United Nations*. https://www.un.org/en/ga/screform/.
UN Trade and Development (UNCTAD). 2024. "World Investment Report 2024." June 20. https://unctad.org/publication/world-investment-report-2024.
Union of Concerned Scientists. 2023. "Climate Impacts." www.ucsusa.org/climate/impacts.
United Nations. 1970. "A/RES/2625 (XXV)." *UN General Assembly Resolution 2625*. https://digitallibrary.un.org/record/202170?v=pdf.
United Nations. 2023a. "The Sustainable Development Goals Report: Special Edition."
United Nations. 2023b. "Climate Action." *United Nations*. November 20. www.un.org/en/climatechange/net-zero-coalition.
United Nations. 2024a. "There Is an Exit Off 'the Highway to Climate Hell', Guterres Insists." *UN News*. June 5. https://news.un.org/en/story/2024/06/1150661.
United Nations. n.d.a. "Regional Groups of Member States." Accessed March 26, 2024a. www.un.org/dgacm/en/content/regional-groups.
United Nations. n.d.b. "Summit of the Future 2024 – United Nations | United Nations." Accessed January 29, 2025b. www.un.org/en/summit-of-the-future.
United Nations. n.d.c. "World Summit 2005 | United Nations." Accessed February 4, 2025c. www.un.org/en/conferences/environment/newyork2005.
United Nations. n.d.d. *Declaration and Programme of Action on a Culture of Peace: Resolutions/Adopted by the General Assembly*. UN. Accessed March 21, 2024.
United Nations Climate Change. n.d. "The Global Negotiation Process." *United Nations Climate Change*. Accessed February 3, 2025. https://unfccc.int/about-us/unfccc-archives/the-unfccc-archival-exhibition/the-global-negotiation-process.
United Nations Environment Programme. 2023. "Nations Must Go Further Than Current Paris Pledges or Face Global Warming of 2.5–2.9°C." *UN Environment*. November 20. www.unep.org/news-and-stories/press-release/nations-must-go-further-current-paris-pledges-or-face-global-warming.
United Nations General Assembly (50th sess.: 1995–1996). n.d. *Declaration on the Occasion of the 50th Anniversary of the United Nations: Resolution/Adopted by the General Assembly*. UN. Accessed March 21, 2024.
United Nations General Assembly (55th sess.: 2000–2001). n.d. *United Nations Millennium Declaration: Resolution/Adopted by the General Assembly*. UN. Accessed March 21, 2024.
United Nations General Assembly. 2005. *World Summit Outcome (A/RES/60/1, 24 October 2005)*.
United Nations High Commissioner for Refugees. 2023. "UNHCR – the UN Refugee Agency." *UNHCR*. UNHCR – the UN Refugee Agency. October 24. www.unhcr.org/refugee-statistics/.
United Nations Human Rights. 2017. *Office of the High Commissioner, Afghanistan: 10,000 Civilian Casualties in 2017*. Accessed April 23, 2025. https://www.ohchr.org/en/press-releases/2018/02/afghanistan-10000-civilian-casualties-2017-un-report-suicide-attacks-and.
United Nations Office for Disarmament Affairs (UNODA). 2023. "Lethal Autonomous Weapon Systems (LAWS) – UNODA." https://disarmament.unoda.org/the-convention-on-certain-conventional-weapons/background-on-laws-in-the-ccw/.
United States Environmental Protection Agency. 2024. "Climate Change Indicators in the United States: Fifth Edition." June. www.epa.gov/climate-indicators/climate-change-indicators-united-states-fifth-edition.
United States Holocaust Memorial Museum. 2015. Darfur. https://encyclopedia.ushmm.org/content/en/article/darfur, accessed 15 March 2025.
"Universal Declaration of Human Rights (1948)." n.d. *OHCHR*. Accessed March 21, 2024. www.ohchr.org/en/resources/educators/human-rights-education-training/universal-declaration-human-rights-1948.
U.S. Department of State. 2017. "Protocol and U.S. Representation Abroad (MQ116)." January 20. https://2009-2017.state.gov/m/fsi/tc/fslstraining/c48109.htm.

U.S. Mission. 2025. "President Donald J. Trump Inaugural Address." *U.S. Embassy in Romania*. January 20. https://ro.usembassy.gov/president-donald-j-trump-inaugural-address/.
US State Department. 2022. "24th Anniversary of the 1998 Embassy Bombings." August 22. www.state.gov/24th-anniversary-of-the-1998-embassy-bombings/.
Vasquez, John A. 2009. *The War Puzzle Revisited*. Cambridge, England: Cambridge University Press. https://doi.org/10.1017/cbo9780511627224.
Vattel, Emmerich de. 2004. "Diplomatic Classics: Selected Texts from Commynes to Vattel." In *Diplomatic Classics: Selected Texts from Commynes to Vattel*, edited by Geoff Berridge, 189. Basingstoke, UK: Palgrave Macmillan.
Védrine, Hubert. 2005. *Francois Mitterand: Un Dessin, Un Destin*. Paris: Gallimard.
Ventre, Daniel. 2012. *Cyberwar and Information Warfare*. EPUB. Edited by Daniel Ventre. Wiley-ISTE. www.wiley.com/en-us/Cyberwar+and+Information+Warfare-p-9781118603512.
Vincent, R. J. 1986. *Human Rights and International Relations*. Cambridge University Press.
Vine, David. 2021. *The United States of War: A Global History of America's Endless Conflicts, from Columbus to the Islamic State*. Oakland: University of California Press.
Viola, Lora Anne, Duncan Snidal, and Michael Zürn. 2015. "Sovereign (In)equality in the Evolution of the International System." In *The Oxford Handbook of Transformations of the State*. Oxford: Oxford University Press.
Voeten, Erik. 2019. "Making Sense of the Design of International Institutions." *Annual Review of Political Science* 22 (2019): 147–63.
Vucetic, Srdjan. 2011. *The Anglosphere: A Genealogy of a Racialized Identity in International Relations*. Stanford CA: Stanford University Press.
Wacquant, Loïc. 1999. "How Penal Common Sense Comes to Europeans." *European Societies* 1 (3): 319–52.
Waever, Ole. 1993. *Securitization and Desecuritization*. Centre for Peace and Conflict Research.
Wæver, Ole. 1996. "European Security Identities." *Journal of Common Market Studies* 34 (1): 103–32.
Walker, Stephen G. 1990. "The Evolution of Operational Code Analysis." *Political Psychology* 11 (2): 403–18.
Waltz, Kenneth Neal. 1979. *Theory of International Politics*. New York: McGraw-Hill.
Wan, M. 2010. "Review: Articulating the Sinosphere: Sino-Japanese Relations in Space and Time." *The Journal of Japanese Studies* 36 (1): 153–8.
Wang, Haidong, Katherine R. Paulson, Spencer A. Pease, Stefanie Watson, Haley Comfort, Peng Zheng, Aleksandr Y. Aravkin, et al. 2022. "Estimating Excess Mortality Due to the COVID-19 Pandemic: A Systematic Analysis of COVID-19-Related Mortality, 2020–21." *The Lancet* 399 (10334): 1513–36.
Watch, Human Rights. 2003. "World Report 2003: Iraq and Iraqi Kurdistan." www.hrw.org/wr2k3/mideast4.html.
Watson, Adam. 1984. *Diplomacy: The Dialogue between States*. London, England: Routledge.
Watson, Adam. 1992. *The Evolution of International Society: A Comparative Historical Analysis*. Routledge.
Watson, Adam. 2020. *Diplomacy: The Dialogue between States*. London, England: Routledge.
Watts, Sheldon. 1999. *Epidemics and History*. Yale University Press. https://yalebooks.yale.edu/book/9780300080872/epidemics-and-history/.
Weldemichael, Awet Tewelde. 2019. *Piracy in Somalia*. Cambridge University Press.
White House. 2018. "Remarks by President Trump to the 73rd Session of the United Nations General Assembly." September 25. https://trumpwhitehouse.archives.gov/briefings-statements/remarks-president-trump-73rd-session-united-nations-general-assembly-new-york-ny/.
White House. 2022. "Biden-Harris Administration's National Security Strategy." www.whitehouse.gov/wp-content/uploads/2022/10/Biden-Harris-Administrations-National-Security-Strategy-10.2022.pdf.
White House. 2025. "Withdrawing the United States from the World Health Organization." January 21. www.whitehouse.gov/presidential-actions/2025/01/withdrawing-the-united-states-from-the-worldhealth-organization/.
Wicquefort, Abraham. 2004. "The Ambassador and His Functions." In *Diplomatic Classics: Selected Texts from Commynes to Vattel*, edited by Geoff Berridge, 122–37. Basingstoke, Hampshire and New York: Palgrave Macmillan.
Widakuswara, Patsy. 2023. "Biden Meets Sunak Amid Differences on Cluster Munitions for Ukraine." *Voice of America (VOA News)*. July 10. www.voanews.com/a/biden-sunak-to-discuss-ukraine-ahead-of-nato-summit/7173972.html.

Wiener, Antje. 2009. "Enacting Meaning-in-Use: Qualitative Research on Norms and International Relations." *Review of International Studies* 35 (1): 175–93.
Wiener, Antje. 2018. *Contestation and Constitution of Norms in Global International Relations*. Cambridge University Press.
Wiener, Antje, Anthony F. Lang, James Tully, Miguel Poiares Maduro, and Mattias Kumm. 2012. "Global Constitutionalism: Human Rights, Democracy and the Rule of Law." *Global Constitutionalism* 1 (1): 1–15.
Wight, Martin. 1936. "Christian Pacifism." *Theology* 33 (193): 12–21.
Williams, Michael C., and Iver B. Neumann. 2000. "From Alliance to Security Community: NATO, Russia, and the Power of Identity." *Millennium* 29 (2): 357–87.
Wilson, Woodrow. 1918. "Address to a Joint Session of Congress on the Conditions of Peace." *The American Presidency Project*. January 8. Accessed February 13, 2025. www.presidency.ucsb.edu/documents/address-joint-session-congress-the-conditions-peace-the-fourteen-points.
Winston, Carla. 2023. "International Norms as Emergent Properties of Complex Adaptive Systems." *International Studies Quarterly* 67 (3): sqad063.
Wolfe, Cary. 2009. *What Is Posthumanism? Posthumanities*. Minneapolis, MN: University of Minnesota Press.
Woods, Ngaire. 2023. "Multilateralism in the Twenty-First Century." *Global Perspectives* 4 (1): 68310.
Wootliff, Raoul. 2018. "Full Text of 'Singapore Agreement' Signed by Trump and Kim." June 12. www.timesofisrael.com/full-text-of-singapore-agreement-signed-by-trump-and-kim/.
World Bank. 2024. "Annual Report 2024." www.worldbank.org/en/about/annual-report.
World Economic Forum. 2024. "Strategic Intelligence." https://intelligence.weforum.org/topics/a1Gb0000000LHOoEAO/key-issues/a1Gb0000004beMwEAI.
World Health Organization. 2023. *World Health Statistics 2023: Monitoring Health for the SDGs, Sustainable Development Goals*. World Health Organization.
World Meteorological Organization. 2023. "State of the Global Climate 2023." Accessed March 15, 2024. https://wmo.int/publication-series/state-of-global-climate-2023.
World Trade Organization. 2015. "World Trade Report 2015." https://digitallibrary.un.org/record/4038635?v=pdf.
World Trade Organization. 2024. "WTO Annual Report 2024." www.wto.org/english/res_e/publications_e/anrep24_e.htm.
Wright, Katharine A. M. 2019. "Telling NATO's Story of Afghanistan: Gender and the Alliance's Digital Diplomacy." *Media War & Conflict* 12 (1): 87–101.
Xinhua News Agency. 2017. "Full Text of Xi Jinping's Report at 19th CPC National Congress." *Xinhua*. October 18. www.xinhuanet.com/english/special/2017-11/03/c_136725942.htm.
Yoon, Junghyun. 2023. "Supply Chain Security in the Age of Techno-Geopolitics: 'Fab 4' Case in the Semiconductor Industry." *The Korean Journal of International Studies* 21 (1): 27–60.
Young, Gran R. 1996. "Institutional Linkages in International Society: Polar Perspectives." *Global Governance: A Review of Multilateralism and International Organizations* 2 (1): 1–23.
Young, Robert. 2016a. *Postcolonialism: An Historical Introduction*. Wiley Blackwell.
Young, Robert. 2016b. "Front Matter." In *Postcolonialism*, i–xxx. Chichester, UK: John Wiley & Sons, Ltd.
Yusim, Mark. 2018. "Savonarola as a Reformer in Francesco Guicciardini's 'History of Italy'." *Istoriya* 9 (9).
Zacher, Mark W. 2001. "The Territorial Integrity Norm: International Boundaries and the Use of Force." *International Organization* 55 (2): 215–50.
Zagzebski, Linda Trinkaus. 2012. *Epistemic Authority: A Theory of Trust, Authority, and Autonomy in Belief*. Oxford University Press.
Zartman, I. William. 1989. *Ripe for Resolution: Conflict and Intervention in Africa*. Oxford University Press.
Zartman, I. William. 1995. "The Role of Justice in Global Security Negotiations." *American Behavioral Scientist* 38 (6): 889–903.
Zartman, I. William. 2000. "Ripeness: The Hurting Stalemate and Beyond." In *International Conflict Resolution after the Cold War*, 225–50. Washington, DC: National Academies Press.
Zeng, Fanxu, Jia Dai, and Jeffrey Javed. 2019. "Frame Alignment and Environmental Advocacy: The Influence of NGO Strategies on Policy Outcomes in China." *Environmental Politics* 28 (4): 747–70.

Zhou, Jianren. 2019. "Power Transition and Paradigm Shift in Diplomacy: Why China and the US March towards Strategic Competition?" *The Chinese Journal of International Politics* 12 (1): 1–34.

Zonova, Tatiana V. 2007. "Diplomatic Cultures: Comparing Russia and the West in Terms of a 'Modern Model of Diplomacy'." *The Hague Journal of Diplomacy* 2: 1–23.

Zürn, Michael. 2020. "Unravelling Multi-Level Governance Systems." *British Journal of Politics and International Relations* 22 (4): 784–91.

Index

abbreviations xii
actors: agency of 4, 5, 8, 232; cities as foreign policy actors 238; diplomatic actors 177; great power(s) as 29, 49, 76, 96, 152, 157–8, 165; middle powers as 112, 150, 163; non-state actors 5, 9, 41, 58, 90–1, 136, 176; unitary actor assumption 165
adaptive toolbox (heuristics) 128
Adenauer, Konrad 110, 147
Adler, Emanuel 81
Adler-Nissen, Rebecca 105
agenda 2063 65
agenda-setting (in mediation) 113
aggression (crime of) 93
agreements: landmark agreements 108; written agreements 21–22, 204; signing of (Munich) 129; international organizations making 196
AI (Artificial Intelligence): generative AI 174; towards an international agency for 162; algorithmic bias 185, 234; algorithmic governance 185, 235–6
Alberti, Leon Battista 221
Algiers 146
alliances (military) 141, 158, 205
Amarna Letters 18, 22
ambassador(s): Greek 18; Medieval 19; Resident Ambassador 20
anarchical society 49
anarchy (international system) 5, 49
ancient Greece 27, 40, 196
annexation 33, 61
anthropomorphisation 125
appeasement 129
appropriateness, logic of 12, 130
Aristotle 104, 163
Aron, Raymond 202, 214–16
arts (in diplomacy) 130
Assange, Julian 89
Asylum, Diplomatic 88–9
attacks (on diplomats/premises) 83, 86–7
authority: agential power 147; epistemic power 13, 201–2; of international organizations 104
Aztec 28

background (of diplomacy/contexts): background categories (crises) 137; background knowledge 12, 97, 197; background structures 230, 235; contestation of 165; ideas 110; layers 82; procedural background provisions 82
balance of power 28, 47, 158, 213
bargaining power 183
Barnett, Michael N. 105, 111
Bauman, Zygmunt 44
Behavioural markers (of a diplomat) 89
Belarus 85
Bercovitch, J. 113
Berridge, Geoff 114
bilateral trade negotiations 109
black-boxing the state 109
blending (digital/traditional diplomacy) *see* engagement hybridisation
border disputes 57, 149, 192
bounded rationality 12, 128
Boutros-Ghali, Boutros 113
BRICS 160
British (interests in Greece) 108
bureaucracy/bureaucratic administration 64, 102
Butterfield, H. 161
Buzan, Barry 54, 161
Byzantine diplomacy 24–5

Cable, Diplomatic 89, 103
Callières, François de 110, 112
Cameroon 56, 87
career diplomats 69, 130, 194
Carr, E. H. 190–1
causes (of success/failure of mediation) 114
ceremony (in diplomacy) 25
chairpersonship (in multilateralism) 109, 161
Chamberlain, Neville 129
change: epochal change 190; peaceful change 190; rules change (longue durée) 136; technological change 92, 164, 208
Charter of the United Nations 57, 93, 140
Cheap talk 104, 107, 123
Chile 84, 159

China 3, 24, 43, 52, 70, 92, 152, 198, 217; Macartney Embassy to 32
Churchill, Winston S. 107, 216
cities as foreign policy actors 238
civil wars 55, 94
classical realism 158
classics (diplomatic writings) 48, 114
climate action 66, 197
closed communication 100
closed fist (metaphor) 101
coal and steel community (European) 145–6, 207
collective security 33–4, 150
colonialism 48, 153
co-management (crisis) 192–3
communication: communicative action 134; communicative genre 82, 90; communicative rules 103; communication lines (embassy/capitals) 83, 87; crisis communication (digital) 174; digital communication 181, 187; facilitating strategies (mediation) 113; institutionalised communication 7; real-time communication (digital) 174–5; reciprocal communication (dialogue) 12; social media 69, 107, 165, 175–6, 184–5; strategic communication 174
communities (political/security) 141–2
Compact, Global Digital 76
Comprehensive Test Ban Treaty 105
Concert of Europe 29, 82
confidentiality (in digital negotiations) 173, 184
conflict management: Conflict parties 113–16; Conflict resolution 3, 27, 45, 184
Confucius 203
Congress of Vienna (1815) 32, 62, 158, 204
constructivism/constructivists 5, 161
contestation (of norms/backgrounds) 91, 131, 152
contexts of diplomacy: background layers 81; foreground layers 82, 92; interplay with tasks 101; structural contexts 11; substantive dimensions 81
continuity (of diplomacy) 38
continuum (relations) 140, 149
contraction (of diplomacy) 11, 54
convention(s): Anti-Genocide Convention (1948) 93; Vienna Convention on Diplomatic Relations (1961) 81, 203
COP (Conference of the Parties) 108
COVID-19 26, 40, 62, 178, 184
Crimean Peninsula 54, 116
crimes (ICC jurisdiction): aggression 93; crimes against humanity 59, 85, 93, 151; ethnic cleansing 59
crisis/crises: crisis co-management 192–3; crisis diplomacy 5, 204, 230; crisis management 137; digital crisis management stages 176; institutional crises 191–2, 195; inter-epoch crises 191; inter-state 191, 196; intra-state 55, 94; moments of openness (Kairos) 147; policy crises 191, 194, 230; polycrisis 191; permacrisis 190; sudden escalation vs slow escalation 137; systemic shocks 231; war in Ukraine 34
Cull, Nicholas J. 179
cultural differences (negotiation) 110
customary law 83
cyber-diplomacy 163, 186
Czech Republic 55, 75

Da Vinci, Leonardo 225, 227
Daladier, Edouard 129
decisions/decision-making: diplomatic decision-making 186, 230, 236; functional decision-making organ (coal/steel) 146; stop searching for alternative options 128
Declaration, Schuman 146
Declaration, Singapore 144
deep fakes 165
deepest layer (nomic) 136
deliberation 75, 94, 119, 232
demand (for global governance) 11, 168, 199
Der Derian, James 5, 38, 43
deteriorating (relations) 92, 118
development: developing countries 64; sustainable development 65, 92, 106, 142
Dewey, John 223
digital age 161, 175, 207, 216
digital communication 183, 186
digital crisis communication 174, 178
digital diplomacy 88, 175, 181, 187, 210, 231; digital public diplomacy 88, 179–82, 209; digital sovereignty 217; digital turn 173
digital forensic research lab 179
digital technologies 76, 173, 188
dimensions (of diplomacy): multilateralism dimensions 3, 34, 197; power dimensions 13, 201; Shils' dimensions of tradition 38–41
directive strategies (mediation) 113
disciplinary boundaries 10
disinformation 174–5, 206
disputes (international): border disputes 57, 149, 192; intra-state disputes 55, 93
dissemination (knowledge/information) 105–6
distance (relations) 43, 140, 148
domestic level (negotiations) 161
duty to protect (Vienna convention) 83
dynamics: Hobbesian dynamic 54; organizational routines 127; performative and relational dynamics (digital) 177; political dynamics 204

Earth Systems Council (proposed) 196
East Asia 62, 159, 167
Eastern Europe 91, 96, 102, 153
East Germany 110
economic diplomacy 9, 167, 229
economy, international political 61–3
Ecuador 86, 89
education (diplomatic) 229, 231

272 *Index*

Egypt 18, 45, 87, 116, 159
embassy/embassies: mission premises 86, 88; soviet embassy 87; us embassy attacks 87
emerging technologies 9, 231
emotional dimension (decision-making) 129–30
empirical illustrations (mediation) 112
encrypted (diplomatic cables) 103
engagement: bilateral engagements 140; digital engagement 179, 185; diplomatic engagement 7, 18, 183, 201, 230; global engagement 4; hybridisation 180; in-person engagements 184; tactical engagement 52
English School 5, 49, 90, 161
enlargement (EU) 105, 147
enmity (France/Germany) 148
environmental diplomacy 11, 67, 229
epistemic power 11, 201
equality: equal terms (UNGA) 149; human equality 161; Sovereign equality 12, 90, 149–50
equilibrium, systemic 38, 52
estrangement (addressing through mediation) 38, 43
Ethiopia 55, 148
ethnic cleansing 59
EU (European Union): EU enlargement 105, 147; EU resilience 147; European diplomacy 19, 29, 48; European economic community 146; European unification process 97, 147; idea of Europe 96
evolution (of diplomacy): evolution of International Society (Watson) 49; historical evolution 17
exclusion (from diplomacy) 42
expansion (of diplomacy) 54
external messaging 100–1, 104

fake news 165
fast and frugal heuristics 128
feedback loops (digital diplomacy) 177
foreground (of diplomacy/contexts) 10, 81
Foreign Policy: Foreign Policy Analysis (FPA) 4–5; cities as foreign policy actors 238; digital feminist foreign policy 210–1; economic diplomacy and 9, 167, 229; Russian foreign policy 106, 160
formal decisions (UNFCCC) 108
formal legal structures 230
Former Heads of State (as mediators) 115
Foucault, Michel 164
Fourth Industrial Revolution 76
fragmentation (international relations) 11, 44, 217
framework(s): legal frameworks 7, 18, 203; power nexus framework 47, 51; rule-based systems 230; varieties of knowledge framework 201; world order frameworks 157
France: French ambassador 31; French foreign office 146; French occupation (Greece) 29
freedom(s): freedom from fear 65; freedom from want 65; fundamental 93
front-stage visibility (digital) 188
functional integration 146

functionalist logic 146
functional perspective (diplomacy) 229
fusion of horizons (Gadamer) 40

Gadamer, Hans-Georg 11, 37, 38–52, 117, 119, 240
game theory 108, 109, 124, 183, 240, 241, 244; diplomatic game 136; rules of the diplomatic game 136; two-level game 109, 161, 183
gardening (of positions) 55
General Assembly (UNGA) 33, 34, 58, 59, 65, 66, 68, 74, 75, 82, 83, 93, 94, 95, 97, 104, 115, 116, 140, 149, 158, 186, 196
geopolitical context 17, 21, 34, 48, 210, 230
geopolitics 67, 96, 98, 185
German reunification 55, 119, 135
Germany 48, 56, 57, 61, 69, 73, 87, 91, 96, 101, 102, 111, 124, 129, 132, 133, 135, 145, 146, 147, 148, 150, 151, 192; Nazi Germany 33, 129, 159, 216; West Germany 110
gift-giving, diplomatic and courtly 23, 24, 25
global compact, UN 61, 74, 76, 162
global economy 61, 62, 64, 76
global engagement 4
global governance 10, 11, 13, 34, 50, 53, 67, 76, 88, 166, 195, 228, 230, 236, 239
global health diplomacy 9, 72, 167, 224
global south 64, 85, 151, 152, 159. 177, 179
Goffman, Erving 73, 180, 182, 239
good governance 64, 65, 95
governance xv, 3, 7, 8, 9, 10, 11, 12, 13, 17, 32, 33, 34, 44, 50, 51, 63, 64, 69, 88, 111, 166, 185, 187, 203, 205, 209, 217, 218, 224, 227, 228–36, 231, 240, 241; algorithmic governance 185, 231, 233, 236; global governance 10, 11, 13, 34, 50, 53, 67, 76, 88, 166, 195, 228, 230, 236, 239; health governance 3, 11; nuclear governance 166; post-conflict settings 9, 46; post-liberal cyberspace 163
Grammar rules (digital diplomacy) 179, 180
grandstanding (of leaders) xiv, 194
great powers *see* actors, great power(s)
Greece 11, 29, 63, 108; Ancient Greece 22, 27, 35, 40, 196; French occupation 29; Grecian Affairs (London Conference) 29
Guantanamo Bay 89, 105
Guicciardini, Francesco 13, 48, 202, 212, 213, 218
Guide to Diplomatic Practice (Satow) 31, 48, 89
Guinea 87, 154

Habitus of Restraint 97
Habsburg Monarchy 31, 47, 48
Hammerskjöld, Dag 153
health (global) 9, 62, 69, 71, 72, 91, 167, 194, 224; health governance 3, 11
hegemony 29, 31, 157, 158, 163, 165; liberal hegemony 163, 165

heuristics 12, 109, 131, 138, 230; fast and frugal heuristics 128
hierarchies (in international relations/diplomacy) 8, 24, 27, 91, 136, 153, 154, 155, 163, 186, 189, 224
high authority (Coal/Steel) 146
historical analysis 5, 6, 7
historical context 10, 17, 21, 240
historical evolution (of diplomacy) 11, 17, 18, 21, 221
historical examples 89, 33, 50, 204
historical meanings 11, 37, 38, 41, 52
history 10, 19, 29, 30, 43, 50, 90, 95, 96, 106, 107, 118, 123, 127, 131, 133, 147, 149, 201, 202, 203, 205, 214; diplomatic history 19, 127, 203; of diplomacy 19, 127, 203; epidemics and history 70; history and human relations (Butterfield) 161; of international relations 50, 95, 214; of world politics 48, 133
Hobbesian dynamic 49, 50, 51
Holbein the Younger, Hans 41, 42, 43
holistic preparation (diplomatic education) 231
Holmes, Marcus 173, 180, 181, 182
Holsti, Ole 128
Honours System (English, Princely India) 32
horizontality (in diplomatic relations) 12, 140, 149, 150, 154, 155
host country/state 83, 84, 85, 88, 106
human equality 161
humanitarian crises 137; humanitarian reasons for intervention 33, 34, 59
human relations 43, 184, 204, 205, 225
human rights 3, 9, 11, 54, 60, 61, 64, 65, 74, 75, 76, 93, 94, 105, 111, 117, 134, 157, 161, 162, 167, 195, 196, 197, 210, 211, 229, 233; human rights council (proposed) 196; international human rights law 75
human security 64, 65, 75, 82, 111, 112
human trafficking 56, 74
Hussein, Saddam 128, 129, 130, 131
hybrid approach (engagement) 184

ICC (International Criminal Court) 58, 59, 60, 74, 93, 119, 131, 149
Idea of Europe 95, 96, 239
ideologies 28, 48, 163
Ikenberry, G. John 162, 163
ILC (International Law Commission) 83, 149
images and identities (digital diplomacy) 174, 178, 181, 210
impact (of diplomacy/tech/etc.) 11, 26, 50, 96, 104, 108, 133, 149, 150, 164, 165, 173, 174, 176, 177, 178, 179, 180, 181, 228
impartiality (of mediator) 12, 38, 46, 114, 115, 119
implementation (of agreements) 65, 66, 71, 24, 88, 108, 114, 132, 144, 145, 187, 207, 218
incentives (mediation) 113, 141, 143, 214, 245

inclusive (multilateralism) 45, 46, 65, 95, 111, 179, 183, 197
India 3, 24, 32, 55, 57, 61, 62, 68, 89, 132, 141, 142, 152, 157, 160, 166, 168, 187, 190
Indonesia 46, 61, 87, 115, 142, 198, 211
Industrial Revolution, Fourth 76
influence 6, 8, 9, 11, 12, 13, 17, 18, 19, 21, 24, 27, 28, 30, 34, 35, 43, 47, 48, 50, 51, 52, 63, 84, 96, 102, 106, 107, 126, 127, 146, 153, 157, 159, 160, 166, 167, 173, 174, 179, 180, 181, 183, 184, 185, 186, 187, 188, 189, 201, 202, 203, 204, 205, 206, 207, 208, 209, 212, 214, 216, 217, 218, 219, 224, 230, 231, 232, 234, 236, 241, 242, 243, 244; critically engaging structures of 231; diplomatic influence 17, 18, 21, 24, 27, 30, 35, 47, 50, 106, 127, 153, 175, 181, 184, 186, 187, 201, 212, 214, 218, 224, 243; epistemic power as 165, 201; of good governance 64, 65, 95; great power influence 30, 157, 160; of Monnet 146, 147, 206, 207; of non-state actors 9, 11, 173, 188, 224; precolonial Africa 21; strategic influence 8, 13, 24, 185, 216, 236
influencers (vaccinations) 185
informal (negotiations/moments) 6, 61, 90, 107, 109, 110, 114, 125, 143, 149, 151, 155, 159, 173, 182, 183, 186, 187
information 7, 23, 24, 25, 67, 89, 102, 105, 107, 111, 113, 114, 115, 130, 174, 176, 177, 178, 179, 182, 184, 186, 187, 205, 208, 210, 219, 224, 234, 239; accurate information 103; classified information 103; credible information 113, 115; information-retrieving function 102; misinformation 165, 174, 175, 176, 178, 183, 184, 185; strategic use of 174, 175, 239
innovation 7, 9, 10, 19, 21, 23, 35, 40, 41, 43, 45, 57, 62, 66, 70, 76, 120, 162, 179, 190, 220, 230; Pandemic Treaty 71, 198; technological innovation 23, 40, 76, 162, 190; tradition and 35, 41, 43, 230
institutional crises 13, 191, 195, 196, 199, 230
institutional growth (crisis management) 177
institutional logics 225
institutional structures 202, 224, 229, 231
institutions, international 11, 50, 57, 69, 102, 153, 157, 192, 197, 240; crises of 57, 190, 192, 196; legitimacy of 34, 41, 58, 195, 196, 197, 199, 235; primary institutions 161; secondary institutions 161; UN sidelined xiv; Vienna Convention and 11, 81, 82, 83, 83, 85, 86, 87, 88, 89, 98, 102, 106, 203
instructions (diplomats) 18, 22, 23, 31, 100, 102, 123, 175
Instrumentalised (appeasement) 129
integration 24, 44, 49, 50, 51, 52, 62, 63, 74, 96, 98, 145, 146, 147, 163, 173, 174, 175, 177, 178, 180, 182, 185, 186, 187, 188, 192, 206, 207, 229, 236, 239; agents of 146;

deeper/broader 49, 147, 192, 229; functional integration 146; integration scheme 62, 239
intellectual exercise (diplomacy) 218, 223
intellectual traditions 10, 225
intelligence analysis, AI-driven 13, 185, 186, 188, 189, 199, 205, 206, 208, 218, 232, 233, 234, 236
intelligence gathering 35, 202, 203, 218
intensive diplomacy 34, 188
interaction capacity 185, 231
interactions 5, 6, 7, 9, 10, 12, 17, 18, 20, 21, 27, 32, 39, 40, 43, 47, 49, 53, 66, 96, 110, 116, 134, 160, 173, 177, 182, 183, 184, 185, 187, 194, 203, 204, 205, 208, 209, 210, 211, 224, 230, 231, 232, 234, 235, 238, 239, 240, 242
interdependence 9, 43, 49, 51, 70, 224
inter-epoch 13, 190, 191, 192, 193, 194, 195, 197, 199
interests 4, 5, 8, 9, 19, 24, 29, 30, 33, 34, 37, 38, 44, 47, 49, 50, 51, 52, 53, 57, 62, 71, 75, 90, 91, 96, 104, 110, 111, 116, 143, 137, 154, 183, 198, 202, 206, 207, 212, 214, 215, 218, 223, 242, 243, 244; national interest 4, 5, 38, 44, 49, 50, 52, 63, 67, 71, 115, 154, 202, 214; short-term state interests 11, 49
interfering (domestic affairs) 88
intermediary activity (mediation) 112
internal messaging 12, 100, 101, 102, 119, 120
international community 33, 59, 131, 132
international cooperation 33, 48, 72, 94, 134, 145
international criminal court *see* ICC
international crises 57, 132, 190, 193, 199
international dimension (conflict) 112
international institutions *see* Institutions, International
international law 34, 49, 59, 61, 63, 73, 75, 83, 93, 111, 133, 141, 149, 190, 203; international human rights law 89, 160
international negotiations 95, 134, 146, 173, 174, 182, 183, 185, 203, 234, 236, 239
international order *see* order, international
international organization 94, 141
international rescue committee 194, 195
international sanitary regulations (1951) 69, 72
international society 49, 50, 53, 103, 161, 243
interpersonal dynamics 51, 245
intervention (humanitarian/military) 26, 30, 33, 34, 43, 55, 57, 59, 63, 89, 128, 132, 233, 249, 153, 193, 202, 212, 232, 239
intrusion (mission premises) 83
investigations 85, 154, 161
inviolable (mission premises) 83, 86, 89
invitations (multilateral gatherings) 197
IOM (International Organization for Migration) 73
IOs *see* institutions, international
Iran 55, 86, 117, 134, 142, 144, 145, 168; Iran Nuclear Deal 145, 183, 187
Iraq 55, 56, 87, 115, 128, 129, 130, 132, 192, 200
Irredentism in European Politics (Kornprobst) 33, 123

Israel 3, 26, 45, 55, 57, 58, 59, 75, 77, 85, 86, 113, 114, 155, 157, 159
issue areas 11, 13, 54, 60, 61, 67, 75, 76, 77, 99, 136, 146, 192, 194
Italy 20, 61, 129, 150, 155; renaissance Italy 212, 213

Japan 23, 24, 25, 55, 61, 118, 143, 168, 192, 217
Jean Monnet *see* Monnet, Jean
Johnstone, Ian 134
Jönsson, Christer 110, 120, 158
judgement (Machiavelli) 102
judgements 123, 130, 138, 192, 193, 194, 199
Julian Assange *see* Assange, Julian
jurisdiction 19, 68, 83, 84, 85, 93; civil and administrative jurisdiction 83; criminal jurisdiction 83, 84; universal jurisdiction 84, 85
justification, public 169
juxtapositions (Self/Other) 103, 133, 148, 155, 192, 227

Kairos (rhetorical theory) 147
Kazakhstan 168
Kennan, George F. 102, 103, 203, 204, 206, 207, 208
Kenya 56, 86, 116, 123, 143, 175; Westgate Mall attack 175
Kissinger, Henry 11, 35, 38, 43, 51, 52, 53, 118, 152, 158, 203, 204, 216, 245
knowledge 11, 12, 13, 37, 38, 42, 52, 69, 90, 97, 111, 127, 131, 152, 163, 168, 201, 202, 203, 204, 205, 206, 208, 209, 212, 219, 224, 232, 234, 235, 236, 239, 242; acquired knowledge 205; background knowledge 12, 97, 127, 168; control of 13, 212, 218, 232; dissemination of 201, 202, 239; experiential knowledge 202, 204, 205, 206, 207, 218, 239; knowledge as influence 201, 202, 203, 204, 205; knowledge production 201, 209, 219, 234, 235, 236; objectual knowledge 202, 206, 207, 208, 218, 239; practical knowledge-how 201, 202, 205, 206, 207, 239; propositional knowledge 201, 202, 203, 204, 206, 207, 218; strategic knowledge 163, 202; tacit knowledge 205, 224; varieties of knowledge 202–9
Kornprobst, Markus 55, 57, 71, 72, 77, 81, 91, 97, 98, 101, 106, 111, 123, 136, 138, 149, 154, 155, 160, 161, 168, 169, 192, 200
Kosovo 55, 113, 115, 128, 193, 200
Kyoto Protocol (1997) 68, 108, 109
Kyrgyzstan 168

Langhorne, Richard 18, 19, 20, 21, 22, 23, 24, 27, 30, 32, 36, 92
Latin America 28, 55, 56, 70, 84, 89, 131, 153, 159, 160, 166, 184, 196, 210, 216, 217

law 116; global health law 71; international law 34, 49, 59, 61, 63, 73, 83, 93, 111, 133, 141, 149, 160, 190, 203; legal frameworks 7, 18, 206; legal rules 89; military law 97, 160, 162; private international law 28; Rome Statute 58, 74, 92, 249, 151; Satow's Guide 110, 112; Vienna Convention 11, 81, 82, 83, 84, 85, 86, 87, 88, 89, 98, 99, 102, 106, 203, 230
Lawson, George 161
layers (of contexts) 81
leaders 5, 18, 23, 26, 29, 40, 48, 52, 62, 91, 104, 105, 106, 107, 108, 114, 119, 125, 128, 129, 130, 144, 147, 150, 154, 183, 192, 194, 204, 211, 214, 242; agency of 147; individual decision-makers 128, 130; plays diplomatic cards 147, 148, 150; portraying as Hitler 129
League of Nations 11, 33, 44, 69, 146, 149, 150, 241, 245
learning (techniques) 119; diplomatic lesson (appeasement) 129; from one another 119; lessons learned (crisis) 176, 177
legitimacy 7, 8, 9, 10, 13, 18, 26, 28, 30, 32, 34, 35, 37, 41, 58, 11, 114, 116, 177, 195, 196, 197, 199, 201, 202, 210, 212, 214, 218, 223, 224, 225, 227, 228, 230, 231, 232, 233, 234, 235, 236, 237, 242, 244; constructing legitimacy 218; of international institutions 8, 34, 58, 196, 197; of international norms 41, 225, 236; reputational security 177
lenses 10, 38, 82, 95, 96, 98, 111, 155, 164, 212, 230, 242; conceptual lenses 10; episteme as lens 95, 98, 157, 164, 239; methodological lenses 5, 7, 10, 229, 230
liberal international order 34, 163, 167
liberal norms 32, 34, 162
liberation (struggle) 99, 146, 174, 241
limitations 6, 12, 19, 34, 110, 159, 169, 181, 182, 183, 186, 194, 213, 228, 233, 235; of diplomatic capacity 12, 168, 183; of psychological approaches 12; of scholarly perspectives 110
Linklater, Andrew 106
logics of action 123, 127, 133, 128, 141, 241; functionalist logic 146, 147; institutional logics 4, 225
London Conference on Grecian Affairs (1827–32) 29
long Telegram (Kennan) 207
long-term trends 51, 245
loss (perception of) 128
Louis XIV, King 29, 31

Macartney Embassy 32
Machiavelli, Niccolò 35, 47, 48, 53, 102, 203, 205, 212, 219
making (diplomacy/relations/order) 4, 34, 95, 99, 157, 165, 167, 201, 218; making agreements 12, 52, 182, 186, 187, 201, 204; making judgements 123–39; making order 157–69; making relations 141–56
management 8, 9, 13, 17, 27, 28, 30, 35, 45, 49, 51, 67, 73, 106, 107, 124, 137, 138, 161, 175, 176, 177, 180, 181, 182, 188, 190, 191, 193, 194, 197, 199, 205, 206, 214, 215, 224, 235, 237; conflict management 17, 27, 28, 30, 35; crisis management 13, 49, 51, 138, 175, 176, 177, 181, 188, 190, 191, 192, 193, 194, 197, 199, 200, 205, 206, 235, 239; digital crisis management stages 176; perception management 180; risk management 124
Maximise (utility) 12, 124, 240
meaning 5, 7, 11, 22, 27, 31, 37, 38, 39, 40, 41, 52, 102, 118, 147, 161, 165, 175, 188, 201, 202, 208, 209, 210, 218, 219, 224, 227, 233, 240, 242, 243; making new meaning 40, 102, 240; meaning-making exercises 5, 165, 175, 188, 201, 218, 219; pre-established meaning 147
mediation 5, 6, 7, 11, 12, 37, 38, 43, 44, 45, 46, 47, 52, 53, 86, 100, 112, 113, 114, 115, 116, 119, 120, 123, 149, 208, 224, 225, 227, 228, 229, 230, 231, 234, 244; approaches 45; success and failure of 114; types of 43, 114
mediator/mediators 8, 44, 45, 46, 112, 113, 114, 115, 116, 208, 209, 238; experience of 46, 114, 115, 208; former Heads of State as 115; impartiality of 45, 46, 114, 115; mediator and parties 114; power of 45, 112, 113, 114, 115, 208, 209; trust-building 51, 180, 183, 235
Meinecke, Friedrich 11, 38, 48, 52, 53
messaging 12, 88, 100, 101, 102, 104, 107, 119, 120, 123, 144, 173, 174, 175, 176, 177, 178, 180, 181, 185, 187, 188, 206, 210, 211, 229; effectiveness of 175–82; external messaging 100, 102, 104; internal messaging 100, 101, 102; messages (sending/receiving) 18, 30, 87, 100, 103, 107, 177; public messaging 101, 104, 106
methodological approaches/lenses 5, 7, 10, 229, 230
Metis 147, 155
Mexico 61, 85, 87, 113, 150, 210
MFA *see* Foreign ministry
microfoundations 125
Middle East 3, 6, 28, 52, 55, 56, 62, 113, 115, 159, 167, 191, 204, 217
Middle powers 112, 150, 163, 165, 167
migration 3, 9, 11, 28, 46, 54, 61, 72, 74, 75, 76, 105, 137, 166, 192
military (capabilities/alliances) 30, 25, 48, 60, 97, 150, 157, 158, 190, 207, 214, 216, 244
military functions (peacekeeping) 93, 243
misinformation 165, 174, 175, 176, 178, 183, 184, 185, 198, 208
mission premises (embassy) 83, 86, 88
Mitchell, Christopher 112

Mitrany, David 96, 146, 147
Mitrovica (post-conflict) 169
Modern Diplomacy 11, 17, 18, 39, 41, 42, 88, 203, 219
Modern European diplomatic system 36
Monnet, Jean 146, 147, 206, 207
Morgenthau, Hans 5, 158, 159
multi-track diplomacy 117
Munich Agreement (1938) 128, 129, 131
music diplomacy 118
Musk, Elon 60, 190
Mussolini, Benito 129, 150
Myanmar 87, 157, 191, 194

narratives 12, 13, 38, 43, 45, 46, 53, 131, 173, 174, 175, 176, 177, 178, 181, 183, 184, 185, 188, 189, 201, 202, 205, 209, 210, 211, 212, 214, 218, 219, 230, 231, 233, 234, 236, 238, 242, 244; framing geopolitical narratives 218; global narratives 175, 177; impact of 177, 179; state narratives 173, 189; strategic narratives 12, 188
national identity 30, 148, 209, 210, 218
national interest 4, 5, 38, 44, 49, 50, 52, 63, 67, 71, 154, 202, 214
nations 20, 36, 82, 87, 92, 94, 104, 112, 129, 141, 147, 149, 153, 177, 194, 239; powerful nations 136; small nations 149
nation-state 9, 24, 66, 75, 89, 96, 110, 140, 147, 153, 154, 240
NATO (North Atlantic Treaty Organization) 44, 55, 57, 119, 128, 135, 141, 142, 293, 207, 210, 238, 246
natural disasters xiv
navigating (diplomacy/power) 32, 35, 38, 39, 40, 41, 52, 180, 214, 217
Nazi Germany 33, 102, 129, 159, 216
negotiation(s) 6, 7, 8, 9, 12, 13, 20, 22, 23, 24, 29, 30–35, 39, 40, 41, 44, 51, 52, 68, 71, 83, 95, 104, 107–14, 118, 119, 120, 234, 244, 259, 161, 173, 174, 176, 182–89, 197, 201–6, 114, 117, 234, 235, 136, 139, 242, 245; approaches to 44, 146; bilateral trade negotiations 109; digital negotiations 13, 182, 185, 187, 188; international negotiations 95, 134, 173, 174, 183, 185, 203, 204, 231, 234, 236, 239; informal negotiation rounds 110; limits of scholarly perspectives 110; pandemic Treaty negotiations 71; Putnam's two-level game 109, 161, 183; strategic bargaining 12; UNFCCC COP negotiations 108, 184; Utrecht Negotiations 29; voluntary negotiations 113
neorealism 243
networked world 219
networks 6, 8, 9, 44, 56, 60, 69, 85, 110, 119, 162, 163, 165, 169, 175, 188, 203, 217, 218, 234
Neumann, Iver B. 24, 91, 99, 120, 137, 141, 147, 155, 169

NGOs (Non-Governmental Organizations) 11, 62, 66, 67, 76, 88, 105, 110, 113, 120, 136, 137, 152, 176, 177, 195, 197
Nicolson, Harold 19, 20, 22, 23, 27, 28, 30, 32, 48, 92
norm contestation 131, 163
norms 4, 5, 7, 8, 11, 12, 17, 32, 34, 37–43, 49, 50–53, 76, 88, 131, 134, 138, 157, 160, 161, 162, 164, 173, 174, 175, 188, 203, 224, 228, 230, 240–44; Diplomatic norms 11, 32, 38, 188; Emergent properties Liberal norms 34, 162; Publicly controlled rules 22; Shared norms 11, 38, 41, 43, 49, 52, 53, 131; Unwritten norms 12; Universal jurisdiction norm 84, 85
North Korea 55, 118, 143, 149
nuclear diplomacy, digital 176, 183, 187, 198
nuclear governance 166
nuclear non-proliferation regime 136
nuclear prohibition treaty 58, 91, 111, 112, 166
nuclear weapons tests 58, 105, 143, 167

objectual knowledge 201, 202, 206, 207, 208, 218, 239
OECD (Organisation for Economic Co-operation and Development) 257, 267, 195
Olaf Scholz 133
open communication 116, 117, 135, 188
open hand (metaphor) 101
operational code 128
order, international 3, 5, 6, 8, 11, 21, 30, 34, 38, 43, 49, 50, 51, 93, 158, 160–64, 200, 206, 212, 228; crisis in world order 168; developing international society 49, 50, 53; evolution of 21, 35, 50, 159; global order 34, 48, 49, 51, 189, 218, 227, 237, 244; international order making 157, 159, 160, 161, 162, 163, 164, 166, 169; liberal international order 34, 163, 167; multiplex world order 166; new global order 135, 159; ordering outcome (balance of power) 158; ordering the world 166; post-liberal order 163; post-liberal cyberspace 163; polycentric order 165; polarising world order 165; primary institutions of order 161; rule-based systems 230; systemic stability 37, 38, 53
outcomes 12, 45, 50, 62, 67, 108, 109, 110, 111, 146, 182, 186, 197, 216, 218, 224, 236; yielding tangible outcomes 197
outreach (digital diplomacy) 180

Pact for the Future (2024) 76, 197
Pacte de Famille (1761) 31
Pakistan 55, 87, 142, 168, 198
Pan-Africanism 95, 154
pandemic Treaty negotiations 71
pandemic, COVID-19 26, 40, 62, 63, 70, 71, 92, 176, 177, 178, 183, 184, 200, 211

Paris Agreement (2015) 3, 44, 68, 108, 109, 198, 241
parties (conflict) 109, 114, 115, 116, 238; Parties to UNFCCC 68
pattern(s) 6, 10, 19, 20, 30, 54, 71, 72, 89, 94, 143, 157, 186, 194, 197, 206; Diplomatic representation 250; Digital disruption patterns 173, 174
Paul, T. V. 57, 160
peace 3, 12, 26, 28, 29, 30, 46, 47, 51, 57, 60, 65, 66, 71, 72, 75, 76, 77, 81, 82, 83, 86, 92, 93, 94, 98, 108, 113, 114, 116, 128, 129, 140, 141, 144, 150, 183, 190, 191, 192, 193, 196, 200, 204, 216, 238, 239, 242, 243; an Agenda for peace 60, 113; conciliatory peace 146; diplomatic peace 60, 113; peace and war (Aron) 214, 216, 244; peace concepts 94; peace research 95
peacekeeping 93, 243
perception management 180
perceptions (of loss/gain) 128
performance 13, 64, 91, 120, 137, 180, 181, 182, 188, 196, 205, 224; performing diplomatic tasks 100, 101; Performance plummeted (multilateralism) 197; threatens legitimacy (multilateralism) 197
performative dimensions (diplomacy) 230
Permacrisis 13, 190
Persona Non Grata 85
perspectives 10, 11, 12, 37, 40, 41, 43, 45, 51, 52, 117, 127, 130, 145, 160, 173, 181, 202, 212, 230, 232, 233, 231, 240; posthumanist perspectives 234; scholarly perspectives 110, 145; theoretical perspectives 10
philosophy 203, 205, 208, 210, 211, 212, 219, 223, 224; philosophy of diplomacy 223–37
piracy in Somalia 56
pitting groupings (polarisation) 158
pivotal transformations (in diplomacy) 17
place branding 219
places (for negotiations) 113
plague 69
platforms (digital) 9, 40, 70, 165, 173–85, 187, 188, 189, 206, 209, 210, 211, 217, 231, 236
Plato 227
plurilateral diplomacy i
Poland 57, 75, 129, 148
polarity 12, 157, 158, 165, 166, 168, 190, 230, 235
policy 3, 4, 5, 6, 10, 13, 26, 28, 32, 33, 36, 61, 77, 90, 96, 97, 100, 101, 103, 104, 108, 117, 132, 133, 135, 138, 142, 144, 149, 159, 179, 182, 187, 188, 190, 191, 192, 193, 195, 196, 197, 199, 204, 205, 207, 208, 210, 211, 214, 230, 241, 242, 243; foreign policy 3, 4, 5, 6, 10, 28, 32, 33, 36, 37, 101, 103, 104, 132, 133, 135, 144, 149, 159, 182, 188, 192, 193, 194, 204, 207, 210, 211, 214, 241, 243; policy crises 13, 191, 192, 194, 195, 199, 230; policy fields (multilateralism) 10, 61, 77, 197; policy formation 10, 100; policy making body (UNGA) 65, 66, 93, 95, 115, 158; policy of diplomatic prestige 26; policy review (US) 264
political communities 4
political dominance 260
political psychology 109, 124, 128, 124, 128, 130, 139, 243
political theory 10
political trivia 23
politics 4, 5, 6, 10, 13, 29, 33, 34, 39, 48, 53, 54, 63, 67, 72, 75, 77, 82, 83, 94, 95, 96, 99, 103, 107, 110, 113, 119, 132, 133, 134, 135, 136, 137, 138, 143, 145, 146, 149, 150, 152, 154, 155, 158, 161, 162, 164, 175, 185, 190, 193, 194, 195, 197, 198, 199, 207, 214, 215, 216, 219, 224, 227, 236, 240, 241, 242, 243, 244; of crisis management 175; of exceptionalism 233, 234; power politics (state and great power) 48, 54, 63, 241; of public justification 246; study of political leaders 254; of violence 193; world politics 53, 72, 95, 103, 110, 113, 134, 135, 138, 152, 155, 158, 190, 197, 199, 242, 244
Polycentrism 165
Polycrisis 13, 190, 191
polylogue 12, 100, 117, 118, 120, 135
Polyplexity (nuclear governance) 12, 157, 166, 167, 168
populist governments 75, 192
posthumanism/posthumanist 232, 233, 234
post-liberal order 163; post-liberal cyberspace 163
post-WWII period 5, 13
power 3–8, 11, 17–26, 28, 32, 34–35, 37–38, 41, 43, 45, 47, 48, 50–53, 57, 60, 67, 70–72, 76, 89, 94, 101–2, 105, 109–10, 114, 136, 150, 153, 163, 173–74, 179, 201, 205, 206, 208, 209, 212–13, 216, 217–19, 223–24, 227–28, 230, 232–34, 241–43; agential power ('Metis') 147, 155; balance of power 18, 25, 27–28, 32–33, 35, 43, 47, 158–59, 161, 206, 212–13, 216, 238, 241, 243; diplomatic power 12–13, 201–2, 212, 218, 231, 236; distribution of material capabilities 165; epistemic power 13, 201–2, 212, 218–219, 230, 234, 236, 239, 242; great powers 29–30, 33, 49, 54, 60, 76, 96, 97, 111–13, 143, 150, 152, 157–60, 163–66, 168–69, 190–91, 198, 238, 241–42; hidden forms of power 136; middle powers 112, 150, 163, 165, 167; power asymmetries (digital) 185; power nexus 47, 51; power shifts 3, 7, 11, 13, 43, 67, 201, 206; power struggles 49–50; power through knowledge production 201, 236; power transitions 13, 190, 199; powerful nations 136; soft power 12, 47, 179, 180, 210, 218, 243; strategic power 13, 201–2, 212, 216, 218–19, 232, 234, 242, 244; symbolic power 13, 26, 27, 42, 201, 202, 209, 212, 218, 219, 236, 242, 244; thirty years' war example (*see* war); unipolarity 158, 190

practical knowledge-how 201–2, 206
practice (of diplomacy) 36, 48, 185, 229; diplomatic practice (Kleiner) 87; ethics and practice 9, 205; a guide to diplomatic practice (Satow) 48; practice of diplomacy (de Callières) 48; practice of everyday life (de Certeau) 147; practice turn xiv; renaissance diplomacy (Mattingly) 20; warfare & diplomacy in pre-colonial west Africa (*see* war)
practitioners 41, 89, 146, 174, 179, 229–230
precautionary principle (health) 71
precedence rivalry 31
prestige (diplomatic) 26
prevent crises (diplomacy) 190
preventive diplomacy 28
primary institutions 161
prism (of episteme) 149
procedural dimensions (of contexts) 81–82
procedural strategies (mediation) 113
processes 4–5, 12, 43, 45–46, 88, 94, 105, 111, 123, 130, 134, 136, 140–41, 147, 161, 164, 165, 173, 180–82, 186–88, 192–93, 209, 224, 228, 231–32, 235–36, 238; negotiation process 111, 113–14, 183–84, 186–87; polarisation processes 165; recognition processes 7; reflective process 177; shaping processes (multilateral) 40, 140
production, knowledge 202, 209, 212, 234, 235, 236
professional (diplomat) 228, 230, 242
projection (digital diplomacy) 180–82
promises (pact for the future) xiv, 60; diplomatic promises (peace) xiv, 95, 97, 193; league of nations 11, 33, 44, 69, 146, 149–50, 241, 245
propaganda 28, 151, 207
propositional knowledge 201–7, 218, 239
prospect theory 128
Protagoras 227
protection 9, 19, 24, 35, 73, 83–85, 87, 111, 198; Responsibility to Protect (R2P) 33, 59–60, 93, 106, 198
proximity (relations) 12, 44, 140–42, 145, 148–49, 153–55, 164, 201, 230
psychological approaches (to decision-making) 12, 127–28, 130, 138, 240
psychology 4, 10, 28, 109, 123–24, 127, 128, 130; political psychology 109, 124, 127–28, 130, 139, 239, 242
public diplomacy xiv 4, 12–13, 88, 100, 104, 106–7, 123, 173–75, 179, 180, 184, 188, 219, 229, 242–43; digital public diplomacy 88, 173, 179–82, 188, 209; global public diplomacy xiv
Putnam, Robert 108–9, 161, 183, 262

qualitative research (norms) 268
quarantine measures 71
quest for certainty, the (Dewey) 252

racial ideologies 249
racial prejudgements/prejudices 99

Raison d'état 11, 19, 29, 37–38, 47–53, 230, 243, 245
Raison de système 11, 37–38, 48–53, 230, 243, 245
Rana, Kishan S. 120
ranking (diplomatic) 31
rational institutionalism 160–61, 263
rationality 127, 233; bounded rationality 12, 128
realism (in IR) 5, 158, 214, 223, 243; classical realism 158, 243; neorealism 243
reality xv 3, 5, 41, 43, 58, 63, 102, 105, 125, 174, 208, 212, 227, 235, 242; making a global reality 105; political realities 212
real-time communication (digital) 173–75, 181
reason (and emotion) 128–29
rebuilding functions (peacekeeping) 93; society-rebuilding 93; state-rebuilding 93
recognition 8, 10, 23, 26, 41, 43, 50, 55, 66, 100, 132, 155, 169, 186, 188, 212, 214, 224, 225, 228, 236; processes of 7; West German recognition of East Germany 100
reflective practitioner 178
reform x, 34, 47, 120, 142, 195, 196; diplomatic reform 121, 248; UN reform x, 34, 142, 195–96
refugee 9, 73–75, 92, 111, 223, 266
regime(s) 55, 58, 68, 84, 103, 113–14, 116, 128–29, 132, 136, 143, 148, 161, 168, 238, 247, 254, 263; nuclear non-proliferation regime 136, 161
regionalism, African 247
regional powers 157, 160, 168, 190
regional relations 120
regulation(s) 9, 69–70, 83, 91, 256, 260; International Health Regulations 69–70, 91, 256; International Sanitary Regulations 69; Vienna Regulation (1815) 83
relational dynamics (digital diplomacy) 177
relationist understandings (IR) 155
relations, diplomatic 8, 11–12, 21, 23, 27–28, 30–31, 36–37, 43, 45, 81–82, 88–89, 98–99, 107, 110, 140–45, 151, 154–55, 161, 164, 189, 201, 203–4, 230, 239, 249; between states 21, 30, 62, 88, 90, 92, 105, 107, 118, 143–45, 148–49, 153, 155, 158; bilateral relations 144; deteriorating/stabilising/improving 91–92, 118; horizontality/verticality continuum 12, 140, 149–50, 154–55, 230; making and unmaking relations 140; proximity/distance spectrum 12, 44, 140–42, 145, 148–49, 153–55, 164, 201, 230; regional relations 120; track-two diplomacy 117–18, 245; transnational politics 264; unorthodox relations 161; US-Iranian relations x, 144
religious communities 117, 245
renaissance 19, 21, 26, 35–36, 62, 65, 205, 212–13, 225, 227, 249–50, 255, 259, 264
report(s) 18, 20, 23, 25, 65–66, 70–71, 77, 86, 104–5, 247, 249, 252, 256, 261–62, 266–68; Annual reports (IOs) 105, 268; Human Development Report (UNDP) 65; reporting capacities (WHO) 71; Reporting style

(Resident Ambassador) 23, 35; report of the Secretary-General 60, 195; World Migration Report 256; World Report (Human Rights Watch) 105

representation 4–6, 13, 17–19, 21, 30, 34–35, 41, 153, 196, 202, 208–9, 211–12, 218–19, 230–31, 234, 236, 241–42, 244, 250, 256, 259, 266; diplomatic representation 21, 153, 236, 242, 250; problems of (UN) 34; of regions (UNSC) 34

reproduction (diplomatic norms/practices/knowledge) 11, 52–53, 120, 259

reputational security 177, 251

Resident Ambassador 19–21, 23, 35–36, 241

resilience 37–38, 40, 43, 50, 52, 147, 175, 177–81

resolving conflicts 17

resolving grievances 27, 51

response (crisis) 9, 46, 70–72, 131, 176, 183, 189, 194, 196, 236

Responsibility to Protect (R2P) 33, 59–60, 93, 106, 196

restraint 12, 37, 56, 93–94, 97–98, 136, 238, 246, 248; habitus of restraint 97, 135, 136, 248

revolution(s) xiv, 3, 76, 86, 107, 144, 148, 164, 199, 239–40, 242; fourth industrial revolution xiv, 76

revolutionary diplomacy 164, 247

rhetoric 62, 186, 205, 215, 247; rhetorical action 263; rhetorical field theory 258; rhetorical weapon (appeasement) 129; theory xiv, 4–5, 10, 35–36, 81, 96, 98, 101, 108–9, 120, 124, 128, 130, 133, 135, 147, 155, 161, 181, 201, 208–9, 212, 214–15, 218–19, 227, 229, 231, 233, 240–41, 244, 246–49, 252, 254–65, 267

Richelieu, Cardinal 19–20, 23, 35, 39, 47–48, 203, 206–7, 213, 251, 262

risk(s) 4, 6, 13, 18, 24, 45–46, 51, 59, 70, 87, 174–77, 181–84, 186–87, 198, 208, 212, 215, 219, 235–36, 256–57; risk-prone/risk-averse 124, 128, 192

role (of diplomats/actors/etc.) 8, 37–39, 44, 46, 51, 77, 88, 109, 163, 188

Rome 18, 22, 28, 34–36, 58, 74, 93, 113, 149, 151, 204–5, 212–13, 241, 250, 261–62; Renaissance Rome 36; Rome Statute (ICC) 58, 74, 93, 149, 151; Sack of Rome (1527) 212–13, 250

Ruggie, John Gerard 95, 164, 263

rules x, 7, 9, 12, 22, 27–28, 33–34, 36, 49, 60, 66, 76, 81–83, 88–92, 96, 103, 128, 131, 136, 138, 149, 151, 158, 160, 162, 164, 166–68, 179, 180, 217, 218, 224, 240, 243, 245, 248; communicative rules 103; legal rules 89; publicly controlled rules (negotiation) 22; rule-based systems 230; rules of the diplomatic game 136

Russia xiv, xv, 3, 21–23, 33, 50, 55, 57–58, 60–61, 63, 67, 73, 85, 87, 96–98, 102, 105–6, 108, 111, 116, 118, 123, 132–33, 142, 143, 151–52, 155, 157, 159–60, 168, 177, 179–80, 190–92, 195–96, 198, 238, 243, 248, 252, 254, 257, 262, 268–69; Russian aggression 55, 142; Russian Foreign Policy 253; Soviet embassy 87; Soviet Union 51, 57, 102–3, 110, 117–19, 125–26, 135, 150, 152–53, 155, 158–59, 207, 214, 238, 245

Sack of Rome (1527) *see* Rome
Satow, Ernest Mason 31, 36, 48, 89, 263
Saudi Arabia 61, 67, 73, 116, 157, 168, 190
Schuman, Robert 146–47, 206–7, 263
science 3–4, 54, 69, 75–76, 118, 123, 164, 167, 189, 208–9, 225; Science and Technology for Development (UN Commission) xii, 76
SCO (Shanghai Cooperation Organisation) xii, 160
scope (of diplomacy) 11, 175
secret diplomacy xv, 259
Secretary-General (League of Nations) 146
Secretary-General (UN) 60–61, 76, 113, 125, 146, 153, 195, 249
security xv, 5, 8, 50–51, 54, 57, 61, 63, 72, 75, 81, 90, 92, 97, 112, 128–29, 137, 166–67, 182, 185, 187, 191–93, 196–99, 207, 214, 219, 243–44, 247–48, 259, 265; cybersecurity 9, 184, 187, 206, 208; human security 64–65, 67, 75, 82, 254; national security xv, 51, 75, 87–88, 97, 112, 125–26, 152, 159, 198, 256, 267; peace and security 57, 72, 128–29, 191–93, 196–97, 243; reputational security 177, 251; security communities 141–42, 246, 262, 268; security council (UNSC) x, xiii, 34, 57–60, 72, 87, 90, 93, 96, 98, 131–32, 142, 145, 151, 196, 243, 245, 249, 255, 257, 260, 266; security issues (mediation) 112
self and other (juxtapositions) 165
sense-making (in crisis management) 173, 175, 188, 193, 200
separate skill set (digital diplomacy) 231
Serbia 128, 192–93
settlement (mediation) 33, 57, 112–13, 133, 193, 243; WTO dispute settlement 62, 198, 249
Sharp, Paul 4–6, 11, 38, 43, 45, 52, 92, 155, 161, 166, 201, 247, 260, 264
Shils, Edward ix, 11, 37–39, 40–41, 52, 264
shocks 147, 250; exogenous shock 147; systemic shocks 230–31
Simmel, Georg 11, 38, 43–46, 52–53, 244, 264
Simon, Herbert 128, 264
Simple heuristics 128, 254
Singapore 63, 144, 246, 250, 264, 268; Singapore Agreement (Trump/Kim) 268; Singapore Declaration 144, 264
Skinner, Quentin 205, 259, 264
Slaughter, Anne Marie 43, 259, 264
social construction 111, 262; social construction power 111
social facts (IOs disseminating) 105–6

social media i, iii, 69–70, 88, 104, 107, 165, 174–78, 181–85, 189, 205–6, 210–11, 239, 250, 252, 256, 262, 264
sociology 10, 123, 247, 255, 259, 262, 264
soft power 12, 47, 179–80, 210, 243, 259, 261–62
Somalia 54, 56–57, 69, 97–98, 194–95, 267
South Africa 46, 61, 115, 117–18, 132, 143, 150–52, 160, 168, 260
South Asia 62, 166
South, Global 64, 85, 120, 151–52, 156, 159, 177, 179, 254–55
Sovereign equality 12, 90, 93, 98, 149–50, 153–54
sovereignty 9, 19, 30, 32–33, 35, 45, 47, 49–51, 53, 57, 59, 83, 123, 161, 196, 203, 217, 224, 231, 235, 236, 239, 244, 246, 249, 256, 259, 261, 262–63; digital sovereignty 217, 249; not absolute privilege 59
Soviet Union: Soviet embassy (Berlin) 87; *see also* Russia
space (epidemic) 261
spaces (post-conflict) 247
Spain 19, 29, 31, 102, 153, 212; Spanish ambassador 31
spheres of influence 96, 102, 107, 160, 167
spill-over (functional integration) 146
sports diplomacy 118
Srebrenica x, 193
stability xv, 3–9, 11, 19, 24, 26, 30, 35, 37–39, 41, 44, 47–53, 60, 63, 160, 203, 207, 212, 215–16, 224, 235, 245; systemic stability 37–38, 47–53, 245; stabilising force (tradition) 41; stabilising relations 140, 216
statecraft xv, 4, 6, 13, 27, 35, 38, 40–41, 48, 53, 120, 201–3, 205–6, 212–19, 224, 230, 235–36, 242, 244, 250–51, 253, 255, 257
state(s) iii, x, xiv–xv, 4–9, 11–13, 18–21, 23–29, 32–35, 37–38, 41–44, 47–50, 53–61, 63–64, 66–68, 70–72, 74–75, 77, 82–84, 86, 89–91, 93, 95–97, 100–3, 105–9, 111–13, 115–16, 118, 125–26, 128, 135, 137–38, 140–43, 145, 147–51, 153, 155, 158, 160–65, 168, 174–75, 179–82, 184–88, 191–93, 197–98, 200, 202, 203, 208–9, 212, 214–16, 217–19, 223–24, 236, 238–40, 242–45, 251–52, 261–62, 267; great powers (*see* power); host state 23, 81, 83–84, 87–88, 98, 102, 106–7, 242; individual states 9, 49, 59; key states (CTBT ratification) 105; making relations between 140; middle powers 112, 150, 163, 165, 167, 247; nation-state 9, 29, 66, 75, 89, 96, 110, 146–47, 153–54, 240; non-state actors 5, 9, 111, 41, 54, 58, 60–61, 68, 71–72, 90–91, 136, 152, 155, 162, 173, 175–76, 188, 224; powerful states 107, 136, 152–53; responsibility of 9, 59; state actors 67, 136, 152, 185, 241; state interests 4, 9, 11, 19, 29, 37, 47, 49–52, 218, 243; state leaders 47, 106, 128; state narratives 13, 173, 189; state representatives 19, 71; statesmen 35, 48, 202, 206, 214–15; unitary actor state 163
Statute, Rome 58, 74, 93, 149, 151
strategic bargaining 12
strategic communication 174, 188, 218, 243, 265
strategic environment 51
strategic narratives 12, 260
strategic power 13, 201–2, 212, 216, 218–19, 232, 234, 242, 244
strategic responses (digital crisis) 38
strategic vision 11, 38, 48, 52, 206, 208

tactical engagement 11, 52
tactical skill (Kissinger) 51
tact (of a diplomat) xiv, 12, 81–82, 89–90, 92, 98, 230
Tajikistan 168
Taliban diplomacy 161, 264
Tanzania 152
tasks of global diplomacy (part III / chapter 6) vii, 100; core tasks 12; different kinds of performing 100–1, 242; relate tasks to contexts ix, 12, 46, 100–1, 211
teaching (diplomacy) 105
techniques (for learning) x, 119; negotiation techniques 230; sophisticated techniques (digital) 165
technological acceleration 174, 219, 248
technological change 92, 164, 208, 230
technological innovation xiv, xv, 40, 76, 162, 190
technology ii, xii, xiii, xv, 26, 44, 54, 60, 75–76, 88, 162, 166–67, 178, 182, 184, 190, 198, 204, 206, 208, 217–19, 233, 241, 246, 249, 253, 261, 263
tension(s) xv, 3, 7, 12, 20, 27, 29, 34, 37–38, 43, 51, 66, 98, 143, 149, 155, 174–77, 184, 204, 224, 228, 245; key tension (expansion/contraction) 54; localized tensions 51; notable tension (mediation explanations) 66
termination (crisis management) 176
territorial aggrandisement 129
territorial change (violent/peaceful) 55
territorial conquest 55
territorial disputes 55
territorial revisions 129
terror attack (Westgate) 175, 264
terrorism 55, 56
Tigray (Ethiopia) xiv, 55, 149
topoi 250
track-change diplomacy 182, 246
trade 9, 18–21, 41, 44, 49–50, 61–63, 74, 92, 106, 163, 168, 192, 197–98, 240, 253; bilateral trade negotiations 109
tradition(s) ix, 6, 10–12, 21, 22, 25–26, 32, 35–43, 52–53, 115, 203–5, 209, 211, 215, 223, 225, 228–30, 240, 251, 257, 264; dimensions of (Shils) 39, 41; intellectual traditions 10; reproduction

Index   281

and reinterpretation 11, 53; Stabilising force 41; traditional channels ii; traditional definitions (crisis) 191; traditional diplomacy 72, 76, 235; traditional great-power diplomacy 76; traditional negotiations 188, 205, 239
transformative diplomacy (Twitter) 177, 252
transgressions 246
transnational corporations 88, 110, 264
transnational dialogue iii
transnational politics 264
treaties 7, 9, 18, 21–23, 27–29, 31–32, 58, 67, 75, 93, 101, 166, 201–4, 206, 213, 218, 224, 227, 239, 241–42; Comprehensive Test Ban Treaty (CTBT) xii, 105–6, 252; Iran Nuclear Deal 183, 187, 248; misplacing texts of 23; negotiation of (nuclear prohibition) 112; Pandemic Treaty 71, 198; terms of treaty 22, 89, 93; Vienna Convention 8, 11, 81–89, 98–99, 102, 106, 203, 230, 249
Trinidad and Tobago 58, 73, 149
Trump, Donald J. 44–45, 50, 60, 62, 91, 104, 143–45, 165, 195, 198, 249, 251, 253, 255, 265, 267–68
trust 5, 7, 33, 40, 44–46, 107, 116, 173, 175, 176–79, 181, 183–84, 188, 211, 239, 268; trust-building 12, 51, 174, 178–79, 209–10, 212, 235, 258
Trusteeship Council (UN) 196
Turkey 46, 61, 103, 125–26, 168, 215
turn (digital, practice) ii, viii, xiv, 173, 189, 246
Twenty Years' Crisis 1919–1939 (Carr) 250
Twitter/X 144, 175–78, 180, 183–84, 210–11, 247, 252, 256–57, 260, 264–66
two-level game theory 109, 161, 183, 248, 251, 260, 262, 264
typhoid 69

Ukraine ii, xiv, 3, 33, 43, 34, 50, 55–58, 60, 63, 85, 96–98, 105, 107, 116, 123, 133, 142, 155, 159–60, 177–79, 191–92, 195–96, 248, 251–54, 257, 259–60, 269
ultimatums (mediation) 113
UN (United Nations) xiii, xiv, 55, 59, 65–66, 68, 98, 153, 195–96, 258, 264–67; UN Charter 33–34, 57, 92–93, 113, 123, 131, 140, 149, 195–96, 240, 243, 245; UN Commission on Science and Technology for Development xii, 76; UN General Assembly (UNGA) xiii, 65–66, 93, 95, 115, 158, 255; UN Global Compact 61, 74, 248, 264; UNHCR (UN High Commissioner for Refugees) xiii, 73, 266; UN Peacekeeping 93, 243, 249; UN Security Council (UNSC) xiii, 34, 57, 59, 91, 129, 133–34, 240, 245; UN sidelined 192; UN System 57–58; UN Reform x, 34, 142, 195, 196, 255, 266
UNDP (United Nations Development Programme) xiii, 65, 72, 74
UNFCCC (United Nations Framework Convention on Climate Change) xiii, 68, 108, 266
unification (Europe) 62, 95, 145, 147, 192
unilateral state action 49–50, 63, 192, 224
unipolarity 158, 190, 258
unitary actor (state) 163
United Arab Emirates (UAE) 67, 69, 116, 168, 190
United Kingdom (UK) 56, 60, 69, 105, 118, 129, 132–33, 147, 151
United Nations *see* UN
United States (US) x, xv, 3, 25, 33, 43, 46, 48, 50, 55–57, 59, 60–63, 67–69, 73, 75, 86–89, 103–5, 107, 111–12, 116–18, 125–26, 128–29, 132–33, 141, 143–46, 149–53, 155, 157–58, 165, 168, 196, 200, 214, 216–17, 238, 243, 245, 248, 253–54, 261–62, 265–67; The Crisis of American Foreign Policy 36; Digital diplomacy (*see* digital diplomacy); US Air Force 126, 127; US diplomats (attacks on) ix, 87; US-Iranian Relations x, 144; US Navy 126; US State Department 89, 181, 267; US/UK excluded from surveillance 87
Unity of Europe 3, 91, 145, 148
universal jurisdiction 84–85, 258
unmaking relations 163
unorthodox diplomatic relations 161
unwritten norms 12, 230
US State Department *see* US State Department
Uzbekistan 168

vaccinations 179, 258
varieties of knowledge 201, 250
Vattel, Emmerich de 114, 248, 252, 267
Versailles Conference 146
verticality (in diplomatic relations) x, 12, 140, 150–51, 154–55, 230
Vienna Convention on Diplomatic Relations (1961) 8, 11, 81–89, 98, 99, 102, 106, 203, 230, 249; compliance record 84, 86–88; overhaul/new convention calls 88; provisions of 83–85, 91–92, 95, 98, 116, 144, 150; spying and 85, 87–88
Vienna Regulation (1815) 83
virtual seminar/summits 180
visibility (front-stage) 188
vision (strategic) 11, 38, 48, 52, 206, 208
Vitruvian Man (Da Vinci) ix, 13, 225–27, 236, 254, 259, 261
voluntary negotiations 262
voting (UNGA) 149–50, 158, 186

war 8, 19, 22–23, 25–26, 28–34, 40, 54–60, 65, 71, 75–77, 85, 94, 96–98, 102, 105–6, 109, 116, 128–29, 131–32, 143, 149, 151, 157, 159–60, 169, 190, 195–96, 200, 207, 214–16, 219, 238, 241, 243, 244, 247, 250–51, 254, 257–59, 262–63, 267; against Poland 129; American Revolutionary War 69; Civil wars xiv, 55–56, 87, 113, 116, 131, 152, 200; Cold war 44, 50–52, 57, 64, 85, 87, 94, 117, 119, 124–25,

134–35, 141–42, 145, 150, 152, 155, 158–60, 164, 168, 195–96, 204, 207–8, 215–16, 238, 245–46, 249, 253–54, 257, 260–61, 268; costs of war 55, 90; Hegemonic war 169, 190; Napoleonic Wars 29, 158, 204, 238; post-9/11 Wars 56, 247; Russo-Ukrainian War 50–51, 63, 142, 194–95; Saddam Hussein wars 128; Sudan civil war xiv, 55–56, 87, 194; territorial wars 55; thirty Years' War 29, 47, 50, 96, 206; wars of territorial conquest 55, 157; World War I 11, 17, 23, 32–33, 36, 48, 54–55, 58, 69, 73, 96, 127, 241; World War II 11, 33, 36, 54–55, 58, 69, 73, 76, 95–96, 106, 129, 132–33, 145–47, 150, 162, 190–92, 207, 238, 243; Yemen War 55, 200

war crimes 33, 58–59, 60, 85, 93, 151

warfare & diplomacy in pre-colonial West Africa 21, 264

Watson, Adam 7, 11, 38, 49, 52–53, 92, 116, 243, 267

West Africa 56, 67, 69, 72, 159, 257, 264

West Germany 110

Western-Centric World 247

WHO (World Health Organization) xiii, 69–72, 256, 267–68; WHO Constitution 69; WHO funding 71, 198; WHO reporting capacities 71

Wicquefort, Abraham de 115, 267

Wight, Martin 49, 161, 268

WikiLeaks 88–89

Wilson, Woodrow 32–35, 48, 89, 239, 241, 268

Win sets (negotiation) 109

World Politics xiv, 13, 72, 83, 135, 190, 197, 199

World Summit Outcome (2005) ix, 59, 93, 266

World War I *see* war

World War II *see* war

WTO (World Trade Organization) xiii, 12, 50–51, 61–62, 191, 198, 249, 261, 268

X (Twitter platform) *see* Twitter

Yellow fever 69

Yemen War *see* war

Yugoslavia 55, 83, 108, 132–33, 142, 193

Zaporizhzhia 55

Zimbabwe 73, 99, 153–54, 252, 260

For Product Safety Concerns and Information please contact our EU representative GPSR@taylorandfrancis.com
Taylor & Francis Verlag GmbH, Kaufingerstraße 24, 80331 München, Germany